# DIAL HOUSE abc GUIDE FOOTBALL GROUNDS

## JON LADD

**DIAL HOUSE**

First published 1995
Second edition 1996
Third edition 1997
Fourth edition 1998

ISBN 0 7110 2601 7

Published by Dial House

an imprint of Ian Allan Publishing Ltd, Terminal House, Station Approach, Shepperton, Surrey TW17 8AS.
Printed by Ian Allan Printing Ltd, Riverdene Business Park, Molesey Road, Hersham, Surrey KT12 4RG.

Code: 9708/C3

**Dedication**
To my wife Liz and daughter Daisy — the two coolest people I know, both of whose beauty, patience, support and sense of humour makes my life complete — this book is dedicated with all my love.

**Note to readers**
All '08xx' numbers are charged at the premium rate of 50p/min.

*Rear cover:* Anfield. Aerofilms

---

# ACKNOWLEDGEMENTS

Once again I have to say that this book would not have been completed without the efforts of many, many people (whether that is a good or a bad thing I'll leave you to decide). One of the best things about doing this book is that it reaffirms my faith in human nature that so many people are prepared to go out of their way to provide information and assistance to me. So to all the club secretaries, stewards, fanzine sellers, police officers and supporters, I offer my very grateful thanks and appreciation.
One or two people who have acted above and beyond the call of duty and to whom I would like to give very special thanks:
• Liz Bulbeck who introduced me to the sexy world of mailmerges and who, once again, managed to wheedle information out of some clubs which they appeared remarkably unwilling to give out;
• John Mist, a hero in the beer, pies and fanzines department as well as a great geezer to spend four hours in a car travelling to and from Carlisle with. From Kingstonian to Stockholm and all points in between, if there is a match on Misty's up for it;
• Stuart Evans for whom 1998/99 will be the year in which he completes the 92 club (don't forget Brighton at Priestfield); one of the few people I know who thinks the idea of spending one day of the Christmas holidays going to matches at Exeter and Bristol was only spoilt by the fact that he couldn't take in a third game on the same day;
• Jason Manning from top Brit band NUMB. Still unsigned, still brilliant;
• Richard Jones and Alex Murphy at *Total Football* for not only providing support throughout the year but mainly for producing such a great magazine, which I would get whether or not there was any connection with this book;
• Peter Waller, Nick Grant and Zoe Schofield/Little at Ian Allan Publishing for continuing to have faith in this book and giving limitless help and support;
• Big cheers also to Paul Days at Sunderland AFC, The Mill Tavern Awayday Travellers (wherever next boys?), Graham Loader at Hob Nob Anybody?, John Cosgrove at Two Together, Paul Mullen at Monkey Business, Andy Medcalf at the UNOFFICIAL Hull City WEB SITE; and Danny Baker and Danny Kelly for entertaining me every week on the way to and from matches and providing a football fan's alternative to David Mellor on Saturday evenings (for which fact alone they should be given a Sony Award).

# CONTENTS

# INTRODUCTION

Welcome to the fourth edition of the *abc Guide to Football Grounds*. As with all the other versions, let me start off by saying the key word in the first sentence is 'guide'. This book is not a bible and given that clubs change things like their kit with the sort of frequency normally only associated with managers at Crystal Palace, then there are bound to be one or two things that become out of date between this going to the printers and it reaching your hands.

If you have bought a previous copy of this book, although the format remains the same, you should find much of the content updated (there are over 65,000 'different' words from the previous edition).

1997-8 was a strange season for football. We saw several new grounds opening, which on the whole offered fans improved — if slightly more sterile — facilities than their predecessors. The Reebok Stadium at Bolton was, without doubt, the most innovative of designs, but the Stadium of Light won hands down in terms of atmosphere and the fact that, because it is by the city centre, fans have the option of doing what they want before they go to the match rather than relying on club facilities. 1998-9 looks like it will be far less of an upheaval, although the new Madejski Stadium promises much. Last season we also lost a dear (if rather shabby) friend in Doncaster Rovers, who deserved so much better than what they got. I can only hope that somehow the problems they have resolve themselves and that our paths cross again in happier circumstances in the near future. Working on the principle that every cloud has a silver lining, it is nice to be looking forward to watching league football at The Shay again in 1998-9. It may not be the Maracana, but it is much improved on the ground Town had when they were relegated to the Conference and the warmth of the welcome you are likely to receive will help you to turn a blind eye to any shortcomings.

Tragically 1997-8 also saw the death of a football fan outside a ground. This only illustrates that some of the problems associated with the game (and, to be honest, life as a whole) have not disappeared completely — and sadly I doubt they ever will. I think Bill Shankly was one of the greatest managers the world has ever seen, but his quote about football being more important than life and death is nonsense.

It's difficult to guess what next season holds for us all. I am writing these notes before the World Cup Finals and am filled with blind optimism and complete dread in equal proportions. Hopefully, we will continue to see an improvement in the way that we are treated as supporters (though no doubt we will still be viewed by many clubs as £20 notes on legs). Certainly, during my time in researching each edition of this book, I have noticed a marked improvement in attitudes to both home and away supporters, although I maintain that if a supermarket treated you the way certain football clubs do (namely with a mixture of suspicion and contempt) then you would do your shopping elsewhere pretty quickly. There's the problem, though: you, I and most importantly the clubs know that the majority of us can't change football clubs like we do washing powder and because of this loyalty we can be taken advantage of.

Enjoy the book; I hope it proves to be some use to you. Remember the scores I give to each ground are based on my experiences of one or two visits in a season. What you may encounter may be very different (either for better or worse) from what I came across and, if you feel this is the case or if there are any points that you feel I have missed out then, please don't hesitate to write to me care of: Ian Allan Publishing, Riverdene Business Park, Molesey Road, Hersham, Surrey, KT12 4RG and I will endeavour to put things right for the next edition. Similarly, fanzine editors; I have sought out your publications in all four corners of the country, but if I have either not mentioned you or given you what you feel is too brief or an inaccurate review then please send me a copy care of the publishers at the above address and I will try to put it right next time.

Finally, by way of a thankyou for ploughing through this introduction, let me give you a tip which alone is worth the cover price of this book if you drive to games and you live in the northwest or south. If you want to avoid the hell hole that is the M6 at Birmingham (especially true for mid-week matches when, if your average speed between Junction 5 and 12 is in double figures, you have to consider yourself lucky), then come off the motorway at Junction 15 (just after Keele service station), take the A500 towards Stoke and then the A50 (dual carriageway and in some places three lanes wide) to Uttoxeter and Derby which will allow you to pick up the M1 at Junction 24 (obviously if you are travelling south to north just reverse these instructions). The mileage it adds to your journey is negligible, but each time I have used it, I reckon I have saved myself 30min to one and a half hours.

One other brief note: early in 1998 a section of the M62 was reclassified as the M60. I have been told that there may follow another large junction renumbering exercise early in 1999. With this in mind, I have left references to the M62 (which are still up on the signs) within the road directions. Have a fantastic season all the best.

*Jon Ladd*
*May 1998*

## The *Total Football* Experience Ratings

For the second time I have attempted to allocate each club a score out of 100. Let me straight away make it clear that this is not simply a mark for spectacular stands but rather a grading on the facilities offered, the attitude of the club towards visiting spectators, programmes, fanzines, the pricing structure, the food and drink you can get in and around the ground, or in short what the Irish would call The Craic. There is no secret formula to work out how this figure was arrived at; it's just a number I scrawled on a scrap of paper each time I left a ground (for clubs who are changing grounds it's basically what their last ground would have got plus a figure which represents the improvements in facilities that the new stadium will offer). It should give you a good feel for what each ground is like, but it's worth remembering that it's based on my experiences on a given day, and that yours may be different. If you feel strongly enough about a grade (be it that you think it is too high or too low) then feel free to write to me and say so. I'll keep an eye open for whatever you say on my next visit, and if I agree with you I'll change the grade and if I don't, I won't. I'll be honest that I was a bit surprised when I looked at the final tables, but that's the way I felt when I left each ground and I didn't want to change my gut feeling for each place.

# PUBLISHER'S NOTE

The views and comments in this book are made as a result of the author's practical knowledge and a visit to the grounds. Changes may have been made since the author's visit.

The Publisher would like to hear comments and suggestions from all supporters — home and away — concerning the Premiership and Nationwide League grounds.

Football clubs are selling a commodity and do not like unfair criticism. As with all businesses, most complaints are acted on and the higher up the chain one goes, the greater is the likelihood of this happening, but a football club obviously does have financial restrictions on the extent of its facilities.

Furthermore, football is a mass market business; it reflects wider social and economic developments and frequently football clubs have been forced to make changes in order to accommodate this.

The author of abc Guide to Football Grounds is an enthusiast who is writing for the average fan who would like to be treated well but who realises that there have to be restrictions. The author has visited each ground in the book in the last 18 months and has first-hand knowledge of what actually happened during his visit.

Obviously some clubs are disappointed with their entry — it may have been just a case of harassed staff or police on the day or they may be disappointed by general criticism — but of the 93 grounds we have listed, we received corrections, which we have been happy to incorporate, from the following clubs:

| | |
|---|---|
| Arsenal | Bournemouth |
| Aston Villa | Bradford City |
| Barnet | Brentford |
| Birmingham City | Brighton & Hove |
| Blackpool | Albion |
| Bolton Wanderers | Bristol City |

| | |
|---|---|
| Bristol Rovers | Plymouth Argyle |
| Burnley | Port Vale |
| Bury | Portsmouth |
| Cambridge United | Preston North End |
| Cardiff City | Queens Park |
| Carlisle United | Rangers |
| Chelsea | Reading |
| Chester City | Rochdale |
| Chesterfield | Rotherham |
| Colchester United | Scarborough |
| Coventry City | Scunthorpe United |
| Crewe Alexandra | Sheffield United |
| Crystal Palace | Sheffield |
| Darlington | Wednesday |
| Derby County | Shrewsbury Town |
| Everton | Southend United |
| Fulham | Southampton |
| Gillingham | Stockport County |
| Halifax | Stoke City |
| Hartlepool United | Sunderland |
| Huddersfield Town | Swansea City |
| Hull City | Swindon Town |
| Ipswich Town | Torquay United |
| Leeds United | Tottenham Hotspur |
| Leicester City | Tranmere Rovers |
| Leyton Orient | Walsall |
| Lincoln City | Watford |
| Liverpool | Wembley Stadium |
| Luton Town | |
| Macclesfield Town | West Bromwich |
| Manchester City | Albion |
| Mansfield Town | West Ham United |
| Middlesbrough | Wigan Athletic |
| Millwall | Wimbledon |
| Northampton Town | Wolverhampton |
| Norwich City | Wanderers |
| Notts County | Wrexham |
| Oldham Athletic | Wycombe |
| Peterborough | Wanderers |
| United | York City |

---

The following clubs did not reply when we sent them a copy of their entry:

| | |
|---|---|
| Barnsley | Nottingham Forest |
| Exeter City | Oxford United |
| Manchester United | |

We hope that the information provided is accurate and we would be happy to incorporate their corrections in the future.

---

The following clubs did not want to be associated with this book, mainly due to the tone of their entry:

| | |
|---|---|
| Blackburn Rovers | Grimsby Town |
| Charlton Athletic | Newcastle United |

We would like to reiterate that this book is not intended to knock football clubs. It is intended to be a useful but humorous guide for a public which deserves the best possible service (and in order for football to reach the same heights of service of many sports abroad it needs substantial improvements in many instances, as long as these can be afforded). The views and comments therefore are those of a fan committed to football.

A note also has to be made on behalf of the police and stewards at football matches: they do a difficult job and it is not surprising that there are occasional instances when this strain shows.

# ARSENAL

**ADDRESS:** Arsenal Stadium
Avenell Road, Highbury
London N5 1BU

**TELEPHONE No:** 0171 704 4000

How posh are Arsenal? Well when you get put on hold (for a couple of hours) you don't get Greensleeves, you get Mozart... Ooooo La-di-dah Gunner Graham!! (Or should that be Gunner Wenger?)

**TICKET OFFICE:** 0171 704 4040

**FAX:** 0171 704 4001

**WEB SITE:** www.arsenal.co.uk (official)

**CLUBCALL:** 0891 20 20 20

**NICKNAME:** The Gunners

**RECORD ATTENDANCE:**

73,295 v Sunderland Div 1 9 March 1935 (Surprisingly a 0-0 draw)

**CLUB COLOURS:**

**HOME:** Shirts: Red, Red/White sleeves;
Shorts: White; Socks: White with Red tops

**AWAY:** Shirts: Yellow with Navy hoop;
Shorts: Navy; Socks: Navy and Yellow hoops

**KIT SPONSORS:** JVC

**MANUFACTURERS:** Nike

## GROUND INFO

If you can't get one of the (fairly generous) away allocation tickets then you might be struggling (at least from official sources). The club introduced a 'Ticket Retail Scheme' in 1997-8 which gives registered members the opportunity to buy tickets from exactly two calendar months before the game. Non-TRS fans can buy any remaining tickets one month before a match. Occasionally you may get 'returns' on a matchday but the demand for these far outweighs any supply. There are a good few touts around on matchdays who seem to charge about £30-£40 for the cheapest ticket (normal price £13.50).

**CAPACITY:** Stands: 38,900; Terrace: Nil

**AWAY FANS:** Clock End South Corner: 1,800;
Total: 1,800

This can be increased to include the Clock End Block T (an extra 1,100 spaces) or the whole of the Clock End (capacity 6,000) if the level of visiting support demands. Let's get the bad things out of the way first. The Clock End is only covered from row eighteen, so if you're at the front and the weather doesn't look too clever either wear a coat or try to swap tickets with a mate. If your mate seems keen to swap, this probably means he's got tickets

at the back of the West Stand Lower tier from where the view is dreadful. Second moan is that there are no concessions for away fans.

However, the point remains that adult tickets at Highbury are amongst the cheapest for away supporters in the Premiership. Other than the limited problems previously stated, the view is excellent and the facilities for away fans are impressive. You get the feeling that Arsenal want visiting supporters at the ground and don't simply see them as a way of making a few extra quid for a sub-standard service. It must break Gooners' hearts when they go on their travels and get regularly fleeced, and, while I'll confess that the thought of sad Arsenal fans is not one that normally fills me with grief, I am forced to admit that on this occasion Arsenal are right and the rest of football needs to catch up with their attitude.

**DISABLED FACILITIES:** 184 spaces (including 92 for helpers) are available in front of the East Stand towards the Clock End, and there is no charge for either disabled fans or helpers. Most places are allocated to Arsenal season ticket holders but there are usually some available on a match-to-match basis. However, it is essential to pre-book, as you should for one of the 54 places available for match commentaries for the blind. The club do not have any special parking facilities, which is a real nuisance given the general lack of places in the immediate ground area. It's probably as well to be a little bit cautious when Nigel Winterburn's about too.

**PROGRAMME:** £2.00

**FANZINES:**

| | |
|---|---|
| The Gooner | £1.50 |
| One-Nil Down, Two-One Up | £1 |
| An Imperfect Match | £1 |
| Up The Arse | £1 |
| The Highbury Wizard | 50p |
| The Highbury High | £1 |

## TRAVEL

**NEAREST RAILWAY STATION:**

Finsbury Park (from King's Cross and the north) (0171 922 9091)

**NEAREST TUBE STATION:**

Arsenal (Piccadilly Line). The club's famous manager Herbert Chapman persuaded London Underground to change the name of the station from Gillespie Road to Arsenal. This was done to honour the club and not, as some scurrilous Spurs fans have suggested, because otherwise the Arsenal fans wouldn't know when to get out!

Getting back onto the tube after matches can be slow. The police don't let the fans go directly into the station, but line them up by the side. To prevent people cutting in the queue there are crash barriers which everybody likes to try and climb over, which tend to topple over in big crowds. Finsbury Park (Piccadilly Line) and Highbury & Islington (Victoria Line) are also walkable if you want to avoid the crowds.

## BY CAR:
**NORTH:** Leave the M1 at J2 and follow signs for the City. Keep going for about seven miles until you see Holloway Road tube station. Once you have passed the tube station, take the third left; this will take you into Drayton Park. 0.75 mile later turn right into Aubert Park, the third left will then take you into Avenell Road.

**SOUTH/EAST:** Cross the Thames at London Bridge, and follow signs for Bank of England, and then Angel (Islington). When you get to a major set of traffic lights, turn right (signposted 'The North') and after a mile you will come to the Highbury Roundabout. Take a deep breath and go straight across. This takes you into the Holloway Road, where the third right takes you into Drayton Park Road. Then as north.

**WEST:** Take M4 to J1, then take the A315 to Chiswick. One mile down the A315 turn left onto the A402 to M41, A40(M), and the A501. At Angel, turn left and continue to Highbury Roundabout. Then as south.

**PARKING:** There is very restricted parking at Arsenal, with a residents' parking scheme in operation. Do not think that a blind eye will be turned if you park without a permit, because you will certainly end up being towed away. It can be worth parking a little away from the ground and travelling in on the tube; otherwise there normally is somewhere to leave the car around Finsbury Park.

## FUTURE DEVELOPMENTS
On Thursday 12 March 1998 Arsenal unveiled a £120 million bid to buy Wembley stadium (this compares very favourably to the £90 million that was on the table from the National Stadium Committee). The club insisted that this was not a publicity stunt, but withdrew from the bidding before the end of the month. In truth what it succeeded in doing was highlighting the fact that either Highbury needs to be redeveloped (the club's number one choice) or it needs to find another site. The main problem with developing Highbury are the residents, who don't want either the local skyline dominated by bigger stands or an extra 15,000 fans going past their front doors every fortnight. The ball is in Islington Council's court and my gut feeling is that planning permission will be granted during this season. If it is not, expect the search for a new site (outside Islington) to be progressed with urgency and a possible move happening in 2000.

## OTHER INFORMATION
The most popular away pub is probably the Finsbury Park Tavern, though it can get a little hairy at times and a better bet can be either the World's End on Stroud Green Road or The Bank of Friendship on Blackstock Road; the latter has an excellent — but small — garden where some scenes from *Fever Pitch* were filmed. For grub you can't get better than The Arsenal Fish Bar (also on Blackstock Road). Without a doubt, this is the best Chinese chippie in London although, bizarrely given the nationality of the proprietors, the best thing on a fantastic menu is the chicken curry and chips. It is as well to stock up here anyway, as in my experience the food in the ground is not really all that good (although to be fair I have tasted a lot worse). Still, at least the toilets are very posh — full of Arsenal Club Crests which of course is VERY important to away fans.

*Total Football* **Experience Rating: 89**

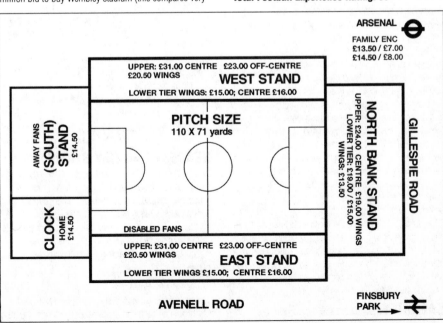

ARSENAL
FAMILY ENC
£13.50 / £7.00
£14.50 / £8.00

UPPER: £31.00 CENTRE   £23.00 OFF-CENTRE
£20.50 WINGS   **WEST STAND**
LOWER TIER WINGS: £15.00; CENTRE £16.00

**PITCH SIZE**
110 X 71 yards

AWAY FANS (SOUTH) STAND £14.50

CLOCK HOME £14.50

UPPER: £24.00 CENTRE £19.00 WINGS   NORTH BANK STAND   LOWER TIER: £19.00 / £15.00 WINGS: £13.50

GILLESPIE ROAD

DISABLED FANS

UPPER: £31.00 CENTRE   £23.00 OFF-CENTRE
£20.50 WINGS   **EAST STAND**
LOWER TIER WINGS £15.00;  CENTRE £16.00

**AVENELL ROAD**

FINSBURY PARK

ARSENAL ARSENAL ARSENAL ARSENAL ARSENAL ARSENAL

# ASTON VILLA

**ADDRESS:** Villa Park
Trinity Road
Birmingham B6 6HE

**TELEPHONE No:** 0121 327 2299

**TICKET OFFICE:** 0121 327 5353

**FAX:** 0121 322 2107

**WEB SITE:** www.astonvilla@fc.co.uk (official)

**CLUBCALL:** 0891 12 11 48

**NICKNAME:** The Villains

**RECORD ATTENDANCE:**

76,588 v Derby FA Cup 6th 2 March 1946 (L 3-4)

## CLUB COLOURS:

**HOME:** Shirts: Claret with Blue sleeves;
Shorts: White; Socks: Claret/Blue

**AWAY:**
Shirts: Turquoise with Black panel, White piping
Shorts: Black with Turquoise panel, White piping; Socks: Turquoise

**THIRD:** Shirts: White; Shorts: Claret; Socks: White

**KIT SPONSORS:** tba

**MANUFACTURERS:** Reebok

## GROUND INFO

The away fans are sited in R Block of the North Stand, which has what you might describe as a holographic roof — when the rain comes down, supporters find themselves getting soaked when they might have believed they were under cover.

You may find it a bit of a problem getting into the ground, if you have not got a ticket. I got the run-around from the stewards and ticket office, all of whom appeared to think it a bit of a wheeze to send fans round and round the ground in search of the elusive selling point. For the vast majority of matches you will probably find that (despite what you may be told initially) you can actually pay on the turnstile. Having entered the ground, stop and ponder a moment as to whose bright idea it was to put the programme hut and the food serving hatches right at the top entrance of the corridor by the entrance to the actual seats. There again, you may feel that your time will be better spent fighting through the masses and heading for your seat. (A little tip, go to the toilet before you start this epic voyage, as if you get to your allocated position only to find that you've got to go through it all again to relieve yourself it may just ruin your day!) In all seriousness, getting in and out can get a little hairy at times, so be warned and be careful.

**CAPACITY:** Stands: 39,339; Terrace: Nil

**AWAY FANS:** North Stand Lower Tier (R Block) 2,671;
North Stand RR block: 448
Total: 3,119

The prices aren't too bad although the lack of concessions is not pleasing. If you get the choice then definitely sit towards the back/middle of the stand as the first three or four rows of seats are so low that you feel you are actually looking up at the pitch. In addition, the closer to the front you are, the more susceptible you are to both the elements and the occasional pastie kindly donated from the home fans above you.

## DISABLED FACILITIES:

There are 40 spaces available for wheelchair-bound supporters, with disabled fans being admitted for nothing and helpers paying the standard match day price of £15. There are no special parking facilities. Match commentaries for the blind are available, pre-booking for which, as with the disabled spaces, is essential.

A lift has been installed in the Witton Lane (aka Doug Ellis) Stand for elderly and disabled supporters. Obviously it is a great logistical feat for someone to press a button and so 'applicants requiring the use of this facility should speak to the Operations Manager'.

## PROGRAMME: £2.00

The very grandly titled *Aston Villa News & Record*. Initially it appears that this is a good one and probably is — but for home fans only.

## FANZINES:

| | |
|---|---|
| *Heroes and Villains* | £1 |
| *The Holy Trinity* | £1 |
| *The Witton Wag* | £1 |

The typeface of *Heroes and Villains* seems to get smaller and smaller and the layout uglier and more cramped with every issue, but the quality of it just keeps improving. Cheaper, better and a far longer read than the programme, a definite one to buy. Fanzine sellers seem to act as unpaid guides to Villa fans as, on my last visit, three people came and asked the seller for directions to various parts of the ground.

## TRAVEL

### NEAREST RAILWAY STATION:

Witton (0121 643 2711 — Birmingham New Street)
This is less than a quarter of a mile from the ground. Trains run every 30min and are heaving from about 1.45. Alternatively try Aston which has trains every 20(ish) minutes on which you can sometimes even get a seat. It is further from the ground (0.75 mile) but the ground is signposted and you can always follow the crowds.

**BUS:** Birmingham Central (Midland Road) (0121 200 2700 — Centro Hotline)
Best bet from Birmingham city centre is the Number 7 which you can get from outside McDonalds on the High

Street, ie NOT the one right by New Street station which stops on Trinity Road.

## BY CAR:
**FROM ALL PARTS:** M6 to J6 (Spaghetti Junction). When you exit the motorway, follow the signs for Birmingham NE. At the roundabout, take the fourth exit on to the A38 (signposted Aston) and half a mile later turn right into Aston Hall Road. Turn right at the end of Aston Hall Road for Witton Lane (B4137) and the ground is 200yd on the right.

**PARKING:** Asda Car Park in Aston Hall Road, or by Aston Villa Leisure Centre.

## FUTURE DEVELOPMENTS
Villa Park is another ground which is desperately in need of having an increased capacity as, at present, it seems to be about 10,000 short of what the fans demand. The club recognises this and there are plans to increase the capacity to around 50,000, bringing the Trinity Road Stand up to the height of the other three stands. The planning application is being heard by the local Authority late summer 1998, if successful work is scheduled to start early 1999.

## OTHER INFORMATION
Villa is the terrain of the West Midlands police force whose strict football watch code tends to be something of a bugbear for visiting fans, who inevitably come away from Villa Park with tales of being pulled out for no apparent reason, as well as being antagonised by excessive body searches etc. As a general rule, if you get told to jump by one of these boys in blue then don't stand there arguing, just do it.

The old Aston Tavern — where you could always be assured of a warm welcome — (yeah right!) — is now closed and derelict and it is worth noting that the majority of the pubs in the immediate vicinity have a real 'home' feel to them.

With the fast and frequent train service to Witton from New Street, it can be as well to stay around Birmingham city centre if you fancy a pre- or post-match pint. The Villa Fish Bar on Manor Road does an excellent portion of chips which, no doubt, your mum would like; however, just a little further up the road is Tony's Burger Bar, home of the Motherfucker and Daddyfucker (three and four burgers in a bun respectively) which she would probably be less keen on; alternatively there are plenty of mobile snack bars around the ground, including one which is done up like a mock Tudor cottage.

If you have got the time to hang around the city for a bit (especially after a night game) a top bet is the Witton Island Balti which does fantastic food at a good price.

Inside the ground the food improved beyond recognition last season and the new Balti pie might be an idea copied from local rivals Walsall but is none the less more than welcome. I can only presume that there has been a change in caterer or catering supplier as the pastie inside the ground was also fantastic. They still don't seem to have sussed out the drinks though; the tea was OK but my hot chocolate was tepid and tasted like someone had added two handfuls of sand in it for good measure — truly awful.

Providing he is still with the club, keep your ears peeled for the tannoy blasting out a song before the match called 'Dwight Yorke, Dwight Yorke'. It's played to the tune of 'New York, New York' and start spreading the news, it's simply tragic!

Finally no mention of Aston Villa is complete without reference to club mascot Hercules the Lion (aka Gavin Lucas) who, during a match, mauled Miss Aston Villa. The club (which states that Hercules had been warned about his provocative actions earlier in the season) failed to see the funny side — although the fans seemed to — and Gav was sacked!!! Tschh!

***Total Football* Experience Rating: 79**

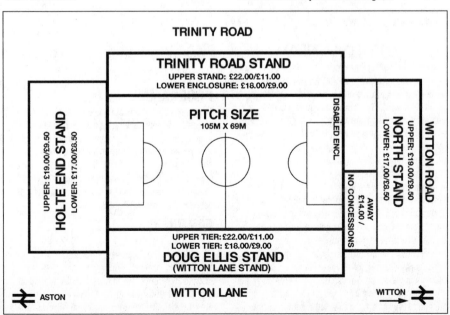

# BARNET

**ADDRESS:** Underhill Stadium
Westcombe Drive
Barnet
Herts EN5 2BE

**TELEPHONE No:** 0181 441 6932
**TICKET OFFICE:** 0181 449 6325
**FAX:** 0181 447 0655
**CLUBCALL:** 0891 12 15 44

**WEB SITE:**
www.twotogether.demon.co.uk
(unofficial).
Several good pages from the chaps who bring you the club fanzine

**E-MAIL:**
john@twotogether.demon.co.uk
All round good bloke, who will help/give advice if he can.

**NICKNAME:** The Bees

**RECORD ATTENDANCE:**
11,026 v Wycombe Wanderers Am Cup QF
23 February 1952 (W 2-0)

**CLUB COLOURS:**
**HOME:** Shirts: Amber and Black;
Shorts: Black; Socks: Amber & Black hoops
**AWAY:** Shirts: Grey with Black and White trim;
Shorts: Black/Grey; Socks: White/Black

**KIT SPONSORS:** *Loaded*

**MANUFACTURERS:** Errea
Who are generally despised by the local fans for their inability to get replica tops into the club shop.

## GROUND INFO

Away fans are sited in the temporary South Stand. Though as this is now seeing its fourth season of action, the description 'temporary' seems to be used in the loosest sense of the word. This is an area of some 1,000 uncovered seats which are an absolute delight to sit in when the weather is hot and sunny. Sadly, as some of you may have noticed, football in England is a winter sport which means that visiting supporters often have to endure sitting on wet seats and getting drenched.

If you are playing the Bees in winter, pray that you take enough down with you for the club to open the East Terrace since this is at least covered. Alternatively you might want to take along a youngster and thus be able to grab a place in the family stand.

The club no longer offers away supporters concessions (thanks a lot Mr Kleanthous) as it had done during even the bleakest of financial times (obviously this is the club's way of thanking those of you who dug into your pockets when the 'Save Barnet' collection buckets

were going around at various league grounds). However, to even things up somewhat, other than the Family Stand, Barnet fans no longer get concessions either, unless they are club members (Hm, so that should be appealing to the 'floating fan' — still, being sited just outside North London the club are obviously banking on the fact that there are no other teams to watch.....except Arsenal, Tottenham, Watford etc). To be fair to those in charge, if you do live in the area then it is worth becoming a member, especially for juniors who can then get free admission to the ground. This very progressive attitude makes the fact that visiting fans get stung by the Bees even more irritating and less easy to comprehend.

To be honest, the only thing steeper than the prices at Underhill is the pitch, but at least the playing surface is moving in the right direction as in the club's amateur days it used to have a 9ft slope between one goal and the other.

Be aware that a lot of games are deemed all-ticket due to the ground's small capacity, with no tickets being available on the Saturday of the match. So it is essential to check with the club before you travel to ensure you will get in.

**CAPACITY:** Stands: 1,902; Terrace: 2,115;
Total: 4,017

**AWAY FANS:** South Stand: 915;
East Terrace (overflow only): 450;
Total: 1,365

**DISABLED FACILITIES:** There are 12 spaces for wheelchair-bound fans and helpers, these being in the family enclosure of the ground. Admission is via the Barnet Lane gate and is free for disabled supporters, however, helpers now pay the full whack. Places should be pre-booked. The toilet facilities at the ground are much improved from previous years. There are no match commentaries available for the visually impaired and the club advises that parking facilities for disabled supporters are no longer available.

**PROGRAMME:** £1.50.
The sponsorship deal with *Loaded* was heralded with the statement that journos from the magazine would submit weekly articles for the programme and that *Loaded* would also feature monthly reports on the club's (mis)fortunes. There is no doubt as to who got the better end of the deal here (clue: I don't think it was the readers of *Loaded*) and along with a general sprucing up, this was one of the better programmes in 1997/98.

**FANZINES:**
*Two Together* £1.00
This seems to have improved immensely, with the editors focusing a lot of pages on the fight to secure the new stadium and it is well worth reading if only to keep up to date on the latest shenanigans. Quite a bit of humour too, even if some of this remains very much 'in' jokes, which

will sail right over the casual reader's head.

## TRAVEL

### NEAREST RAILWAY STATION:
New Barnet (Great Northern Line from Moorgate on weekdays, King's Cross weekends) (0171 922 6061)

### NEAREST TUBE STATION: High Barnet
(Northern Line)

### BUS: London Transport (0171 222 1234)

### BY CAR:
**FROM ALL PARTS:** M25 or A1 to the intersection of the two (J23 of M25). Take A1081 St Albans Road (signposted Barnet). As you approach Barnet town centre the road merges with the A1000. Continue along this road past High Barnet tube turning right 0.25 miles later into Fairfield Way, and then into Westcombe Drive for the ground. An alternative if coming from the south is to go up the A1 to Stirling Corner and turn right on to the A411 Barnet Road. Turn right after 0.25 miles into Barnet Gate which becomes May's Lane along which after one mile you can turn right into Barnet Lane for the ground.

**PARKING:** There is on-street parking around the ground, or you can park at High Barnet tube. If you opt for the latter be careful as it is a very, very tight left turn off the A1000. And the seemingly ever increasing pile of headlight/reflector glass in the gutter is a testament to those who took it just a bit too fast.

The other hassle with parking here is that, because you have to turn right to get out, it can take a bit of time to escape after the match. Fortunately as there are plenty of sets of traffic lights along the road you don't have to rely entirely on the legendary courtesy of London drivers.

## FUTURE DEVELOPMENTS
The good news for the club is that the FA has given it a one-year extension in which to get the ground up to the minimum required standard (at one stage they faced expulsion from the league at the end of the season); the bad news is that the club's plans for a multi-sports complex, including a 10,000 seat stadium which would offer parking for 700 at Copthall, Mill Hill, are being strongly opposed by local group Keep Copthall and Open Space (KCAOS). A public inquiry is being held to review the plans which means that, even if everything goes its way, the club will be incredibly lucky to move in to its new accommodation before the start of the 1999-2000 season.

## OTHER INFORMATION
The Old Red Lion by Fairfield Way is the nearest pub to the ground. Away fans are always welcome, and if the weather isn't too inclement there are tables outside where you can sit and inhale the fumes from the traffic on the Great North Road. Otherwise walk down Barnet Hill for the Queen's Arms, which is big and OK, or the Weaver, which is smaller and nicer. Between the two is a bookies for your fixed odds. The nearest chip shop is Fresh Fry, 3min walk from the ground by the Weaver.

The food in the ground is a bit hit and miss: the pies are OK (Peter's pies) but my burger was an awful combination of fat, gristle and sinew, which was so bad it was almost jettisoned before it was finished. The Bovvie was a good bit better and helped to wash the taste of the food away for which I will be eternally grateful.

The team now emerges onto the pitch to the strains of 'We've Got The Power' by Snap; ironic really as the PA seems to fade in and out (though you'll be impressed by the size of the speakers on the Main Stand!) which means you can hardly hear it.

*Total Football* Experience Rating: 68

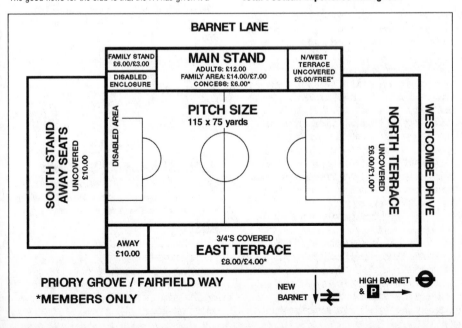

# BARNSLEY

**ADDRESS:** Oakwell Ground
Grove Street
Barnsley
S71 1ET

**TELEPHONE No:** 01226 211211
**TICKET OFFICE:** 01226 211211
**FAX:** 01226 211444
**CLUBCALL:** 0891 12 11 52
**WEB SITE:** http://www.yorkshire-web.co.uk/bfc
(semi official?) Rubbish

**NICKNAME:** Colliers, Tykes, Reds

**RECORD ATTENDANCE:**

40,255 v Stoke FA Cup 5th 15 February 1936 (W 2-1)

**CLUB COLOURS:**

**HOME:** Shirts: Red; Shorts: White; Socks: Red
**AWAY:** Shirts: White with Green flashes;
Shorts: Green; Socks: Green

**KIT SPONSORS:** ORA Electronics

**MANUFACTURERS:** Admiral

## GROUND INFO

The myth — Plucky Barnsley battling their way into the Premiership, their fans urging them on, not caring if they won or lost but just enjoying the experience.

The reality — I have to say that without a shadow of a doubt my trip to Oakwell was the worst day out of last season. So much so that it is difficult to know where to start on what is a fairly sorry tale.

Food and drink is dealt with in the 'Other Information' section of this entry so I'll content myself with the 'facilities' (and I use the word loosely) offered at the ground on my visit.

For £15 you get to sit on a plastic seat which has just been laid on terracing and from which you seem to spend more time looking at the neck of the bloke in front of you rather than the game. Stand up to try and see what's going on and you will be fairly swiftly told that if you don't sit down again you will be ejected (together with possibly such endearing comments as 'and I'll have my — insert the expletive of your choice — eye on you'. If it rains the club will offer you the opportunity to sit in what appears to be a see-through bin liner, for which they will have the effrontery to charge you £1.

The toilets are disgusting and the away end is filled with ridiculous signs; for example, the Ladbrokes hut (which, when I visited, would only hand out betting slips one at a time) is adorned with a sign stating that 'spectators must not climb on this building' — no really!!! I thought that was the way to the seats. In a way you have to commiserate with some of the home supporters who saw prices hiked through the roof after

promotion. The vast majority of fans bought season tickets but, where there was the opportunity to pay on the day, areas such as the archaic West Stand went up from £12.50 to £20.00 for the Upper Tier and from £11.00 to £17.00 for the Lower Tier.

**CAPACITY:** Stands: 19,007; Terrace: Nil

**AWAY FANS:** Total: 2,036

**DISABLED FACILITIES:** Barnsley was the first club in the league to construct a purpose-built stand for disabled fans and this holds 55. Admission to this stand is free for disabled fans, with their helpers paying £8. In addition, when the new Ora and East Stands were built, facilities for disabled supporters were also constructed. Phone the club to book a place. Matchday commentaries for the visually impaired are available and again these should be pre-booked. There are specific parking areas by the ground for disabled supporters.

**PROGRAMME:** £1.80

Went up 30p in 1997-8 (20%) but, it has to be said, that this is an excellent offering with a superb away section. This includes a diary of events and some very good general interest articles as well as the compulsory 'Tommy Tyke Sez' piece which is written in the local dialect. Definitely worth the outlay.

**FANZINES:**

| | |
|---|---|
| *South Riding Fanzine* | 50p |
| *Dizzy Heights* | 50p |
| *Better Red Than Dead* | 80p |

*South Riding* used to be an excellent read but I didn't see it on sale on my last visit. *Dizzy Heights* reflected the optimism of supporters and was not bad value for money although nothing special — to be fair though, I did see the first edition so the quality may have improved since then.

I didn't see a copy of *BRTD* when I went to the ground last season but I am assured that it lives on. From past experience of the mag I'd say don't be put off by the uninspiring title as, unlike many fanzines, it (rightly) concentrates on the contents rather than a snazzy front page.

## TRAVEL

### NEAREST RAILWAY STATION:

Barnsley (0114 272 6411 — Sheffield Enquiries)
The train station at Barnsley is one of the nicest buildings in the town and looks like a new shopping centre.

### BUS:

East bus station (01704 515151)
The phone number is advertised as 'the number that isn't a lottery', which is very handy because if they hadn't told me I would have wasted a quid selecting one number which doesn't appear on a lottery ticket in an attempt to win a rollover jackpot.

You can take either a 115,116 or 117 from the station to Pontefract Road and walk up to the ground from there. Watch out for the bus stops which have revolving information boards on them. These seem to have been specially designed to pitch anyone who leans on them on to the ground (much to the amusement of the locals).

## BY CAR:
**NORTH/SOUTH/WEST**: M1 to J37, and travel towards Barnsley on the A628 (Dodworth Road), keeping in the right-hand lane. After 0.25 miles you get to a crossroads and some traffic lights; turn right here (signposted Wakefield A6133, Pontefract and Doncaster). Continue along the A6133 (NB: 30mph restrictions on the dual carriageway) until you get to a crossroads where you see the Coach & Horses opposite you. Turn left, and then right by the next traffic lights into Oakwell Lane. At the bottom of this road turn left and immediately right into Grove Street. The ground is on your right.

**EAST:** Take the A628, first crossing the River Dearne and then driving past Beevor Hall. Turn right 200yd past the Hall into Grove Street and the ground is on your right.

NB: As you approach the town you'll see signposts for the ground, and, to be fair, these do take you to the Oakwell....eventually. If you don't fancy a tour of picturesque Barnsley then follow the instructions given above.

**PARKING:** There are car parks at both ends of the ground (£2). Stick to the main one that you see as you turn into Grove Street rather than the one by the away supporters' terrace entrance (unless you want to see 6,000-odd people hit the road before you). (It may be an idea to cover up your colours on the walk from the away end.) There is also plenty of street parking around, although if you go for this, make sure your handbrake is in good order and that you've been practising your hill-starts!

## FUTURE DEVELOPMENTS
The club is currently developing proposals for a new Spion Kop Stand. However, these are at a very early stage with no completion date available.

## OTHER INFORMATION
If I tell you that a couple of people I was talking to were apparently refused entry into a club on the day before a match because the bouncers felt that their southern accents might be responsible for provoking the locals into an attack you'll get the picture.

You'll not get into the Mount pub on Pontefract Road (the nearest pub to the ground) on match days, and you will probably not want to get into the Yorkshireman, the Old Courtyard and the Emporium in the town centre. The Beer Engine is a good meeting place for visiting fans, although I have heard reports (though not witnessed it myself) of people getting grief from home supporters between here and the ground.

There are a couple of chip shops in the town which, whilst nothing special, are certainly miles better than what is served inside Oakwell. However, inside the ground you do have the pleasure of the staff who will greet you with a miserable 'yeah what do yer want' and an exasperated sigh if you dare not have the right change with you.

Having re-read this entry I do appreciate that many fans may feel I haven't given the club a fair crack of the whip. However, all I can say is that, when I went to Oakwell, I got the distinct feeling that away fans were neither welcomed nor wanted, and this view has been borne out by other supporters I have spoken to. My abiding memory of my last visit was of seeing a visiting supporter getting punched full in the face as he left the ground for seemingly no more than having a replica shirt on.

*Total Football* **Experience Rating: 43**

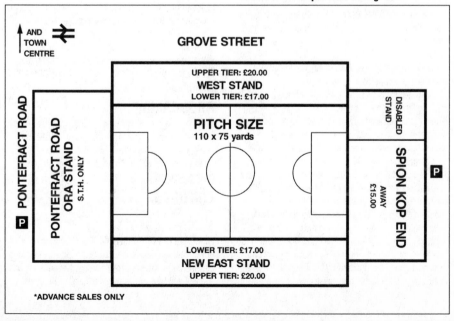

*ADVANCE SALES ONLY

# BIRMINGHAM CITY

**ADDRESS:** St Andrew's
St Andrew's Street
Birmingham B9 4NH
**TELEPHONE No:** 0121 772 0101
**TICKET OFFICE:**
0121 772 0101 (Ext 5)
**FAX:** 0121 766 7866
**CLUBCALL:** 0891 12 11 88/tickets
0891 33 29 88
**WEB SITE:** www.bcfc.com
**NICKNAME:** The Blues
**RECORD ATTENDANCE:**
67,341 v Everton FA Cup 5th 11 February 1939 (D 2-2)
Various other record/fact books tend to give the
attendance as either 68,844 or 66,844.

**CLUB COLOURS:**
**HOME:** Shirts: Blue with White trim;
Shorts: White; Socks: Blue
**AWAY:** Shirts: White with vertical Black fade stripe;
Shorts: Black; Socks: White;
**KIT SPONSORS:** Auto Windscreens
**MANUFACTURERS:** Pony

## GROUND INFO

One can only hope that the club has more luck with its
developed stadium than it has had in the past. Perhaps
top of the bad luck table is the time when the fire brigade
was called to put out a brazier, but when they arrived
instead of going for the traditional method of using water,
they doused it liberally with petrol instead, and virtually
gutted one of the stands in the process. Actually, with the
old stadium, gutting one of the stands would have
probably done upwards of £13.20 in damage.

St Andrew's has undergone the kind of face-lift that
Joan Collins only dreams about! Gone are the sprawling
terraces to be replaced by superb sweeping stands, which
are impressive to behold, although the touting of the .
redeveloped ground as the 'Old Trafford of the Midlands'
may be stretching it slightly. I've got to say I do miss the
sight of the old Kop which ran the full length of the pitch,
but I am just a sad traditionalist, and you won't hear the
Blues fans who go to the ground week-in week-out
complaining much. They still manage to create a fairly
good atmosphere there as well, and their rendition of
'Keep Right On To The End Of The Road' doesn't seem to
have been too muffled. The Railway Paddock suffers a bit
in comparison to the standards of the Tilton and Kop
Stands but it still offers a reasonable view of the action

for visiting supporters even if the toilets are a bit on the
dodgy side.

It's just a shame that amongst all the redevelopment
the club hasn't managed to find it in its heart to offer
concessions to away fans; still I don't suppose we can
have everything in this old life can we? Home fans do get
concessions if they are members of the club's Beau
Brummie scheme (and it should give fans money off for
inflicting such a dodgy pun on them!) or within the family
enclosure.

**CAPACITY:** Stands: 25,000 (reduced to 20,000
unti February 1999); Terrace: Nil
Capacity after February 1999; 30,000.

**AWAY FANS:** Railway Paddock: 3,600; (subject to
change because of redevelopment).
There have been problems for away fans in the not too
distant past, and it would be a blatant lie to say that St
Andrew's is one of those grounds where you'd stroll
around after a night match flashing your replica top to
some of the locals. However, the club has made a
concerted effort to weed out the problem and the vast
majority of the home fans seem to recognise what is
acceptable taunting and when the line has been crossed
(and get their point across). In fact, the only problems I
heard of last year were the Trevor Francis' son incident
and another where a fan threw a mobile phone at a
linesman. The phone hit him in the ear (and — at the
risk of being called flippant — at least makes a
difference from a pastie and it is good to talk).
The stewarding too has improved and there is more of a
'how can I help' rather than a 'not my job' attitude.

**DISABLED FACILITIES:** There are 90
spaces for wheelchair-bound fans available at the ground,
which means that pre-booking is required. The club
states that the cost for disabled fans and their helpers is
'to be decided'. As it was also unable to say whether
match commentaries were available you get the feeling
that the facilities for the disabled is an area on which Ms
Brady has still to work her magic touch.

**PROGRAMME:** £1.70.
Had a bit of a revamp last year and, to be fair, the quality
of writing did improve somewhat. However, it still is a
catalogue for all those lovely Birmingham City
accessories with which you need to fill your life (even
more so than other programmes).

**FANZINES:**
| | |
|---|---|
| *Blues News* | 65p |
| *Wake Up Blue* | £1 |

I think (but I may be wrong) that *The Heathen* is no
longer with us. *WUB* has therefore taken on the mantle of
praising the Golds, David Sullivan and Karren Brady one
moment and then vilifying them the next. Still, in the

copy I saw, our Trev seemed to be drawing the line of fire. Not happy people....

## TRAVEL

### NEAREST RAILWAY STATION:

Bordesley (0121 643 2711 — Birmingham New Street) Although New Street (£3ish cab fare itself or Moor Street [20min walk]) offer the better services and are more likely stopping off points.

**BUS:** Birmingham Central — Midland Road (0121 200 2700 — Centro Hotline)
The best bet from the city centre is the 97 or 96.

### BY CAR:
### FROM ALL PARTS:

M6 to J6 (Spaghetti Junction) and take the A38 Aston Expressway. After 1.5 miles you get to the second exit from the Expressway; leave at this point and take the first exit at the roundabout on to the Dartford Middleway A4540 (signposted Bordesley). Go straight over the next three roundabouts and 0.75 miles later turn left into Kingston Road. At the bottom of Kingston Road turn left into Coventry Road and keep to the left for Cattell Road and the ground.

**PARKING:** Considering St Andrew's is virtually in the middle of Birmingham, parking around the ground is pretty easy. The main car park is now for permit holders only, although there are other car parks in the area that you can get into on a match day.

## FUTURE DEVELOPMENTS

It has been announced that the Railway End will be redeveloped during the summer and will hopefully be open for business in February 1999 (capacity 8,200). It has been stated that this will house both home and away fans (which may make for an interesting atmosphere) with the visitors likely to get 2-4000 seats. This position is subject to review by the club. The net effect is that the ground capacity will be increased to c30,000.

## OTHER INFORMATION

It's difficult to know what to make of the team of the Golds, David Sullivan and Karren Brady. Certainly St Andrew's is a better stadium since their arrival (and Birmingham a better team) and the club is much more responsive to the fact that fans' needs and requirements must be sought and addressed. However, there is a downside to this in that the 'team' is incredibly commercially aware.

Having said this, I believe that there is a love for the club that is growing at its heart (perversely, probably, the most obvious signs of this are the occasional outbursts of anger — you don't get cross about something you don't care about). Perhaps the key thing is that City fans seem generally happy although there remains that good old fashioned streak of footie pessimism that makes them wonder how long it is going to last.

If you fancy a drink it can be as well to stick to the city centre, although they do serve a very good pint at the, admittedly basic, Brighton Arms in Small Heath which is a 10min walk away. The recent success of the Blues means that old favourites like the Roost on Cattell Street are now 'members only' on match days.

There is a moderate choice of food available outside the ground. The mobile with the sign stating that they sell 'most excellent burgers' isn't necessarily telling the completely unfettered truth. Once inside, the standard does improve markedly with a very tasty steak and kidney pie although as with many things about the club it is not the cheapest you'll ever find.

Finally, hats off to Birmingham who had perhaps the greatest marketing offer literature that I have seen in the last few years when their Blues Superstore gave supporters the chance to 'meet the Gold brothers and the PG Tips Monkeys' — make your own punchline!!

***Total Football* Experience Rating: 79**

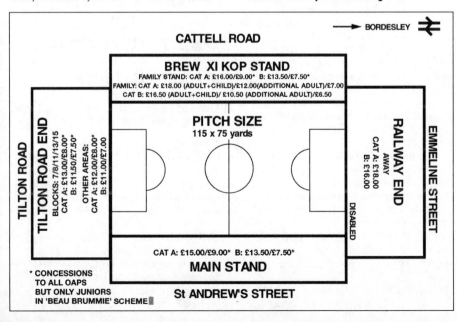

CATTELL ROAD

→ BORDESLEY

**BREW XI KOP STAND**
FAMILY STAND: CAT A: £16.00/£9.00* B: £13.50/£7.50*
FAMILY: CAT A: £18.00 (ADULT+CHILD)/£12.00(ADDITIONAL ADULT)/£7.00
CAT B: £16.50 (ADULT+CHILD)/ £10.50 (ADDITIONAL ADULT)/£6.50

**PITCH SIZE**
115 x 75 yards

TILTON ROAD

TILTON ROAD END
BLOCKS: 7/8/11/13/15
CAT A: £13.00/£8.00*
B: £11.50/£7.50*
OTHER AREAS:
CAT A: £12.00/£8.00*
B: £11.00/£7.00

RAILWAY END
AWAY
CAT A: £18.00
B: £16.00

DISABLED

EMMELINE STREET

CAT A: £15.00/£9.00* B: £13.50/£7.50*
**MAIN STAND**

* CONCESSIONS
TO ALL OAPS
BUT ONLY JUNIORS
IN 'BEAU BRUMMIE' SCHEME

**St ANDREW'S STREET**

# BLACKBURN ROVERS

**ADDRESS:** Ewood Park
Bolton Road
Blackburn
BB2 4JF

**TELEPHONE No:** 01254 698888

**TICKET OFFICE:** 01254 671666

**FAX:** 01254 671042

**WEB SITE:** www.rovers.co.uk

**E-MAIL:** enquiries@rovers.co.uk

**CLUBCALL:** 0891 12 11 79

**NICKNAME:** Rovers or Blue and Whites.

## RECORD ATTENDANCE:
61,783 v Bolton FA Cup 6th 2 March 1929 (D 1-1)

## CLUB COLOURS:
**HOME:** Shirts: Blue and White halves;
Shorts: White; Socks: White
**AWAY:** Shirts: Orange; Shorts: White;
Socks: Orange/White

## KIT SPONSORS: C.I.S. Insurance

## MANUFACTURERS: Asics

# GROUND INFO

Ewood Park is one of those grounds that suddenly appear from nowhere as you drive into the heart of the home town, and the stadium that Uncle Jack built is incredibly impressive on first (and even subsequent) sight.

Once inside you won't fail to be impressed by the away facilities which really do offer everything you could want (the bar even serves shorts). A minor gripe may be that the TVs that the club has installed are sited too near to the actual entrance for the seats, which can cause congestion.

The ground itself is quite strange: three magnificent stands and one distinctly old looking one with pillars a plenty to block the view and a bleak hill (Higher Croft) behind it. Incredibly this is NOT the one that is given to visiting supporters and the away section (the Darwen End) offers away fans plenty of leg room, a good view and zero hassle from either stewards or home fans.

On the plus side, the club offers concessions to visiting fans which exactly mirror those given to Rovers' supporters but, on the minus side, it does operate a twin categorisation pricing strategy (which ultimately costs the club first place in this guide).

## CAPACITY: Stands: 31,367; Terrace: Nil

## AWAY FANS: Darwen End: Upper Right 1,500;
Darwen End: Lower Right 2,300;

Total: 3,800

This figure can be increased to the whole of the Darwen End (approximately 8,000) if demand is sufficient.

## DISABLED FACILITIES: Brilliant! The front row of each end of the ground is allocated to disabled fans and their helpers (a grand total of 822 places!), visitors are welcome, and the design means you can actually get to be near your mates which makes a welcome change from the unspoken attitude of 'Goodness gracious me! Do disabled supporters have "normal" friends?' Although there is plenty of room you should think about pre-booking as admission is free for disabled fans with helpers paying standard matchday prices. There is supervised parking at the ground. Headphones are available for matchday commentaries at the Blackburn End, and again these should be pre-booked. If you can't organise a set of headphones, bring a radio and tune in to Radio Rovers (1404AM) for match commentaries.

## PROGRAMME: £1.50
The *Blue 'n' White*, as the programme is called, shows continued improvement with an excellent five-page visitors' section and several general interest articles. Even the 'pure' Blackburn articles aren't (always) written with a rose-coloured tint and are worth checking out.

## FANZINES:
| | |
|---|---:|
| *Loadsamoney* | £1 |
| *4,000 Holes* | £1 |

Apart from having one of my favourite fanzine titles (named after the number of holes in Blackburn according to the Beatles in *A Day in The Life*) FTH really offers very little inside its nice shiny cover and *Loadsamoney* is a far better bet both in terms of quality and quantity of writing.

# TRAVEL

## NEAREST RAILWAY STATION:
Blackburn Central (01772 259439 — Preston Enquiries)

## NEAREST BUS STATION:
Blackburn Central (01254 51112)
The number 346 (Darwen) bus runs from both the station and the town centre to the ground.

## BY CAR:
**NORTH/WEST:** M6 to J31, take the A666 (Oooer! Yon tarmac hath the number of the beast!) towards Samlesbury and Blackburn. As you travel along the road you will see signs for Nova Scotia and Ewood. Go past the Infirmary and 0.5 mile later turn left into Kidder Street; the ground is on your right.
**SOUTH:** M6 to J29. When you leave the motorway turn left onto the A6 (signposted Chorley), turning left after a mile onto the B5256. Turn right onto the A6061 by the Fielden Arms pub (Livesey Park Road) and continue for approx two miles.
You will climb a hill, and as you descend it you will

see the ground loom up in front of you. Continue to the bottom of the hill and turn right at the roundabout on to the Bolton Road for the stadium.

NB: This way takes you on about 5-6 miles of winding narrow roads, and it may be as well, if the traffic is bad, to go in via the north directions.

**EAST:** M65 to J6. When you leave the motorway go straight over at the exit roundabout, and take the next left into Whitebirk Road, then right onto the A679 Accrington Road (signposted Audley). After 1.5 miles the road (now called Lower Audley Street) is crossed by two roads — Park Road and Great Bolton Street. Turn left into the second of these, this is the A666 (signposted Bolton Road, Ewood), then as north.

**FROM ALL PARTS:** With the opening of the new motorway, there is now an alternative route to the ground, namely: M6 to J29, then onto the M65 towards Blackburn — leave the M65 at J4 (A666) and follow signs towards Blackburn. Ewood Park is about one mile down the road on the right-hand side.

**PARKING:** The car parks at the ground are for permit holders only. There is a free car park on the first roundabout as you head towards Blackburn town centre from the ground on the Bolton Road.

## FUTURE DEVELOPMENTS

There has been talk of The Walker Steel Stand being rebuilt at some point in time to bring it in line with the rest of the ground although, at present, this seems to be — according to the information I got from the club — very much in the planning stages.

## OTHER INFORMATION

The town is famous for its curry houses, and if you've got the time you should go into Darwen for a particularly fine one. If your tastes are simpler, check out the excellent meat and potato pies sold from the window of a converted house opposite the ground.

If you fancy a pint then it is worth climbing the hill that leads out of the town for about 0.75 mile to the White Bull, the Brown Cow or the Moorgate; the third of these is a bit small, but all serve a decent pint.

Whatever your tastes, the new Ewood Park is well worth a visit, if just to see how the other half lives, and it may go some way towards convincing doubters that the arrival of all-seater stadia does not necessarily mean the onset of all things dreadful: good food (although be warned the mobile pie sellers are more expensive by 10p a pie than the serving hatches), good drink and good attitude. It also offers a chance for a betting game. All round the outside of the pitch are blue seats for stewards to sit on. However, the stewards don't actually go to these till five minutes before the end of the game by which time half of them have been scattered to the four winds by balls going out of play, So you and each of your mates pick a stool, stick a quid into the pot and the first (or last) one hit takes the lot.

Although the ground isn't always full, the club is very proud of the fact that they are 'the Town's team' and this is perhaps reflected by a survey which looked at each league club's population and their average gate and came to the conclusion that Blackburn are the second most successful club in attracting local fans with a whopping 20.4% of the population attending every game.

Finally, for the collectors of trivia among you, in 1994, when Rovers were redeveloping the ground, workmen found what they thought was a footie but turned out to be someone's severed head which had been there for 15 years!! Given that the murderer was tracked down and convicted this probably is a warning to any fans to stay in line for, like the Mounties, the Blackburn Old Bill 'always get t'man'.

*Total Football* **Experience Rating: 92**

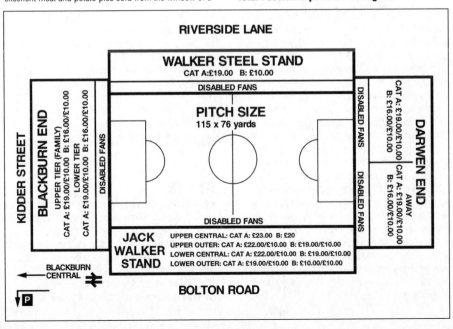

RIVERSIDE LANE

WALKER STEEL STAND
CAT A:£19.00  B: £10.00

DISABLED FANS

PITCH SIZE
115 x 76 yards

DISABLED FANS

BLACKBURN END
UPPER TIER (FAMILY)
CAT A: £19.00/£10.00  B: £16.00/£10.00
LOWER TIER
CAT A: £19.00/£10.00  B: £16.00/£10.00

DISABLED FANS

KIDDER STREET

DISABLED FANS

DISABLED FANS

DARWEN END
CAT A: £19.00/£10.00  B: £16.00/£10.00
AWAY
CAT A: £19.00/£10.00  B: £16.00/£10.00

JACK WALKER STAND
UPPER CENTRAL: CAT A: £23.00  B: £20
UPPER OUTER: CAT A: £22.00/£10.00  B: £19.00/£10.00
LOWER CENTRAL: CAT A: £22.00/£10.00  B: £19.00/£10.00
LOWER OUTER: CAT A: £19.00/£10.00  B: £10.00/£10.00

BLACKBURN CENTRAL

P

BOLTON ROAD

# BLACKPOOL

**ADDRESS:** Bloomfield Road
Blackpool
Lancashire
FY1 6JJ

**TELEPHONE No:** 01253 405331

**TICKET OFFICE:** 01253 404331

**FAX:** 01253 405011

**E-MAIL:** bfc@cyberscape.net

**WEB SITE:**
www.cyberspace.net/users/bfc/

**CLUBCALL:** 0891 12 16 48

**NICKNAME:** Seasiders

**RECORD ATTENDANCE:**
38,098 v Wolves Div 1 17 September 1955 (W 2-1)

**CLUB COLOURS:**
**HOME:** Shirts: Tangerine; Shorts: Tangerine;
Socks: Tangerine
**AWAY:** Shirts: Royal Blue; Shorts: Royal Blue
Socks: Royal Blue
Never dare call the kit 'orange' unless you want to be subjected to a 10min rant (and while we're at it, it's probably as well to avoid the term 'donkey lashers' to describe the locals as well).

**KIT SPONSORS:** Telewest Communications

**MANUFACTURERS:** Lotto

## GROUND INFO

With the forthcoming demise of Springfield Park, Wigan, Blackpool looks ready to take on the mantle of worst ground (facilities-wise) in Britain. With each passing year, the ground looks older and more decrepit and a visit only goes to remind you how long ago the side's glory years really are. The away terrace is basic (the toilets are not nice at all and uncovered which means that when the wind and rain get up — and remember Blackpool is one of England's best tourist resorts so this is virtually compulsory — it can be a very bleak place to be). On the brighter side the club has reintroduced concessions for visiting supporters, although I think it is a bit of a pity that these do not mirror those offered to home fans who go into the paddocks to the tune of £2 less.

Stewarding is very laid back and, for the majority of matches, the police presence seems negligible. On the whole, providing you keep within reason you will be allowed to go your own way. If you do need assistance, then the stewards seem happy (and, more importantly, able) to help.

**CAPACITY:** Stands: 3,041; Terrace: 8,254;
Total: 11.295

**AWAY FANS:** Spion Kop: 1,482; East Paddock (North): 1,050; Total: 2,532

**DISABLED FACILITIES:** There are spaces for 12 wheelchair-bound fans in the South Stand by the players' tunnel, and there is no admission charge for disabled fans, with their helpers paying £10.00 (£5 concessions). The club states that pre-booking is not required, but given the limited number of places it is better to be safe than sorry. Match commentaries for the blind are available (but only three spaces so book early). There is also plenty of parking at the ground, with some spaces allocated for the use of disabled supporters.

**PROGRAMME:** £1.70
At last, something that has improved at the ground over the last few years. From being a truly dreadful rag, it has now got a nice layout combined with a fair content.

**FANZINES:**
*Another View From The Tower*                £1
I'm guessing that this has been born out of the old Blackpool fanzine *A View From The Tower* (amazing deduction Holmes, whatever led you to that conclusion?). If this is not true, it certainly has one amazing similarity to its predecessor — that it never seems to be on sale in the ground.

## TRAVEL

**NEAREST RAILWAY STATION:**
Blackpool South Shore/Blackpool North (01772 259349) South Shore is the nearest railway station to the ground, but only has about a third of the trains serving it that North does. If you end up at South Shore, turn left as you leave the station and follow your nose (just keep crossing car parks and you can't miss the ground). From North it's probably as well to cab (£4), bus or tram it. Scrooges should turn right as you leave the station, go through the subway to Talbot Road. Walk all the way down to the North Pier Prom where you should turn left. Go past the Tower, to Central Pier then turn left into Lytham Road for Bloomfield Road and the ground.

**NEAREST BUS STATION:**
Blackpool Transport (01253 23931)
Talbot Road, two miles

**BY CAR:**
**FROM ALL PARTS:** M6 to J32. At J32 exit onto the M55; continue to the end of the motorway, and carry straight on along the spine road (Yeadon Way). Go straight over the first two roundabouts, then when you get to a mini-roundabout, turn right and the ground is 0.5 mile on the right.

NB: If you are driving to the ground from the town/beach area, then head towards the Tower (driving from the Pleasure Beach area) along the sea front. Turn right off the Promenade then left onto Lytham Road. Continue until you get to some traffic lights beyond which is the Old Bridge pub, at which you should turn right into Bloomfield Road and the ground is 250yd on the left. If in any doubt head towards 'Rigby' car parks (signposted in green).

**PARKING:** There is a large (3,000 space) pay-and-display adjacent to the ground (Rigby Car Park), which is cheap and easy to get away from (£2ish in 'high season'; £1ish in 'low season'). Some on-street parking is also available.

## FUTURE DEVELOPMENTS

In the late 1980s Blackpool first announced that they were going to build a new ground. Initial plans to redevelop Bloomfield Road were thwarted by the council and the club decided to move to Whyndyke Farm (at the end of the M55) a couple of miles outside town. Plans were submitted for a 25,000-seat stadium with (the now infamous) retractable roof which would sit at the heart of a leisure complex. In November 1997 following numerous problems (disagreements/jail sentences etc), the land owners at the site announced the deal was dead in the water. The club says that the 'Coliseum' will still be built, though when and where is much less clear.

## OTHER INFORMATION

Blackpool is one of those places where football almost seems secondary to the day out (heresy!). Don't go to the place with any ideas other than to simply enjoy the day/night/weekend. You always tend to get one or two people who get sniffy at the fact that there are 3ft by 2ft signs for fart powder, and yes it is tacky, but more importantly, it's fun, and besides, where else in the world would you find a shop that is half dedicated to selling

spectacles with the other half selling marital aids? (The window display is wild!!!)

There are rakes of pubs (although not that many very close to the ground) and it must be said that some of these seem to view footie fans as if they were a disease. However, their attitude does seem to soften in the low season, and even in high season there are very few who will not take your money off you.

Inside the ground the food is passable and, if you are going out of the tourist season, is probably better than some of the chip shops where you are never sure how old the stock is. The tea is hot but weak, and you might opt for the hot blackcurrant instead, which is fine. Two things bound to turn you off, though, are, firstly, the fact that away fans pay a premium on food and, secondly, that the home fans seem to have a lot better choice (including ice creams on hot days when all you have to look forward to are warm soft drinks).

If the match is dull you can always spend your time looking at the Tower which has a hypnotic light going round and round it. Also keep an eye/ear open for the newspaper seller who spends about two hours before a game circling the outside of the ground, and the full 90min of the match walking round the perimeter of the pitch uttering only one sound — 'Herehhhh'. Apparently this translates as 'Get your copy of the *Gazette* here, fine townsfolk'. This man is an absolute hero, and every time he passes the home fans he gets a cheer and a response of 'Herehhhh', which always makes him smile, and which he always acknowledges with a nod of the head.

The staff in the club shop are excellent, and have plenty of time for away as well as home fans, although in keeping with the town's ambience they do have some particularly garish souvenirs on sale, top of the list being a Sir Stanley Matthews toby jug/tea mug in luminous orange.

***Total Football* Experience Rating: 63**

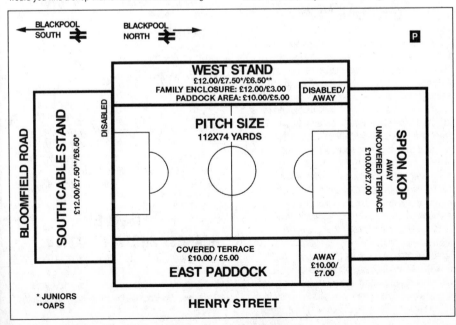

BLACKPOOL SOUTH

BLACKPOOL NORTH

P

**WEST STAND**
£12.00/£7.50*/£6.50**
FAMILY ENCLOSURE: £12.00/£3.00
PADDOCK AREA: £10.00/£5.00

DISABLED/ AWAY

**PITCH SIZE**
112X74 YARDS

DISABLED

BLOOMFIELD ROAD

**SOUTH CABLE STAND**
£12.00/£7.50**/£6.50*

**SPION KOP**
AWAY
UNCOVERED TERRACE
£10.00/£7.00

**COVERED TERRACE**
£10.00 / £5.00

**EAST PADDOCK**

AWAY
£10.00/ £7.00

* JUNIORS
**OAPS

**HENRY STREET**

# BOLTON WANDERERS

**ADDRESS:** Reebok Stadium
Burnden Way
Lostock
Bolton
BL6 6JW

**TELEPHONE No:** 01204 673673
**TICKET OFFICE:** 01204 673601
**FAX:** 01204 673773
**WEBSITE** www.boltonwfc.co.uk
(Official)
**E-MAIL:** tba
**CLUBCALL:** 0891 12 11 64
**NICKNAME:** The Trotters
**RECORD ATTENDANCE:** 69,912

v Man City FA Cup 5th 18 February 1933 (L 2-4)
There have been numerous instances of capacity crowds
of 25,000 at the Reebok since its opening. The first of
these was for the visit of Manchester United in the
Premiership on 20 September 1997 (D 0-0)

## CLUB COLOURS:

**HOME:** Shirts: White with Blue side panel;
Shorts: Navy Blue; Socks: Navy Blue
**AWAY:** Shirts: Yellow; Shorts: Yellow;
Socks: Yellow

**KIT SPONSORS:** Reebok
**MANUFACTURERS:** Reebok

## GROUND INFO

As with the McAlpine Stadium, Huddersfield, the Reebok
Stadium is more than just four stands, it is a genuine
thing of beauty and when you see it for the first time it is
likely to induce awe, goosebumps and envy in equal
proportions. The brilliant concave roofing and bowl
design means that it would look more in place in Spain
or Italy than just off the M61. It is difficult to know what
to make of the 25,000 capacity. Certainly for the money
spent on the stadium (£30 million), you might expect
more and some feel that it shows a lack of self belief by
those in charge at the club in that it suggests they can
never really compete in terms of support with the
Manchester or Merseyside big clubs. On the other hand
perhaps it is simply that those in charge of the
development have opted against a cram them in policy;
certainly the leg room is better than you would find at
many other grounds, and whilst 25,000 isn't a massive
capacity it does mean that the ground is always either full
or nearly full which gives it an excellent atmosphere.
Other facilities which are being constructed at the site
include a bowling alley, multiplex, and in keeping with
Bolton's proud tradition....a supermarket!! Fortunately for
visiting supporters this one is going to be outside the
stadium rather than between them and the pitch as was
the case at Burnden.

**CAPACITY:** Stands: 25,000
**AWAY FANS:** South Stand: 3,000

This can be increased to the full capacity of the South
Stand (5,200) if appropriate.
The visitors' end at the Reebok has all the facilities you
would expect from it: unrestricted views (even the first
row of seats is raised so that you are looking down on
the pitch instead of being level with it), bars, a bookies,
decent toilet facilities, TVs for pre-match entertainment.
Slightly less expected is that the club has priced this very
reasonably (just £13 for a lower tier seat) and also that
concessions are given in all parts of the ground. An
added bonus is that the shape of the ground means that it
doesn't take too many visiting fans to get a decent
atmosphere going.

**DISABLED FACILITIES:** There are positions
for wheelchair-bound supporters in all parts of the
ground, numbering just under 200 in total. Wheelchair
users and visually impaired supporters are admitted free
of charge, with helpers paying standard rates. Places
should be pre-booked. Matchday commentaries are
available as are parking facilities (both of these should be
pre-booked).

**PROGRAMME:** £2.00
A mightily unhandy A4 size. I didn't really think it would
have been possible for the last season effort to get any
worse, but it did and of the 36 pages in the copy I
bought, only three could be said to be of any interest or
relevance to visiting supporters — this really is one to
give a wide berth to.

## FANZINES:

| | |
|---|---|
| *White Love* | £1.00 |
| *Tripe 'N' Trotters* | £1.00 |

A quick word of thanks to the (anonymous) person who
sent me a copy of *Tripe 'N' Trotters* with the note that not
all Wanderers fans glory in the Munich air disaster
(certainly the behaviour of Bolton supporters at Old
Trafford on the 40th anniversary of the event seemed to
mirror that feeling). However, let us not praise *T&T* for
being civilised, instead let us praise it for being a funny
and incisive publication which is well worth a buy to
catch up with the glory of having a new ground and the
pain of watching a team on the verge of relegation.

## TRAVEL

**NEAREST RAILWAY STATION:**
Bolton Trinity Street (0161 832 8353 Manchester
Enquiries)
The construction of Lostock Halt is due to commence
during the 1998-9 season, this will be sited just behind the
West Stand.

## NEAREST BUS STATION:

Trinity Street: Tel 01772 886633 (Stagecoach Enquiries) There are several services that run from around Bolton to the new stadium, but these 'specials' are very much for home fans only. Visiting supporters should either get the number 11 from outside the court house on Black Horse Street (on a Saturday these are at 12.25pm arriving at 1pm or 1.55pm arriving at 2.30pm) or splash out a fiver or so on a cab.

## BY CAR:

**FROM ALL DIRECTIONS:** M61 to J6. Take the A6027 Horwich Link Road for 0.3 mile and you will come to a roundabout; visiting fans follow 'Car Park' signs. Basically you see the ground as you come down the motorway.

**PARKING:** The good news is that there is parking for up to 2,000 fans around the ground (including a separate section for away fans), with another 3,000 planned at various other parts of the leisure complex. This slightly less pleasing information is that it will set you back £5 to use one of them!! The trouble is because this is an out of town stadium there are very few roads around which you can park in, so start saving. Even these extravagant fees do not ensure you a quick start to your journey. There was a fairly impressive snarl-up on my visit which meant that although I got away after about two minutes, a mate who was parked a little way away had 25min before he got out of first gear.

## FUTURE DEVELOPMENTS

None at present.

## OTHER INFORMATION

If you fancy a beer before the match then, unless you go inside the ground where they serve McEwans and John Smiths at £1.95 a pint, you can be struggling. The Beehive is for home fans only and Bennigans Americans Tavern seemed to be shut when I went there. You can go into Bolton, but if you do, be careful as some of the locals can be a tad inhospitable (although the Bromilow Arms on Lostock Lane is fairly welcoming). If you want to be assured of a good and hassle-free drink, consider nipping down the B5288 for five miles to Wigan (see the Wigan entry for more details), although if you do take this option be warned that the roads can get a bit chocka before the match so allow yourself enough time.

The food inside the Reebok is surprisingly good, although because there was only one hatch serving away fans, it did get very crowded (which in turn blocked the gangways to the seats which made the problem worse etc etc). Please note that, while the club finds £20 notes an acceptable form of payment for tickets, the same is not true when you are trying to buy food and they stick to the rules fairly strictly although no doubt after 20min queuing for a pie and a tea only to be turned away for having such money you'll be happy to know that 'I don't make the rules mate, but you know... Never mind eh...' (yes, I do actually). If you do actually manage to purchase a pie, then you'll be impressed with the nice touch that it actually comes with a fork, so ending that unsightly scramble to get it all into your mouth before your fingers receive second degree burns from the filling.

There can be no denying that the new Reebok Stadium is a massive improvement on Burnden (it even boasts separate tunnels for home and away teams) and what is equally refreshing to report is that there seems to have been a modernisation of attitudes from both club and home supporters towards visiting fans. I still heard of some fans encountering problems at the ground last year but on a far lesser scale than in previous seasons.

*Total Football* **Experience Rating: 76**

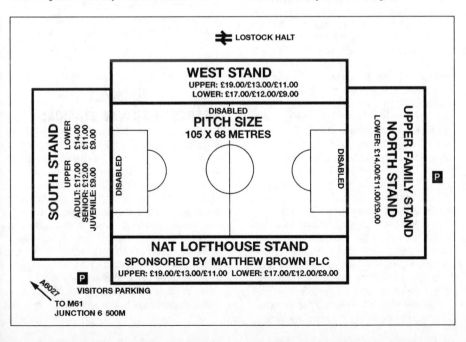

**LOSTOCK HALT**

**WEST STAND**
UPPER: £19.00/£13.00/£11.00
LOWER: £17.00/£12.00/£9.00

DISABLED
**PITCH SIZE**
**105 X 68 METRES**
DISABLED
DISABLED

**SOUTH STAND**
UPPER LOWER
ADULT: £17.00 £14.00
SENIOR: £12.00 £11.00
JUVENILE: £9.00 £9.00

**UPPER FAMILY STAND**
**NORTH STAND**
LOWER: £14.00/£11.00/£9.00

P

**NAT LOFTHOUSE STAND**
**SPONSORED BY MATTHEW BROWN PLC**
UPPER: £19.00/£13.00/£11.00  LOWER: £17.00/£12.00/£9.00

A6027

P
**VISITORS PARKING**

**TO M61**
**JUNCTION 6 500M**

BOLTON WANDERERS BOLTON WANDERERS BOLTON WANDERERS

21

# BOURNEMOUTH

**ADDRESS:** Dean Court
Bournemouth
Dorset BH7 7AF

**TELEPHONE No:** 01202 395381

**TICKET OFFICE:** 01202 395381

**FAX:** 01202 309797

**WEB SITE:** www.afcb.co.uk (official)

**E-MAIL:** enquiries@afcb.co.uk

**CLUBCALL:** 0891 12 11 63

**NICKNAME:** The Cherries

**RECORD ATTENDANCE:**
28,799 v Man Utd. FA Cup 6th 2 March 1957

**CLUB COLOURS:**
**HOME:** Shirts: Red/Black pinstripes
Shorts: Black; Socks: Black
**AWAY:** Shirts: Green and Black stripes; Shorts: Green;
Socks: Green

**KIT SPONSORS:** Seward Rover MG

**MANUFACTURERS:** Patrick

## GROUND INFO

Where do we start? Is it by applauding the club for offering excellent concessions for both home and away fans or is it by booing them roundly for having introduced without doubt the most complex ground pricing in the Football League? Given that fans are expected to utter the sentence 'I'll have a ticket for the Family Stand, Premium Section Category A game please,' I think possibly the latter. At least away fans' concessions are static regardless of the match: £5 on the terrace (hooray) but nothing for a seat (hiss). A little thing to think about. When AFCB nearly went to the wall, fans from other clubs dug into their pockets to try and help out. Presumably the clubs with the biggest followings gave the most money, so how do Bournemouth say thank you? They up the price for these same people (big club = category A) to go in the ground. Thanks.

The view from the away terrace is somewhat obscured by the fact that the pillars that the fencing was attached to remain (20 pillars and no roof — someone's having a laugh!!). The away seating at Dean Court is restricted to the front five rows of A Block and is designated only for families, OAPs and disabled fans.

If you go onto the away terrace you will see an old boy lurking at the back who resembles a disreputable Santa Claus. He is a local who the club allows to come to every match free of charge (and who used always to bring his greyhound with him before it went to the giant dog kennel in the sky) but rather than the option of a roof over his head he prefers the open end. Slightly eccentric but a true footie fan and nice to see that — in some instances — the club shows its appreciation of his support.

**CAPACITY:** Stands: 3,140; Terrace: 7,360
Total: 10,500

**AWAY FANS:** A Block Stand: 150; Brighton
Beach End (uncovered terrace):
2,620; Total: 2,770

## DISABLED FACILITIES:

There are spaces for approximately 15 fans in a specially designed shelter by the South Stand. The club states that disabled fans receive complimentary tickets and that helpers pay a concessionary amount. Pre-booking is required and there are disabled parking facilities at the ground. There are no matchday commentaries available for the blind, although the club is still hoping to introduce them at some point in time.

Bournemouth is one of the few clubs which, if disabled away fans turn up on the day, will let them into the Brighton Beach End, provided they feel there are not likely to be any problems through overcrowding. If you do take this option, expect to pay full whack and accept a moderate view, although you should be all right using the toilets as these are fairly spacious.

**PROGRAMME:** £1.60

This seems to have taken a step backwards last year. Apart from an excellent trivia and statistics page on the visiting side, I found very little to read.

## FANZINES:

Community Service        £1

December 1997 saw the last ever edition of Not the 8502; however, before the tears were dried on the passing of this cracking little fanzine, it was announced that several of the people responsible for putting it together were going to launch a new effort, and thus Community Service was born.

## TRAVEL

### NEAREST RAILWAY STATION:

Pokesdown or Bournemouth Central (01202 292474) Pokesdown is about 0.75 miles from the ground but only has about one train every hour. It is fairly pointless asking the locals for directions as they will look at you as if you are some kind of weirdo. 'No football team here mush' seems a standard reply. Turn right as you leave the station and take the first right into Gloucester Road. As you go down this road you'll see the floodlights on your left.

If (as is likely) you end up at Bournemouth then either try and catch a bus (25, 68 or 33) to the Queen's Park or prepare to hike up to the Asda at which you should turn left into Holdenhurst Road which eventually leads to Littledown Avenue and Thistlebarrow Road. Note if you walk: allow yourself 20-25min to get there.

**BUS:** Central Bus Depot (01202 673555) Get either a 33, which drops you off right by the ground, or a 25 or a 68 and get off at the Queen's Hotel.

## BY CAR:

**NORTH and EAST:** A338 Wessex Way towards Bournemouth. Turn left off the A338 at the King's Park exit (signposted Football Traffic). Take the first left at the mini-roundabout into Littledown Avenue (do not take the next exit signposted King's Park and Parking), then immediately right into Thistlebarrow Road. The entrance to the ground is at the bend of the road.

**WEST:** A3049 through Bournemouth continuing until you cross the A338 Wessex Way dual carriageway. At the next roundabout turn left into Holdenhurst Road, and at the following roundabout take the second exit into Littledown Avenue. Then as north.

**PARKING:** There are a couple of large car parks by the ground. The one immediately opposite is the club car park and will cost you £1.00 for the pleasure of being boxed in after the match. Alternatively 50yd further on is a pay-and-display car park (60p for four hours) where drivers find their own space and where you will not be blocked in. Take your pick. There is some on-street parking in the area.

## FUTURE DEVELOPMENTS

Now that the club's existence has been secured, attention is being switched into how to improve the facilities offered. Initially it was considered that Dean Court would be redeveloped. However, these plans appear to have been put on to the back burner and the focus is now on building a new stadium/leisure facility off the A338 Wessex Way. A site for this between the hospital and Tesco Supermarket has been earmarked but everything is still in the planning stage.

## OTHER INFORMATION

The Queen's Park on Holdenhurst Road is the only pub in the immediate area but it is welcoming enough, serves a decent beer and last time I was in, the fruit machine seemed to be on permanent payout. The Dean Court Supporters Club at the ground will allow in up to 100 away fans (although the Club advises advance booking). Alternatively try the town centre, which has got a far wider choice for both food and drink. For food undoubtedly the star place last season was the Cockney Grub House (turn into Sea Road by Lloyds Bank and it's 50yd down the road). Awful turquoise decor and a hideous 'Cockney' tape that is so infectious you can't help singing 'Maybe It's Because I'm a Londoner' in your best Dick Van Dyke accent even if you've travelled from Carlisle, but it does serve great food (pie and mash, bangers and eels as well as a chip shop menu) all reasonably priced. Friendly staff and the owner Ern is a good old boy. The nearby pub, the Portman, seemed welcoming enough for away fans.

Inside the ground the pies are fairly hot, although more pastry than meat, and the tea comes in nice big cups. If you do want to eat though, make sure you don't offer £20 notes, which are not accepted (because you know that all footie fans are master forgers).

One final thing to keep an eye open for. On the way to the ground you may see a house with life-size cardboard cut outs of characters from Star Wars in it (these are considered to be a criminal deterrent which suggests that the average thief in Bournemouth is hardly likely to pull off the Brinks Mat job because they might encounter real people).

*Total Football* **Experience Rating: 58**

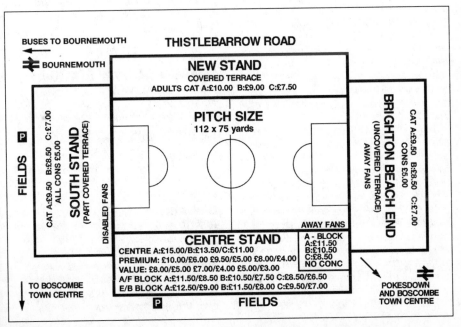

BUSES TO BOURNEMOUTH

BOURNEMOUTH

**THISTLEBARROW ROAD**

**NEW STAND**
COVERED TERRACE
ADULTS CAT A:£10.00  B:£9.00  C:£7.50

**PITCH SIZE**
112 x 75 yards

FIELDS

CAT A:£9.50  B:£8.50  C:£7.00
ALL CONS £5.00

**SOUTH STAND**
(PART COVERED TERRACE)

DISABLED FANS

**BRIGHTON BEACH END**
(UNCOVERED TERRACE)
AWAY FANS

CAT A:£9.50  B:£8.50  C:£7.00
CONS £5.00

AWAY FANS

**CENTRE STAND**
CENTRE A:£15.00/B:£13.50/C:£11.00
PREMIUM: £10.00/£6.00 £9.50/£5.00 £8.00/£4.00
VALUE: £8.00/£5.00 £7.00/£4.00 £5.00/£3.00
A/F BLOCK A:£11.50/£8.50 B:£10.50/£7.50 C:£8.50/£6.50
E/B BLOCK A:£12.50/£9.00 B:£11.50/£8.00 C:£9.50/£7.00

A - BLOCK
A:£11.50
B:£10.50
C:£8.50
NO CONC

TO BOSCOMBE TOWN CENTRE

POKESDOWN AND BOSCOMBE TOWN CENTRE

**FIELDS**

# BRADFORD CITY

**ADDRESS:** Valley Parade,
Bradford
West Yorkshire
BD8 7DY
**TELEPHONE No:** 01274 773355
**TICKET OFFICE:** 01274 770022
**FAX:** 01274 773356
**CHATLINE:** 0930 191196
**E-MAIL:**
bradfordcityfc@compuserve.com
(club)
**E-MAIL:** www.legend.co.uk/citygent
**NICKNAME:** The Bantams
**RECORD ATTENDANCE:**
39,146 v Burnley FA Cup 4th 11 March 1911 (D 1-1)
**CLUB COLOURS:**
**HOME:** Shirts: Claret and Amber stripes;
Shorts: Black; Socks: Black
**AWAY:** Shirts: Blue; Shorts: Blue;
Socks: Blue
**KIT SPONSORS:** JCT 600
**MANUFACTURERS:** Beaver International

## GROUND INFO

Valley Parade is a strange ground in that it is built on an incredible slope — that'll be the Valley I guess — which means that on one side of the ground — the Sunwin Stand — fans go through the turnstiles and find themselves at the top of the stand and having to walk down to their seats, whereas on the opposite side — the CIBA Stand (where the Old Midland Road Terrace used to be) — is actually built on supports and if visiting fans end up here, they can look forward to the sort of climb that normally requires two base camps before they can sit down.

The Symphony (ex HSG Packing Case, ex Charlie Brown) Stand is for away supporters and despite being only seven or so years old it seems ancient compared with the rest of Valley Parade. The bottom tier is particularly poor, with pillars aplenty and the rows of seats being fairly shallow so you end up with a perfect view of the bloke-in-front-of-you's neck. Just to complete the scenario, if you are at the back of the lower tier the upper tier restricts your view of the far goal (but apart from that it's perfect). The upper tier is better but still not really that much to write home about. Mind you it has to be said that this is not the only stand that has restricted views, with the Sunwin Stand having three big pillars and the Diamond Seal Kop a further two. If you get the

choice, use the CIBA Stand (although as this is only used as an overflow you may not get a say in the matter).

VP has a scoreboard with a clock counting down the time left in the half. Underneath the figures is the word 'remaining', which does help resolve those maddening confusions encountered at other grounds when you look at the clocks and then need to work out whether they mean that five minutes have gone or if there are five minutes remaining!

**CAPACITY:** Stands: 10,748; Terrace: 7,234;
Total: 17,982

**AWAY FANS:** Symphony Stand: 1,840;
CIBA Stand (if required): 1,800; Total: 3,640

**DISABLED FACILITIES:** There are 49 places for disabled supporters which are sited in the Sunwin and CIBA Stands, disabled fans and helpers both paying £6.50. Admission is £13.00 but this includes the cost of one helper (although if you don't take anyone with you don't expect the charge to be halved). Pre-booking is required. Matchday commentaries for the visually impaired should be pre-booked. Parking facilities are available at the ground.

**PROGRAMME:** £1.80
The price rose by 20% last season and most of this money seems to have been spent on improving the style without too much thought being given to the content. It suffers in comparison with being bought at the same time as one of Britain's best fanzines (see below).

**FANZINES:**
*City Gent* £1
The voice of Bantam Progressivism is a top-notch fanzine which is worth buying no matter who you support. All 1997-8 issues were excellent.

## TRAVEL

**NEAREST RAILWAY STATION:**
Forster Square (0345 484950 — Leeds Enquiries) Forster Square has a limited service and it is as well to aim for Bradford Interchange (same telephone number).

**NEAREST BUS STATION:**
First Bradford and Keighley & District (01274 732237) Too many buses to list stop at Manningham Lane which is just up from the ground. Basically, any Shipley or Saltaire bus will see you right.

**BY CAR:**
**NORTH:** A650. Turn left onto the Ring Road then first right by the hospital into Midland Road. The ground is then about 0.5 miles on the right.
**SOUTH:** M1 to J42, then M62 towards Bradford, exiting at J26 onto the M606 towards Bradford. At the end of the motorway take last exit onto Rooley Lane (signs Airport). McDonalds is now on your left. At

second roundabout turn left into Wakefield Road. Stay in middle lane. Over two roundabouts staying in middle lane (signs Shipley and Skipton) onto Shipley Airedale Road which then becomes Canal Road. Just after Staples Office Equipment showroom (on left) turn left into Station Road and left again into Queens Road. Up hill to traffic lights and turn left into Manningham Lane. After SAVE petrol station (on left), turn first left into Valley Parade for stadium.

**EAST/WEST:** M60 to J26. Pick up M606, then as south.

Whichever way you travel in, the ground is fairly well signposted (to avoid anxiety it is as well to know that no sign at a roundabout means carry straight on).

**PARKING:** Street parking and car parks by the ground. The car parks aren't cheap at £2.50. The ground is in the Manningham area of the city, which is not overly renowned as being a long-stay car park, so do watch out where you leave your vehicle.

## FUTURE DEVELOPMENTS

The Diamond Seal Kop remains one of the last great end terraces in English football and although it is obvious that it is living on borrowed time it is harder to see why; it's safe, the facilities are good and the fans love it (oh well, we can't be having that now). The club will hang onto it as long as it can but plans for a 5,000 seater replacement have been mooted.

## OTHER INFORMATION

Campbells, which is the pub at the ground, is for home supporters only. Other than this the nearest pub to the ground is the Belle Vue, but you're better off either walking a little further down Manningham Lane to Nellie Dean's or sticking to the city centre. This also boasts hundreds of curry houses; as a general rule of thumb, the

less it looks as if you'd like to eat in the place, the better it will be. My own favourite is the Chand Balti House, but other top tips (courtesy of the bloke I bought my fanzine from) include The Karachi, Nawaabs and The Amir.

Inside the stadium the food is fairly good (although they weren't doing their famed Mexican Flan on my last visits — a bitter blow.

If you find yourself with some time on your hands and fancy something a bit different then the National Museum of Photography is well worth a visit.

I can't let this opportunity pass without thanking City chairman Geoffrey Richmond for the stand he took against David Mellor as to whether the dismissal of Chris Kamara in 1997-8 was racially motivated. It would be ridiculous to suggest that there are no racists who watch City, but the club has done more than many to promote an environment where anyone can feel safe watching a game.

The physical signs of the 1985 fire have long since gone, and all there is to show for it is a fairly discreet sculpture on the side of the stand.

However, there is still an atmosphere at the ground which can probably best be described as sombre. If you get to the stadium before the main bulk of the crowd, it can be oppressive, yet very moving. What happened at Valley Parade seems almost forgotten by many and is often only referred to in passing when mention is made of the Taylor Report (even then, it is inevitably referred to after Hillsborough and Heysel). While it would be obscene to try and 'grade' these disasters, it is essential that we as supporters never forget that the fire occurred, and that we ensure the clubs are not allowed to forget the lessons of that afternoon.

*Total Football* **Experience Rating: 67**

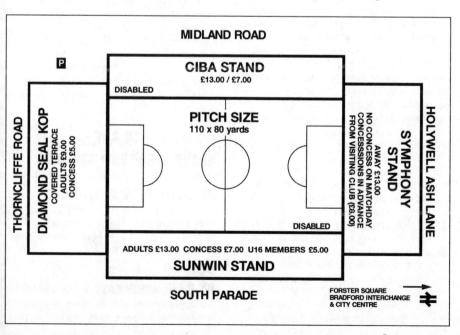

MIDLAND ROAD

P

CIBA STAND
£13.00 / £7.00

DISABLED

THORNCLIFFE ROAD

DIAMOND SEAL KOP
COVERED TERRACE
ADULTS £9.00
CONCESS £5.00

PITCH SIZE
110 x 80 yards

NO CONCESS ON MATCHDAY
CONCESSIONS IN ADVANCE
FROM VISITING CLUB (£3.00)
AWAY £13.00

SYMPHONY STAND

HOLYWELL ASH LANE

DISABLED

ADULTS £13.00  CONCESS £7.00  U16 MEMBERS £5.00

SUNWIN STAND

SOUTH PARADE

FORSTER SQUARE
BRADFORD INTERCHANGE
& CITY CENTRE

# BRENTFORD

**ADDRESS:** Griffin Park
Braemar Road
Brentford
Middlesex TW8 0NT

**TELEPHONE No:** 0181 847 2511

**TICKET OFFICE:** 0181 847 2511

**FAX:** 0181 568 9940

**WEB SITE:**
www.redweb.co.uk/brentford

**E-MAIL:** brentford@saqnet.co.uk

**CLUBCALL:** 0891 12 11 08

**NICKNAME:** The Bees

**RECORD ATTENDANCE:**
39,626 v Preston FA Cup 6th 5 March 1938 (L 0-3)

**CLUB COLOURS:**
**HOME:** Shirts: Red/White stripes;
Shorts: Black; Socks: Black
**AWAY:** Shirts: Blue/Yellow;
Shorts: Blue; Socks: Yellow

**KIT SPONSORS:** GMB

**MANUFACTURERS:** Super League

## GROUND INFO

The entrance to the away end is tucked in between a row of houses, and once in the visitors' section you will find it looks like a multi-storey car park basement, with the 'roof' of the terracing actually being the bottom of a tier of seats. There are two big pillars which can block your view, and the toilets are not the nicest you'll ever come across (still, there must be something decent about the place as, on my last visit to the ground, one of the main topics of conversation with Brentford fans was their campaign to get the stand re-allocated to home supporters). At £14 a seat it is not great value for money, and the concession of £11 whilst a nice gesture isn't really much better. I can't really seem to get to grips with Brentford. On the one hand my recent visit saw me — and a lot of other fans — enduring not one but two body searches and a bit of a lairy attitude as we approached the turnstiles, but then once inside everyone was left in peace by the stewards and when I asked a steward a question nothing was too much trouble for him.

One of the best things about being in the away end is that you don't have to look at the garish Bees 'murial'. Given that clubs are trying to get fans into the ground earlier, it's got to be questioned whether Brentford will insist this season on playing a sub 'Chas and Dave' version of Ole Ole crossed with Aïda on the entrance of the teams, as this seems to provide the ideal excuse for

drawing that last pint out for another five minutes and getting in at just after three.

**CAPACITY:** Stands: 8,920;
Terrace: 3,843;
Total: 12,736

**AWAY FANS:** Brook Road Stand 636;
Brook Road Terrace: 1,627;
Total: 2,263

**DISABLED FACILITIES:** There are 18 places (this figure includes nine spaces for helpers) in the South Stand E Block which are free of charge to both disabled supporters and their helpers. Pre-booking is required, but be warned there are no parking facilities available. The club reports that match commentaries are available for the partially sighted. These are positioned in the Braemar Road Stand A Block and once again should be pre-booked. Good toilet facilities are available at the ground, plus you can also get to food serveries without too much hassle.

**PROGRAMME:** £1.50
Not cheap but worth buying. There is a decent enough away team spread, and enough home team news to be interesting without being overly obscure to other than the most die-hard of Bees fans. Added to which there are normally a couple of well above average general interest articles.

**FANZINES:**
| | |
|---|---|
| *Voice of the Beehive* | 50p |
| *Thorne in the Side* | 50p |
| *Beesotted* | 80p |

Only *Beesotted* was on sale during my last visit and it has to be said that it seems to have come on in leaps and bounds from previous seasons. While perhaps it can't be considered a classic, it is still worth getting hold of (if only to see what David Webb has been getting up to recently — this varies but tends always to involve getting up the home fans' noses).

## TRAVEL

**NEAREST RAILWAY STATION:**
Brentford (0171 928 5100 — Waterloo Enquiries)

**NEAREST TUBE STATION:**
South Ealing (Piccadilly Line) (one mile)
Without wanting to sound like your mother, if you go to South Ealing (turn right as you leave the stadium) watch out when you are crossing the A4! It can be a bit hairy.

**BUS:** London Transport (0171 222 1234)

**BY CAR: NORTH/EAST:** Take the A406 North Circular Road (heading west) to Chiswick. At Chiswick Roundabout take the third exit onto Great West Road and continue straight on for 0.75 miles before turning left on to the A3001 Ealing Road. The ground is 0.5 miles on the right.

**WEST:** M4 to J2. When you leave the motorway there is a set of traffic lights. Do a U-turn at these onto the A4 (heading west). After 0.3 miles turn left into Ealing Road (A3001). The ground is 0.5 miles on the right.

**SOUTH:** Take the A205 South Circular Road (heading west) until you cross the Thames; turn left into Kew Bridge Road (A315). Turn right after 0.25 miles into Ealing Road (A3001) and the ground is 0.25 miles on the left.

## PARKING:
There is street parking around. Otherwise those coming from the north, east or south can take the Ealing Road past the ground and take the second turning on the left into Layton Road where there is a car park. This is also where supporters' coaches park. For those coming from the west, Layton Road is first right after you turn onto Ealing Road.

## FUTURE DEVELOPMENTS
The club plan to put a roof over the Ealing End of the ground, although they did say that this was not imminent, and may be delayed as they do not want to cover an area which may require development in the short/medium-term. A further option would be to close the area and redevelop it with a purpose-built stand. The general opinion is that the progression towards all-seater status would be driven by the club's league position and the level of grants available. There was also some talk of redeveloping the toilets in the New Road Stand.

## OTHER INFORMATION
No trip to Griffin Park is complete without doing the 'Brentford Four': that is the pubs that stand at each corner of the ground. Start off at the Royal Oak on New Road (you have to do this because after 1.30pm they don't let anyone else in), then, pop into the Griffin and Princess Royal before finishing off at the New Inn which is not only the best one to meet up with your fellow away fans, but also serves incredible sandwiches, which will help soak up the alcohol that you have indulged in. An alternative to the New Inn for food is the chip shop opposite the Griffin which is fairly reasonable (if you are going to a night match and fancy something different there is a great Nepalese restaurant between the tube and the ground).

Inside Griffin Park the pies are large, hot and very tasty, but don't have the staying power to last the journey from silver tray to mouth without falling apart. Naturally no forks are provided so be prepared to do a pig in a trough impression if you want to fill your stomach. For those with a sweeter tooth, confectionery can be bought from a little hut between the Braemar and Ealing Road terraces which luxuriates in the grand name of the 'Community Tuck Shop' (I say Bunter you fat owl let's go and watch the Bees play); sadly chomp bars are no longer available they were deemed deadly weapons after Brentford fans in their thousands took to waving them at players (and it has to be said occasionally heaving them on to the pitch).

I know a few people who don't really like Griffin Park but these tend to be people who have only recently started coming to games — the atmosphere can be raucous but is rarely threatening. The attitude of home fans is very much one of 'we don't care how badly the team is playing we are here to have a sing and enjoy ourselves'. Favourite ditties are 'We are Bees' (I don't know why but this always makes me giggle) and 'Hey Jude' (where a lot of fans struggle on the last, and very high 'better'). Be prepared to have a sing back or have your allegiances/abilities/sexual orientation questioned.

*Total Football* **Experience Rating: 66**

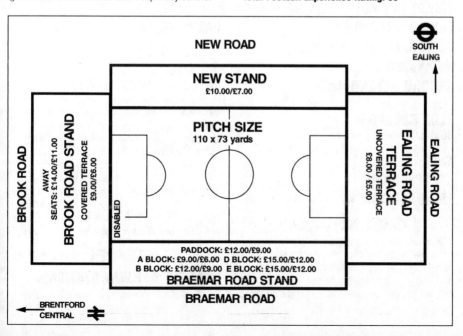

# BRIGHTON & HOVE ALBION

**ADDRESS:** Priestfield Stadium
Redfern Avenue
Gillingham
Kent
ME7 4DD

**ADMIN ADDRESS:** 118 Queens Road
Brighton
BN1 3XG

For the second season running as this book goes to print it is unclear where Albion will be playing. The options are: Gillingham (where the final season of their lease agreement is), Withdean, a slightly run-down athletics stadium near Brighton, or even another ground share, this time with Woking. Although the Withdean option is the favourite among the fans, I have a feeling that there would be too much to do to get the ground up to scratch. I believe Tony Scally at Gillingham has said he is prepared to let Albion break their contract providing they move back to the town and, although it has been stated that the club might continue to pay the rent at Gillingham while playing elsewhere, with the club having announced losses last year (to May 1997) of £1.4 million I don't know whether such a move would be practical.

I do expect the club to return to their home town in 1999-2000 but until then they will have to keep undertaking the 150-mile round trip to Priestfield. Should they move to Withdean write to me c/o Ian Allan enclosing a SAE and I will send you an updated entry.

**TELEPHONE No:** 01273 778855

**TICKET OFFICE:** 01273 778855

**FAX:** 01273 321095

**CLUB CALL:** 0891 800 609

**NICKNAME:** Seagulls

**RECORD ATTENDANCE:**
36,747 v Fulham Div 2 2 December 1958 (W 3-0)

**CLUB COLOURS:**
**HOME:** Shirts: Royal Blue & White stripes;
Shorts: Royal Blue; Socks: White
**AWAY:** Shirts: Red; Shorts: Red; Socks: Red

**KIT SPONSORS:** tba

**MANUFACTURERS:** Super League

## GROUND INFO

Priestfield is a fairly tidy football ground — for Gillingham; for Brighton it is a morgue and a place to be detested. There are still numerous instances of Brighton fans going in the away end because they refuse to accept it as their 'home'. To be honest the majority of Gillingham fans dislike having Brighton there as much as the Seagulls hate being there. The point is, however, surely it is better to have Brighton playing at Priestfield than the very real danger 18 months ago of the club folding.

Bad news for visiting supporters is that you still get stuck in the corner terrace of the Gillingham End with its lack of cover and poor views. Generally you won't get any hassle if you want to go in the Main Stand or the multi-pillared New Gordon Road Stand although it should be noted that, due to the small crowds the club was attracting, the bronze sections of the New Stand were frequently closed on matchdays.

The club does offer absolutely brilliant concessions for home and away supporters.

**CAPACITY:** Seats: 3,525;
Terrace: 7,136; Total: 10,661

**AWAY FANS:** Redfern Avenue Corner
Terrace:1,320; Main Stand: 100; Total: 1,420

## DISABLED FACILITIES:

There are 56 spaces for disabled supporters in front of the Main Stand. Admission for disabled fans together with one helper is free. Places should be pre-booked. There may be the possibility to arrange parking, but this is not guaranteed. No matchday commentaries for the visually impaired.

**PROGRAMME:** £1.70

A fairly run-of-the-mill affair which is distinguished by a couple of general interest articles, one by Tony Millard (but what the hell is that pose he is in in the accompanying photo??) and an 'Independant (sic) View' which on my last trip was an excellent piece by Paul Camillin of Scars & Stripes.

## FANZINES:

| | |
|---|---|
| Seaside Saga | £1 |
| Scars & Stripes | £1 |
| Build a Bonfire | £1 |

Scars & Stripes hit the ground running and is an excellent publication which is well written and a very good place to keep up to date with the happenings and hopes at the club. Given all the work that the fans did to keep their club alive you feel it is almost a duty to buy a fanzine; fortunately with S&S this duty is also a pleasure. One of the top five in the division.

I'm not normally one for local papers, but mention must go to the Argus/Sports Argus, which have also been campaigning strongly on the BHA (Bring Home Albion) front. The paper is shipped in from Sussex on matchdays and is worth getting just as another gesture of support.

## TRAVEL

**NEAREST RAILWAY STATION:**
Gillingham (01732 770111)

## NEAREST TUBE STATION:
Surrey Quays (East London Line)

**BUS:** Maidstone & District (01634 281100)

## BY CAR:
**FROM ALL PARTS:** M2 to J4. When you leave the motorway follow the signs for the A278 (Gillingham). At the third roundabout turn left onto the A2. After 1.5 miles turn right onto Nelson Road (A231). Just after the bus station turn right at the lights into Gillingham Road, continue past the Livingstone Arms and the ground is on your right.

**PARKING:** There is no official parking at the ground; however (due to the small size of the crowds), the side streets, are likely to furnish you with a place without too much trouble even up to 2.55pm on a match day.

## FUTURE DEVELOPMENTS
Under the guidance of Dick Knight you feel that it is a question not if the club is going to return home, but when this will happen. The Withdean Athletics site does remain the prime location and Albion are looking to develop this and move in for a set period (possibly trying to entice Sussex CCC to share the facilities with them). There are plenty of bridges to cross before this becomes a reality — not least of all the protests from the local residents (who have apparently already sent in about 1,500 letters of complaint about the possible scheme). From conversations I have had with those at the club, it would appear that they see Withdean as only a short to medium term solution and that they would hope to have identified their own site and be moved into a purpose-built stadium within three seasons. As for Priestfield itself, expect no changes during 1998-9.

Groundsharing with Gillingham FC is expected to cease at the end of October 1998. Home matches will then be played at Withdean Sports Stadium, Brighton, and will be 'all-ticket' as capacity is only 6,000.

## OTHER INFORMATION
It may sound clichéd but when I went to see Brighton at Priestfield, I wondered whether there was actually a match on. At 2.30pm the streets were deserted and it was only the fact that there was a liberal scattering of fanzine and programme sellers that gave any clue to what was about to happen. In truth everyone seems to try and stick to the pubs, which means all the ones in the local area — the Cricketers, the Livingstone Arms etc — are heaving with noisy Albion fans and are perhaps not the best place to enjoy a pint. Instead wander the 10min into the town centre and pop in at the Southern Belle (near the train station) which is more welcoming for visiting fans. For food try either the Circus Fish Bar or French the Butchers' spit roast chicken (see Gillingham for more details). Once inside Priestfield away fans are served by a small hut, the occupants of which on my last trip looked very seedy. Your encounter with these chaps makes you wonder what the food is going to be like and to be honest it comes as little surprise that it is awful, tasteless and served either incinerator hot or frozen. I strongly recommend sticking with only (melted) chocolate bars.

Finally it was superb to see that Brighton tried at least to give something back in 1997-8 following the massive countrywide support they had the previous year, when they organised Fans Day 2 on behalf of Doncaster Rovers. Again it was great to see supporters link under a common cause, but I have a nagging doubt that the Rovers' story will have a less happy ending than Brighton's.

***Total Football* Experience Rating: 60**

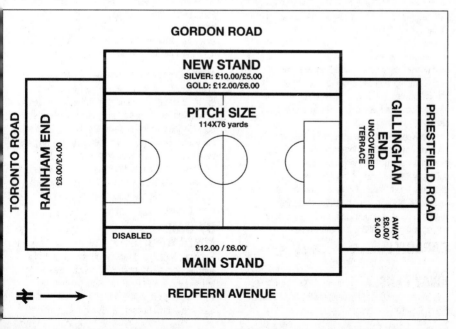

# BRISTOL CITY

**ADDRESS:** Ashton Gate
Winterstoke Road
Bristol
BS3 2JE

**TELEPHONE No:** 0117 963 0630
**TICKET OFFICE:** 0117 966 6666
Oooer, it appears that the ticket hotline has the number of the beast (twice) which may explain why the person on the other end of it seemed to want to make the process of buying a ticket as hellish as they did for me.

**FAX:** 0117 963 0700
**CLUB CALL:** 0891 12 11 76
**WEB SITE:** www.bcfc.co.uk/
**NICKNAME:** The Robins
**RECORD ATTENDANCE:**
43,335 v Preston FA Cup 5th 16 February 1935 (D 0-0)

**CLUB COLOURS:**
**HOME:** Shirts: Red; Shorts: White; Socks: Red
**AWAY:** Shirts: Yellow; Shorts: Green; Socks: Green

**KIT SPONSORS:** Sanderson Computer Recruitment

**MANUFACTURERS:** Uhlsport

## GROUND INFO

Away fans are sited in the Database Wedlock Stand (does this mean that all the home supporters are out of wedlock?).

The away allocation is more than adequate for the vast majority of matches. If you do go into the Dolman or Brunel Ford Williams Stands, you can pretty much guarantee that some kid will sit behind and accidentally kick one of the seats down, but be so impressed by the loud wooden bang it makes that they will spend the next 90min banging it up and down (by the end of the game you will be seriously wondering what sort of noise the little darling's head would make if you bounced it off the seats a bit).

The Wedlock End offers decent facilities and a fairly good view of the action (considering it is one of those seats on terracing efforts which are normally pretty dire), but it is worth avoiding the first few rows if you can as these aren't quite raised enough to give you the proper perspective of the match. Moderate concessions for visiting supporters, though the new three category pricing system for 1998-9 isn't great news.

**CAPACITY:** Stands: 21,200; Terrace: Nil;
Total: 21,200

**AWAY FANS:** Wedlock End: 2,500; Total: 2,500
This can be extended to the whole of the End (capacity 5,500) if demand is sufficient.

**DISABLED FACILITIES:** There are 50 places for disabled fans, and these are sited at the Atyeo and GWR Family Enclosure. Pre-booking is not necessary. Admission for disabled fans is free, with helpers paying £11.00 or £13.00. Parking facilities are available at the ground. Match commentaries are available.

**PROGRAMME:** £2.00
This is an area that the club just can't seem to crack; too many adverts and the stuff that there was to read was fairly dull.

**FANZINES:**
| | |
|---|---|
| *One Team in Bristol* | £1 |
| *Stand Up...* | £1 |
| *Come In Number 7 Your Time Is Up* | 50p |
| *The Cidered* | 80p |

*OTIB* is definitely the pick of the bunch although any of the above is a better read than the club programme (but then a box of matches would be better than the programme). Plenty of digs at the 'Rent Boys' (Bristol Rovers — on account of the fact that they don't own their own ground), and although there will be quite a few that you've heard before you can count on at least a couple of good jokes which you will be able to adapt for your most hated rivals. It is more than just page after page of insults though, and the content seems to have improved an awful lot compared with earlier editions that I have seen.

## TRAVEL

**NEAREST RAILWAY STATION:** Parson Street (0117 929 4255 — Bristol Enquiries)
Parson Street is (contrary to popular belief) still open but the number of trains that stop there is minimal; so you are better off aiming for Temple Meads, which is about 1.5 miles from the ground.

**BUS:** City Line/City Dart (0117 955 3231)
In my experience, the bus drivers in Bristol are among the worst for pulling out in front of cars at bus stops; and as you slam on the brakes and your shoulder gets pulled out of its joint by your seatbelt, the driver will rub salt in the wound by either belatedly indicating or giving you a wave to thank you for your 'co-operation'.

There are no buses direct from Temple Meads to the ground, and to avoid a longish walk you should take either an 8 or 9 bus to Broadmead, and then a 21 or a 22 to the ground.

**BY CAR:**
**NORTH/WEST:** M5 to J16. Take the A38 (signposted Patchway, Bristol) and keep going along this road until you see signs for Taunton (A38); follow these and this will take you across the River Avon. Bear left into Winterstoke Road, then turn left into Marsh Road and right into Ashton Road.

**EAST:** M4, M32 into Bristol City Centre, picking up the signs for Taunton (A38), then as north/west.

**SOUTH:** M5 to J18. When you leave the motorway, pick up the A4 (Portway), cross the swing bridge and bear left into Winterstoke Road. Then as north.

Whichever way you are going in, watch out for the road signs which seem to change for no given reason, eg one minute you will see a motorway indicated in the left-hand lane, and 20yd up the road it will have miraculously changed to the right-hand lane. (Another favourite is for the signs for a particular area to stop for no obvious reason other than to worry drivers that they have missed their turn-off.)

**PARKING:** The car park at the ground is for permit holders only; otherwise there is a Do-It-All/ Curry's right by the ground which has a decent car park and a Sainsbury's along Winterstoke Road, and plenty of parking on side streets around the ground.

## FUTURE DEVELOPMENTS
None planned.

## OTHER INFORMATION
The pubs in the immediate vicinity of the ground (the Wedlock, the Rising Sun) are very much for home fans only. Last season I ended up at the Robins, which is 5min walk from the ground. Again this has a predominantly home feel about it, but the landlord there was happy to serve away fans who respected the place/the other supporters, and I've got to say that I will go there again (although it would be even better if some of the records on the jukebox were binned).

If you decide to go into the city, it's worth taking the bus as otherwise it's a bit of a walk. The centre itself is a little disappointing, and on my visit there seemed to be an atmosphere which at times, especially for night matches, almost bordered on the hostile.

As with many grounds, fans are banned from taking such deadly weapons as umbrellas into the ground, but unlike most places there is actually a little hole in the wall (in which a steward is incarcerated) where you can deposit your brolly for the duration.

There are a couple of excellent chip shops by Ashton Park near the ground. This is at the opposite end of the stadium to the away seats but I would recommend paying them a visit because, once inside the Gate, although you do have a fairly wide choice of food, the quality of it leaves a lot to be desired (taste, flavour, texture etc). Still at least, as one of the people selling it pointed out to me 'it really isn't that expensive' (Hmm thanks, I'm sure my colon really appreciated the cost savings!!!).

The attitude of some of the stewards at the club seemed to improve a bit in 1997-8 and, from discussions, it seems that City are trying to make the place more friendly/accessible to visiting fans (much of this it has to be said has been instigated from the very top and Scott Davidson deserves the thanks of all away fans). On my visit there last year I had no hassle at all. That being said, I still know of quite a few fans who have had problems during their away days here. To be honest, much of what I have heard about has occurred away from the ground (and therefore outside of the club's control), but the most worrying thing is that the stories that came to me did not occur at big matches but rather at run-of-the-mill games where you would expect no problems. What I don't want to do with this entry is give you the impression that Ashton Gate is a no-go area or that the fans are animals, because that simply is not true. However, I would recommend that you exercise perhaps slightly more caution than you would do normally.

*Total Football* **Experience Rating: 56**

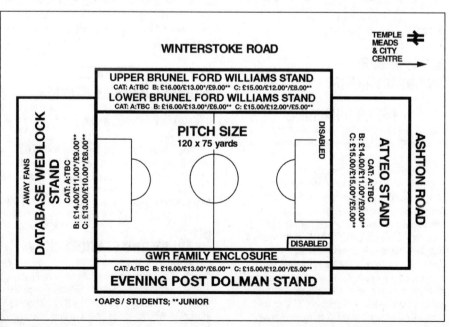

**WINTERSTOKE ROAD**

TEMPLE MEADS & CITY CENTRE

**UPPER BRUNEL FORD WILLIAMS STAND**
CAT: A:TBC  B: £16.00/£13.00*/£9.00**  C: £15.00/£12.00*/£8.00**
**LOWER BRUNEL FORD WILLIAMS STAND**
CAT: A:TBC  B: £16.00/£13.00*/£6.00**  C: £15.00/£12.00*/£5.00**

**PITCH SIZE**
120 x 75 yards

DISABLED

DISABLED

**AWAY FANS**
**DATABASE WEDLOCK STAND**
CAT: A:TBC
B: £14.00/£11.00*/£9.00**
C: £13.00/£10.00*/£8.00**

**ATYEO STAND**
CAT: A:TBC
B: £14.00/£11.00*/£9.00**
C: £15.00/£15.00*/£5.00**

**ASHTON ROAD**

**GWR FAMILY ENCLOSURE**
CAT: A:TBC  B: £16.00/£13.00*/£6.00**  C: £15.00/£12.00*/£5.00**
**EVENING POST DOLMAN STAND**

*OAPS / STUDENTS; **JUNIOR

# BRISTOL ROVERS

**ADDRESS:** The Memorial Stadium
Filton Avenue
Horfield
Bristol
BS7 0AQ
**TELEPHONE No:** 0117 977 2000
**TICKET OFFICE:** 0117 977 3200
**FAX:** 0117 977 3888
**CLUBCALL:** 0891 12 11 31
**WEB SITE:** There are a plethora of Gas web sites. Pirates.Net is probably the best place to start surfing at www.personal.u-net.com/~coley/rovers/index.htm (check out the ultimate internet guide).

Although the club shares with the Bristol Rugby Union Club, it maintains its own offices away from the ground (the telephone numbers for which are given above). The registered offices are at: The Beeches, Broomhill Road, Brislington, Bristol, BS4 5BF.
Alternatively the supporters' club can be contacted at: 199 Two Mile Hill Road, Kingswood, Bristol, BS15 7AZ. Telephone: 0117 961 1772

**NICKNAME:** The Pirates
## RECORD ATTENDANCE:
38,472 v Preston FA Cup 4th 30 January 1960 (D 3-3). At the Memorial Ground; 9,173 v Northampton Div 2 Play-Off 1st Leg 10 May 1998 (W3-1)

## CLUB COLOURS:
**HOME:** Shirts: Blue and White quarters;
Shorts: White; Socks: Blue
**AWAY:** Shirts: Yellow/Black;
Shorts: Black; Socks: Black

**KIT SPONSORS:** Cowlin Construction
**MANUFACTURERS:** Cica

## GROUND INFO
The Memorial Stadium itself is quite weird. The Centenary Stand (where the away fans are sited) is a throwback to the old seats and paddock style. The Scoreboard End of the stand and this area is undeveloped. The Clubhouse Terrace is open to the elements (with what appears to be a series of lock-up garages abutting it), so at least you can laugh at (or sympathise with) the home fans getting soaked at the same time as you are suffering. The New West Stand at first glance looks quite impressive, being a mixture of seats, executive boxes and, once again, paddock. However, once you look slightly closer you notice that there are only four rows of seats in it, and it is obvious that this has been built with the Rugby Club in mind rather than the potential League requirements should

Rovers get promoted.
**CAPACITY:** Stands: 1,796*
Terrace: 7,404**;
Total: 9,200
* Includes 270 seats in 'suites'.
** Includes 500 in Family Terrace scheduled to open in 1997/98, and 740 on visitors' terrace.
**AWAY FANS:** Centenary Terrace: 740
Great concessions. If, as an away supporter, you fancy staying dry then it is as well to arrive early if you hope to get into the Centenary Stand which seems to climb almost vertically into the air.

## DISABLED FACILITIES:
There are 30 places available to wheelchair-bound supporters which are sited in the West and Centenary Stands. The club advises that pre-booking is required — contact the club secretary. Parking facilities are available at the ground. Admission is free of charge for wheelchair-bound supporters, with helpers paying £4.50. Matchday commentaries for the visually impaired are available (huzzah) although there are only facilities to provide these for two supporters (oh).

**PROGRAMME:** £2.00
A terrific well-laid out read for home supporters but offers little for visiting fans.

## FANZINES:
> The 2nd of May    £1
> Black Arab    £1
I believe that the *Black Arab* is the third incarnation of the *Trumpton Times* (named after Twerton Park) and *Wot No Quarters!* (named after Rovers' diabolical kit in the 1996-7 season). It remains a great fanzine to buy, read and then leave on the train on the way home for someone else to enjoy. *The 2nd of May* continues to improve.

## TRAVEL
### NEAREST RAILWAY STATION:
Filton or Stapleton Road (0117 929 4255 — Bristol Enquiries) Great Western Trains (0345 484950 Customer Services)
Filton is approximately one mile north of the ground and Stapleton Road a mile and a half to the south of the ground. The chances are, though, that you will end up at one of the city's 'big two' stations, Parkway or Temple Meads. Both are a good couple of miles away but do offer reasonable bus services to the ground (or about £5 taxi fares).

**NEAREST BUS STATION:** City Line/City Dart (0117 955 3231)
From the City Centre, Nos 73 and 74 run along Filton Avenue, directly past the Memorial Ground. Services 71 and 72 stop in Ashley Down Road, a short walk from the ground. Services 75, 76 and 77 stop in Gloucester Road,

almost opposite Filton Avenue, and will mean a short walk to the ground. If you are going to an evening match, it is worth knowing that for reasons known only to themselves, the bus company add a '5' at the start of the number, ie 573, 574 etc.

## BY CAR:

**NORTH:** A38 towards Bristol. This goes through the Filton area of the city. Once through Filton the road forks in two. To the right the road becomes B4468 (signposted Golden Hill) but you want the LEFT fork, still keeping on the A38. Take the third left (this is the first major road on the left) into Muller Road and the first right into Filton Avenue for the ground.

**EAST:** M32 to J2. Take the fourth exit from the roundabout (in effect turning right) signposted to the A38, bear right at fork into Muller Road B4469. Bear immediately right then continue for approximately one mile following signs to Horfield and Southmead until you see a church on your right-hand side (after six sets of traffic lights), either turn left (Downend Road) and first right into Ellicott Road, or take the following left into Filton Avenue, both of which lead to the ground.

**WEST:** It's probably as well to go M5 J17 and follow signs for Patchway. This will lead you onto Highwood Road at the top of which is a roundabout. Take the third exit onto the A38 then as north.

**SOUTH:** A37 into Bristol continuing straight (not right) onto the A4. Turn right onto the A4044 Temple Way continuing for approximately one mile before taking the A4032 Newfoundland Street (following the signs for M32). Follow the M32 to J2, turn left onto Muller Road, then as east.

**PARKING:** There is parking at the ground for 320 vehicles, but not for away fans. Street parking abounds.

## FUTURE DEVELOPMENTS

In May 1998 the Memorial stadium was purchased by the Memorial Stadium co in which Rovers have a 50% stake. However, the dream remains for the Gas to have their own stadium in the future. A site at Severnside has been earmarked (the land being donated by ICI). However, at present there remain differences to be resolved regarding the building of the road infrastructure to support the ground. If/when these problems are resolved it is the intention to build a 20,000 all-seater stadium.

## OTHER INFORMATION

There are absolutely hundreds of pubs along the Gloucester Road (the main road five minutes from the ground) from which you can really take your pick, although I'd think twice about going into the Duke of York or the Victoria. Make sure you do get in the ground before kick-off if just to witness the team's morale building 'huddle' before the match in which they even include the mascot (you're doing a great job son, just keep peppering the club mascot with weak penalties).

The food in the ground is excellent "Proper Cornish — Real (including Vegetarian) Pasties" and the pies are also a rare treat. Drinks are so-so.

I don't know what it is about Rovers, but I always feel it is a great away day. Friendly fans, good pubs and food mean that even the ground's shortfalls can be forgiven.

Finally, be warned that the Rovers' fans' version of the 1950s hit 'Goodnight Irene' is dreadfully addictive; at best it will be in your mind for weeks afterwards, and at worst you will join in with them as their team scores a last minute winner against you (don't worry what your mates will say, as they'll probably be singing it too).

*Total Football* **Experience Rating: 80**

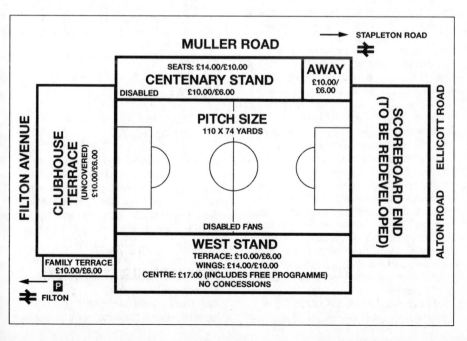

# BURNLEY

**ADDRESS:** Turf Moor
Brunshaw Road
Burnley
BB10 4BX

**TELEPHONE No:** 01282 700000
**TICKET OFFICE:** 01282 700010
**FAX:** 01282 700014
**CLUBCALL:** 0891 12 11 53
**WEBSITE:** www.clarets.co.uk
**NICKNAME:** The Clarets
**RECORD ATTENDANCE:**
54,775 v Huddersfield FA Cup 3rd 23 February 1924
(W 1-0)

**CLUB COLOURS:**
**HOME:** Shirts: Claret with three White pinstripes
across the chest and Blue sleeves;
Shorts: Claret; Socks: Blue
**AWAY:** Shirts: Blue with Yellow chest stripe and
sleeves; Shorts: Yellow; Socks: Yellow

**KIT SPONSORS:** P3 Computers
**MANUFACTURERS:** Adidas

## GROUND INFO
First a piece of good news: prices for 1998-9 remain the
same as those last year which makes Burnley a fairly
reasonable ground to visit.

Whichever way you enter Burnley the first view of Turf
Moor is likely to be an impressive one as it nestles at the
bottom of a hill and dominates the rows of terraced
houses which stretch out like sheets of tarpaulin all
around it (oooer I'm getting a bit flowery here!!!!).

The New East Stand aka Bee Hole End (why does this
sound so incredibly rude? and why am I so childish that
whenever I go to Turf Moor I always have to ask a Claret
if they are going up the Bee Hole that afternoon?) and the
redeveloped Longside Stand have changed the face of
Turf Moor for ever (not least because you can now walk
three quarters of the way round the ground without
having to take massive detours through housing estates).
I remember going to Burnley a good few years back and
thinking the Bob Lord Stand (named after the
controversial club chairman who was the first in such a
position to be given a high media profile and thus the
person we've got to thank for the likes of Ken Bates, Alan
Sugar and Deadly Doug Ellis etc) was a vision of the
future. Now it stands opposite the new Longside (North)
Stand and it looks distinctly tatty (and for some reason
the seats in the directors' box look like rows of toilets
with the seats up).

The away section of the Endsleigh Stand is OK in
terms of leg room and view — provided that you sit
towards the front. It has the added advantage of having a
roof that actually covers the fans.

The attitude to concessions is strange. None of the
visitors' turnstiles advertise the fact that concessions are
available. Officially this is because no concessions are
available after midday for a 3pm kick-off and 4.30pm for
an evening match. However, if you go into the ticket office
and speak very nicely to them you might persuade them
to let you have a reduced price ticket.

**CAPACITY:** Stands: 19,399; Terrace: Nil
Total: 22,524
**AWAY FANS:** Endsleigh Stand: 4,125
You can't fail to see the warnings as you enter the ground
that bad language 'can and will' result in you getting
ejected, although more puzzling is the fact that there don't
appear to be any of these signs around the home
turnstiles. Presumably this is because any Claret would
rather die than sully his/her mouth with an obscenity.

**DISABLED FACILITIES:** There are 21
places available in the North Lower and East Lower
stands. These must be pre-booked (at the same time
organise a parking space). Admission is free of charge
for disabled supporters and £10 for helpers. There are 10
seats for the blind near the press box in the Bob Lord
Stand at concessionary prices. Either pre-book your
space via your own club, or get in touch with the
Community Officer at the club (Dean Ramsdale) on
01282 700011.

**PROGRAMME:** £1.70
Despite being an impressive size (56 pages), away fans
will probably have this tucked away in their back pocket
after about five minutes. The only decent thing is the
write-in quiz, which is based on the day's visitors;
therefore if you can be bothered to enter and providing
the club puts your name in the draw — which I'm
positive they would — could lead to you being £20
better off.

**FANZINES:**

| | |
|---|---|
| The Claret Flag | 60p |
| Kicker Conspiracy | £1 |
| Who Ate All The Pies | £1 |
| Bob Lord's Sausage | £1 |

None of the four above mentioned fanzines were on
(obvious) sale on my last visit to Turf Moor. From
previous seasons I remember The Claret Flag as being a
fair enough read (although it did tend to get a bit Rovers
obsessive at times) and if you see one then at 60p it is
worth the gamble.

## TRAVEL
**NEAREST RAILWAY STATION:**
Burnley Central (01282 423125)
If your team's supporters have something of a
'reputation', expect to be escorted back to the station and

34

lined up outside until your train arrives. Whilst outside, if my experience is anything to go by, you'll be advised by the police that anyone who steps off the pavement will be 'in trouble', ie given a severe wigging until precisely 20sec after your train has left the station. So be on your best behaviour!

**BUS:** Central bus station (01282 423125)

## BY CAR:

**NORTH:** Follow the A682 to the town centre and take the first exit at the roundabout (by the Gala bingo club) into Yorkshire Street. Continue through traffic signals into Brunshaw Road for the ground.

**EAST:** A646 to A671 then along Todmorden Road towards the town centre. At the traffic lights turn right into Brunshaw Road.

**SOUTH/WEST:** Leave M6 at J29 signposted M65. Take the M65 to J10 and follow signs to Towneley Hall. The road goes past the ground.

There are signs for the ground (there are also some rogue signs which suggest the way to go to 'Turd Moor' which you can obviously ignore) but these tend to be actually on the turning or roundabout exit rather than before them which means it is very easy to go sailing past. Because Turf Moor lies in a valley the easiest thing to do is to get into the town centre and navigate by the floodlights.

**PARKING:** As you approach the town centre you will see signs for away and home parking. The away parking is, I believe (the signs never seem to actually lead anywhere), at Burnley Cricket Club ( £1.50) on Belvedere Road and the home parking is at Fulledge Rec Ground (£1). Alternatively there is a plethora of side streets.

## FUTURE DEVELOPMENTS
The club may look to redevelop the Endsleigh Stand in the future, but this is dependent on both demand and the finances being in place to undertake this without adversely affecting the team.

## OTHER INFORMATION
If you follow the signs for the away parking you'll see two pubs opposite each other, the Sparrow Hawk and The Talbot, and these are a good bet for a drink and a meeting point with fellow journeymen.

Insofar as food is concerned let me give you a very big tip, avoid the Carolina Chicken on Brunshaw Road which was serving perhaps one of the worst deep fried chickens it has ever been my misfortune to taste.

The Park View chippie which is down the side road by the Park View pub serves a good portion of chips but awful gravy. Still, it's miles better than the food on sale in the ground which consists of mush-filled pies and weak tea (and whatever you do don't be tempted to go for the squash which comes in those horrible 1960s cinema containers and which has less taste than Big Ron Atkinson). In fact the only thing to recommend the tea bar — and this is for chaps only — are the girls who serve there, who take the word flirty to new heights (last time I was there two of them were massaging each other and suggesting that a similar service might be more popular than the pies. After one bite out of the pie I had to agree with them!). There is a sign on the opposite wall to the tea hut which reads 'top class refreshments'; if only it gave directions how to find them.

The stewards are a very mixed bunch, ranging from the petty to the excellent. The latter can be distinguished by the fact that they all seem to smell of wintergreen and will spend a good hour telling you how the club is about to turn the corner.

***Total Football* Experience Rating: 71**

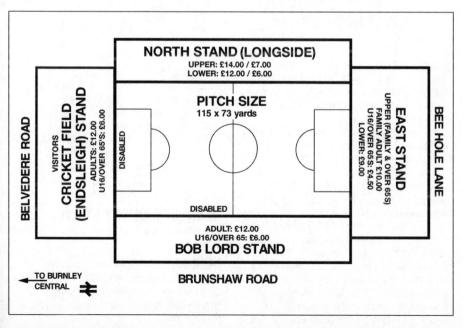

**NORTH STAND (LONGSIDE)**
UPPER: £14.00 / £7.00
LOWER: £12.00 / £6.00

**PITCH SIZE**
115 x 73 yards

BELVEDERE ROAD

VISITORS
**CRICKET FIELD (ENDSLEIGH) STAND**
ADULTS: £12.00
U16/OVER 65'S: £6.00

DISABLED

DISABLED

**EAST STAND**
UPPER (FAMILY & OVER 65S)
FAMILY ADULT £10.00
U16/OVER 65S: £4.50
LOWER: £9.00

BEE HOLE LANE

ADULT: £12.00
U16/OVER 65: £6.00
**BOB LORD STAND**

TO BURNLEY CENTRAL

**BRUNSHAW ROAD**

# BURY

**ADDRESS:** Gigg Lane
Bury
Lancashire BL9 9HR

**TELEPHONE No:** 0161 764 4881

**TICKET OFFICE:** 0161 705 2144

**FAX:** 0161 764 5521

**CLUBCALL:** 0930 190003

**WEBSITE:**
http://www.buryfc.creations.co.uk/
main.htm (unofficial)

**NICKNAME:** The Shakers

**RECORD ATTENDANCE:**
35,000 v Bolton FA Cup 3rd 9 January 1960 (D 1-1)

**CLUB COLOURS:**
**HOME:** Shirts: White; Shorts: Royal Blue;
Socks: Royal Blue
**AWAY:** Shirts: Red; Shorts: Black;
Socks: Red
Even given that it seems compulsory for away kits to be artistically challenged, Bury's latest effort is worthy of mention. A red shirt with the letters 'BFC' printed in various sizes all over it, it looks like something that a kid has drawn in a school book and then doodled over. Horrible (but no doubt it will sell thousands).

**KIT SPONSORS:** Birthdays

**MANUFACTURERS:** Super League

## GROUND INFO

The club has tidied up the ground a lot in the last few years, although from the outside it still looks a little bit run down. Another commendable point is that while improvements have been made, the ground doesn't have the look of an out-of-town superstore about it that many grounds do. On the minus side there are still plenty of pillars which can restrict your view.

If you decide not to go into the official away allocation (and if you are an away fan and choose to do this you will need to be discreet or face ejection) then it's worth noting that other than the 'Ceme' end there are very few areas of the ground which have cash turnstiles. This obviously leads to double queuing (at the ticket offices and the turnstiles) and as these lines of people aren't the fastest moving things in the world you'll come across, it's worth giving yourself an extra five minutes.

Stewarding at the club fluctuates between the awful and the excellent and I saw examples of both on a recent visit. On the one hand a gaggle of stewards stood halfway up the stairs at Door B of the Main Stand looking into the car park making such profound judgements as 'I don't like the way that lad's running across the car park, if he gives

anyone the slightest trouble then we'll get him out'. On the other hand they took a kid's autograph book and rounded up players to sign it for him. Err on the side of caution.

It's also worth noting that Bury are one of the few clubs which insists that gangways are kept clear. This means no wandering towards the exits during the last couple of minutes then making a dash for it when the final whistle goes.

**CAPACITY:** Stands: 9,340; Terrace: 2,500;
Total: 11,840

**AWAY FANS:** West Stand: 2,676
The club has in the past (on rare occasions) also made the Cemetery End available to visiting fans if there is sufficient demand.

**DISABLED FACILITIES:** There are places for 20 wheelchair-bound supporters in the South Stand (home supporters) plus further room for eight wheelchair-bound supporters in the West Stand for visitors. Each place also has room for one helper. Disabled supporters are admitted at no cost and the club advises me that it also provides 'one free escort' which is a good give-away in anyone's language. Pre-booking is required. Match commentaries for visually impaired fans are available in the Main Stand. Parking facilities are also available at the ground.

**PROGRAMME:** £1.80
This went up 20% in price last season but, to be fair, its content and style improved by about 50% and it was one of the better ones in the division. Plenty of little snippets and general interest pieces.

**FANZINES:**
| | |
|---|---|
| *Dead and Bury(ed)* | 50p |
| *Where Were You At The Shay?* | 60p |
| *The Hatchet* | 50p |

1997-8 saw the birth of a new fanzine at Gigg Lane, *Dead and Bury(ed)*. I didn't manage to get hold of a copy myself but talked to a couple of fans who were raving about it. It even got a favourable review in the club programme (I'll leave you to decide whether this is a good or bad thing). I actually got hold of a back copy of *WWYATS* last season and it is a fair enough read. If *DAB* can better this, it will do well (although hopefully it will be a lot easier to get hold of).

## TRAVEL

**NEAREST RAILWAY STATION:**
Bury Interchange (from Manchester Victoria — 0161 832 8353)

**BUS:** Bury Interchange bus station (0161 228 7811)
If your journey takes you into Manchester you could enjoy a nostalgic trip on the tram from the City to Bury. From the centre of Bury you can take either a 90 or a 92 bus to the ground.

## BY CAR:

**NORTH:** M66 to J2. Turn right onto the A58 Rochdale Road (signposted Bury) and after 0.5 mile turn left on to Heywood Street (B6219). After another 0.5 mile turn right into Wellington Road. Continue until you get to the T-junction with Manchester Road (A56) at which you should turn left. Turn left again after 0.5 mile into Gigg Lane and the ground is on the right.

**SOUTH/EAST/WEST:** M66 to J3. Turn left onto Pilsworth Road. After 1.25 miles you will get to a T-junction and turn right (A56 Manchester Road). A mile later turn right into Gigg Lane.

Alternatively: leave the M60(previously the M62) at J17 and take the Bury Road (A56) towards the town. After three miles turn right into Gigg Lane.

It should be noted that there were signposts put up for Gigg Lane last season so your trip shouldn't be too difficult.

**PARKING:** There is plenty of street parking around the ground, although be warned: all the side streets are cobbled which can be potentially damaging to any dodgy exhausts, loose fillings etc. Otherwise take the A56 Manchester Road towards Bury (ie from north, turn right onto Manchester Road, and from other directions continue straight past the Gigg Lane turning) and either turn right into Keighley Street, where there is a small car park by the Tech, or continue to the T-junction with Angouleme Road (A58). Within 0.75 mile there are three car parks on your right, the furthest of which is 1.5 miles from the ground.

## FUTURE DEVELOPMENTS

Bury used to be the butt of many a visiting fan's jokes with references to Bury/Cemetery End, 'Giggle' Lane, and the fact that one of the most popular songs sung by the locals went 'Tiptoe through the Ceme' to the tune of 'Tiptoe through the Tulips'. But the reopening of the South Stand means the ground is over three-quarters of the way to becoming all-seater. There remain plans afoot to finish off the job by converting the Cemetery End and it is projected that this will be, er, undertaken (see? you just can't help making dodgy puns!) in 1999; although having said this, initially this work was planned to be completed in 1996.

The club suggests that the approximate capacities during and post-construction will be 11,500 and 12,500.

## OTHER INFORMATION

For a pre-match pint try either the Pack Horse or the Staff Of Life, both of which are on Manchester Road, on the right as you leave Gigg Lane. An alternative is to try the Swan and Cemetery which is up the Manchester Road heading away from the centre. For connoisseurs of fine cuisine why not sample the delicacy for which the town has won numerous championships — black pudding?

Food at the Lane is average, although the choice of pies is restricted to meat and potato or nothing. The pasties/sausage rolls/hot dogs probably are better value/tasting. Bovvie is excellent (and they have pepper on the side).

Bury ground share with Swinton RLFC and the previously barren pitch has seen a marked improvement with the move to summer rugby. Talking of the Rugby Club, you won't fail to be impressed by their crest which is painted along with Bury's on the Main Stand. It's that ferocious king of the beasts, the lion, although its status is possibly diminished somewhat by the fact that this particular version bears a striking resemblance to the one from the Wizard of Oz and also appears to be cross-eyed! Grrrrr!

***Total Football* Experience Rating: 72**

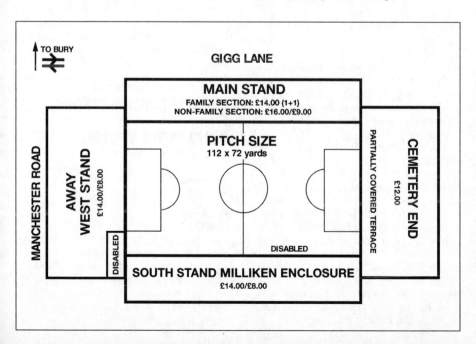

# CAMBRIDGE UNITED

**ADDRESS:** The Abbey Stadium
Newmarket Road
Cambridge CB5 8LN

**TELEPHONE No:** 01223 566500
**TICKET OFFICE:** 01223 566500
**FAX:** 01223 566502
**ABBEY UPDATE:** 0891 555 885
**WEBSITE:**
http://www.geocities.com/Colosseum/
4422/cufc.html (unofficial)
**NICKNAME:** The U's
**RECORD ATTENDANCE:**
14,000 v Chelsea Friendly 1 May 1970 (W 4-3)

**CLUB COLOURS:**
**HOME:** Shirts: Amber and Black quarters; Shorts:
Black; Socks: Black and Amber hoops
**AWAY:** Shirts: Sky Blue with Royal Blue collar and
sleeves; Shorts: Royal Blue; Socks: Royal Blue

**KIT SPONSORS:** tba
**MANUFACTURERS:** Patrick

## GROUND INFO

Let's get this straight from the start, Cambridge's drop from first to second place in the list of great away days in no way suggests that the club's standards have slipped but that those at Sunderland have risen beyond belief. The Abbey Stadium remains a fantastic away day that I would unreservedly recommend that all spectators enjoy.

The away facilities are fairly basic: there is an uncovered terrace and just under 400 seats in the Habbin Road Stand. There are a couple of pillars in the stand which may obstruct your view (although other than for sell-outs the club has no objections to you moving to find a better space) but it does have the advantage of having great acoustic qualities which mean that if there are more than 50 of you singing it can sound like a Wembley final.

The concessions offered to visiting supporters mirror those that are given to home fans and on occasion when the travelling support is less of an army and more of a battalion the club may shut the terracing. However, rather than try and make a fast buck out of those who make the journey the seats in the stand are priced at terrace levels.

Before a visit to the Abbey it is worth brushing up on your country code, as the visitors' entrance is not on the main road, but via a hike through fields negotiating swing gates and stiles! There is a path laid down but as this is about the width of two people you can imagine what it gets like after the final whistle goes, and you're in for a particularly pleasant time if there has been a drop of rain which reduces the fields to marshland very rapidly.

Due to the low walls surrounding the stadium, the gamblers amongst you might like to organise a little sweepstake amongst your friends about how many times you will see the ball hoofed out of the ground.

**CAPACITY:** Stands: 3,216;
Terrace: 6,315; Total: 9,531

**AWAY FANS:** Habbin Stand (Seats): 366;
South Terrace (Uncovered):
1,950; Total: 2,316

**DISABLED FACILITIES:** There are spaces for 18 disabled supporters between the Main Stand and North Terrace. Disabled fans are admitted free of charge, with helpers being charged £8.

All places must be pre-booked. There is a limited amount of car parking available at the ground for disabled fans, available on a first come first served basis. Due to the lack of general parking in the area, it is as well to try and be one of the first there! No match commentaries are available for the visually impaired.

**PROGRAMME:** £1.50
Continuing to get better year by year and worth buying for Steve Greenhall's column alone (possibly the only interesting Company Secretary I know). There have been improvements in the information about the visitors with at least four or five pages of general interest articles which will easily fill the time that you are eating (yet another) bacon roll.

**FANZINES:**
*The Abbey Rabbit*                    £1
The *Abbey Rabbit* and the club seem to be back on a more even keel following their lovers' tiff in 1996-7. The *Rabbit* continues to be a good source of information, but does suffer (if 'suffer' is the right word) from the fact that the club is fairly open with supporters, which means there aren't many skeletons to be discovered in cupboards. A reasonable read but nothing more.

## TRAVEL
### NEAREST RAILWAY STATION:
Cambridge (two miles) (01223 359602)

### NEAREST BUS STATION:
Cambridge city centre (01223 423554)
From Cambridge railway station take the Street Shuttle to the city centre (Emmanuel Street), and from there take either a 3 or a 3a to the ground.

### BY CAR:
**NORTH:** Cross the M11 at J14. Take the A1307 (Huntingdon Road) towards the city centre. At the bottom of the A1307 turn right onto Mount Pleasant Street, then after a (jinking) 0.25 mile turn left onto the A1303. After a further 1.75 miles turn right onto the A1134. Carry on for about 0.3 mile till you get to a roundabout at which you should turn left onto the A1134 Newmarket Road. The ground is 0.75 miles on the right.

**EAST:** A1303 Newmarket Road. Go past the airport and you will come to a roundabout. Continue straight on following the A1134 (note the left turn is also the A1134, do not follow this as it is just part of a master plan by the good people of Cambridge to get you lost); the ground is 0.5 mile on the left.

**SOUTH:** M11 to J11. Take the A1309 which becomes the A1134 (heading towards the city centre). Turn right onto the A603 (Lensfield Rd), go straight over the first major roundabout then right at the second roundabout onto the A1134 Newmarket Road. The ground is 0.75 miles on the right.

**WEST:** A1363. Continue through the north end of the city till you reach the junction with the A1134. Turn right here and then after 0.3 miles left at the roundabout onto the A1134 Newmarket Road. The ground is 0.75 miles on the right.

**PARKING:** Parking has eased somewhat since the club purchased the 'Corona' site at the back of the ground. However, finding a place can still be a chore although there are side streets which can be used.

## FUTURE DEVELOPMENTS

If it was up to me — and the general consensus of visiting fans I have talked to — the Abbey would stay exactly the same as it is now and glory in its imperfections and character, all of which contribute to the excellence of a trip here. However, progress means that there are likely to be changes in the medium term future and a planning application for ground development is due for submission in late 1998, although even if this is passed there are likely to be no changes this season.

## OTHER INFORMATION

Still no news about the Globe 'disco pub' reopening so

the options are to either wander down Newmarket Road to the Wrestlers (5-10min), go into the city centre and find one of the many excellent watering holes there, or alternatively pay £1 and go into the supporters' club bar. The latter is probably the best option as you'll enjoy a decent pint and not have the trauma of trying to rediscover the ground.

There is a chip shop by the Wrestlers, but if you can stave off your hunger wait till you get into the ground and enjoy one (or more) of United's legendary bacon rolls. I can't begin to describe how good these are other than to recount this true story. Last season Sky was doing some filming at the ground on a Saturday at 2.50pm and wanted to get a shot of someone eating a bacon roll. They approached a track-suited bloke and asked if he would mind being the subject of this action to which he recoiled in horror saying 'No! No! I'm playing in five minutes' time!!! The boss thinks I'm out here warming up, but I just couldn't resist it...' Brilliant (and understandable).

One minor curiosity/ annoyance is that, although the tea is boiling hot, it is served in cups that are guaranteed to transfer the heat directly to your fingers. The cold coke, however, is served in insulated cups (obviously third degree burns being preferable to a slightly chilled hand!).

The toilets are very dark, although you will probably be able to make out the Cambridge Clubcall signs which are on the walls. As these toilets are for away fans, I'm not sure whether they think you are likely to have a spiritual 'conversion' in them or whether it is just misplaced advertising.

*Total Football* **Experience Rating: 93**

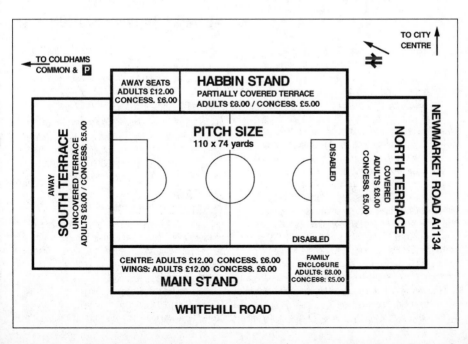

TO CITY CENTRE

TO COLDHAMS COMMON & P

AWAY SEATS
ADULTS £12.00
CONCESS. £6.00

**HABBIN STAND**
PARTIALLY COVERED TERRACE
ADULTS £8.00 / CONCESS. £5.00

**PITCH SIZE**
110 x 74 yards

DISABLED

**SOUTH TERRACE**
AWAY
UNCOVERED TERRACE
ADULTS £8.00 / CONCESS. £5.00

**NORTH TERRACE**
COVERED
ADULTS £8.00
CONCESS. £5.00

NEWMARKET ROAD A1134

DISABLED

CENTRE: ADULTS £12.00 CONCESS. £6.00
WINGS: ADULTS £12.00 CONCESS. £6.00
**MAIN STAND**

FAMILY ENCLOSURE
ADULTS: £8.00
CONCESS: £5.00

**WHITEHILL ROAD**

# CARDIFF CITY

**ADDRESS:** Ninian Park
Sloper Road
Cardiff CF1 8SX

**TELEPHONE No:** 01222 398636
**TICKET OFFICE:** 01222 398636
**FAX:** 01222 341148
**CLUBCALL:** 0891 12 11 71
**CLUB SHOP:** 01222 666699
**WEBSITE:**
http://www.styrotech.co.uk/ccafe/
**NICKNAME:** The Bluebirds
**RECORD ATTENDANCE:**
61,556 Wales v England 14 October 1961 (D 1-1)
57,800 v Arsenal Div 1 22 April 1953 (D 0-0)

**CLUB COLOURS:**
**HOME:** Shirts: Blue; Shorts: White; Socks: Blue
**AWAY:** Shirts: Yellow; Shorts: Blue; Socks: Yellow

**KIT SPONSORS:** tba
**MANUFACTURERS:** tba

## GROUND INFO

Although the club has undertaken some improvements at Ninian Park, the overwhelming impression you are left with is of a once great ground in decay. In truth the stadium looks worse from the outside than it does when you are in it; for example the back of the Canton Stand appears to be full of huge holes, but when you get inside you find that the club has put up a false wall at the back which means that it is similar to many other (small) stands that you will see around the country, although it does only stretch 80% of the way behind the goal. The fact that neither the Grangetown Terrace nor the paddock in front of the Popular Bank is open (other than for big games) adds to the air of disrepair.

If you are going to a match, try to get a seat at the back of the section because those at the front have been built on an old paddock area, and do not give the best view. In addition, regardless of where you are, there isn't masses of leg room. The club does offer excellent concessions to both home and visiting supporters.

In some ways the atmosphere has got a lot better at and around the ground over the last couple of seasons. Part of this may be due to falling attendances and the poor performances of the team, but equally part is down to the efforts of the club and the supporters. My own opinion is that there is still an 'air' about the place but this may simply be down to old experiences at the ground, and certainly when I went down last season neither myself nor any away fans had any hassle. If you can't get a ticket for the away end then while you shouldn't avoid going to

the match, it is probably as well to stick to the Grandstand and be circumspect.

**CAPACITY:** Stands: 12,367;
Terrace: 2,234; Total: 14,601

**AWAY FANS:** Grangetown End: 2,234
Total: 2,234

**DISABLED FACILITIES:** There are places for 20 supporters in front of the Canton Family Enclosure. Admission for both wheelchair-bound supporters and (one) helper is free. Pre-booking is required. There are no matchday commentaries nor special parking facilities at Ninian Park.

**PROGRAMME:** £1.60
A fairly run-of-the-mill affair.

**FANZINES:**
*Watch The Bluebirds Fly*     30p
*The Thin Blue Line*     50p
*The Thin Blue Line* is the best read if you want to know what is going on with the club (don't expect this to make particularly heart-warming reading though). One very different publication you may come across is the football(ish) adult comic *Bluebird Jones*. This was — it is no longer produced — a bizarre mix of comedy (from the hilarious to the embarrassing) and issues (nothing was considered untouchable and it was very thought-provoking). You may see some old copies (although I think only five were produced) knocking about (and I believe there will be a 'best of...' at some time in the future). If you do see a copy, then buy it.

## TRAVEL

**NEAREST RAILWAY STATION:** Ninian Park Halt (from Cardiff Central) (0345 484950)
Ninian Park Halt is right behind the ground. This is on the City Line (from Cardiff Central). Not the most frequent of services (there are three trains on Saturdays after matches at 16.47, 17.17 and 18.34) but to save a longish walk it is useful to brave the scrum and try and get on one.

**BUS:** Cardiff bus station (01222 396521)
From the bus station catch a City Circle No 1 bus from stand E4 which will drop you right outside Ninian Park. On the way back you'll need to pick up a number 2 (urrgh) from the opposite side of the road.

**BY CAR:**
**FROM ALL DIRECTIONS:**
M4 to J33. Pick up the A4232 for about six miles until you see a roundabout signposted for Barry (this is the second exit on the A4232). Turn left at this roundabout into Leckwith Road and continue for about 0.75 mile. The football car park is on your right.

Note: some people suggest getting off at J29 on the M4 and taking the A48/A4161 through Cardiff. This is a shorter (in miles) route but takes you on a tortuous trip through the city. Do yourself a favour and don't bother.

**PARKING:** There is a large car park on Sloper Road, and street parking; the latter is not recommended as there are restrictions on all surrounding roads that are rigorously enforced. If when you are approaching the ground you go left at the Cowbridge Road East/Lansdowne Road fork, there are two car parks (£1.50) within a mile or so. To get to these, turn either left into Llandaff Road or, slightly further on, left into Severn Road.

## FUTURE DEVELOPMENTS

Of principal interest to the club and its fans at present seems to be not what Cardiff will do but whether Wimbledon will relocate to the city. Many people feel that if they do then it could sound the death knell for the club as more people are tempted away from Ninian Park. Despite the fact that Sam Hammam is a generally good egg, you need only to talk to the fans at Cardiff to realise that franchising can't be the way forward if we want to keep our traditional league structures.

As for City themselves, don't expect too much. There has been talk of relocating to Cardiff Bay (an area which I understand was rejected by Glamorgan County Cricket Club as a site for a new ground). However, there is nothing concrete and the Development Corporation's charter runs out in 1999 which means that plans are going to have to be drawn up very quickly if the club wants to take advantage of any financial benefits the construction of such a stadium in this area might bring.

## OTHER INFORMATION

The Ninian Park is right by the ground, but in truth this really is a home pub. If you are an away fan, may I suggest that it would not be wise to walk into the Ninian with your England replica top on offering to buy pink gins for everyone. A better bet is to walk down Leckwith Road (heading towards the city) and after about 10min you come to the Canton area of the City. This boasts a wide choice of pubs including the Canton Cross Vaults (OK), the Admiral Napier (OK) and the Kings Castle (probably the best of the bunch), which has an excellent Balti House next to it. There is also the Canton Fish Bar which does good potato and pineapple fritters, but they poured cold gravy onto the chips and then microwaved the lot (a heinous crime!). There is also a couple of bookies around although the Ladbrokes is opposite a Baptist Church (bizarrely, last time I was down there they were giving out balloon animals for Jesus), and it can be a bit disorientating watching your red hot tip go down to the background of the church band that they have outside.

Inside, the food is edible and they do serve a decent and reasonably priced large cup of tea. The toilet facilities are fairly grim and the small entrance/exit means that there is always a bottleneck at half-time.

Ninian Park is a weird place and quite a few older fans might travel there with a feeling of some trepidation remembering what it was like in the past. It still can get a bit hairy on occasions but my last visit was everything a day out should be, a good couple of beers and a laugh then a match at a ground where the club seemed happy that you had come and did not rip you off for the privilege.

*Total Football* **Experience Rating: 71**

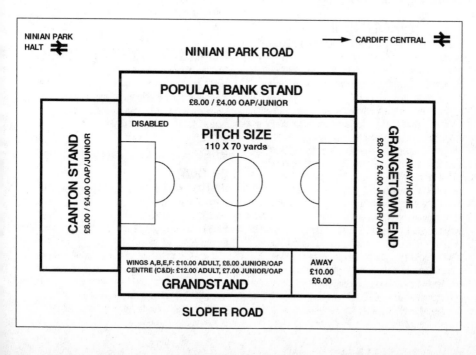

# CARLISLE UNITED

**ADDRESS:** Brunton Park
Warwick Road
Carlisle CA1 1LL

**TELEPHONE No:** 01228 526237

**TICKET OFFICE:** 01228 526237

**FAX:** 01228 530138

**RED FOX CLUBLINE:** 0891 230011

**E-MAIL:**
carlisleunited@easynet.co.uk

**WEBSITE:** www.cufconline.org.uk
(unofficial)

**NICKNAME:** The Cumbrians

**RECORD ATTENDANCE:**
27,500 v Birmingham FA Cup 3rd 5  January 1957
(D3-3); v Middlesbrough FA Cup 5th 7  February 1970
(L 1-2)

**CLUB COLOURS:**

**HOME:** Shirts: Blue, with White/Red markings;
Shorts: White; Socks: White with Blue/Red trim

**AWAY:** Away: Gold with Red and Green 'deckchair'
inserts
Shorts: Gold with Red and Green trim;
Socks: Gold with Red and Green trim

**KIT SPONSORS:** Eddie Stobart

**MANUFACTURERS:** Red Fox (own brand)

## GROUND INFO

The first thing you notice about the ground are the weird
floodlights, which look as if someone has stolen the top
of the pylon where the bulbs should be and rather than
replace them the club has attached bike lights down the
side of the pylon.

Away fans are sited in the north end of the East Stand.
If you can, avoid blocks 1 & 2 as when you look out you
will get a good view across not the pitch but rather the
old Petteril Terrace. As a result you will get a crick in
your neck looking up to try and see the action. The other
end of the stand finishes about level with the edge of the
Warwick Road penalty area. Presumably the club intends
moving the pitch at some point during the development
of the ground and everything will return to normal, but at
present it just looks as if the stand has been built about
20ft out of place. Still, providing you do avoid these
blocks then at least you can be assured of a good view of
the pitch and some protection from the biting wind.

There were no signs up offering away fans
concessions when I visited, but some supporters told me
that they had got them when they had asked for them
(though they never received the extra discount where, if

you bring two kids, the second only pays half the
concessionary rate, ie £3), while others had gone through
the home fans' entrance to the stand and (after a quick
word with the stewards) transferred across to the away
seats.

**CAPACITY:** Stands: 7,986 Terrace: 8,664;
Total: 16,650

**AWAY FANS:** East Stand Blocks 1-4: 2,000

**DISABLED FACILITIES:** There is a
dedicated section in the new East Stand with full facilities
Admission is by prior arrangement only. The club admits
one helper per wheelchair-bound supporter, neither of
whom is charged for admission. There are no match
commentaries for the blind but local radio covers every
match.

**PROGRAMME:** £1.50
Although this was the 1996-7 Programme Monthly
divisional programme of the year I can't see it repeating
the feat this season. Still, it is better than average and,
despite the 'pen pics' nature of the away section, has
enough general interest articles to get you through half-
time. If you go to the club shop you can not only pick up
the day's programme but also, for some unknown reason,
seemingly any Bournemouth home programme including
their matches against Southend and Watford which must
really pull in the passing trade.

**FANZINES:**

| | |
|---|---|
| What The Fox's Going On | 50p |
| Land Of Sheep And Glory | £1 |
| Cumberland Sausage | £1 |

None of these were on sale during my last trip to the
ground.

## TRAVEL

**NEAREST RAILWAY STATION:** Carlisle
Citadel (1.5 miles) (01228 44711)
This is about 15min walk from the ground and although
you may find you want to stretch your legs after getting to
Carlisle, it is also worth knowing that a cab (of which
there are loads outside the station) won't cost you more
than £2.50.

**BUS:** CMS Buses (01946 63222)

**BY CAR:**

**NORTH/SOUTH:** Take M6 to J43 then the A69
Warwick Road into Carlisle. The ground is 1.25 miles on
the right.

**EAST:** A69 into Carlisle. After the A69 crosses the M6,
the ground is 1.25 miles on the right.

If you intend filling up with petrol for the way back
there are only two petrol stations on the left-hand side
between Brunton Park and the motorway; so if you have
time when you arrive it is best to do it on the way into
Carlisle because after the match the roads get very
choked up.

**PARKING:** There is a sizeable car park behind the ground. Drive past the ground about 0.25 mile and turn right into Victoria Drive and right again into St Aidans Road (along which there is street parking). At the bottom of St Aidans Road there is a golf club; drive into here and keep going and the car park is on your right. The trouble with this is that it puts you behind the traffic heading out of the City, so expect delays.

There is on-street parking but if you go for this option it is best to park on the motorway side of the ground in order to avoid being held up as the police direct the traffic leaving the club car park onto the main road. Also, if you do park-up by the ground and fancy a walk into town, be warned: it is a fair hike.

## FUTURE DEVELOPMENTS

Michael Knighton has got a blueprint to turn the ground into a 28,000-seat stadium although this will take longer than initially planned. Given that the Petteril End is hardly ever used at the moment and seems to be in a stage of disrepair, it seems sensible that this would be the next area of the ground to be developed. However, the fact that Brunton Park has a 16,000+ capacity and the team is getting average attendances of around the 6,000 mark, there does not seem to be any rush to get this completed.

## OTHER INFORMATION

If you've never been into Carlisle take the 15min walk into the city and give yourself a pleasant surprise; it is not the wilderness some people would have you believe, but clean and filled with interesting buildings. If you can stay a night — there are loads of cheap B&Bs on the Warwick Road — it is well worth doing as the Border City has a definite sense of excitement about it. I can't really describe it other than it is how I imagine a saloon in the Wild West might have felt. Not threatening but definitely a slight lawless atmosphere about it.

For eating if you want to go a bit posh try the Old Arcadian on English Street, near the courts (and very conveniently, if you travel up on a January evening, right by the Damart thermal underwear shop). It's like a cross between somebody's house and a Victorian theatre foyer. The average age of the clientele seems to be mid to late 90s but the staff do a very reasonable all-day breakfast at £3.75 and a cracking Cumberland sausage with chips and all the trimmings at £3.95. Otherwise there are plenty of chip shops in the town centre which do, amongst other things, haggis and black pudding in batter. The food inside the ground has improved beyond belief over the last couple of seasons and the Scotch pie (spicy mutton) is a must try; if you've still got a gap then add a Brunton Pastie, which is also excellent. Hot drinks are good (although the spoons are the smallest that I've ever seen and capable of holding only about three grains of sugar).

If you do fancy a beer then the Beehive is the closest pub, but tends to be quite a 'home' venue. Ten minutes down the road is the White House — miles bigger with a rocking atmosphere.

Finally, if you want to have your ego massaged, check out one of the female stewards who searches away fans on the way in. As she does your trouser legs she will smile knowingly and say 'My, that's a huge... pocketful of change you got there' which leaves you feeling very chuffed with life (providing you're a bloke).

Older supporters who remember the stuffed fox that used to be laid on the centre spot before United's games by a man in blue and white top hat and tails (who was, if my memory serves me correctly, a local dustman) will now notice its absence from the field of play. However, if you want to pay a trip down memory lane then just pop into the lobby of the ground where 'Olga' now resides.

*Total Football* **Experience Rating: 73**

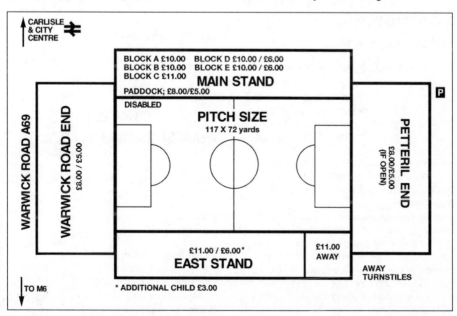

# CHARLTON ATHLETIC

**ADDRESS:** The Valley
Floyd Road, Charlton
London SE7 8EL

**TELEPHONE No:** 0181 333 4000

**TICKET OFFICE:** 0181 333 4010

**FAX:** 0181 333 4001

**WEBSITE:**
http:/www.charlton-athletic.co.uk

**E-MAIL:**
info@charlton-athletic.co.uk

**CLUBCALL:** 0891 12 11 46

**NICKNAME:** The Addicks

Charlton seem to change their nickname as often as some teams (Charlton, for example) change grounds. Have also been known as the Valiants and the Robins at various points during their illustrious lifetime.

Perhaps the most interesting is The Addicks, which is thought to be a derivation of the word haddock, and which came about when, in days of yore, one of the Charlton directors owned a fish and chip shop and all visiting team officials were given a free haddock supper by the club.

**RECORD ATTENDANCE:** 75,031 v Aston Villa FA Cup 5th 12 February 1938 (D 1-1)

**CLUB COLOURS:**
**HOME:** Shirts: Red; Shorts: White; Socks: Red
**AWAY:** Shirts: Off White; Shorts: Black;
Socks: Black and White

**KIT SPONSORS:** Viglen

**MANUFACTURERS:** Le Coq Sportif

## GROUND INFO

Entrance to The Valley is ticket controlled, and although away fans do have their own ticket booths by the South Stand, this still inevitably leads to having to queue twice to get into the ground. The view from the South Stand isn't too bad although there are a couple of pillars (as there are in the North and West Stands) and it isn't over generous on leg room. The stand seating everywhere except the West Stand starts from about six feet up, and this means that no matter where you go you get a decent view of the pitch.

If you remember The Valley from a few years back when it had the old banked terracing, then to see a compact all-seater ground can be a bit depressing. If you are a Charlton fan who has in the past had to travel to Selhurst Park and Upton Park to see your team, then it's probably the most beautiful sight you could imagine.

The club does offer away supporters concessions — which should be applauded — although a mighty £4

discount on £13 isn't that much to write home about. More irritating is the fact that home fans who have exactly the same (or better) facilities get a far better deal. For example if a grandfather, father and son go to the North (home) Stand, they will pay £23 to get in (£18 if dad is a member). If the same people go into the South (away) Stand they will pay £31.

**CAPACITY:** Stands: 20,000

NB This figure is post final development of the West Stand. Should this be delayed the capacity will remain at 16,000.

**AWAY FANS:** South Stand: 3,073;
Total: 3,073

**DISABLED FACILITIES:** There are spaces for 70 wheelchair-bound fans with their helpers in the East (30), West (20) and South Stands. Disabled facilities for away fans are at the back of the Jimmy Seed Stand. Disabled fans are admitted free with helpers but you must book in advance. Similarly, if you want a parking space by the ground you must pre-book this. The club do offer match commentaries for the blind, and state that whilst pre-booking is not essential, it is recommended.

**PROGRAMME:** £1.80

Grew in size last season although it can still only be classified as average.

**FANZINES:**
*The Voice Of The Valley* £1.50

*Voice of the Valley* remains a shining example to all football fans and fanzine editors as to just what can be achieved if people really put their minds to it. Formed out of anger at the fact that the club was playing at Selhurst Park, the lads who put this together were instrumental in keeping the club's plight in the local and national spotlight and the fact that the club returned to its rightful home is in no small part down to the chaps who put this together. The 1997-8 version fortunately returned to a pocket friendly A5 format and can be bought both inside (in home areas) and outside the ground.

## TRAVEL

### NEAREST RAILWAY STATION:

Charlton: (0171 928 5100 — London Bridge Enquiries) You can catch trains to Charlton from any of the following London main-line stations: Waterloo East, Charing Cross, London Bridge. If you are going to a match mid-week you can also get on board at Cannon Street; be warned though that some of the trains which go via Lewisham may not call at Charlton. There are two trains an hour.

**BUS:** London Transport (0171 222 1234)
177 and 180 buses stop on Woolwich Road which is a two-minute walk from the ground.

Alternatively grab a 53, 54 or 380 which will drop you off about five minutes away.

## BY CAR:

**NORTH:** A1 into London. At the roundabout by Highbury and Islington tube station go straight over on to the A1200 (signposted Shoreditch). When you reach Shoreditch pick up and follow the signs for Whitechapel, and once there, take the A13 (signposted Limehouse and Tilbury). Turn right to cross the Thames via the Blackwall Tunnel then continue on to the A102/A102(M). After one mile turn left onto the A206 Woolwich Road and then right after one mile into Charlton Church Lane. First left into Floyd Road and the ground is 200yd on the right.

**EAST:** A2 into London, continuing past Eltham to Kidbrooke at which point take the A102(M) (signposted Blackwall Tunnel). After one mile turn right onto the A206 Woolwich Road, then as north.

**SOUTH:** M23/A23 into London until you get to Kennington. Turn right onto the A202 Camberwell New Road (signposted Camberwell, Peckham) and carry on for 3.5 miles until the road merges with and becomes the A2. Continue for 2 miles then turn left at the roundabout on to the A102(M). Then as east.

**WEST:** M4/A4 into Central London. As you approach Hammersmith, turn right following signs for A306 Hammersmith Bridge. Cross the river and continue for two miles then turn left on to the A205 Richmond Road. After one mile this merges with the A3; follow A3 to Kennington and by Oval tube station turn right into Camberwell New Road (A202). Then as south.

**PARKING:** Some street parking, but watch out because there is a tow-away scheme in many of the roads near the ground. If you want off-street parking then take the A206 past the ground following signs for Woolwich Free Ferry, next to which there is a car park (about 1.5 miles from the ground). It should be noted that with the construction of the Millennium Dome the local council has decided to introduce further parking restrictions which may have some impact on where you can leave your vehicle (although it has been stated that these restrictions may be lifted/reduced on matchdays).

## FUTURE DEVELOPMENTS

Stage 2 of the West Stand development is due to be completed before the start of the 1998-9 season. This will take The Valley over the 20,000 mark and will signal the completion of the ground's reconstruction from the decaying shell it had become following the club's departure. to a fairly impressive stadium for the 1990s.

## OTHER INFORMATION

Historically, the club has been very strict about what is allowed into the ground. In 1919 one of its own supporters was banned from attending matches because he insisted on bringing in a haddock nailed to a piece of wood, which he waved in the air for 90min.

The Watermans Arms and McDonnells are both at the corner of Woolwich Road and Charlton Church Lane, but it's much better to wander down Woolwich Road for about 0.25 miles to the Horse & Groom. Nothing special in terms of décor, it makes up for this by being a good honest boozer with a very friendly landlord and landlady.

For food, the Kebab House on the corner of Floyd Road and Charlton Church Lane does excellent chips, although its burgers aren't fantastic. Once inside the ground the mince and onion pies aren't bad even if they do have a tendency to fall to pieces on that long journey between silver tray and mouth.

In general a trip to The Valley is a good day out, though the pricing structure sticks in the throat. If you are into doing other things as well as going to the match you should note that the Millennium Dome site and the Thames barrier are within easy visiting distance.

*Total Football* **Experience Rating: 54**

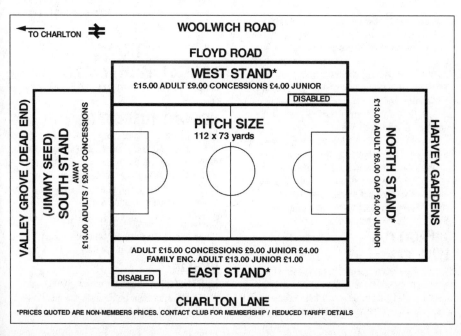

TO CHARLTON

WOOLWICH ROAD

FLOYD ROAD

**WEST STAND***
£15.00 ADULT £9.00 CONCESSIONS £4.00 JUNIOR

DISABLED

**PITCH SIZE**
112 x 73 yards

VALLEY GROVE (DEAD END)

(JIMMY SEED)
**SOUTH STAND**
AWAY
£13.00 ADULTS / £9.00 CONCESSIONS

**NORTH STAND***
£13.00 ADULT £6.00 OAP £4.00 JUNIOR

HARVEY GARDENS

ADULT £15.00 CONCESSIONS £9.00 JUNIOR £4.00
FAMILY ENC. ADULT £13.00 JUNIOR £1.00

DISABLED

**EAST STAND***

CHARLTON LANE

*PRICES QUOTED ARE NON-MEMBERS PRICES. CONTACT CLUB FOR MEMBERSHIP / REDUCED TARIFF DETAILS

# CHELSEA

**ADDRESS:** Stamford Bridge
Fulham Road
London SW6 1HS

**TELEPHONE No:** 0171 385 5545

**TICKET OFFICE:** 0171 386 7799

**FAX:** 0171 381 4831

**CLUBCALL:** 0891 12 11 59

**WEB SITE:** www.chelseafc.co.uk

(official and absolutely brilliant, the standard by which all others must be judged)

**NICKNAME:** The Blues

**RECORD ATTENDANCE:**

82,905 v Arsenal Div 1 12 October 1935 (D 1-1)

**CLUB COLOURS:**

**HOME:** Shirts: Blue, White under sleeves;
Shorts: Blue; Socks: White

**AWAY:** Shirts: White, Blue trim;
Shorts: White, Blue trim; Socks; Blue/White

**KIT SPONSORS:** Autoglass

**MANUFACTURERS:** Umbro

## GROUND INFO

Welcome to Stamford Bridge, I hope you've brought your wallet... Chelsea remain one of the most expensive sides to watch in the division and the news that the club has increased season ticket prices for 1998-9 by over 40% in some instances (netto) does not augur well for away fans.

Actually in 1997-8 away fans did not do too badly, especially for category 'A' matches where prices mirrored those charged to home supporters in the half-finished West Stand who don't even have a roof over their heads. The East Stand offers a great view of the action (although the first couple of rows should be avoided if possible).

If you don't have an away ticket, then you can be struggling as the only place that non members can get in is the West Stand.

For those of you who remember the fairly intimidatory atmosphere of the old West Stand, fear not as nowadays it seems to be chock-a-block with Scandinavian and Italian tourists who seem to view watching a Chelsea game along with going to Madame Tussauds and Carnaby Street as a 'must do' on their trips to London (sometimes they will cheer as well).

**CAPACITY:** Stands: 35,629; Terrace: Nil

**AWAY FANS:** East Stand Lower Tier: 1,608 Chelsea offer all clubs the opportunity to extend this to the whole of the Lower Tier — 3,200 — if required. It should be noted that for 1998-9 the first section allocated to away fans will be the North (Matthew Harding) end of

the Lower Tier rather than the South (Shed) End.

**DISABLED FACILITIES:** There are 40 places at the ground for disabled supporters, these being sited in the front row of the East Stand Family Section. In addition, there are five places in the Upper Tier of the North Stand for club members only. Prices are £9 for disabled fans and £24 for helpers. The club stated that matchday commentaries were not available but I do know that these are provided on Radio Chelsea (1494 AM). No designated parking is available, which means either shelling out for the club car park or the lottery of trying to find a place on the street.

**PROGRAMME:** £2.50

No this is not a misprint: in 1997-8 Chelsea charged £2.50 for every match programme. This is a fairly slick publication for home fans but there is little or nothing of general interest which will appeal to away fans.

**FANZINES:**

| | |
|---|---|
| *The Red Card* | 80p |
| *The Chelsea Independent* | £1 |
| *In the Net* | £1 |

*The Chelsea Independent* seemed to return to some past glories with a change of editor last season, although on occasion a smug 'holier than thou' tone still rises to the surface. *Red Card* remains for me what a fanzine should be about. OK, so in the odd article the standard slips but in every issue you'll always find stuff that is funny, angry and interesting; it also contains the odd article from the bloke who used to put together the (now defunct?) *Cockney Rebel* fanzine — these are unlike anything that you'll have ever come across in a fanzine before and simply a fantastic read. *In The Net* appears to be just reprinted pages from various internet sites and can be left alone.

## TRAVEL

**NEAREST RAILWAY STATION:** Putney Bridge (a long old walk) (0171 262 6767 — Paddington Enquiries)

**NEAREST TUBE STATION:**

Fulham Broadway (District Line)

When using the District Line make sure you get on a Wimbledon train, not one to Richmond, Olympia or South Ealing. The tube does not stop at West Brompton, the station before Fulham Broadway, at weekends, so you want the first stop after Earl's Court.

**BUS:** London Transport (0171 222 1234)

The number 14 stops directly outside the ground. The 91, 295 and 28 stop outside Fulham Broadway.

**BY CAR:**

**NORTH:** M1 to J1. Turn right on to the A406 North Circular Road (travelling west). Continue for four miles to Hanger Lane roundabout (or gyratory system to give its full belly-dancing title) and go straight over into Hanger Lane. After two miles you will see Gunnersbury Park and shortly after, the Chiswick roundabout. Take the second exit onto the A4. At the next roundabout (Hogarth) take the first exit, which keeps you on the A4 Great West Road. After one mile you reach Hammersmith. Follow the one-way system until you are almost travelling back in the direction you have come, and turn immediately left into Fulham Palace Road (A219). After 1.5 miles turn left onto Fulham Road (A304), the ground is 1.25 miles on the left.

**WEST:** M4 to J1 continuing straight on to the A4. After one mile you come to Hogarth roundabout, then as north.

**SOUTH:** A24 into London. At the crossroads with the A214 (by Tooting Bec station) turn left onto Trinity Road. Continue for 1.75 miles then turn left onto the A3. After one mile the road splits into two; take the right-hand lane (Upper Richmond Road) then go right at the next crossroads into Putney High Street (A219). Take this road and cross Putney Bridge, then 0.25 mile later turn right onto the A304 Fulham Broadway and the ground is 1.25 miles on your left.

**EAST:** A12 to A406 North Circular Road (travelling west). Continue along the A406 until you get to the end of the M1. Then as north.

**PARKING:** Street parking off the Fulham Road is the only real choice, but be aware that the Fulham Road can be closed by the police just before and/or just after matches.

There is a 200-space car park at the ground but at £10 a match you'll probably find it better value to park away from the ground and take a tube to the stadium.

# FUTURE DEVELOPMENTS

The club has had problems with the local council about how often it will be able to use its new West Stand when completed; the council says only on matchdays, the club want to use it everyday. Until these issues are resolved this stand will remain only half built, awaiting an upper tier and roof. The club advises that it hopes this work will be completed in late 1999 and states that this will raise the capacity to '42,000' (or was this a Freudian slip and it has revealed its new ticket prices). 1997-8 saw the opening of numerous food outlets and bars around the ground.

# OTHER INFORMATION

The vast majority of the pubs in the area have a real home feel about them and it is probably better either to stop for a drink a couple of tube stops away or to go for a mega pose pub on the Kings Road. Alternatively if as you're walking towards the ground from the tube you turn right up a side road as you pass the fanzine stalls then you will come across the Pickled Pelican which is OK if there are not too many of you and where the brilliant bar staff serve drinks at an incredible rate of knots.

For food there are plenty of chip shops on the Fulham Road but if you fancy something different then go to the Lost Café (in the basement behind the Red Card stall). Run by a Brazilian, it offers everything from English breakfast to lasagne, cannelloni and salads as well as snacks.

Once inside the ground — that is providing you manage to walk down the dire concrete concourse that leads to the away seats without being blown away by the wind tunnel that seems to have been created — it's a case of you don't get what you paid for. When you cough up £2 (again not a misprint) for a pie and £1 for a tea, then you would expect them to be hot and tasty; sadly the ones I was served with failed miserably on both counts.

*Total Football* **Experience Rating: 68**

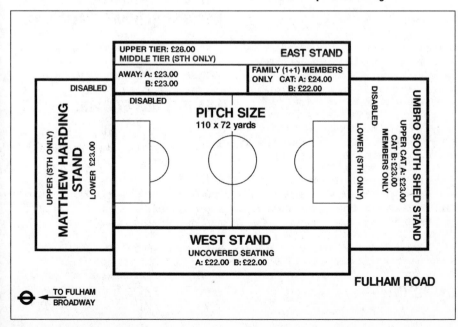

UPPER TIER: £28.00
MIDDLE TIER (STH ONLY)

EAST STAND

AWAY: A: £23.00
B: £23.00

FAMILY (1+1) MEMBERS
ONLY  CAT: A: £24.00
B: £22.00

DISABLED

DISABLED

PITCH SIZE
110 x 72 yards

DISABLED

MATTHEW HARDING STAND
UPPER (STH ONLY)
LOWER £23.00

UMBRO SOUTH SHED STAND
UPPER CAT A: £23.00
CAT B: £23.00
MEMBERS ONLY
LOWER (STH ONLY)

WEST STAND
UNCOVERED SEATING
A: £22.00  B: £22.00

TO FULHAM
BROADWAY

FULHAM ROAD

# CHESTER CITY

**ADDRESS:** Deva Stadium
Bumpers Lane
Chester CH1 4LT

**TELEPHONE No:** 01244 371376
**TICKET OFFICE:** 01244 371809
**FAX:** 01244 390265
**CLUBCALL:** 0891 12 16 33
**WEBSITE:** www.chester-city.co.uk.
**NICKNAME:** City or Blues

**RECORD ATTENDANCE:**
20,500 v Chelsea FA Cup 3rd Rep 16 January 1952
(L 3-2 AET). At Deva: 5,638 v Preston North End Div 3
2 April 1994 (W 3-2)

## CLUB COLOURS:
**HOME:** Shirts: Blue & White stripes;
Shorts: White; Socks: Blue with White turnover
**AWAY:** Shirts: Claret & White;
Shorts: Claret & White; Socks: Claret & White

**KIT SPONSORS:** Saunders Honda

**MANUFACTURERS:** Super League

## GROUND INFO

Within the East Stand there is a family section which offers the same concessions as the home section of the West Stand. Visiting supporters can phone the club in advance and obtain tickets for this area with the relevant discount for kids. The club is (still!) apparently reviewing the possibility of offering away fans concessions but at the moment hasn't decided on whether to embark on what some might consider a radical move.

A trip to the Deva illustrates all that is both right and wrong with football and out-of-town stadia in the 1990s. The staff are generally helpful (and the majority are — rightly — embarrassed that visitors do not get concessions) and you get a half decent view of the game wherever you go. The trouble is that because it is out in the back of beyond, there are no basic facilities for supporters (pub, bookies, chippie; hell, even a newsagent wouldn't go amiss), which takes away some of the spontaneity and atmosphere from the ground. This means a day at the football becomes more of a chore than something you do for enjoyment. One little point that it is worth while being aware of is that if you go to a night match at the Deva and fancy a wander around the ground before going in, it is as well to take a davy lamp with you as the words 'outside illumination' seem to be a mystery to the club (this is especially true at the back of the West Stand).

**CAPACITY:** Stands: 3,408; Terrace: 2,592;
Total: 6,000

**AWAY FANS:** South Terrace: 1,296:
West Stand 600: Total: 1,896
If the away support warrants it, they can be given the whole of the West Stand, increasing their total seating allocation to 1,274.

**DISABLED FACILITIES:** There are 32 spaces for disabled fans (and 40 helpers — does that mean you get to go to a game with 1.25 friends — splendid!) which are spread in pockets along the East and West Stands, with the club having installed ramps to these at the side of the pitch. Away fans are admitted although pre-booking is required. Disabled fans are admitted free, with helpers paying the standard matchday price. Match commentaries for the blind are available (10 places), but these too should be pre-booked. There are disabled parking facilities at the ground, just speak to one of the stewards.

**PROGRAMME:** £1.50
Not a bad read for either home or away fans.

## FANZINES:
| | |
|---|---|
| *Hello Albert* | £1 |
| *The Onion Bag* | 80p |

Both *Hello Albert* — so called because the first PA announcer that Chester had, used to start the afternoon's proceedings with the message 'Hello Spion Kop! Hello Albert (Albert being a friend of his in the crowd) — and the *Onion Bag* have their fair share of downbeat humour. *Hello Albert* tends to have one or two excellent articles but also some definite space fillers (including a very self congratulatory Fan Profile).

## TRAVEL

**NEAREST RAILWAY STATION:** Chester (1.5 miles) (0151 709 9696 — Liverpool Enquiries)
This is a good couple of miles from the ground and taking a cab can be an expensive affair because there always seem to be traffic jams around the area (which really helps that metre spin round).

**NEAREST BUS STATION:**
Chester Interchange (01244 602666)
Bus 1a runs from the Exchange to the ground every half an hour, and it's worth being on one as it is a long walk from the city centre.

**BY CAR:**
**NORTH:** M56/A41/A5116 into the city centre. At the second roundabout take the third exit (in effect turning right) into St Martins Way (signposted A548 Queensferry). About 0.5 mile later you will pass a car park on your left. Take the next right after this onto the A548, Watergate and travel past the top end of the dreadfully under-utilised Chester Racecourse into Sealand Road. Turn left at the traffic lights (this is where the old ground used to be) into Bumpers Lane, and the ground is at the bottom of this road.

NB: An alternative route is to come in on the A56. If you do this, follow A548 Queensferry signs into Watergate, then as above.

**EAST:** A51 into Chester. Turn left into Union Street (A483), and about one mile later at the next roundabout take the third exit into Nicholas Street. After 400yd turn left into Watergate (A548), then as north.

**SOUTH:** A483 into Chester, taking the first exit at the roundabout by the castle into Nicholas Street, then as east.

**WEST:** A55 to the roundabout with the A483, then the first exit (signposted Handbridge and Chester) onto the A483, then as south.

The drive through the city is never particularly quick due to the amount of tourist traffic. Unless you get in the right lane first time every time, it is quite easy to get forced off track. If this happens it is worth knowing that while the ground isn't signposted itself, if you head for first the Racecourse and then Sealand Industrial Estate you will get to where the old ground was. Turn off at the T-junction by the out-of-town stores for Bumpers Lane and the ground is about 1 mile down the road.

**PARKING:** The football ground is one of the few places in Chester where you can get a parking spot without any hassle. Away fans pay £1.50, though the club pointed out that season ticket holders can park for free. Watch out also for the Le Mans style racing start come the final whistle — dodgy!

## FUTURE DEVELOPMENTS

As the ground was only completed in August 1992, there are no immediate plans for change, although the foundations have been laid to cater for future extensions as and when required. It is the intention of the club to retain the traditional two stands and two terraces for as long as they are allowed to.

## OTHER INFORMATION

At one time Chester was reputed to have the most pubs per square mile in Britain. This title has now been relinquished, but there are still enough good watering holes in the city to make a visit there pleasurable. However, the nearest pub to the ground, the Watergate by the Racecourse, is still a good 20min walk away. Alternatives you might plump for are the pleasantly named 'Axe' and 'Headless Woman'. If you prefer something a little less gruesome, you can do an awful lot worse than driving past the turn-off to the ground heading away from the City and continuing for 1.5 miles until you get to the rather pleasant Elms.

If once you have got to the ground you decide you can't be bothered venturing anywhere then you do have the option (providing you are happy to pay a hefty £1.50) of getting signed in at the Chester City Social Club.

City fans tend to revel in their Englishness and it is one of the few grounds in which anti-Welsh chants appear to be a part of every game regardless of who the visitors are (although to be fair to the club the language always appears to be fairly moderate). I was once told (this may or may not be true) that Henry IV passed a law that any Welshman found in Chester after the hours of darkness could be summarily beheaded, but the attitude in the Deva does seem to have settled somewhat from these 'short sharp shock' days.

For food you have the choice of inside the ground (an apparent plan to serve food outside the ground has come to nothing), the city centre or nothing. The 'meat pot' that appears on the menu isn't some exotic local delicacy but simply a very decent meat and potato pie. Hot drinks are scalding but bland and grainy and spoon rationing is the order of the day as only about three are laid out to meet the requirements of the masses.

*Total Football* **Experience Rating: 54**

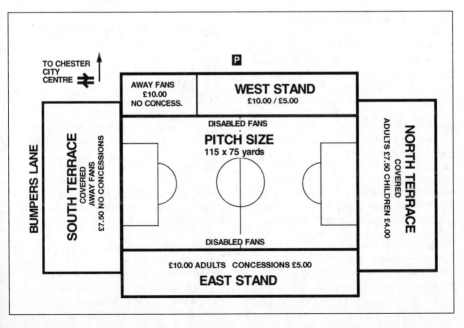

# CHESTERFIELD

**ADDRESS:** The Recreation Ground
Saltergate
Chesterfield
Derbyshire S40 4SX
**TELEPHONE No:** 01246 209765
**TICKET OFFICE:** 01246 209765
**FAX:** 01246 556799
**CLUBCALL:** 0891 55 58 18
**WEB SITE:**
http://www.spirenet.demon.co.uk/
Aspire is an unofficial (but excellent) web site for the club.
**NICKNAME:** The Spireites
**RECORD ATTENDANCE:**
30,968 v Newcastle Div 2 7 April 1939 (W 2-0)
**CLUB COLOURS:**
**HOME:** Shirts: Royal Blue with Blue fading to White stripes; Shorts: Royal Blue with White; Socks: Royal Blue
**AWAY:** Shirts: Red; Shorts: Red; Socks: Red
**THIRD:** Shirts: White; Shorts: Royal Blue; Socks: White
**KIT SPONSORS:**
**Home:** Kenning Car, Van & Truck Rental
**Away:** GK Group (Ford)
**MANUFACTURERS:** Super League

## GROUND INFO

When I was there, the Main Stand looked very unkempt from the outside, with flaky paint on rusty metal being the order of the day. Inside, the seats are wooden and appear to have been hewn out of the stand itself; you are unlikely to get to half-time before you start shifting from one buttock to another in an attempt to get more comfortable. There is also one large pillar in the away section which can lead to a restricted view.

The facilities are basic, and there tend to be long queues for half-time tea and pies. The gents' toilets are particularly horrible, being of a trough-in-the-floor variety, but just to add a bit of spice, the trough actually encircles the whole floor, so you have to step over it to enter. Once inside it doesn't take long to notice both that the trough is fairly shallow, and that the floor seems horribly wet considering there is a roof over it...

The away terrace is open, and to get in you have to queue up outside what appears to be a sandstone castle wall on which is the biggest sign advising 'visiting supporters only' that you'll ever come across.

Sadly the same cannot be said for the sign for away concessions, because there isn't one. I believe some turnstile operators are sympathetic to kids going in with their parents but don't count on it.

**CAPACITY:** Stands: 2,674; Terrace: 6,280; Total: 8,954

In actual fact, the ground is much bigger than the capacity suggests. However, the lack of exits from the Compton Street Terrace means that the figure is restricted in order to meet safety requirements.

**AWAY FANS:** Cross Street: 2,300; Main Stand: 885; Total: 3,185

**DISABLED FACILITIES:** There are 30 spaces available for home and away supporters by the Saltergate wing of the Main Stand. The club has advised that pre-booking is required for this.

Disabled supporters are admitted free of charge, with helpers paying £8.50.

Matchday commentaries for the blind are available and a limited radio service. There are no parking facilities at the ground.

**PROGRAMME:** £1.60

Looks very nice but is a dreadful read. Over 20 pages out of 36 were adverts or sponsorship etc. Those articles there were tended to be about a third of a page long and dull as ditchwater (simply because the writers did not have a chance to expand on anything but the mere basics).

**FANZINES:**
*Beyond the Call of Duty*     80p
Apparently BTCoD is the re-incarnation of *The Crooked Spireite.*

## TRAVEL

**NEAREST RAILWAY STATION:**
Chesterfield (01332 257000 — Derby Enquiries)
**BUS:** Busline: 01246 250450
**BY CAR:**
**NORTH:** M1 to J30. Take the A619 from the exit roundabout and continue into the town centre where you should pick up signs for Old Brampton. Following this road will bring you onto Saltergate and the ground is on your right.
**SOUTH:** A61 into Chesterfield. Turn left at the roundabout with the A617 and left again at the next roundabout with the A617 Markham Road. At the following roundabout take the fourth exit into Foljambe Road. At the end of this road is Saltergate and the ground is directly in front of you.
**EAST:** A617 to town centre. Turn left at the roundabout with the A619, then as south.
**WEST:** A619 into town centre. As you enter the town there is a crossroads with the A632; turn left at this into Old Hall Road and right at the bottom of this road into Saltergate. The ground is 0.5 mile on your left. NB: If you

miss the turn into Hall Gate Road, which is easy enough to do, take the first exit at the next roundabout into Foljambe Road, then as south.

**PARKING:** Chesterfield appears to be a town of about a million car parks, with 18 to my knowledge within 0.75 mile of the ground. One of the best ones (if only because it is free, and probably the closest to the ground) can be found on the left as you drive 0.25 miles along Saltergate past the ground (heading away from the town centre). The pay-and-display car parks tend to be reasonable, costing about £1 for four hours and I must say on my last couple of trips I have been arriving as someone with time on their tickets has been leaving and they have handed them over for nowt.

## FUTURE DEVELOPMENTS

The club is desperately looking to relocate, but a planning application on a site at Brimington was turned down by the Borough Council. There are possibilities that the club may move to the old coking plant site at Wingerworth or (and by far the least popular) Wheeldon Mill (which has already been looked at). Regardless of which (if either) of these schemes comes to fruition, the club is looking towards a 15,000-seat stadium. If one of these does get the nod then I reckon the earliest you could expect to see the club playing there is 2000-1. Until then everything stays as it is at England's oldest football ground.

## OTHER INFORMATION

There are quite a few pubs on Saltergate; those that spring to mind are the County Hotel (Stones), the Barley Mow (Wards), the Manhattan (Whitbread) — which is right next to the Gardeners (Mansfield) — and Local Heroes (which used to be the Golden Lion). To be honest none are really that special and it is probably better to wander five minutes into the town centre, where every other building seems to be a pub and there is bound to be something to suit your taste. The Saltergate Club by the ground is members only, although dependent on the match you will probably be able to get in (provided you are not in a big group).

There are no chip shops in the immediate vicinity of the ground and the fairly large drum shop which was on the corner has disappeared. However, there is now a piano repairer and tuner; which is great news if you are Richard Clayderman but not so good if you are either Cozy Powell or a hungry football fan! The Saltergate sandwich shop does some hot snacks, and without being fantastic, is probably better than what you can expect once inside the ground.

Don't miss the ballboys who form a guard of honour for the teams as they come onto the pitch, then position themselves around the centre circle as the captains toss up, before dispersing like a ripple in a pond to their various points around the ground.

No trip to Chesterfield is complete without checking out the crooked spire, which dominates the skyline, like something from a fairy tale. Apparently the spire's shape is due to the devil lashing out in rage as he flew over Chesterfield having had a nail driven into his foot by a Bolsover blacksmith who was reshoeing him. Well, either that or the fact that the eight-sided spire was made out of green timber which distorted under the weight of the heavy lead covering.

Chesterfield is a nice enough place but you tend to get the feeling that the football club would rather it didn't have to bother with away fans (except presumably for the ones they employ as I saw several Man Utd stickers in the offices) which can make this a bit of a irritating day.

*Total Football* **Experience Rating: 48**

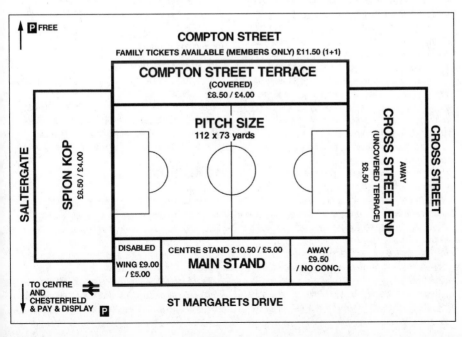

# COLCHESTER UNITED

**ADDRESS:** Layer Road,
Colchester
Essex CO2 7JJ

**TELEPHONE No:** 01206 508800

**TICKET OFFICE:** 01206 508802

**FAX:** 01206 508803

**U's LINE:** 0891 737300

**WEB SITE:** http://www.cufc.co.uk/
(official). Absolutely top rate.

**NICKNAME:** The U's

**RECORD ATTENDANCE:** 19,072 v Reading
FA Cup 1st 27 November 1948 (D 1-1)
Imagine: an FA Cup tie, a massive crowd, the match
nicely balanced, what happens next? Well, on this
occasion the game was abandoned at half-time. For the
stats fans amongst you, the rearranged tie was played the
following Saturday and the U's went down 2-4.

## CLUB COLOURS:
**HOME:** Shirts: Blue and White stripes;
Shorts: Blue; Socks: White
**AWAY:** Shirts: Yellow with Navy sleeves;
Shorts: Navy/Yellow; Socks: Navy/Yellow

**KIT SPONSORS:** Home: Guardian Direct
Away: Ashbys Tea & Coffee

**MANUFACTURERS:** Patrick (UK) Ltd

## GROUND INFO

In 1996-7 Colchester opened their Clock End Stand (a
stand so small that the lettering CUFC is crammed into
one corner as there are not enough rows of seats for it to
be spread across the whole stand). Amazingly the club
then managed to secure a sponsorship deal which
appeared to involve Colchester getting two new phone
lines and the stand being renamed The East Coast Cable
Stand; I'll leave it to you to decide who got the better
deal. What this does mean, however, is that some spaces
have been made for away fans in the Main Stand,
although these are at a premium.

It can be worth trying to get one of these as the
terrace, although covered, is only nine steps deep and the
angle of it means that, unless you are on the front step, it
is quite easy for the near goalline to disappear behind
people's heads. There are also plenty of pillars around,
which doesn't help matters (but this is true everywhere in
the ground). Still, the roof at least means that you can get
a decent atmosphere going. The club does also offer
excellent concessions for all fans in all parts of the
ground which make the (lack of) facilities more
acceptable.

There always seems to be a lot of stewards round the
away fans but to be fair, although they might not look it,

these are a decent bunch of blokes, and (perhaps more
surprisingly) the supervisor makes sure that common-
sense prevails all round. There are normally a couple of
policemen around, but they too are very laid back, and
the (true) story goes that one day the away team didn't
have any supporters, so the officer in charge got a couple
of 'his lads' round to cheer the visitors on because 'A
match isn't a match without a bit of banter!'

**CAPACITY:** Stands: 1,940; Terrace: 5,615;
Total: 7,555

**AWAY FANS:** Layer Road End (Terrace 1): 580;
Layer Road End (Terrace 2): 515;
East Coast Cable Stand Block E: 196;
Total: 1,297

**DISABLED FACILITIES:** There are spaces
for six wheelchair-bound fans at the ground, and
although pre-booking isn't essential, it is strongly
recommended. Unless it is considered dangerous due to
the size of the crowd, the club will consider letting
supporters in wheelchairs into the front of the terrace,
although many supporters may find this unsatisfactory as
this isn't quite wide enough to allow the wheelchair to be
positioned straight on to face the pitch. There are special
toilet facilities behind the main stand.

There is no charge for disabled supporters and one
helper is also admitted free of charge.

The club does offer match commentaries for the
visually impaired; contact them direct for full details and
to pre-book a spot. There is space for only one visually-
impaired supporter and helper; the remaining two
positions are occupied regularly by home supporters.

No parking facilities are available at the ground.

**PROGRAMME:** £1.80
This has apparently won awards in the recent past,
although as these were from the Commercial Marketing
Managers Association I don't know whether this is
something that the club should brag about or deny all
knowledge of. Non members of the Commercial
Managers Association may well come to the same
conclusion as me that this is fairly dull and trite.

## FANZINES:
*The Blue Eagle* £1
You know how some fanzines are very politically correct;
well, go to the other end of the scale, and you have *The
Blue Eagle* — I could never imagine a thing like the
*Chelsea Independent* running a naked women feature, for
example. The point is that despite (or perhaps because
of) the fact that it doesn't really care if it offends on
occasion (oh dear, dangerous football writing, whatever
next) it is a funny, angry and generally excellent read.
Buy one if this sounds appealing; avoid it if it doesn't.

# TRAVEL

## NEAREST RAILWAY STATION:

Colchester Town (01206 578261)
Slightly further away but with a better service is Colchester North (01206 564777). Layer Road is really in the middle of nowhere, so the train station is not to be recommended unless you like walking.

## BUS:
Eastern National (01206 571451) Either a 64 or a 64a will drop you outside the ground.

## BY CAR:

NB: Fulham fans may want to take especial note of this item as last year the coach they were travelling in managed to drop them off at Cambridge rather than Colchester.

**SOUTH:** A12 towards Colchester town centre until you reach the roundabout with the A604. Take the third exit into Spring Lane and continue along this road as it becomes Church Lane and The Commons until you get to a T-junction. Turn right into Norman Way and go straight over the crossroads into Boadicea Way. At the bottom of Boadicea Way there is a T-junction. Turn left onto Layer Road and the ground is 0.3 miles on your left.

**NORTH/WEST:** A45/A12. Take the A1232 Ipswich Road into the town centre. To avoid the one-way system turn left before the castle onto the A1224 Queens Street. At the next major roundabout turn onto the B1022 Maldon Road. Continue for one mile then turn right into Boadicea Way. Then as south.

**PARKING:** Street parking. One of the best places to leave your car is by the Shrub End playing fields around Boadicea Way.

As you drive down Layer Road, watch out for some residents-only parking schemes which are not to be trifled with — some of the residents in question are part of Colchester garrison and any out-of-place car is quickly identified and acted upon. Rather than returning to find a ticket, or your car's been towed away, you're more likely to find that your transport home has been reduced to a pile of smouldering metal in a controlled explosion!

# FUTURE DEVELOPMENTS

In February 1998 the club commissioned a feasibility study (in liaison with Colchester Borough Council) to be undertaken by McAlpine's to establish whether it was viable to build a 'community stadium' either at Layer Road or at another site. At the time of going to press the results of this were not available which suggests that everything will remain as is during 1998-9.

# OTHER INFORMATION

The ground is a bit out of the way, and it as well to stick to Colchester town centre (especially for food). There are plenty of decent pubs in the town, with perhaps the most welcoming for away fans being the Castle, which has a painted sign outside proclaiming 'Wanderers welcome'. There is one pub near the ground itself, this being the Drury Arms, which serves a decent pint and is always buzzing on match days (although service is fairly quick and away fans will get no hassle). Because there aren't a plethora of turnstiles at the ground, although it's only a 10min yomp from the Drury to Layer Road, if you want to be sure of seeing kick-off allow yourself 20min.

The away fans are served by a minuscule tea hut which serves equally small hot dogs and burgers, but no pies. Apparently the U's fans are campaigning for pies to be available in the ground, but as yet there has been no real success. The tea is OK, — sadly as the stirrers are smaller than the cups you end up dipping your fingers in to retrieve it.

***Total Football* Experience Rating: 61**

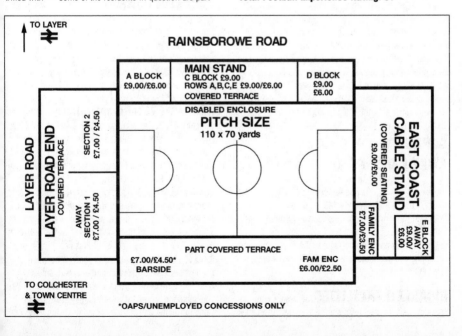

# COVENTRY CITY

**ADDRESS:** Highfield Road Stadium
King Richard Street
Coventry CV2 4FW

**TELEPHONE No:** 01203 234000

**TICKET OFFICE:** 01203 234020

**FAX:** 01203 234099

**CLUBCALL:** 0891 12 11 66

**WEB SITE:** www.ccfc.co.uk (official)

**E-MAIL:** chris.m@ccfc.co.uk

**NICKNAME:** The Sky Blues

**RECORD ATTENDANCE:**
51,455 v Wolves Lge Div 2 29 April 1967 (W 3-1)

**CLUB COLOURS:**

**HOME:** Shirts: Sky Blue and Navy stripes White side panels; Shorts: Sky Blue; Socks: Sky Blue

**AWAY:** Shirts: Purple and Yellow stripes; Shorts: Purple; Socks: Purple

**KIT SPONSORS:** Subaru-Isuzu

**MANUFACTURERS:** Le Coq Sportif

## GROUND INFO

A fairly decent away allocation means that Highfield Road is one of the — ever fewer — Premiership grounds at which it is still relatively easy to turn up on the day and get in (although it goes without saying that for 'big' matches you should take the normal precautions). Once inside the ground, everything seems a bit cramped and the leg room is fairly tight (you may well end up with nice lines across your knees where your legs have been pressing against the seat in front of you).

A real downer is the fact that the club appears to have discontinued offering away supporters concessions. Certainly these used to be available but on the price listing that the club sent me these had been scored out. On the brighter side, the categorisation of matches has also been stopped.

**CAPACITY:** Stands: 23,627; Terrace: Nil

**AWAY FANS:** Mitchell and Butlers Stand Upper Tier: 2,823; Mitchell and Butler Stand Lower Tier: 1,325; Total: 4,148

Coventry is one of the most organised and helpful clubs for fans in not only the Premiership but the whole of the league. Queries and problems are dealt with promptly and efficiently, and the stewards will go out of their way to help.

**DISABLED FACILITIES:** There are two separate areas for disabled supporters — the M&B Clock Stand and the Main Stand. The first of these areas tends to be allocated to visiting supporters. The new East Stand is also fully accessible to disabled supporters, including the executive areas and lounges. There are also 10 headsets available for the visually impaired. Cost of admission is £5 for wheelchair-bound or visually-impaired supporters and £11 for helpers. Pre-booking is generally required (although I have been told the club is very accommodating to spur of the moment visits). One area which definitely requires pre-booking, due to the limited number of spaces, is parking.

**PROGRAMME:** £2.00

Unfortunately this remains probably the worst in the Premiership. Slightly smaller than most and definitely much less interesting.

**FANZINES:**

*In Dublin's Fair City* £1
*Sent to Coventry* £1

I must have been to Highfield Road about 20 times in the last 10 or so years and only once have I seen a fanzine being sold, and it was neither of these two.

## TRAVEL

**NEAREST RAILWAY STATION:**
Coventry (01203 555211)

**BUS:** West Midlands Transport (01203 559559)
Take either a 17 or a 27 from the station or any one of 17 different routes from the city centre (look for Gosforth Green buses).

**BY CAR:**

**NORTH/SOUTH/WEST:** M6 to J2. Take the A4600 (signposted City Centre). Follow this until it becomes Walsgrave Road. Shortly after this the road forks in two by the Walsgrave pub; take the left-hand lane and at the next roundabout take the third exit. Continue along Walsgrave Road until you get to a set of traffic lights just past a road bridge. Turn right at these lights into Swan Lane; the ground is 100yd on the left.

**NORTH/WEST (alternative):** M45/A45 towards Coventry city centre. Turn left on to the A4114 (Allesley By-Pass) and take the third exit at the next roundabout, continuing along the A4114 Holyhead Road (signposted City Centre). After 1.75 miles turn left onto the inner ring road (A4053) and carry on for 1.5 miles, then turn left into Sky Blue Way (A4600). When this road forks in two, take the left fork into Walsgrave Road, then take a left by the traffic lights before the railway bridge into Swan Lane. The ground is 100yd on the left. Alternatively exit M40 at J15, A46 for 10 miles, then B4110 (as East).

**EAST:** M45 till you pass the Peugeot Talbot plant; at the next roundabout take the third exit, onto the A423. After about 1-mile you get to another roundabout where you should turn onto the B4110 (signposted 'Stoke'). Continue all the way down this road (there are loads of sets of lights) till you get to a T-Junction. Turn left here (Walsgrave Road) then immediately right into Swan Lane for the ground.

**PARKING:** There is a small coach and car park on the opposite side of the road to the Swan Lane turning by the ground, which is good for getting away from. Alternatively head down the A4600 (Sky Blue Way) onto the inner ring road and there are car parks almost immediately on the left or right of this; these are about 1.25 miles from the ground. There is some street parking available, although this is restricted in the immediate ground vicinity.

## FUTURE DEVELOPMENTS

The club has announced the construction of a new 40,000-seat stadium by the gasworks at Foleshill. Other than the 'normal' leisure facilities, this will include a retractable roof and a pitch which can be rolled out of the stadium on Teflon castors (thus allowing the grass to have normal exposure to sunlight etc). The plans and models of this new construction are awe-inspiring and one can only hope that it makes a successful transition from the drawing board.

## OTHER INFORMATION

The Sky Blue Tavern (formerly the Mercers Arms) by the ground has home and away bars and is excellent for having a pre-match drink with your mates, although they have started charging £1 for away fans to get in which isn't best pleasing. Other than that, it's a bit of a walk to find anywhere to go for a drink. If you walk away from the ground from the visitors' section of the Sky Blue Tavern and bear left into Hamall Lane East (about 5min walk), there is a chip shop which sells reasonable, well-filled chip batches (rolls). This is worth a visit if only to avoid

hunting down a food outlet and then queuing interminably for below average grub inside the ground.

Whilst the vast majority of clubs seem only too happy to embarrass their supporters occasionally, Coventry is in a class of its own in this respect. Naturally there's a mascot (a grubby elephant), but the fun really starts with the music. First there is *'Sky Blue City'* played when the team comes out at the start of a match (and at half-time), which is the 1987 Cup Final song, and a cross between Bucks Fizz and Slade. The chorus of 'Go for it, go for it City. Sky Blues — shooting to win' is horribly insidious and will lurk around your consciousness for months afterwards (if you have been to Coventry before, you're probably humming it now — sorry!). Almost as bad is the 'chant', written by one Jimmy Hill to the tune of the Eton Boating Song. The fans have resigned themselves to this and actually sing it of their own volition, and after every Coventry goal the club blast about five bars (played on a whiny electric guitar) out of the PA system.

WOMEN! Fancy a swear? How about acting abusively or throwing missiles? If so, Highfield Road is the place for you. There are masses of signs telling spectators about unacceptable behaviour, but as these are all addressed to gentlemen, presumably you've got *carte blanche* to behave in any manner you choose!

Finally, the club have asked that the following be included as information that fans may require (all 01203 std). Ticket Office Fax: 234023. CC Bookings: 578000. Comm. Fax:234015. Comm Dept (exec suites/conference bookings): 234010. Catering Dept (Sunday Lunch bookings/parties/weddings): 234055. Souvenir Shop: 234030.

*Total Football* **Experience Rating: 64**

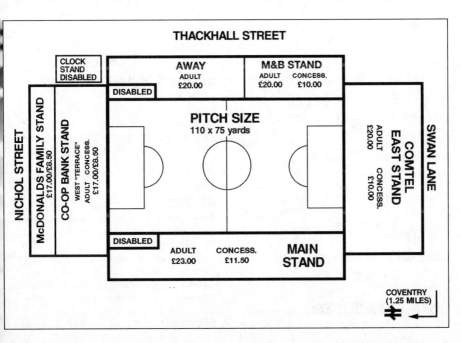

# CREWE ALEXANDRA

**ADDRESS:** Gresty Road
Crewe
Cheshire CW2 6EB
**TELEPHONE No:** 01270 213014
**TICKET OFFICE:** 01270 252610
**FAX:** 01270 216320
**CLUBCALL:** 0891 12 16 47
**NICKNAME:** The Railwaymen
**RECORD ATTENDANCE:**
20,000 v Spurs FA Cup 4th 30 January 1960 (D 2-2)
**CLUB COLOURS:**
**HOME:** Shirts: Red with White chest panel;
Shorts: White; Socks: Red
**AWAY:** Shirts: White and Orange with white trim;
Shorts: White; Socks: White

**KIT SPONSORS:** LC Charters
**MANUFACTURERS:** Adidas

## GROUND INFO

Despite the fact that three sides of the ground have been developed over recent years there is only one area where there are no pillars which obscure the view from at least some of the seats (although this is not a major problem elsewhere). It may come as somewhat of a surprise if you haven't been to Gresty Road before to discover that, this being the case, it remains the area allocated for away supporters. Seasoned campaigners, however, may be a little less shocked as there is a very friendly and laid back attitude about the place which makes it a very undemanding away ground.

The club remains consistent as the prices charged to visiting supporters mirror those for the home fans. For those in the vicinity of the ground, there is a scheme in operation whereby if you buy your tickets in advance from the club there is a £1 reduction in both adult and concessionary prices. I haven't put it to the test but I have been informed that if you buy a ticket for the away area in advance (from Crewe) then you will also get the discount.

If you prefer an along-the-pitch view of the game then any part of the ground should be considered safe. The most vocal Alex fans can be found in the Paddock or at the Gresty Road End of the Ringways Stand but, if for some reason this is where you decided you wanted to go, it would be a very odd day if you encountered any personal animosity.

**CAPACITY:** Stands: 4,710; Terrace: 1,000;
Total: 5,710

**AWAY FANS:** Gresty Road Stand: 972
**DISABLED FACILITIES:** There are seven places for wheelchair-bound supporters (plus seven for helpers) in the Family Stand, with a further seven spaces in the Ringways Stand, and for visitors 10 spaces (five helpers) in the Gresty Road Stand. There has been a change of pricing policy at Gresty Road this season and rather than both disabled supporter and helper paying half price, disabled fans are now admitted free of charge with helpers paying £10 (a saving regardless of whether you go on your own or with someone). Pre-booking is essential. The club provides special parking facilities at the ground and match commentaries for the visually impaired are also available; these too must be pre-booked.

## PROGRAMME: £2.00

Perhaps the only real area of complaint with a day out at Crewe is the programme. It has gone up from £1 to £1.30 to £1.50 to £1.80 in the last four seasons (an 80% rise in four years and 20% in 1997-8 alone), yet it remains a stodgy and unappealing read with too many adverts and too little of any interest. It is also a very unhandy A4 size. The club points out that it has in the past asked its supporters what they wanted from the programme, so presumably home fans are happy enough with the end product. I'd steer well clear as a visiting fan though.

## FANZINES:

*Super Dario Land!* £1
*Super Dario Land!* (or *SDL* as the cover now proclaims) has got to be one of the most improved fanzines in England. It's more than doubled in size from 16 to 36 pages, retained the same price — whilst sensibly dropping the glossy cover — and with the extra space filled with articles that are incomparably better than those which were previously printed. The other Crewe fanzine, *To Work Upon The Railway*, apparently folded last season.

## TRAVEL
**NEAREST RAILWAY STATION:** Crewe
(01782 411411)
Unbelievable! One of England's busiest stations and you have to dial a Stoke-on-Trent number for enquiries. If you think this is ludicrous dial 01270 532727 (the actual number of Crewe station) and tell them so!

**BUS:** Cheshire Bus: Crewe bus station (01270 505350)

### BY CAR:
**NORTH:** M6 to J17. On leaving the motorway take the A534 (signposted Sandbach and Crewe). When approaching the town you will see Crewe and Alsager College on your right; continue for 0.25 miles past this to the next roundabout, at which you should take the second exit onto the A534 Nantwich Road (signposted to BR station). Take the first left after the station into Gresty Road and the ground is 300yd on the left.
**SOUTH/EAST:** M1 to J16. Take the A500 (signposted

Crewe) then turn right onto the A5020 Weston Road (again signposted Crewe). Continue to the roundabout with the A534 Nantwich Road at which you should take the first exit (signposted BR station), then as north.

**WEST:** A534. Follow the signs for Crewe and Sandbach. Turn right at the crossroads with the B5071 onto South Street. This then merges after 0.25 mile with Gresty Road and the ground is immediately on the left. NB: If you miss this, drive past the station to the roundabout, do an about-turn and have another go.

**PARKING:** There are a couple of car parks right by the ground. Alternatively you can try the British Rail long-stay off the Nantwich Road, but this tends to be a bit pricey. There is also plenty of on-street parking in the side streets off Gresty Road.

## FUTURE DEVELOPMENTS

The club advise that at the end of the 1998-9 season work will begin on demolishing the old wooden Main Stand and replacing it with a 6,500-seat stand. The work will hopefully be completed during the closed season and ready for business at the start of 1999-2000, although some impact on this season cannot be discounted. Once this stand is built, the development at Gresty Road will be completed and the ground will have a 10,000 capacity.

## OTHER INFORMATION

Take advantage of the decent train link and leave the car at home for this match, because although the ground is away from the town centre, there is no shortage of good pubs around.

The Royal Hotel and the Crewe Arms both on the Nantwich Road are a fair size, but also worth a visit is the Barrel on the corner of South Street and Nantwich Road, if only because the landlord goes by the name of Michael Crawford! If you go in here do make sure you say 'Oooh Betty' to him because he's probably never heard that one before and is sure to laugh along with you. There are a few excellent chip shops in Crewe; the Golden Chip Shop on Nantwich Road (by the Royal Hotel), which does great meat and potato pies deserves a mention. However check out the Fish and Chip Shop right by the ground, one of the best things about this place is not only that the food is brilliant but it is also very varied. The owners actually think (!!!!!!!!) about what team are playing and will put on a suitable delicacy from that area, which can range from tea/oat cakes to black pudding to roe.

Staff at the ticket office/club shop are very helpful and a good port of call if you have problems, although someone at the ground must have a black sense of humour as on display all of last season was a poster from a local bookmakers which quoted the price for Crewe to win the division and then (if anything, in slightly bigger print) the price for them to come bottom (and the clubs dare call fans pessimistic).

The stewarding too is highly commendable and there is a very positive attitude towards both home and visiting supporters which means that, given the ease with which most people get to the ground and the facilities offered in and around it, this is one of the better away days in the calendar.

A final oddity at Crewe (apart from the fact that the club crest seems to be a lion playing with a ball of wool) is that the club's very name is highly unchantable, Crewe being one syllable too short and Alexandra (after Princess Alexandra if anyone is interested) being about two too many. The fans get around this with a throaty chant of Alex, which for some bizarre reason always sounds, if you are in the away end, as if they are chanting either a mild obscenity or 'Horlicks'.

***Total Football* Experience Rating: 92**

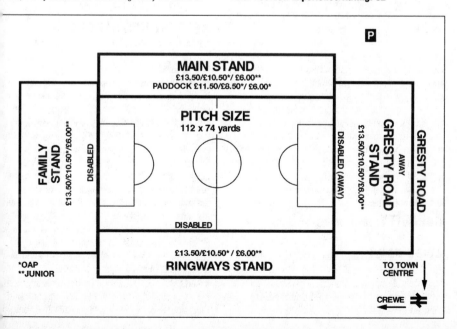

# CRYSTAL PALACE

**ADDRESS:** Selhurst Park
London SE25 6PU

**TELEPHONE No:** 0181 768 6000

**TICKET OFFICE:** 0181 771 8841

**FAX:** 0181 768 6114

**CLUBCALL:** 0891 400 333

**WEB SITE:** www.cpfc.co.uk

**E-MAIL:** palace@cpfc.1.demon.co.uk

**NICKNAME:** The Eagles

**RECORD ATTENDANCE:**

51,801 v Burnley Div 2 11 May 1979 (W 2-0)

**CLUB COLOURS:**

**HOME:** Shirts: Red with Blue panel on each side;
Shorts: Red; Socks: Red

**AWAY**: Shirts: White with Blue panel on each side;
Shorts: White; Socks: White

**KIT SPONSORS:** TDK

**MANUFACTURERS:** Adidas

## GROUND INFO

Selhurst Park seems to be one of those grounds which it always takes ages to get to. It's about 30min to any of the outlying stations from London and, if you go by car, then long traffic jams and snarl-ups seem to be compulsory.

In the third edition of this book I praised Palace saying that the pricing strategy at the club had improved and that admission was not extortionate. Two days after the book had gone to print the club announced that prices for away fans would go up by 42% to £20!! Prices have been frozen for the new season.

The Arthur Wait Stand offers visiting supporters a reasonable view of the pitch, although at £20 it should be palatial but, if you are in the first few rows, then keep your fingers crossed for good weather as you are completely open to the elements in your seat.

One thing that has not changed over the years is the attitude of some of the stewards to visiting supporters. It would be nice to think that one day these people will realise they are not doing you a massive favour by letting you into the hallowed portals of SE25 (although to be fair to the club — there are one or two very very notable exceptions who have gone out of their way to help me and other supporters).

**CAPACITY:** Stands: 26,400; Terrace: Nil;
Total: 26,400

**AWAY FANS:** Arthur Wait Stand: 2,337;
Total: 2,337

Note this is the maximum available in the Stand; if there is insufficient demand then visiting supporters will be allocated 1,724 seats.

**DISABLED FACILITIES:** There are 28 spaces for disabled supporters and their helpers in both the Arthur Wait (for away fans) and Holmesdale Road Stand. Admission is complimentary for disabled fans, with helpers paying half the normal admission price. Pre-booking is required. Match commentaries are available but the club advises that these are 'for the blind only'. There are no parking facilities available but there are wide spaces at the Sainsbury's car park which isn't too far from the ground.

**PROGRAMME:** £2.00

A seven-page section on the visiting team which while undoubtedly repeating a vast number of points that away supporters will already know, is fairly well thought out and interesting. Other than that though, you'll find nothing much to keep you occupied over your half-time cuppa.

**FANZINES:**

| | |
|---|---|
| *Eastern Eagle* | £1 |
| *One More Point* | 50p |
| *The Palace Echo* | £1.30 |

## TRAVEL

**NEAREST RAILWAY STATION:**

Norwood Junction, Thornton Heath, Selhurst
(0345 48 49 50 — Victoria Enquiries)
Norwood Junction is probably the nearest to the ground, but if you are a person who simply follows the crowds at the end of the match then don't be surprised if you end up at one of the other two. Don't get off the train at Crystal Palace (unless of course you enjoy five-mile walks), and there is no tube nearby.

**NEAREST BUS STATION:** London Transport (0171 222 1234)

**BY CAR:**

**NORTH:** M1. Take the A406 North Circular Road (heading west) to Chiswick Roundabout (just before you get there you will see Gunnersbury Park on your right). Take the third exit at the roundabout onto Chiswick High Road, then first left onto the A205 (signposted Kew). After two miles you reach a T-junction at which you should turn left (signposted Putney). Continue until the road merges with the A3, then a mile later turn right onto the A214 (signposted Tooting and Streatham). When in Streatham, turn right onto the A23 Streatham High Road. After one mile turn left into Green Lane (B273) which becomes Parchmore Road. At the bottom of the road turn left onto the High Street. Go straight over at the crossroads with the A212 into Whitehorse Lane and the ground is 300yd on the right.

**EAST:** M25, A20 (signposted London). After approx. four miles turn left onto the A224 (signposted St Mary Cray). After three miles turn onto the A232 Spur Road and follow this until you see Shirley Park Golf Club; then right on to the A215 Shirley Road. Turn right again at the top of this road, then first left into Spring Lane (A215). After 1.5 miles turn left onto the B266, and the ground is 0.5 mile on the left.

**SOUTH:** A23 into London, following the signs for Thornton Heath, turn right onto the A235. (NB: to get to this you need to go through a small one-way system; this is nothing more than an overblown roundabout really.) Once on the A235 turn immediately left onto the B266 Brigstock Road which becomes the High Street, then as north.

**WEST:** M4 to Chiswick, then as north.

**PARKING:** Parking for 500 cars at the Sainsbury's car park just off Whitehorse Lane by the ground. There is also plenty of street parking available. Alternatively, drive down the A212 towards West Croydon and park in one of the two Whitgift Centre car parks.

## FUTURE DEVELOPMENTS

The club has now received planning permission from Croydon Council for the construction of a new Main Stand. However, at the time of going to press, no start date for this work had been set.

## OTHER INFORMATION

For pubs, you would be as well to go to East Croydon (about 10min on the train) where you will find a varied choice. Fairly convenient is the Old Brief 'Ale House' (turn right out of the station and it is about 0.25 of a mile on your left (over one major road). Quite a modern bar, it still manages to serve a decent all-day breakfast. Alternatively, the Clifton Arms is probably the nearest to the ground but away fans tend to drift more towards the Cherry Trees, which is by Norwood Junction railway station. An excellent alternative, which I have been tipped

off about, is the Prince George on Whitehorse Road; great atmosphere, good beer and a big screen TV. The Goat House on Penge Road also gets a thumbs up.

Inside the ground, the pies were warmer than last year. Expect the standard big tea cups/small spoons scenario: the cups themselves are scorching to hold, so either way you are going to end up with burnt fingers (though some may argue that you got those when you bought your tickets). Pies are hot and not too bad. The queues can be a bit slow at half-time and your sense of panic at missing the start of the second half is worsened by the fact that there are announcements made in an ominous tone that 'Would you please care to take your seats as the match/second half will start in 5 minutes'. As you do go to your seat please notice the large signs by the entrance to the stand saying that alcohol is not permitted beyond this point. Don't worry that you might inadvertently break this rule because Palace weren't even selling beer to away fans when I visited.

The toilets under the Arthur Wait are fairly cavernous though you have to go down a series of steps by a pillar to get to them, which can cause congestion. Still, this is probably a better way to spend half-time than having to endure the graceless meanderings of the Palace Crystal Cheerleaders, which are supposed to pass for half-time 'entertainment'.

Perhaps, the most bizarre thing ever seen at Selhurst Park (even more than the most uneagle-like Eagle mascot which has now been immortalised in the Coca Cola adverts was the Fiat 500 they used to wheel out at half-time, at the rear of which was a roller. The back half of the vehicle had such phenomenal weight that it almost used to repair the damage to the pitch... caused by the front half.

***Total Football* Experience Rating: 47**

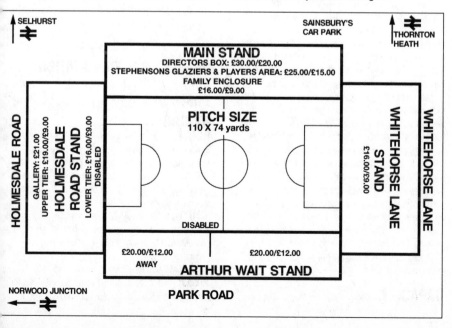

SELHURST

SAINSBURY'S CAR PARK

THORNTON HEATH

**MAIN STAND**
DIRECTORS BOX: £30.00/£20.00
STEPHENSONS GLAZIERS & PLAYERS AREA: £25.00/£15.00
FAMILY ENCLOSURE
£16.00/£9.00

**PITCH SIZE**
110 X 74 yards

HOLMESDALE ROAD

GALLERY: £21.00
UPPER TIER: £19.00/£9.00

**HOLMESDALE ROAD STAND**

LOWER TIER: £16.00/£9.00
DISABLED

**WHITEHORSE LANE STAND**
£16.00/£9.00

WHITEHORSE LANE

DISABLED

£20.00/£12.00
AWAY

£20.00/£12.00

**ARTHUR WAIT STAND**

NORWOOD JUNCTION

**PARK ROAD**

# DARLINGTON

**ADDRESS:** Feethams Ground
Darlington
DL1 5JB

**TELEPHONE No:** 01325 465097
**TICKET OFFICE:** 01325 465097
**FAX:** 01325 381377
**CLUBCALL:** 0891 10 15 55 (50p/min)
**WEB SITE:**
http://www.darlingtonfc.force9.co.uk/
(official)
Brilliant
**NICKNAME:** The Quakers
**RECORD ATTENDANCE:** 21,023 v Bolton
Lge Cup 3rd 14 November 1960 (L 1-2)

**CLUB COLOURS:**
**HOME:** Shirts: Black & White;
Shorts: Black; Socks: Black & White
**AWAY:** Shirts: Red; Shorts: Black;
Socks: White & Black

**KIT SPONSORS:** Darlington Building Society
**MANUFACTURERS:** tba

## GROUND INFO

When you arrive at Feethams you feel as if you have stepped into a different era. In front of the ground is a cricket pitch and there is a large church spire in the background. The River Skerne runs down by the East Stand (apparently the river is the dirtiest in Britain but you wouldn't know it to look at it). All it needs is a policeman wobbling by on a bicycle and the picturesque scene would be complete. In a time of out-of-town super stadia it is fantastic that Darlo have chosen to stay at Feethams, as the ground has a unique character.

Last season the East Stand was constructed. When I went in February, it was still being built but appeared to be a modest but functional stand à la Crewe or Gillingham. Opposite this is the West Stand which is fairly run down. The Polam Lane (aka South End) away allocation covers half the terrace behind one of the goals, and sweeps around to join on to the West Stand, This is an open terrace and can get very, very cold on a January evening. Still, at least the stewarding is good and the welcome that you get from the club is warm (although quite how comforting that will be to you when icy rain is dripping down the back of your neck I don't know).

Outstanding concessions are offered to home and away supporters.

**CAPACITY:** Stands: 4,300; Terrace: 3,450;
Total: 7,750

**AWAY FANS:** Polam Lane (South) End: 600;
Family (West) Stand: 200; Total: 800

**DISABLED FACILITIES:** Last season saw disabled fans stuck in the northwest corner of the ground, by the orange portakabins which were used as dressing rooms (although at least fans had access to a disabled toilet facility). However, with the opening of the new East Stand, this position should improve significantly as there will be a number of specially designed areas for wheelchair access. Admission is free to both disabled fans and their helpers.

**PROGRAMME:** £1.50
A fairly run-of-the-mill affair, but worth buying as all the sellers seem fairly chatty and friendly, although they did seem to have a strange penchant for telling you about their ailments. For example, one talked about 'Jack' whose cyst had burst — hmmm can't wait to try a burger now — and last year for some reason I was told about a verruca that had fallen off somebody's foot. Very strange.

**FANZINES:**

| | |
|---|---|
| *Mission Impossible* | £1 |
| *Where's The Money Gone* | 30p |
| *Darlo, It's Just Like Watching Brazil* | 50p |

I didn't see *WTMG* last season although it is still apparently around. Edited by a 14-year-old lad, the last one I saw was a fair read although a few bits and pieces were well wide of the mark. *Mission Impossible* remains a fantastic read. There are the almost inevitable diary type articles but also loads of general interest stuff. There's a fairly anti-Hartlepool stance, although this isn't allowed to get in the way of putting together an excellent fanzine. Definitely worth hunting out a seller to get your hands on one. *DIJLWB* appeared in the WSC listings last season; I haven't seen a copy, nor had anyone I spoke to.

## TRAVEL

**NEAREST RAILWAY STATION:**
Darlington (01325 355111). 10min from the ground.

**BUS:** United Automobile Services (01325 468771)

**BY CAR:**
**NORTH:** A1(M) to junction with A167 (Great North Road), then follow signs to Darlington Town Centre. Pick up the signs for Northallerton, and this brings you into Victoria Road, then turn right into Feetham. The cricket ground will be directly in front of you and the football ground is behind this.
**SOUTH:** A1(M) to A66(M). Follow signs to Darlington Town Centre. Take the fourth exit at the first major roundabout into Victoria Road and then turn into Feethams.
**EAST:** A67 into town centre, then as north.
**WEST:** A67 into town centre. Take the third exit at the first major roundabout into Victoria Road and then turn into Feethams.

No matter where you are travelling from, the landmark to keep an eye open for is the Safeway Supermarket in the town, which is next to the turning for the ground.

**PARKING:** There is plenty of on-street parking around the ground. If you prefer to go off-street, then there is a car park in Victoria Road, and also plenty available in the town centre which is about a 10-15min walk away.

## FUTURE DEVELOPMENTS

Darlington were taken over by Chaddington last season. The company has said that it intends fully to redevelop Feethams but although plans are 'at an advanced stage' it could/would not inform me of what these were. However, as this is the same company that undertook the redevelopment of the East Stand, fans can feel some assurance that the work will be undertaken in the near future. It is thought that the next area to be developed will either be the West Stand (which will have no effect on away support) or the South End (which may lead to away fans being moved to the West Stand Paddock or a section of the East Stand).

## OTHER INFORMATION

I find Darlington one of the most surprising towns in the country. The first time I went I expected a bleak northeast mining town with an air of depression hanging over it, but nothing could be further from the truth. It's clean, modern (but not just blocks of concrete — it won a prize in the 1997 Britain in Bloom competition) and the people are incredibly friendly. Funnily enough when you get talking to the locals, you'll tend to find that they have got nothing but bad things to say about the team and the town which they make sound like a den of iniquity (which, compared to the old days when it was a Quaker town — make your own oats gag here — it probably is). At first, I thought that there must be a seedy underbelly to Darlington, but I reckon the real reason they put down the place is they want to keep how nice it is a secret from the outside world. It has to be said that Darlo is fairly posh as well. If you travel up the North Road, you will see what you and I might call a butchers shop but here has a sign proclaiming that it is a 'meat purveyors' (there is also a sex shop in the town which has the opening times written on the outside in the type of elaborate gothic script that you'd expect to see in an Oxbridge 'tea shoppe').

There are plenty of good pubs in the town centre. The Falcion (rather quaintly named after a broad curved sword) is a good bet, as it not only serves Cameron's Strongarm Ruby Red Bitter which is excellent, and a good protector against winter chills etc, but also cheap and filling grub.

A little further afield is Breezy's Sandwiches on the North Road; this is well worth popping into if you are passing simply to sample the sausage and bacon sarnies. Inside the ground the horrible away food caravan has gone, but has been replaced with a shed of almost equal grimness. The people serving from it are fairly friendly and obviously happy with the place: 'Tell your mates it's cheap' was the cry as I walked away. At £1 for either a hot dog or a burger this is true, but it has to also be added. The burger lay heavy on my stomach for hours and had an exceedingly adverse effect on my digestive system. If anyone you are with does have one, hope that you'll have reasonable weather on the way back because you'll want all the windows open!

From a visiting fan's perspective, a trip to Darlo is a pretty good day out (and one that will be infinitely better when there is a bit of cover at the ground). Reasonable prices and good treatment.

*Total Football* **Experience Rating: 72**

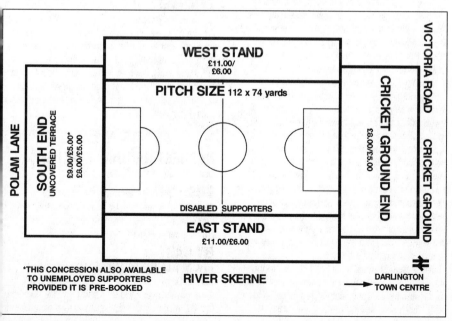

WEST STAND
£11.00/
£6.00

PITCH SIZE 112 x 74 yards

POLAM LANE

SOUTH END
UNCOVERED TERRACE
£9.00/£5.00*
£8.00/£5.00

DISABLED SUPPORTERS

EAST STAND
£11.00/£6.00

VICTORIA ROAD

CRICKET GROUND END
£8.00/£5.00

CRICKET GROUND

DARLINGTON
TOWN CENTRE

*THIS CONCESSION ALSO AVAILABLE
TO UNEMPLOYED SUPPORTERS
PROVIDED IT IS PRE-BOOKED

RIVER SKERNE

61

# DERBY COUNTY

**ADDRESS:** Pride Park Stadium
Derby
DE24 8XL
**TELEPHONE No:** 01332 202202
**TICKET OFFICE:** 01332 209209
**FAX:** 01322 667540
**CLUBCALL:** 0891 12 11 87
**E-MAIL:** press.office@dcfc.co.uk
**WEB SITE:** www.dcfc.co.uk (official)
**NICKNAME:** The Rams
**RECORD ATTENDANCE:**
41,826 v Spurs Div 1 20 September 1969 (W 5-0).
At Pride Park:30,492 v Liverpool Premier League 10 May
1998 (W 1-0).
**CLUB COLOURS:**
**HOME:** Shirts: White; Shorts: Black; Socks: White
**AWAY:** Shirts; Yellow; Shorts: Blue; Socks: Yellow
**KIT SPONSORS:** Puma
**MANUFACTURERS:** Puma

## GROUND INFO

When you arrive at Pride Park, if you look towards the
city centre you can still see the floodlights at the Baseball
Ground. Almost uniquely in this world of out-of-town
stadia, the old ground hasn't been torn down and
replaced with a supermarket but remains in use for
reserve matches. It's about two miles away in distance
but 10 light years away in terms of facilities.

Away fans get the east side of the South (Mansfield
Bitter) Stand which has (as you would expect) good leg
room, cover from the elements (other than the seats right
at the front) and views, as well as decent food/drink
outlets. One gripe is — and I know this sounds stupid
— the turnstiles are dreadfully archaic and completely
out of place. Expect to have to battle your way in.

The club had initially intended that the North Stand
would be reserved for the 'singers' but, to be honest, you
should expect a bit of banter with the home fans, as the
noisiest of these appear to have opted to be next to away
supporters in the East Stand. The acoustics at the ground
are fantastic — helped by the fact that all County fans
seem prepared to sing for their side — and most games
are played in a passionate atmosphere. There is a fairly
high police presence at Pride Park to ensure that this
passion does not get out of hand. Generally they are
pretty tolerant and appreciate that away fans will like a bit
of a singsong, but again there are lines and, if they are
crossed, then ejections will follow.

One of the best things about Pride Park is that there
are touches that give the ground its own personality: the
gap between the West and South Stands (although this is
being filled in) and the North West Corner Stand, which

breaks up the oval sweep of the ground.

One small tip: if you decide to have a wander round
Pride Park before the game take some ear plugs with you
as there is an industrial blower in the West and North
Stand which sounds like a jumbo jet warming up.

There is no smoking in the stands themselves (and
you run the risk of getting thrown out if you ignore this
rule) but you can light up in the concourse beneath each
stand. This, of course, means that the queue for a half-
time cuppa is done in a thick fog which gets worse
depending on how jittery your defence has been looking
that day.

**CAPACITY:** Stands: 30,500; Terrace: Nil;
Total: 30,500

**AWAY FANS:** South East Corner Stand: 2,000
This can be extended to up to 4,800 as appropriate.

**DISABLED FACILITIES:** There are 70
places for home supporters which are sited on all three
sides of the ground. Credit to the club for acknowledging
that, just because you are in a wheelchair, you don't
necessarily want to sit with the home supporters as there
are 30 spaces in the North Stand for away fans.
Admission for disabled supporters and helpers is free,
but must be pre-booked. Parking is available at the
ground.

**PROGRAMME:** £1.80
Fairly predictable. David Moore's column is a good read
and the crossword, which combines questions about
Derby with those about the visitors, is a nice touch.
Other-wise it's all 'pen pics', 'we've met before', and lots
of merchandising adverts.

**FANZINES:**
*Hey Big Spender* £1
A much better read this season (especially as the editors
have restricted the anti-Forest diatribes — and made
them funnier as well), although the seller I was talking to
was saying that it has been less easy to put together this
year because everything has been going well. Respected
by the club and able to get interviews without apparently
selling themselves out.

## TRAVEL
**NEAREST RAILWAY STATION:**
Derby Midland (01332 332051) (one mile).

**BUS:** Derby City Transport (01332 754433)
There will be special shuttles on matchdays. These will
pick up from the city centre and also 'Courtaulds' but
NOT apparently from the railway station.

**BY CAR:**
**FROM ALL DIRECTIONS:** M1 to J25. Head
towards Derby (this is a left turn if you are coming from
the South and right if you are coming from the North) on
the A52. After 5.5 miles (just after you have seen a Travel

Lodge) turn left (signposted The Wyvern and Pride Park) go straight over the next two roundabouts and the ground is on your left. As the A52 is dual carriageway this means that Pride Park is less than 10min from the motorway and a joy to get to compared to the BBG.

Some fans may wish to travel in on the A6; if so, head into the city centre and then pick up the city centre (A6) to A52 (station to Wyvern) link road and the ground is about one mile away on your right. Whichever way you go, Pride Park is well signposted and you can't miss it.

**PARKING:** The away parking is signposted as you approach the ground, but there is one big complaint here: the car park (£3) is by the hospital and about 0.25 miles away from the ground. To get to Pride Park you have to walk by the canal and over some wasteland, which was very poorly policed and where I have heard numerous tales of ambushes of away fans occurring (and they said all seaters were the answer!). A better bet may be to park in the city centre. The walk to and from the ground is like a great migration and, it has to be said, is a lot less hostile. Option three is to park at the Wyvern Centre and walk to the ground. Again it's a fair trek but you may be away quicker. There is also parking for 2,400 home fans at the stadium.

## FUTURE DEVELOPMENTS

Work has started on the infill between the West and South Stands to increase capacity to the 33,000 mark. Scheduled to be completed December 1998.

## OTHER INFORMATION

One of the best watering holes on a trip to the Baseball Ground was the Brunswick by the station; this is probably best avoided now as it is quite a home pub (although it is still almost worth the visit for the fantastic hot rolls they serve there), and a better bet are the Navigation or the Blue Peter, which are near the away car park.

The fittings from the Baseball Hotel have been transported to Pride Park, but admission is members only on matchdays (although if you are passing on any other day you are welcome to have a pint there — which I'm sure countless of you can't wait to do). The beer inside the ground is pricey compared to the centre but drinkable. It can get a bit claustrophobic under the South Stand and the service is (all too predictably) slow on occasions. Mind you the steak & kidney and veg & potato pies (£1.50) were both good (I found the tea at £1 a cup less so).

The police are fairly tolerant, although can and will make arrests/ejections (of both home and away fans) if it is warranted.

There are two big changes at the new ground. Firstly, 'Rammy,' the club mascot, looks a lot less threatening than he used to; in fact, with his Ram's head and goalkeeping top, he hardly frightens any kids anymore. Secondly, although as previously mentioned there is plenty of noise in the ground, the group of fans who used to bleat the theme from MOTD seem to have disappeared.

Pride Park is one of the better new stadia and, although it is out of town, there are facilities which are fairly easily accessible (when in doubt, grab a cab) so in this bright new dawn it is perhaps surprising to hear the tannoy announcements for a 'father and son' to take part in a half-time quiz (presumably the womenfolk are at home preparing their men's dinner!). To be fair the club has said that the competition on other weeks concentrates on mums and daughters, grans and grandsons etc.

Finally of course, whatever else you do on a trip please, please don't forget to take 50p for the meter. You know it makes sense!!

*Total Football* **Experience Rating: 77**

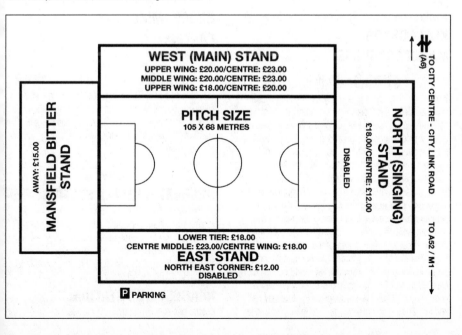

# EVERTON

**ADDRESS:** Goodison Park,
Goodison Road,
Liverpool L4 4EL

**TELEPHONE No:** 0151 330 2200

**TICKET OFFICE:** 0151 330 2300
(Recorded Information)

**FAX:** 0151 286 9112

**CLUBCALL:** 0891 12 11 99

**WEBSITE:** www.everton.com

Official and not too bad, though also check out the rather excellent — and unofficial — toffeeweb on http://mc.blackdown.org/everton/

**NICKNAME:** The Toffeemen

**RECORD ATTENDANCE:**

78,299 v Liverpool Div 1 18 September 1948 (D 1-1)
Goodison Park also holds the English record for a mid-week league match when in 1957 72,077 watched the game versus Manchester United.

## CLUB COLOURS:

**HOME:** Shirts: Royal Blue with White/Amber trim;
Shorts: White with Amber/Blue trim;
Socks: White with Amber/Blue trim

That is unless once again the club manages to get copies of the shirts where the white and amber trim was upside down, thus ensuring that, for the first few months of the season, while fans were wearing the correct colours, players were not (although to be fair to the club, as fans we can only sympathise as we know how difficult it is to keep up with these changes).

**AWAY:** Shirts: White; Shorts: Blue; Socks: White

**KIT SPONSORS:** One 2 One

**MANUFACTURERS:** Umbro

## GROUND INFO

If you are of a certain age — oh no I'm coming over all Denis Norden — you probably remember Goodison as being one of the best stadia you'd visit on your travels. It mixed dominating stands (Including the first three-tier stand in the country) with the peculiarity of having a church in one of the corners. All in all there was something special about Everton. Sadly, in the post-Taylor era, although at 40,185 capacity Goodison remains one of the larger grounds in the country, it has fallen if not into decay then way behind those of other clubs.

Pillars abound (there are about 10 in each of the Bullens Road and Main Stand), and unless you are in the Lower Tier (which is only about 13 rows deep) then expect some kind of obstruction. The motto on the club's crest reads 'nil satis, nisi optimum' or 'only the best is good enough'. Unfortunately many supporters may well find that Goodison is certainly not 'Optimum' especially

as neither is it very 'Cheapum'.

If you are a neutral, or haven't got a ticket for the Bullens Road Stand, where away fans are now sited, then try the top balcony of the Main Stand, although remember not to toss anything over the front — even an empty sugar sachet — as you are so far up that by the time it hits some poor soul underneath it will have gained the weight of a large concrete block.

The stewarding at Goodison tends to be of the strict but (usually) fair variety and I have got to say that in the years I have spent researching this book I have noticed a marked improvement in the way that visiting fans are treated. While you should not expect to be welcomed like a long lost brother, a trip to the ground is not as bad as some would have you believe.

**CAPACITY:** Stands: 40,185; Terrace: Nil

**AWAY FANS:** Bullens Stand Lower: 1,203;
Bullens Stand Upper: 932;
Paddock: 564
Total: 2,699

**DISABLED FACILITIES:** There are 48 places for home supporters (generally taken up by season ticket holders) and 13 spaces for visiting fans in the Bullens Road Stand. These must be pre-booked. Admission is £18.00 for wheelchair-bound supporters and free for helpers (OK so that's one wheelchair and 2,500 helpers please Mr Ticket-Seller!). There is parking available at the ground but there are restricted numbers so again pre-book. Match commentaries are available.

I've had numerous reports from disabled fans that the treatment at Everton is second to none and the club's positive and helpful attitude is to be applauded.

**PROGRAMME:** £2.00

## FANZINES:

| | |
|---|---|
| *When Skies Are Grey* | £1 |
| *Speke From The Harbour* | £1 |

*When Skies are Grey* remains the best club fanzine by a mile with a good mix of humour/nostalgia and opinion. Interestingly enough the fanzine is not so blinkered as to think that fans can do no wrong and is happy to admonish them where it thinks it is needed (lack of passion, attitude of some supporters etc).

## TRAVEL

**NEAREST RAILWAY STATION:** Kirkdale
(0151 709 9696 — Lime Street Enquiries)
In truth you will probably find it as easy to get a bus (£1) or cab (c£3.40) from Lime Street. If you were thinking about walking it from Lime Street, be warned that the 'Just down the road' that you'll be told the ground is fails to include the vital words 'four miles'.

**NEAREST BUS STATION:**
Central bus station (opposite Lime Street station —

0151 709 8600). Numbers 30, 92 and 93 run from the centre to the ground.

## BY CAR:

**NORTH:** M6, M58, M57 to J4, picking up signs for Liverpool A580 (Lancashire Road/Walton Hall Avenue East). After about three miles you will see Walton Hall Park on your right, and shortly after this there is a large intersection with the A5058. Go straight across and then straight on until you see Anfield Cemetery. Turn right by the cemetery into Gwladys Street and the ground is 300yd on the left.

**SOUTH/EAST:** From the M6 exit at J21A onto the M62 to Liverpool. Follow to the end of the motorway and turn right onto the A5058 Queen's Drive (signposted Knotty Ash). After 4.5 miles you get to a roundabout with the A56. Turn left here into County Road. Turn left after 0.75 miles into Spellow Lane, and then left into Goodison Road, and the ground is on the right.

## PARKING:

If when you are coming down Walton Lane you take the first left past Anfield Cemetery into Priory Road, and continue for 0.3 mile (past Stanley Park — price £2.50 with free bus shuttle), there is a big car park on the corner of Priory Road and Utting Avenue. Be warned, you will age waiting to get out of this after a match. You can try street parking, but keep an eye out for residents-only parking areas.

## FUTURE DEVELOPMENTS

At the end of the 1996-7 season Everton fans voted massively in favour of moving out from Goodison (albeit via one of the most leading questionnaires I have ever seen). However, since then there has been a groundswell of opinion to stay at the ground and everything seems to have slowed right down. There is still no decision as to which of the seven sites suggested should be the new home. Wherever it does move to (assuming that this does go ahead), the club is looking for a 60,000 all-seater bowl-shaped two-tier stadium. It is intended that there would be parking for 12,000 vehicles as well as numerous other leisure facilities. However, even if this does get the go-ahead, expect the Toffees to be at Goodison till at least 2000.

## OTHER INFORMATION

If you are looking for a decent pub which serves good food and where away fans are not simply tolerated but positively welcomed, try the Elm Tree (5min from the ground). The landlord is prepared to cater for coach parties, and if you pre-book will even provide a cooked breakfast on arrival. There are plenty of decent fish and chip shops on Goodison Road.

Everton take the field to the theme from 'Z-Cars', but from enquiries I made nobody seemed to know why. (This is about the only problem I had on my last visit, and the club seemed very clued up to dealing with both home and away supporters' needs.) Plenty of people were happy to have a guess (Sergeant Lynch in the series was a big Everton fan, Newtown was meant to be Goodison etc, etc) but the general consensus was that 'It's tradition'; very illuminating!

A little further afield there is the Burger Bar on the concourse outside Lime Street station, where they do an all-day breakfast for £3.50. This has the two essential qualities of food: being great and plenty of it. Inside the ground there is a fair selection. The beer is cheap(ish) and cheerful and the pies are hot and very tasty. If you want something sweet and a bit different try an Eccles cake (pastry and currants) although be warned they do sell out fairly early. One thing that you won't be getting your mitts on are the Everton mints as when the Toffee Ladies do make their ever more rare appearances, they steer well clear of the visiting fans (although I am told this was because their wares often came flying back straight at them).

***Total Football* Experience Rating: 75**

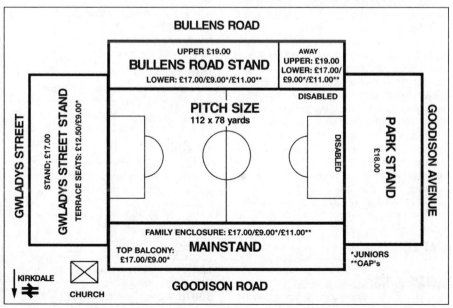

# EXETER CITY

**ADDRESS:** St James Park
Exeter
Devon EX4 6PX
**TELEPHONE No:** 01392 254073
**TICKET OFFICE:** 01392 254073
**FAX:** 01392 425885
**CLUBCALL:** 0891 12 16 34
There is also a newsline which gives out information at the normal national rates on 01392 215544.

**WEB SITE:**
http://www.personal.u-net.com/~ecfc/
(unofficial and well out of date)

**NICKNAME:** The Grecians
All together now: What's a Grecian Urn? About seven bob a week if he's lucky (God bless Sid James, Kenneth Williams, Hattie Jacques *et al*).

**RECORD ATTENDANCE:** 20,984 v Sunderland FA Cup 6th Rep 4 March 1931 (L 2-4)

**CLUB COLOURS:**
**HOME:** Shirts: Red/White stripes, Black trim;
Shorts: White;
Socks: Black/Red trim
**AWAY:** Shirts: Yellow; Shorts: Yellow;
Socks: Yellow

**KIT SPONSORS:** Concept Incorporated
**MANUFACTURERS:** Arrow

## GROUND INFO

The pricing structure at the ground means that away fans pay £1 more than home supporters for uncovered behind the goal terracing, and the same price as home supporters who opt for the along-the-pitch view of the famed Cowshed. There are concessions in the St James Road, provided that Exeter will receive (or have received) them from the visiting club but these are not generally available on the turnstiles. Concessions are available by calling at the matchday office to buy tickets (adults £8.00; OAPs/children £5.00) — just ask for away fans.

The view from the seats isn't too bad, although 75 are classified as 'restricted view' (but not restricted price), but watch out for some of the seats which have extra strong springs in them, and thus are capable of catapulting a cup of tea/programme/coat put onto them as you get yourself comfortable about eight or nine rows back (and almost inevitably onto the lap of the meanest looking person in the ground).

**CAPACITY:** Stands: 1,690; Terrace: 8,880;
Total: 10,570

**AWAY FANS:** St James Road: 960;
Grandstand: 314; Total: 1,274

**DISABLED FACILITIES:** There are 15 places for disabled supporters in 'C' Block who, along with their helpers, are admitted free of charge. The club recommends that these are pre-booked. However, there are no parking facilities at the ground other than for brief (and I do mean brief) dropping off/picking up, which is a bit of a trial. There are no match commentaries available for the blind.

**PROGRAMME:** £1.70
Exeter City have always produced one of the best programmes in the League and 1997-8's Grecian Gazette was no different. It is simply packed with articles that will prove interesting for both home and away fans and, although they do have the dreaded pen pics, this is only part rather than all of the stuff they do on the day's visitors and, rather than lump it all together, there are bits liberally scattered throughout its 40 pages. Top class columns from Mike Blackstone, Norman Sheil and others.

**FANZINES:**
(*There's a) Good Time Coming*
*(Be it ever so far away)* 50p
*Good Time* wasn't on sale last season when I went to the ground; hopefully it hasn't folded as it was an excellent title with all the best bits from its two 'parent' fanzines — *In Exile* and *Exe Directory* — packed in 30+ very readable pages.

## TRAVEL

**NEAREST RAILWAY STATION:**
St James Park Halt, Exeter St David's, Exeter Central (01392 433551)
St James Park Halt is, as the name suggests, a tiny stop just outside the ground. The service there is such that it is likely that you will end up at one of the two other stations, which are a fair walk from the ground.

**BUS:** EWN Buses (01392 427711)
Take note that the Paris Street bus station has now apparently closed. There are no buses that run directly to the football ground, but any letter 'N' bus will take you to the city centre from where it is about a 5-10min walk.

**BY CAR:**
**NORTH:** M5 to J30. Follow signs to Exeter City Centre, this will bring you onto Sidmouth Road which then becomes Heavitree Road. When you get to a large roundabout take the fourth exit (in effect you will be turning right) onto Western Way. At the next roundabout take the second exit onto Old Tiverton Road, then immediately left into St James Road. The ground is 100yd down this road.
**EAST:** Take the A30 into Exeter, this brings you onto Heavitree Road, then as north.
**SOUTH:** A38 into Exeter, following the City Centre

signs until you hit Western Way, then as north.

**WEST:** A30 to A377 (signposted Exeter). Follow the signs to the City Centre until you pick up Western Way, then as north.

## PARKING:
There are three car parks in close proximity to the ground, two off Western Way and one by the Old Tiverton Roundabout. The best bet for off-street parking however is the Dix's Field multi-storey off Paris Street, which is 25yd from the Western Way/Heavitree Road roundabout. From here it is only about 0.5 mile to the ground walking up Western Way.

## FUTURE DEVELOPMENTS

Having hopefully got the most significant of its financial worries out of the way, the club is now capable of looking to the future. Previous thoughts of relocating have (apparently) been shelved and the City Council has now purchased the ground and leased it to the club. Plans have been prepared for a gradual rebuilding at St James Park (starting provisionally at the St James Road End or the Cowshed). However, the precise nature and timing of these changes cannot be divulged, nor work undertaken until funds are made available from the Football Trust. It is likely that, for the majority of next season, things will stay as at present, with the club looking to receive funding and start work in the middle of 1999.

## OTHER INFORMATION

Exeter is a strange place; one half of it is filled with tourists looking up at buildings going 'Gosh, isn't that quaint' and is a bit twee, and the other half is a throwback to 1960s precinct architecture of which there are rows of houses all painted in different colours, which fail to give the place the air of cheeriness they might if they were, for example, on a sea front. Guess which side of the city the football ground is in?

Pubs in the vicinity of the ground include the Fiddlers Pie in Sidwell Street, the Duke of York on the corner of Sidwell Street and York Road, and the Horse and Dray in Blackboy Road. The nearest one to the ground is the Brook Green which isn't too bad. The Centre Spot Social Club is open to members of visiting clubs with membership cards.

The catering at the ground is provided by Ann Corr catering (and I'm not going to make the obvious gag here) and, as with many aspects about the ground, is showing signs of improving. They serve good tasty meat and cheese pasties at £1.25; it's better sticking to cold drinks than hot ones, though, as both my Bovril and tea were dreadful (although the purists amongst you should note that at least they serve pepper with the Bovril). It's worth checking your change, though, as the person who served me had a great deal of difficulty working out that £10 less £1.85 was in fact slightly more than the £1.15 that she wanted to give me.

The incident with the catering staff aside, I have to say that I enjoyed last season's trip to Exeter more than I have done for a good few years. The club seems to have developed a lot more of a relaxed attitude towards visiting fans now that its short-term future has been resolved, which means you can take time to appreciate that the city is a nice one — although the fact that it is twinned with the town of 'Bad Homburg' always makes me giggle for some reason — and the ground has a fantastic character and some nice quirks. These include the fact that the narrow away end is overlooked by rows of houses and the ground is on a slope, which means that between the pitch and the stands you have big grass banks in places. Even the big red sign outside the ground has a nice 'real football' feel about it.

*Total Football* **Experience Rating: 67**

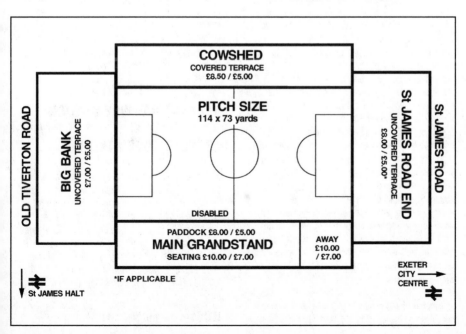

# FULHAM

**ADDRESS:** Craven Cottage
Stevenage Road
Fulham
London SW6 6HH

**TELEPHONE No:** 0171 384 4700

**TICKET OFFICE:** 0171 384 4710

**FAX:** 0171 384 4715

**CLUBCALL:** 0891 44 00 44

**WEB SITE:** www.fulhamfc.co.uk
(official)

**NICKNAME:** The Cottagers

It should be noted that Fulham's nickname is derived from the Craven Cottage, which is a listed building at the corner of the ground.

**RECORD ATTENDANCE:**

49,335 v Millwall Div 2 8 October 1938 (W 2-1)

**CLUB COLOURS:**

**HOME:** Shirts: White, Black collar and cuffs;
Shorts: Black; Socks: White, Red/Black trim

**AWAY:** Shirts: Red and Black squares;
Shorts: White; Socks: Red and Black or White

**SHIRT SPONSORS:** Demon Internet

**MANUFACTURERS:** Adidas

## GROUND INFO

Away fans get the uncovered terrace at the Putney End of the ground. This is high on the club's list of areas to develop, not least because it is apparently collapsing in on itself (although the club has completed initial safety work on it). The Riverside Stand offers a decent view and, since Mohamed Al Fayed has taken over at the club, has had all the seating replaced with — shockingly — ones that you seem now to be able to fit your arse on. However, spaces for (official) away fans are at a premium so make sure you either buy in advance or get there early. If you do go in the Riverside and get chatting to the home fans, then the chances are you might get an invite into one of the bars in the stand which do serve a decent pint.

On the plus side, the number of police at the ground seems to have diminished a bit during the 1997-8 season, which means at least you are only getting searched by one lot of people.

You can also have a good bit of a singsong with the home fans, who have an impressive repertoire ranging from the surreal (I once heard a fantastic version of Edelweiss) to the odd (It's a long way to Tipperary) to the very funny (anything involving camels, Cairo and Mohamed Al Fayed).

Finally hats off to Fulham for the fantastic (over 50%) concessions that they offer to visiting as well as home supporters on the terracing. OK, so the facilities are basic but that doesn't stop certain other clubs from ignoring the fact that away fans don't deserve to be fleeced just because they follow their team.

**CAPACITY:** Stands: 7,000; Terrace: 12,000
Total: 19,000

**AWAY FANS:**
Putney Terrace: 4,000 standing only;

**DISABLED FACILITIES:** There are places for 12 wheelchairs in a covered area along the touchline of the Main Stand. Pre-booking is not essential, but is, in the words of the club, 'advisable'. Admission is free for disabled supporters and £7 for helpers. Match commentaries for the visually impaired are no longer available. There is very limited off-street parking at the ground.

The facilities, once inside the ground, aren't the best you'll come across, although to a degree this is overcome by the fact that if you need assistance the stewards will go out of their way to help.

**PROGRAMME:** £2.00

Went up 33% in 1997-8. However, at least the club can justify these 'Premiership' prices by offering a first rate programme that was, in my opinion, the best in the division last season. It is very well written with an excellent away section as well as numerous general interest pieces and will keep you going well beyond the normal two minute team check.

**FANZINES:**
*There's Only One F In Fulham* £1.30

*TOOFIF* celebrated its 10th anniversary last season and remains one of the fanzines that is really worth buying when you come across it. A nice mix of humour and 'serious' journalism, with a top rate section on some of the mis-information printed about the club by the papers (an area that has grown increasingly with the arrival of Messrs Al Fayed, Keegan and Wilkins).

## TRAVEL

**NEAREST RAILWAY STATION:**
Putney Bridge (0171 262 6767 — Paddington Enquiries)

**NEAREST TUBE STATION:**
Putney Bridge (District Line)

If going on the tube, make sure you get a Wimbledon train. Give yourself a good 15min to walk from the station through Bishop's Park to the ground. NB: Watch out at night matches because the park gets locked at about 8pm. Note: I did hear a couple of stories about visiting fans getting a bit of a hard time when they crossed the Park last season (although this was after a local derby rather than a 'normal' game). For my own part, I've got to say I've never had any problems but it is worth bearing in mind.

**BUS:** London Transport (0171 222 1234)

## BY CAR:

**NORTH:** M1 to J1. Turn right onto the A406 North Circular Road (heading west). Continue for four miles until you get to the Hanger Lane roundabout. Go straight over o to the A406 Hanger Lane. After two miles you will see Gunnersbury Park, and shortly after this is the Chiswick roundabout. Take the second exit onto the A4 and at the next roundabout (Hogarth) take the first exit, continuing along the A4 Great West Road. After one mile you will get to Hammersmith; follow the one-way system until you are heading back in the direction from which you have just come, and turn left onto the A219 Fulham Palace Road. After one mile turn right into Inglethorpe Street, at the bottom of which you should turn left into Stevenage Road and the ground is 100yd on the right.

**WEST:** M4 to J1 continuing straight onto the A4 (heading east). After a mile you will reach the Hogarth Roundabout, then as north.

**EAST:** A12 to A406 North Circular Road, continuing till you get to the end of the M1, then as north.

**SOUTH:** A24 into London. At the crossroads with the A214 (by Tooting Bec station) turn left onto Trinity Road; after 1.5 miles turn left onto the A3. One mile later the road splits in two; take the right-hand lane (Upper Richmond Road) then right at the next crossroads into Putney High Street. Continue across Putney Bridge, then after 0.75 miles turn left into Findlay Street, at the bottom of which turn right for the ground.

**PARKING:** If you are driving to the ground it is as well to park some way away as there is a residents', parking and pay scheme all round the club or the option of very expensive meters (providing you can find a free one).

## FUTURE DEVELOPMENTS

Notwithstanding the fact that the Cottage and part of the Stevenage Road Stand are listed buildings, it would appear that the money Mr Al Fayed is injecting into Fulham means the ground is soon going to receive a (much needed) facelift and plans to develop the Cottage into a 25,000 all-seater stadium are in the process of being released. The replacement of Riverside seats was the first stage and (no doubt to the joy of fans who stand on open terracing) the building of a new club shop the second. It is likely that the Putney End could be next for the treatment which may result in restricted away capacities for at least part of the season.

## OTHER INFORMATION

There can be only one stopping-off place: The River Café outside Putney Bridge Underground station. Run by Italians with pictures of a couple of old Juve and Italy teams on the wall, it offers a full on English style choice of menu. Pick anything you want and it will be fantastic. They serve short fat stubby chips which are out of this world, the service is fast, friendly ('hello', 'bye boys' and smiles seem compulsory), and it is not too expensive (about £3.50 for a good meal). The alternative are the hot dogs at the ground which are £2.50 and tasted dreadful to me.

1997-8 saw the introduction of the (unofficial) Fulham band although, to be honest, this was not as well received as it has been at Hillsborough, with the single drummer facing constant shouts of 'Oi Ringo if you don't stop that bleeding racket I'll take those drumsticks and stick them...'. Even better is the trumpet player who every now and then raises his instrument to his lips with an incredible panache, but then seems to lose his nerve a bit, waves it a around his mouth and then lowers it again, nine times out of 10 without blowing a note. I have been told that he is only just learning how to play the instrument, in which case I would suggest a lot more practice.

***Total Football* Experience Rating: 66**

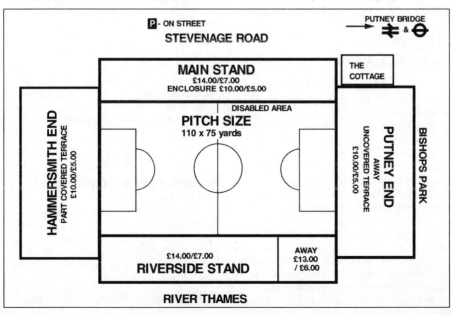

# GILLINGHAM

**ADDRESS:** Priestfield Stadium
Redfern Avenue
Gillingham
Kent ME7 4DD

**TELEPHONE No:** 01634 851854

**TICKET OFFICE:** 01634 576828

**FAX:** 01634 850986

**GILLS HOTLINE:** 0891 332211

**WEB SITE:**

http://ourworld.compuserve.com/hom
epages/gillsf.c/mainpag e/html

**NICKNAME:** The Gills

If you don't want to upset the locals never pronounce this with a hard 'G' (as in what fish breathe through) rather than the soft 'G' (as in the girl's name), as this makes them go into a mighty rage. A lot of Gills merchandise also has the legend 'Home of The Shouting Men' on it; this is neither a nickname nor the club's way of praising its fans but simply a literal translation of the Anglo-Saxon word Gillingham.

**RECORD ATTENDANCE:**

23,002 v QPR FA Cup 3rd 10 January 1948 (D 1-1)
The record attendance actually occurred while Gillingham were a non-league club, as they lost their league status in 1938, and did not recover it until 1950.

**CLUB COLOURS:**

**HOME:** Shirts: Blue; Shorts: Blue; Socks: White
**AWAY:** Shirts: Red; Shorts: Red; Socks: Red
**THIRD:** (for those times when Blue or Red just won't do) Shirts: White; Shorts: White; Socks: White

**KIT SPONSORS:** Kool

**MANUFACTURERS:** Gills Leisure

## GROUND INFO

The New Gordon Street Stand was opened for business in 1997-8 but, while it is good to see some improvements at Priestfield, it is disappointing to report that the new construction has got over 10 pillars in it, which lead to many an obstructed view. Still no need for visitors to worry about this, as there are no pillars on the open terrace that they find themselves on. This is stuck in the corner of the Gillingham Road End and the Main Stand. If you are going on this terrace, make sure you aren't carrying a groin injury because your hips will need to be in tip top condition to get through the very stiff turnstiles.

If you don't fancy getting soaked to the skin (or more radically, you want a decent view of the game) there are some seats available in the Main Stand, although the numbers of these are strictly limited. As a result, it may

be worth trying to buy one from your own club before you travel. Given the incident at the ground last season, any visiting fans who are identified in designated home sections of Priestfield can expect a summary eviction.

The club offers very good concessions to both home and away supporters. Any home fans who go regularly to the ground, but don't attend enough to make a season ticket viable can get additional discounts when they pay for five matches in advance.

**CAPACITY:** Stands: 3,525; Terrace: 9,197;
Total: 12,722

**AWAY FANS:** Redfern Avenue Corner Terrace:
1,800; Main Stand: 100;
Total: 1,900

It should be noted that the capacity of many areas of the ground is under review; thus these figures may be subject to some fluctuation.

**DISABLED FACILITIES:** There are 56 places (including helpers) at the front left of the Main Stand. The pricing system for disabled fans is under review but it is considered a possibility that wheelchair-bound supporters will be admitted free of charge with helpers paying standard match day prices. Contact the club to pre-book a place.

The match commentaries previously provided via Invicta Sport have been discontinued and at present no replacement facility has been established.

**PROGRAMME:** £1.60

Continuing to show improvement during 1997-8 and now in the top half of the 'league'.

**FANZINES:**

*Brian Moore's Head (Looks Uncannily Like The London Planetarium)* £1

Perhaps the most famous fanzine title in the country. However, this is more than just a wacky title, it is 52 pages of great writing which has kept true to the core of the original ideas of fanzines while continuing to improve its content and professionalism. Lots of articles for home and away fans alike and the minimum of 'away days'-type pieces. This is available from the club shop, but has not sold out in the slightest way from having this 'official' link.

## TRAVEL

**NEAREST RAILWAY STATION:** Gillingham (01732 770111).

The easiest way of getting to Gillingham is by train out of either London Victoria or Charing Cross. There are about four trains an hour (two from each terminal) so expect to spend about 75min getting there (delays permitting). From the station it's about 10-15min to the ground. Turn left as you leave and follow the crowds.

**BUS:** Maidstone & District Buses (01634 281100)

## BY CAR:

**FROM ALL PARTS:** M2 to J4. When you leave the motorway, follow the signs for the A278 (Gillingham). At the third roundabout turn left onto the A2. After 1.5 miles, turn right onto Nelson Road (A231). Just after the bus station turn right into Gillingham Road, passing the Livingstone Arms and the ground is on the right.

**PARKING:** The car park at the ground is not for us humble supporters, which means street parking. This is not plentiful; the side streets fill up quickly and can be a nightmare to get away from due to their narrowness and the fact that they are all double parked, so you may find it easier to park-up in the town centre. Midweekers take note — street parking is for permit holders only Monday-Friday 8am-10pm.

## FUTURE DEVELOPMENTS

The development of the new Gordon Stand is the first phase in a complete overhaul of Priestfield. Due to the popularity of the Rainham End it is likely that the uncovered Gillingham End will be the next area improved, though this is not expected to take place until at least summer 1999.

## OTHER INFORMATION

Last season saw trouble at Priestfield, which left a Fulham fan dead after a game which had seen numerous outbreaks of violence. While one cannot overstate the tragedy and futility of the loss of a life, I feel it is right to say that generally, although there are problems on occasion, I find Gillingham a 'safe' ground to go to. It is said that actions speak louder than words so I'd point out here that I have taken my nephew to the ground on several occasions and will do so again in the future.

Naturally the incident has left its scars on the club and I believe that stewarding and policing have both increased and that actions which could be deemed as misbehaviour are likely to be reacted to swiftly and strictly.

On to other (less important) matters. A decent pre-match pint can be found at either the supporters' club bar, or the Cricketers on Toronto Road. If you decide to go into town (a good 15min walk) then the Golden Belle or the Britannia, both of which are right by the station, are worth a visit. If you are looking for food then the Circus Fish Bar, up from the ground, is sizeable and popular. A great alternative is to go to French's the butchers, which is on Gillingham Road and which does a sublime chicken on a spit together with jacket potatoes — they get these from the veg shop they own next door though you can always get chips from Fresh Fry, which is next door. For £4.20 you will get enough for two of you to eat yourselves stupid or four of you to have a decent meal. If it is raining go and sit in your car, otherwise wander 25yd down the hill on Gillingham Road and either sit on the wall outside the mobility shop or turn right into Linden Road, which will take you directly to the away end and scoff away in the ground. Once inside Priestfield, the facilities are fairly basic and, if you haven't popped in at French's, then you will no doubt cast very envious glances at those amongst you who have and who are gorging themselves on the terraces while you decide whether you really want to risk the burgers on offer. Still, at least if you do fast, then you reduce the chances of having to brave the heinous toilets.

*Total Football* **Experience Rating: 69**

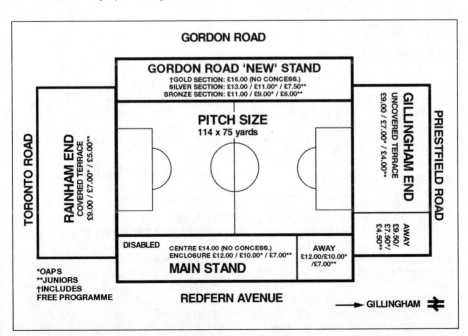

GORDON ROAD

GORDON ROAD 'NEW' STAND
†GOLD SECTION: £16.00 (NO CONCESS.)
SILVER SECTION: £13.00 / £11.00* / £7.50**
BRONZE SECTION: £11.00 / £9.00* / £6.00**

PITCH SIZE
114 x 75 yards

TORONTO ROAD

RAINHAM END
COVERED TERRACE
£9.00 / £7.00* / £5.00**

GILLINGHAM END
UNCOVERED TERRACE
£9.00 / £7.00* / £4.00**

AWAY
£9.50/
£7.50*/
£4.50**

PRIESTFIELD ROAD

DISABLED

CENTRE £14.00 (NO CONCESS.)
ENCLOSURE £12.00 / £10.00* / £7.00**
MAIN STAND

AWAY
£12.00/£10.00*
/£7.00**

*OAPS
**JUNIORS
†INCLUDES
FREE PROGRAMME

REDFERN AVENUE

→ GILLINGHAM

# GRIMSBY TOWN

**ADDRESS:** Blundell Park
Cleethorpes
North East Lincs
DN35 7PY

**TELEPHONE No:** 01472 697111

**TICKET OFFICE:** 01472 605058

**FAX:** 01472 693665

**MARINERS' HOTLINE:**
0891 555855

OK, let's get this over right from the start: the good people of Grimsby are obsessed with two things in life. One is 'Harry the Haddock' (about which more later) and the other is the football trivia question 'Which football club never wins/plays at home?', the answer of course being Grimsby because they play in Cleethorpes. This question is supposed to baffle and amaze you, but because it is as old as the hills, does not. (The fact that there is no such place as Port Vale, and therefore they too satisfy the equation, is the ideal balloon-bursting antidote to use when you are asked this question on your trip.)

**NICKNAME:** The Mariners

**RECORD ATTENDANCE:** 31,651 v Wolves
FA Cup 5th 20 February 1937 (D 1-1)

**CLUB COLOURS:**
**HOME:** Shirts: Black and White stripes;
Shorts: Black; Socks: White
**AWAY:** Shirts: Blue; Shorts: White; Socks: Blue

**KIT SPONSORS:** Dixon's Motors plc

**MANUFACTURERS:** Avec

## GROUND INFO

It isn't often I'll complain when a club offers excellent concessions to visiting fans, but in Grimsby's case I'll make an exception. On my last visit, some fans were talking to their friends and moaning that their kids had had to pay full price to get in. They were somewhat taken aback when the friends said they had got half price tickets at the ticket office so went to the turnstile where they had been charged only to be told that, yes, concessions were available, but only to people who got tickets (from an office less than 50yd away). When questioned further as to why this hadn't been pointed out when dad, mum and two kids had handed over £48 to get in they received a stock 'it's not my job' response. Nice attitude.

Talking of attitudes, we also have the stewards who searched me when I last went to the ground and then had to have a debate as to whether I should be allowed in

with a ballpoint pen — what did they think I was going to do? Draw false moustaches on innocent bystanders?

Then the ground itself: archaic toilets which — especially the portakabin example — may induce nausea when used.

There are pillars in all stands, so away fans can't complain of worse treatment than the Mariners. The exception to this is the John Smith Lower Stand; however, this has the disadvantage of not being fully protected by a roof and also facing the North Sea.

**CAPACITY:** Stands: 8,870; Terrace: Nil

**AWAY FANS:** Osmond Stand: 1,874

**DISABLED FACILITIES:** There are 88 spaces for wheelchair-bound fans in the Main Stand. Call the club to pre-book your place. Matchday commentaries for the visually impaired are available. Admission is free for wheelchair-bound supporters, £5.00 for 'others' and £6.00 for helpers. No parking facilities available.

**PROGRAMME:** £1.50
Unless you are a diehard collector this is, in my opinion, worth avoiding; too many adverts and pictures, and lots of very, very small print.

**FANZINES:**
*Sing When We're Fishing*          80p
My general sense of well-being was further tested on my trip to the ground in 1997-8 when I turned up at 'Imperial Corner' (by the hotel/bar of the same name) and found no sign of Steve Plowes, the esteemed editor of *SWWF* and general all-round good guy. Further enquiries revealed that neither he nor the fanzine had been seen all season (and as this was in April things aren't looking too good). If this publication has folded, it is a real loss as it was always good, angry, educational and funny.

## TRAVEL

**NEAREST RAILWAY STATION:**
Cleethorpes (01302 340222 — Doncaster Enquiries) Cleethorpes is right by the sea front and has a bizarre Disney-type clock spouting out of it. Slightly less appealing is the fact that the station bar is called 'The Number 2'.

**NEAREST BUS STATION:**
Stagecoach (01472 241568)
Take either a 3F, 8X or 9X from the town to the ground.

**BY CAR:**
**NORTH/WEST/SOUTHWEST:** M180 to the junction with the A180 (this is at the end of the motorway). Follow the signs to Grimsby and Cleethorpes. After a while you cross the docks and come to three roundabouts in quick succession. At the third of these (this marks the end of the A180), take the second exit. You will cross over the railway and come onto the Cleethorpes Road (A1098). This becomes Grimsby Road

as you approach Cleethorpes. Continue on this road until you see a drive-through McDonald's which is directly in front of the ground.

**SOUTHEAST:** A1, A46. Continue along the A46, following the signs for Cleethorpes town centre, until you get to a T-junction-come-roundabout, signposted Town Centre to your right and Immingham/Grimsby/M180/A180 to the left (you should also see a memorial hall on your left). Turn left here (onto the Grimsby Road) and the ground is about a mile on your right.

**PARKING:** There is plenty of parking on both sides of the Grimsby Road outside the ground, as well as loads of side streets. If you want a public car park try Cleethorpes town centre.

## FUTURE DEVELOPMENTS

It should be noted that there are still plans to possibly relocate, although these appear to be very much in the early stages of review.

## OTHER INFORMATION

Every time I go to Cleethorpes, I seem to come across another fantastic chip shop. In the town centre there is Steels — a bit up-market, very popular and possibly the best haddock I have ever tasted. Right by the ground is Hobsons — voted No 1 chip shop in the area 1996-7, but this year's recommendation is the County Chip Shop. If you walk from the ground towards the town centre it is about 300yd away. It offers a small haddock and chips for the incredible price of £1 (no, that's not a misprint, I said £1) and for that you get a decent portion of chips and (as with everywhere in the region) a lovely bit of fish. It is ideal for away fans as it is just by the Leaking Boot, which not only serves away fans but positively welcomes them and is a fantastic meeting up place (especially now that they let children with their families into the premises). It is also convenient, as it is right by a William

Hill's if you want to stick your fixed odds coupon on.

The other pubs around the ground (the Imperial, etc) tend to be very much for home fans, so if you don't fancy the Leaking Boot then it is as well to go into the town centre (15/20min) and try one of the numerous pubs there — my own favourite being O'Neills.

There is a McDonald's right by the ground and, while I am partial to the odd Big Mac now and again, I would say that anyone who goes in here and orders a filet-o-fish when they are so near to a cornucopia of piscine magic deserves to have all their taste buds shrivel up.

Inside the ground, the kiosk serves a fair range of pies and sausage rolls. The tea at the ground is another example of where it is served in big mugs with small spoons, so prepare yourself for burnt fingers as you stir your tea.

The club has long since ditched its entry to the stirring refrains of Anchors Aweigh which, although slightly bizarre, did at least have some local connotations given the town's major industry. Rather less understandably, it has been replaced with the William Tell overture (the theme to The Lone Ranger to you and me). Still, at least some traditions hold firm and the club mascots (two salty seadogs) are still weaving up and down the line.

Finally, hats off to the club for the most enigmatic PA announcement of the year when it was broadcast twice during a game that if anybody had lost any 'personal belongings' would they go immediately to a police officer and make themselves known. Unfortunately, as no clues were given as to what these items might be, everyone then spent five minutes going through their pockets checking to see that they had their wallets/car keys etc. When a steward was asked if the club could say what had been handed in the answer came back 'No because then everyone would try and steal it'.

*Total Football* **Experience Rating: 46**

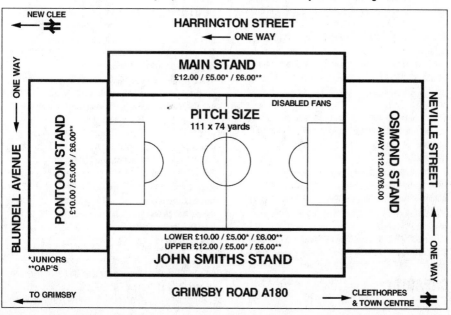

# HALIFAX TOWN

**ADDRESS:** The Shay
Halifax
West Yorkshire
HX1 2YS

**TELEPHONE No:** 01422 345543

**COMMERCIAL TEL + FAX No:**
01422 353423

**TICKET OFFICE:** 01422 345543

**FAX:** 01422 349487

**SHAYMEN HOTLINE:** 0891 22 73 28

**WEB SITE:**
www.geocities.com/Colosseum/
Stadium/3043/ (unofficial)

**NICKNAME:** The Shaymen

**RECORD ATTENDANCE:** 36,885 v
Tottenham Hotspur FA Cup 5th 14 February 1953 (L 0-3)

**CLUB COLOURS:**
**HOME:** Shirts: Blue & White; Shorts: Blue & White;
Socks: Blue & White
**AWAY:** Shirts: Green; Shorts: Green & Yellow; Socks:
Green & Yellow

**KIT SPONSORS:** Nationwide

**MANUFACTURERS:** Riemme

## GROUND INFO

Last season the club operated a fantastic policy whereby admission was £7 for adults 'sit or stand'. There were also brilliant concessions available in all parts of the ground.

1998-9 sees away fans move from the South End of the Shay to the North Terrace, which was opened during the 1997-8 season. At present, this is uncovered — although this may change in the medium/long-term — which means that you will need to wrap up well. It is not so much the cold, as the wind. When I was in Halifax there was a downpour where the rain was coming horizontally.

If you want to sit down then you'll need to get to the ground early to take advantage of one of the limited number of seats in either the Main or Skircoat Stands (the latter is very bizarre as it is neatly subdivided by terracing and seats).

The attitude of those at the club, when I visited, was fantastic and you can only hope that their regained league status does not mean that this will change.

**CAPACITY:** Terrace: 8,750; Seats: 1,750;
Total: 10,500

**AWAY FANS:**
North Stand (Uncovered Terrace): 3,300

**DISABLED FACILITIES:** There are spaces for approximately 20 wheelchair-bound supporters. Away fans will be sited between the North and the Skircoat Stands and home fans by the Main Stand. Admission is free of charge for disabled fans, and standard prices for helpers. Places should be pre-booked with the club as should any parking requirements. Matchday commentaries for the visually impaired are not available.

**PROGRAMME:** £2.00.
Although a well above the average publication for the Vauxhall Conference, this would not fare so well when compared to some programmes in the Third Division. There will possibly be a revamp prior to the start of the 1998-9 season.

**FANZINES:** None

## TRAVEL
### NEAREST RAILWAY STATION:
Halifax (0345 484950)
This is about a 5-10 min walk from the ground.

**BUS:** Halifax (01484 545444 — West Yorkshire Passenger Transport Executive Information)

**BY CAR:**
**NORTH:** A629 through Halifax towards Huddersfield. After you have gone through the town this road becomes Skircoat Road. Either turn left onto Hunger Hill then first right into Shay Skye/Shaw Hill and the ground is on the right; or continue for 300yd and then turn left into Shaw Hill for the ground.
**SOUTH:** M62 to J24. Take the A629 towards Halifax. Continue on the A629 past Halifax General Hospital. Just over 0.5 mile past the hospital, turn right onto Shaw Hill. The ground and car park are 300yd on the left (note: this is quite a concealed entrance).
**WEST:** A646 towards Halifax. Just after you go through the Kings Cross area, the road forks in two. Take the right fork (Skircoat Moor Road) and then the first significant left into Free School Lane. Continue for 1 mile until the road crosses the A629; go straight over at this junction into Shaw Hill. The ground and car park are 300yd on the left (note: this is quite a concealed entrance) .
**EAST:** A58 into the town centre, turn left onto the A629 (signposted Huddersfield) then as North.
No matter from which direction you approach the ground there are signposts which, actually say 'the Shay' rather than just 'football traffic'.

**PARKING:** There is a car park at the ground, the access/use of which is being reviewed for the 1998-9 season. Otherwise there is a car park on the corner of Hunger Hill and Skircoat Road. There is some street parking and a good bet for this is to turn right into Water

Hill opposite the ground, off which there are a number of side/residential streets. If you are feeling flush you could always (for £10) leave your car for a mini-valet at the IMO just by the ground, as the staff are happy to clean your car and then hold on to it till after the match.

Note: there is a voucher system in operation for street parking in the town centre.

## FUTURE DEVELOPMENTS

It is planned to redevelop The Shay into a 15,000 capacity stadium. The first stage in this programme was completed on 30 March 1998 and involved the Trinity Garage End having its capacity increased to 3,000 with new turnstiles also being installed (giving the ground a total capacity of 7,500). This allowed the club to obtain its Grade A certificate (and thus gain admission to the League). The next phase of the project involves improvements to the West Stand and bringing the pitch significantly (about 30ft) closer to the terraces. A two-tier main stand will be built at the south end of the ground; this will include bars and a shop and will cost approximately £2 million. This work will start when funding is available but it is hoped that this will be during, or at the end of, the 1998-9 season. Part of these improvements have been funded by the Halifax Blue Sox (horrible, horrible Americanised spelling) RLFC who will share the ground with the football club from now on.

## OTHER INFORMATION

How times change. Relegated from the Football League in 1992-3 Halifax found themselves needing to win their last match of the 1996-7 season to even retain their Conference place. They beat Stevenage Borough on that day 4-2 and the rest, as they say, is history. Town romped away with the Conference last season and it is good to

see them back in the league.

There is a pub at the ground, The Weavers; this only reopened last season and, at present, signs on the door state that admission is for 'invited guests only'. However, it is hoped that the licensing restrictions may be lifted in 1998-9 and anyone will be able to enjoy a pint there. Alternatively try the Shay, which is on the corner of Hunger Hill, or the Three Pigeons, which is a great Free House on the way to the station. There are loads of pubs in the town centre; the Old Cock serves not only a fair pint but also a good breakfast (providing you are there before 10.30).

Another good choice for food is the Shay Café — on Hunger Hill and opposite the Shay pub. A good honest café, it has an excellent choice of tasty cholesterol-laden grub to suit all palates.

I never really thought I would say this but, if you fancy making a weekend of it, then Halifax is as good a place as any. The moors are fantastic (if a bit bleak) and there are plenty of good places to eat and drink. For the kids, there is the 'Eureka!' centre — a massive science park/activity centre — by the station and the town itself is very clean and a lot bigger than you'd think. If you're looking for stereotypes then, yes, you will see terraced rows of houses clinging to the hillside, but if this place was in somewhere like Gloucestershire rather than Yorkshire it would be bang to the rafters with tourists.

Finally, just inside the entrance to the club, is a large Halifax Town plaque, underneath which is the legend 'A tribute to some nice people'. After a visit to The Shay and the manner in which I and others were treated, you can but agree with the sentiment. A definite must for an away day in 1998-9.

**Total Football Experience Rating: 85**

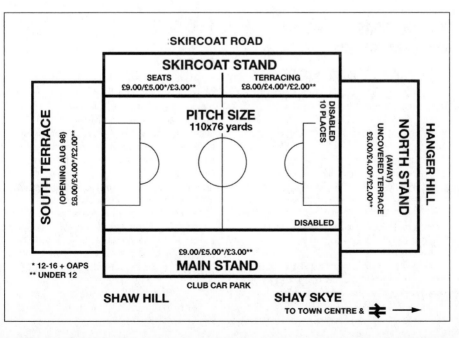

# HARTLEPOOL UNITED

**ADDRESS:** Victoria Park
Clarence Road
Hartlepool TS24 8BZ

**TELEPHONE No:** 01429 272584

**TICKET OFFICE:** 01429 272584

**FAX:** 01429 863007

**THE VICTORIA LINE:** 0891 66 44 47

**WEB SITE:**
Geocities.com/colosseum/Field/1490
(unofficial)

**E-MAIL:** Paul.Mullen@onyxnet.co.uk.
This chap is the all-round good egg who is editor of the Pool fanzine Monkey Business. Very helpful.

**NICKNAME:** The Pool
After their formation in 1908 the club were known as Hartlepools United, but in 1968 they not only lost an 's' but also the 'United'. In 1977 they refound the United, which had fallen down the side of the armchair, but sadly the missing 's' remains unaccounted for and it can only be assumed that it was thrown out with the newspapers by mistake.

**RECORD ATTENDANCE:** 17,426 v
Manchester Utd FA Cup 3rd 5 January 1957 (L 3-4)

**CLUB COLOURS:**
**HOME:** Shirt: Royal Blue and White stripes;
Shorts: Royal Blue;
Socks: Royal Blue
**AWAY:** tba

**KIT SPONSORS:** Camerons

**MANUFACTURERS:** Loki and Ontime

## GROUND INFO

Don't be perturbed by what at first glance appears to be heads on spikes outside the ground. These are, in fact, footballs, which did not (suprisingly) get to their resting place via the hoof of a centre half but are actually part of the ground décor.

Victoria Park, like much of Hartlepool itself, has undergone a degree of regeneration. No longer is the ground three-sided and the Cyril Knowles stand does mean that there is some respite from the bitter wind that whips in off the North Sea (though it is still probably best to pack at least a dozen layers of clothing if you are visiting in anything but the 42min that forms the town's summer season). If you find that the cost of petrol has left you skint by the time you arrive at VP then check out the back of the Rink End Stand as the boundary wall has several view-sized holes in it (though be prepared to fight off the local kids who claim them as their own and also the stewards who are often employed to stand judiciously

in front of them). If you do take this option though, it is as well to take an extra pair of shoes with you as the ones you wear when you cross the park behind the Rink End may well fall foul (literally) to one of the delightful packages that half the town's dog population seem to have left there.

**CAPACITY:** Stands: 4,008; Terrace: 3,263;
Total: 7,271

**AWAY FANS:** Rink End: 741
The seats in the Rink End offer a fair amount of leg room, although the height between each row of seats isn't that impressive and the fact that there are pillars in the stand can also obscure the view. A better bet can be to try the Cyril Knowles Stand which offers a great (and hassle-free) along-the-pitch view at the same price (mind you, at least the Rink End doesn't suffer from blinding you with the setting sun which can happen in the CKS).

**DISABLED FACILITIES:** There are 14 places available in the CKS with admission being charged at £5 for both disabled supporters and their helpers. This is another area where Victoria Park has come on leaps and bounds in the last couple of seasons. The old 'nuclear fallout shelter' at the Rink End of the ground has been boarded up and now proudly announces 'Fibber McGinty's Irish Bar' (to be honest it makes a much better advertising hoarding than place to watch a footie match in). The other big advantage is that the club has recognised that (gasp) disabled fans actually do need to go to the toilet on occasion and there are excellent facilities available.

**PROGRAMME:** £1.50
Went up 15% last season. One of the (many) programmes that I found just indifferent. Buy it, flick through it for five minutes before the game and again at half-time, then stick it in your back pocket and forget it.

**FANZINES:**
_Monkey Business_       £1
_Monkey Business_ is still going strong. You can pick up a copy from the club shop and, although you do have to pay for it separately from the programme, you are not likely to grow old in either of the queues. _MB_ ranges from the often brilliant to the usually good, although there are (very) rare dire bits to it. It tends to have a few press cuttings in it but steers clear of these simply being match reports. Excellent gallows humour, so if you like a good hanging then this could well be for you.

One great thing about the fanzine is that it has a huge advertising hoarding in about the centre of the field which you can see the home team occasionally glimpsing up at and — depending on how well they are playing — either cursing the fact that they know they are being watched and are going to get a slating in the next edition or thanking God that the team has got grass root supporters who are prepared to put their hands in their pockets to keep the club in business.

# TRAVEL

## NEAREST RAILWAY STATION:

Hartlepool Church Street (0191 232 6262 — Newcastle Enquiries)

## BUS: Hartlepool bus station (01429 523555)

## BY CAR:

**NORTH:** A19(T) then left onto the A179 (signposted Hart and Hartlepool). Continue along Hart Road towards the town centre until you reach a crossroads between Hart Road, Middleton Road and Raby Road; turn right into Raby Road. As you drive down Raby Road you will see a swimming pool; 300yd past this turn left into Museum Road, and then left again into Clarence Road. The ground is on your left.

**SOUTH/WEST:** A689 into Hartlepool town centre. You will see a shopping centre and 100yd past this there is a large intersection. Continue straight past the new marina development (on your right with Asda on your left). Left at the following roundabout and then left at the traffic lights onto Clarence Road.

**PARKING:** There is a car park on the Raby Road side of the ground and a large car park by the shopping centre. Also plenty of on-street parking is available.

Whatever you do, don't park at the Asda supermarket by the ground as this is for customers only (and they have patrols to check on you as well).

# FUTURE DEVELOPMENTS

There is a Conference & Leisure Centre being built on the Millhouse Stand side of the ground and it is likely that, while construction work is undertaken, this stand will be closed, meaning that the capacity at the ground will be reduced to 5,000 until February 1999 when the work is (provisionally) due to be completed. This work was initially due to be undertaken last season. However,

the takeover of the club in the summer of 1997 by Increased Oil Recovery (IOR) meant that there has been a one season delay in this. One change that occurred in 1997-8 was that the dog track next to the ground has been demolished.

# OTHER INFORMATION

The story of the people of the town hanging a monkey, which was washed ashore following a shipwreck during the Napoleonic wars, is fairly well known (although this obviously should not stop visiting supporters from shouting 'you hung the monkey' whenever they are in the town).

The Victoria Suite at the ground is for members only. For watering holes, either wander into the town centre (Churchill's and The Park off Park Road are normally quite popular with away fans) or try the Mill House on Raby Road. The Jackson's Landing Marina offers a decent choice but as it is on the sea front (as tends to be the case with marinas) this might not be too appealing in the bleak midwinter.

There is a lack of two major facilities around the ground — and even on first glance in the town centre — namely a chip shop and a national bookies. The first of these faults is somewhat remedied by the fact that the pies inside the ground — despite a strange flat looking appearance — have improved beyond all recognition recently and are now hot and tasty as well as standing up to the ultimate fan's test of being strong enough to — if you so desire — lift the lid off so you can put ketchup in them. The hot drinks also got much better last season (possibly down to the removal of the half pound of dust that you always used to seem to get at the bottom of your cup) and the beef drink was warm and helped keep (a bit) of the chill out.

*Total Football* Experience Rating: 87

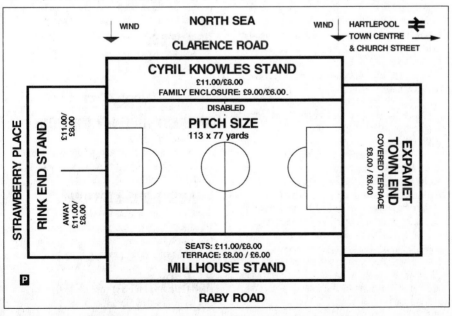

NORTH SEA

WIND → 

WIND | HARTLEPOOL ✈ TOWN CENTRE & CHURCH STREET

CLARENCE ROAD

**CYRIL KNOWLES STAND**
£11.00/£8.00
FAMILY ENCLOSURE: £9.00/£6.00

DISABLED

**PITCH SIZE**
113 x 77 yards

STRAWBERRY PLACE

**RINK END STAND**
£11.00/£8.00

AWAY £11.00/£8.00

**EXPAMET TOWN END**
COVERED TERRACE £8.00 / £6.00

SEATS: £11.00/£8.00
TERRACE: £8.00 / £6.00
**MILLHOUSE STAND**

P

**RABY ROAD**

# HUDDERSFIELD TOWN

**ADDRESS:** The Alfred McAlpine Stadium, Huddersfield HD1 6PX

**TELEPHONE No:** 01484 484100

**TICKET OFFICE:** 01484 484123

**FAX:** 01484 484101

**CLUBCALL:** 0891 12 16 35

**WEB SITE:** http://home.clara.net/a.r.aedy/htfc/index.html (unofficial)

**NICKNAME:** The Terriers

**RECORD ATTENDANCE:**
67,037 v Arsenal FA Cup 6th 27 February 1932 (L 1-2) At Alfred McAlpine Stadium: 19,600 Rugby League Regal Trophy Final 28 January 1995; 18,820 v Middlesbrough Nationwide League Div 1 26 December 1997 (L 0-1)

**CLUB COLOURS:**
**HOME:** Shirts: Blue & White stripes; Shorts: White; Socks: White with Blue hoops
**AWAY**: Shirts: Red & Black stripes; Shorts: Black; Socks: Black

**CLUB SPONSOR:** Panasonic

**MANUFACTURERS:** Pony

## GROUND INFO

It has been said that familiarity breeds contempt, but even now as the Sir Alfred McAlpine Stadium enters its fourth season of existence, the very sight of it, with its ladybird shaped stand roofing, brings on feelings of wonderment. Perhaps this is even more true now that the North Stand has been constructed, which gives the stadium a feeling of completeness.

The ground (which was designated Building of the Year in 1995) was not only the first to comply with the Taylor Report in terms of being all-seated but also to embrace the spirit of change and rebirth that the game has gone through since the mid-1980s.

Having praised the Ground, it should also be said that it is not perfect. For example the first few rows of seats are afforded little protection from the rain by the roof and also, because the club opted for futuristic floodlights in the corners of the ground, whilst you get a good footie feel about the place, you are also slightly exposed to the whistling Yorkshire wind. Still, it's very pleasing to the eye, great acoustically to get a racket going in and something very different to some of the roofless warehouses that have gone up over the last decade. Added to which, the admission price of £12.00 for Adults and £6.00 for concessions are exceptional value for the facilities offered.

**CAPACITY:** Stands: 24,000 (wef August 1998) Terrace: Nil

**AWAY FANS:** South Stand: 4,037; Total: 4,037
It's good to report that the club has not got 'above itself' at the new stadium; the staff are still friendly and helpful and visitors get excellent concessions.

**DISABLED FACILITIES:** There are spaces at various parts of the ground. The best vantage point is from a specially constructed raised platform which seats 16 wheelchair-bound supporters and helpers. Other than that there are 16 designated spaces for disabled supporters (+16 helpers) in the Gardner Merchant (South) stand for away supporters, plus 32 spaces (+32 helpers) in the Lower Tier of the Lawrence Batley Stand. This stand also offers 13 spaces (+13 helpers) with match commentaries for the visually impaired. All areas have good access to facilities. Pre-booking is required only for the raised platform (get in touch with the club at least two weeks beforehand for this area). There are designated parking facilities available at the ground. Ground admission is £7 for both wheelchair-bound supporters and helpers. One thing to be aware of, is that if you are going to the Away section, access is via a fairly steep incline.

**PROGRAMME:** £1.80
One of the most improved programmes last season. It has a good visitor's section and plenty of general interest articles. A minor point was that on the 'Medical Man' page there was a graphic picture of an operation on an ankle ligament. This was definitely not what I wanted to see as I tucked into my meat and potato — mind you, this was less disturbing than Mel Booth of the Examiner's page. Mel writes an excellent column but the leering photo of him that accompanies it is frightening.

**FANZINES:**
| | |
|---|---|
| *Hanging On The Telephone* | 50p |
| *A Slice of Kilner Pie* | 50p |

## TRAVEL

**NEAREST RAILWAY STATION:**
Huddersfield (01484 533481)
The stadium is a bit of a trek from the town centre and the railway station. If you are walking allow yourself a good 20min to get from one to the other.

**NEAREST BUS STATION:**
Huddersfield Central (01484 545444 — Bus Info)
The 201, 202, 203 and 207 drop off on Leeds Road (5min walk) and there are stadium specials (330, 331) which drop off at the Mac itself.

**BY CAR:**
**NORTH/EAST/WEST:** Leave the M60 at J25 and take the A644 and A62 following the signs for

Huddersfield. About a mile away from the town centre you will suddenly see the stadium on the left. Turn either into Bradley Mills Road and then right after 0.25 mile into Kilner Road, or take the following left into St Andrews Way and left after 0.25 mile into Stadium Way.

**SOUTH:** Leave the M1 at J38 and follow the A637/A642 (very windy roads with big drops just feet away so be careful in bad weather) to Huddersfield; at the ring road follow the signs for the A62 (Leeds). Once on the A62 continue until you see at least two car prangs which means you are getting very close to it. Then turn right into St Andrews Road and left into Stadium Road, or next right into Bradley Mills Road and right into Kilner Road.

The fact that on the A62 there are permanent snow warning lights and the council seems to undertake annual maintenance on these in about mid-August in order that they aren't caught out by an early snap of bad weather are reasons enough for you to be warned the roads can get very tricky in winter.

**PARKING:** There is ample car parking at the ground and in the side streets around it, although departing from these can get a bit hairy, and you may wish to park on one of the other roads off the A62 and walk to the ground. Although this will probably take you 10-15min each way you could end up saving yourself a lot of time come 4.45pm/9.30pm.

## FUTURE DEVELOPMENTS

The final bits of scaffolding should come down from the North Stand during the summer and the ground will be fully completed for the 1998-9 season.

## OTHER INFORMATION

There are loads of pubs in the town centre. One of the favourites for away fans is the Head Of Steam by the (very impressive) railway station. If you like sports history, then pop in at the George Hotel, which was the birthplace of Rugby League. Other than the Minstrel, which is renowned amongst some footie fans as being a rough/unfriendly pub, anywhere will do. However, as these are all a 15-20min walk from the ground, then you may prefer Ricky's on the Leeds Road (older fans may know this as the Wagon & Horses). It's friendly and they serve a decent pint. Inside the ground away fans can get John Smiths or Fosters at £1.90 a pint (from an uncovered and crowded concourse). There are also a couple of serveries which serve a tasty and hot meat and potato (but very potatoey) pie which comes not only in a silver dish but also on a paper plate. If you have a sweeter tooth you can stock up on a myriad of toffees and chocolates from the mobile sweet wagon. There are also betting facilities available in all parts of the ground.

On the way into the ground there are a couple of weird signs, the one saying 'Ticket Touting is a criminal offence' is at best optimistic (1st Division relegation strugglers not being renowned as being a place where you'll hear the time worn phrase 'I'll buy any spares').

Finally, the scoreboard at the ground is a good reflection of what is good and bad about the state of football today. On the good side it flashes up latest scores (although as it is behind away fans the majority of them will probably miss this). However, on the other side of the coin it is one of those that insists on flashing up 'dead ball....Goal kick' (with a picture of a boot kicking a ball in case you were unsure of what this meant) at every available opportunity.

This remains a great day out, if you haven't been yet, go.

*Total Football* **Experience Rating: 83**

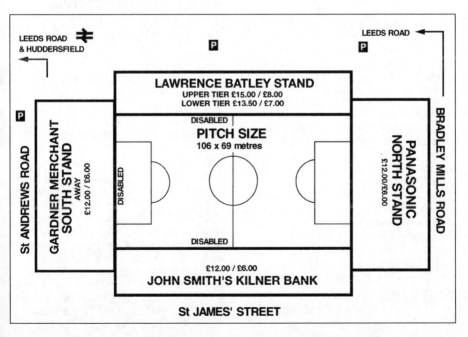

# HULL CITY

**ADDRESS:** Boothferry Park
Boothferry Road
Hull HU4 6EU

**TELEPHONE No:** 01482 327200

**TICKET OFFICE:** 01482 327200

**FAX:** 01482 565752

**WEB SITE:**

http://www.hullcity.demon.co.uk/
Brilliant web-site and a genuinely good bloke.

**E-MAIL:**

andymeds@hullcity.demon.co.uk.

**NICKNAME:** The Tigers

**RECORD ATTENDANCE:** 55,019 v Man
Utd FA Cup 6th 26 February 1949 (L 0-1)

**CLUB COLOURS:**
**HOME:** Shirts: Amber; Shorts: Black; Socks: Amber
**AWAY:** Shirts: White; Shorts: White; Socks: White

**KIT SPONSORS:** tba

**MANUFACTURERS:** Olympic

## GROUND INFO

Away fans have an allocation of 530 seats in the West Stand which are basic, but OK. The club does not encourage visitors to go in the South Stand, but if that is where you desire to put your weary body then you are unlikely to get too much grief.

The away terrace divides into two sections — the North Terrace which is a fairly narrow strip behind the goal that backs on to a KwikSave supermarket, and the North East Section which sweeps up around the corner and joins (surprise, surprise) onto the old East Stand. The view from this section isn't particularly good and you are uncovered as well; the wind and the rain just seem to bounce off the supermarket wall, so you end up getting chilled and soaked from all directions at once.

It has to be said that the club does offer excellent concessions to both home and visiting supporters and it must be tearing its hair out at the fact that the locals do not come in significant numbers to support their side.

I've got to say (and it may just be me being over sensitive here) the club seems to be a lot more insular than it was a couple of years back and, where once you could be sure of a friendly welcome, a few of the stewards and other officials seem a bit anti-away supporters.

**CAPACITY:** Stands: 5,495; Terrace: 7,501;
Total: 12,996

**AWAY FANS:** West Stand: 530;
North Terrace: 1,560; Total: 2,090
Given the dire financial straits that the club found itself in

(again) last season, it is both uplifting and incredible to report that it still offers fantastic concessions to away fans. At £7 an adult and £3 for children for both home and away supporters.

**DISABLED FACILITIES:** Wheelchair facilities for 15 fans are available in between the South and East Stands; bookings are not always necessary depending on the match, but better safe than sorry. There are match commentaries available, and these should be pre-booked, as should a parking space which the club will organise for you. Disabled fans are admitted free of charge, with helpers paying £7.

**PROGRAMME:** £1.50
A run-of-the-mill affair which you can take or leave as you please.

**FANZINES:**

| | |
|---|---|
| Tiger Rag | £1 |
| Amber Nectar | 80p |

Tiger Rag is an excellent fanzine following in a long line of worthy publications (Hull, Hell and Happiness, Look Back In Amber and Cloud Seven to name but three). The only trouble was that it wasn't being sold on my last visit (and at times like these the fans need to keep this excellent mouthpiece going). I did obtain the first copy of Amber Nectar, which was a bit of a curate's egg, in that, at 24 pages, it isn't big enough and, what is more, there was quite a bit of evidence of space filling. On the positive side though there were occasional flashes of anger and humour that hit the spot, and you get the feeling that it will improve as it finds its feet.

## TRAVEL

**NEAREST RAILWAY STATION:**
Hull Paragon (1.75 miles) (01482 223710)

**NEAREST BUS STATION:**
Central bus station (01482 27146)
The bus station is right by Hull Paragon. The best bus to catch is a 66 or any bus heading towards Hessle, of which there are three an hour, and which drop you opposite the ground. (Failing that, a No 2 will do the trick.) There are extra buses back to the station on match days, and these pick up from the away fans/supermarket end of the ground.

**BY CAR:**
**NORTH:** A1 to A1079 Hull turn-off. Follow City Centre signs until you reach the A63. Head towards Leeds on the A63 till you reach Anlaby Road. A mile down Anlaby Road you will reach a roundabout, the first exit from which takes you onto Boothferry Road for the ground.
**SOUTH:** M1, M18, M60. Leave the M62 and turn onto the A63 (signposted Hull). About a mile further on there is a large hotel which serves a decent pint, and football fans provided they aren't too unkempt. Pop in here and if your team have travelled up on the night before you may well bump into them in the reception area (or bar!). By the hotel the road forks in two — take the left fork. About

half a mile further on is the Humber Bridge roundabout. Take the first exit and 1.5 miles down the road is a roundabout, the first exit of which is Boothferry Road.

**WEST:** M60, then as south.

**EAST:** If you can drive across the North Sea you can find your own way to the ground.

## PARKING:
There is a car park by the ground, which belongs to the club; it is, however, pass only.

Two local schools — Francis Askew and Eastfield — are utilised to provide car parks. Each are about 5min walk from the ground and are signposted.

In addition the B&Q car park which is right by the Fina garage and just past the ground is a popular haunt. There is also plenty of street parking.

## FUTURE DEVELOPMENTS

In July 1997 the club announced that it was going to move in with Hull Sharks while Boothferry Park was turned into a 25,000 all-seater stadium. A little over a month later the club was taken over by David Lloyd (of tennis rather than cricket fame) and these plans were put on hold. It is understood that the club still intends to rebuild Boothferry Park, with the football ground being the heart of a leisure complex which will include a tennis centre, swimming pool, gym facilities etc (maybe the supermarket will even get a delicatessen). However, no-one was able to (or perhaps wanted to) give me specific details as to the 'when' and 'how' this would take place, so it is very much a case of watch this space (though I doubt too much will occur in 1998).

## OTHER INFORMATION

The Three Tuns used to promote itself as home fans only, although nowadays you should be able to get in.

If you walk towards the city from the ground you will come across the Silver Cod, which has got a bit of a bad reputation. The only time I've ever been there a few eyebrows were raised at my non 'Ull accent but I didn't get any grief (although I wasn't wearing an away shirt). The Fiveways, on the A63 as you come into Hull, is very welcoming to away fans and serves a belting pint; it makes for an excellent meeting place. Alternatively go into the city centre where there are a rake of places to eat and drink. The Black Boy — one of the oldest pubs in England I think I remember being told — rates a particular mention, though do remember to leave yourself time to get back to the ground. If you go into the centre of Hull you'll find all the usual suspects for burgers, pizzas and fried chicken, although I have yet to find a brilliant chippie. Nearer to the ground, the choice becomes a lot smaller (it can be as well to pop into the supermarket to buy yourself a snack). Alternatively hang on till you get inside the ground because they do serve some excellent grub, not least of all the steak & kidney and the meat & potato pies which both seemed to contain all of the ingredients suggested by their name. They are served piping hot (and believe you me you'll appreciate this) and can be washed down with an excellent cup of Bovril to complete the effect.

Tragically, no longer does the club take to the field to the anthemic strains of 'Tiger Feet' by Mud. In fact there now doesn't seem to be any one tune that belongs to the club and it has been unashamedly flirting with several tracks namely the totally predictable 'Eye of the Tiger', Gloria Gaynor's 'I Will Survive' (which celebrates the fact the club fought off a potential winding up order from the Inland Revenue) and my own favourite 'Tiger Rag' — yes, forget about your 'This is Anfield' signs, a bit of the old Scott Joplin, now there is something to put the wind up the opposition.

*Total Football* **Experience Rating: 51**

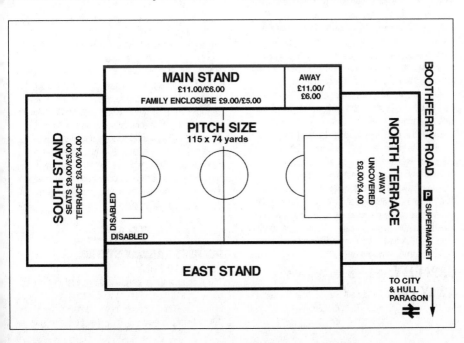

MAIN STAND
£11.00/£6.00
FAMILY ENCLOSURE £9.00/£5.00

AWAY
£11.00/
£6.00

PITCH SIZE
115 x 74 yards

SOUTH STAND
SEATS £9.00/£5.00
TERRACE £8.00/£4.00

DISABLED
DISABLED

NORTH TERRACE
AWAY
UNCOVERED
£8.00/£4.00

BOOTHFERRY ROAD
P SUPERMARKET

EAST STAND

TO CITY
& HULL
PARAGON

# IPSWICH TOWN

**ADDRESS:** Portman Road
Ipswich
Suffolk IP1 2DA
**TELEPHONE No:** 01473 400500
**TICKET OFFICE:** 01473 400555
**FAX:** 01473 400040
**SOCCERLINE:** 0839 66 44 88
**SOCCERLINE:** http://www.itfc.co.uk/
(official)
**NICKNAME:** Town
**RECORD ATTENDANCE:**
38,010 v Leeds FA Cup 6th 8  March 1975 (D 0-0)
**CLUB COLOURS:**
**HOME:** Shirts: Royal Blue; Shorts: White; Socks: Blue
**AWAY:** Shirts: Orange; Shorts: Navy;
Socks: Navy with Orange tops
**KIT SPONSORS:** Greene King
**MANUFACTURERS:** Punch
Despite appearing at strategic points on the kit, it can be confirmed that the word 'Punch' refers to the Suffolk Punch (the creature on the Ipswich crest which is in truth — and perhaps a little harshly considering the quality of the current side — a carthorse) and is not an instruction.

## GROUND INFO
I have always found the atmosphere at the ground to be noisy but relaxed and, if you don't manage to bag one of the tickets for the visitors' section, you can generally be fairly comfortable, so long as you act in a reasonable manner, in any of the other sections of Portman Road. The only problem is that with the club's improved performances last season, it became harder to pick up a ticket for any part of the ground, not just the visitors' section.

The ticket prices at Ipswich are generally very fair (and the club offers brilliant concessions for both home and away supporters).

The club is constantly looking at ways it can attract people to the ground and last season it was having a ladies' day when (and I bet you can work this out for yourself) it was trying to tempt women through the turnstiles. However, one of the ways it was looking at doing this was by offering John Wark as a slave for the day in the raffle — which I would have thought would have had women running a mile in the opposite direction rather than risk having the veteran Town man coming round to 'sort out' their house.

**CAPACITY:** Stands: 22,589; Terrace: Nil
**AWAY FANS:** Cobbold Stand Blocks Sections
V1: 769; V2: 830; A 820;
Total: 2,419

Although the ground always looks very tidy from outside and when you see it on TV, in truth once you're inside it is a bit of a different thing. You are tightly packed into seats and, because the rake of the stand is fairly shallow, it takes a lucky (or exceedingly tall) person to see the near corner of the ground. Added to which, it always seems that the seat number I'm allocated on my ticket is missing which means, if your club has taken a good number of fans with it, then you can spend an irritating amount of time trying to find out where you are meant to be.

**DISABLED FACILITIES:** There are 50 spaces in the Lower Pioneer Stand which are divided 40 for home, and 10 for away supporters. You must have a helper with you for 'safety reasons'. Pre-booking is essential, as for a match commentary.

Admission prices are £12 for helpers (£8.00 concessions), but free for disabled fans. No car parking facilities are available at the ground.

Contact Paul Murray at the club at least two weeks in advance of the fixture to book your seat/commentary.

**PROGRAMME:** £1.80
This seems to be printed on very thin paper, it is a reasonable read as well and the club has obviously invested time and money into content rather than style which does tend to make a nice change.

**FANZINES:**

| | |
|---|---|
| *Dribble* | 50p |
| *Those Were The Days* | 70p |
| *A Load Of Cobbolds* | 50p |
| *Without A Care In The World* | 50p |
| *Score!* | 50p |

Generally Ipswich doesn't have what would be described as fervent support (although I appreciate all Town fans will beg to differ with this), but instead of banding together, zealous supporters have split into a number of factions which means plenty of fanzines but no cohesion. Each of the aforementioned has got good points about it, but it's hard to pick one that stands out above the rest. Perhaps a merging of titles would see a 'must buy' arise from the current situation, although, this being said, *Those Were The Days* does incorporate *Blue,* a previous Town publication, but it would be difficult to say that this had radically improved. It's also worth noting that *Score!* appeared just a couple of seasons back, so even with all these titles someone feels that there is a Town publication gap that needs filling.

## TRAVEL
**NEAREST RAILWAY STATION:**
Ipswich (01473 693396)
This is about a 10min walk from the ground although be warned, the Station Hotel just outside has lured in many innocent travelling fans who have ended up staying in for that 'one last pint before 3.00'. In their befuddled state the

fans forget that getting into your seat at Portman Road is not easy at the best of times, never mind with a last minute surge and needing to go to the toilets (go before you leave the pub) and have missed the first 10-15min of the game.

## NEAREST BUS STATION:
Ipswich Buses (01473 250500)

## BY CAR:
**NORTH/WEST:** Take the A14 (ex-A45) and follow the signs for 'Ipswich West Only'. As you come to Ipswich you will see a large Post House hotel by which there is a set of traffic lights; go straight over at these and then turn right into West End Road. Turn right into Portmans Walk and the ground is 0.25 miles on the right.

**SOUTH:** A12, then take the A1214 following signs for Ipswich West until you get to the lights by the Post House hotel, then as north.

**PARKING:** There are car parks in both Portmans Walk and Portman Road, plus on-street parking in the vicinity of the ground.

Any trip to Ipswich is notable for the hospitality of the people, but maybe this is best illustrated by the very friendly girls you see on and around Portmans Walk, who will peer into your car and wave in a jovial manner at you especially if you are a single male and are going to a night game!

## FUTURE DEVELOPMENTS
There was a major overhaul of the 'access system' (that's 'turnstiles' to you and me) in 1997-8 but nothing major is planned for the current season.

## OTHER INFORMATION
The nearest pub to the ground is the Drum & Monkey on Princes Street, which is normally a popular haunt for visiting supporters. This is a pub I always end up having a beer in, but to be honest, if it wasn't so close to the ground, I'd probably not bother. If you wander further afield then for the most part the pubs you will come across will be friendly and amenable, although as with any town there are always one or two to be avoided. If you're looking for food then there are quite a few burger vans around outside (although there are some far better fish and chip shops in the centre of town). The food inside Portman Road changed in 1997-8 with the introduction of a new catering outfit and, it has to be said that, in my opinion, the move was not for the better. Where the club used to serve cheap hot edible food, the focus now seems to be on tricking customers into buying rubber burgers and flat coke at top of the range prices (a burger and coke left me with less than £2 change out of the fiver that was snatched from my hands). At first I wondered whether I was being fussy but when I saw a bloke of about 30st tossing his pie on the deck I realised that, if this bloke wasn't happy about eating what he was offered, then something definitely wasn't right.

The bleakest part of any trip to Ipswich occurs if you need to go to the toilets. If parts of Portman Road are showing their age then the toilets have not only gone past their sell by date, but are now turning mouldy and lurking at the back of the fridge with a rotten tomato!

Despite a few obvious shortcomings, a trip to Portman Road is, on the vast majority of occasions, a pleasurable experience. While — obviously — there are police and stewards at the club, they have a very laid back attitude and tend to let you get on with your own thing; in fact the only time you'll probably notice them is if you move around while the game is in progress as they seem fairly intent on hanging around in the aisle, watching the game and, as you squeeze past them, their irritation at having their afternoon interrupted may be transmitted via a rather loud tut or exasperated sigh.

*Total Football* **Experience Rating: 75**

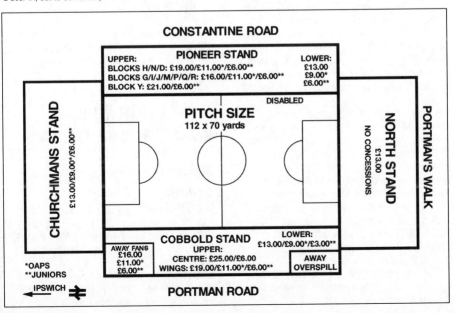

# LEEDS UNITED

**ADDRESS:** Elland Road
Leeds LS11 0ES

**TELEPHONE No:** 0113 226 6000

**TICKET OFFICE:** 0113 226 1000

**FAX:** 0113 226 6050

**CLUBCALL:** 0891 12 11 80

The ticket office number is for credit card bookings only, and Leeds United Ticket Call (0891 12 16 80) is the number the club ask you to dial for enquiries (yes I know this is a premium rate number, and you'll have to wait ages to hear the bit you want to know, but for goodness' sake don't be so selfish…).

**WEBSITE:** www.lufc.co.uk

**NICKNAME:** United or The Peacocks or The Whites

**RECORD ATTENDANCE:** 52,892 v
Sunderland FA Cup 5th Rep 15 March 1967 (D 1-1)

**CLUB COLOURS:**
**HOME:** Shirts: White; Shorts: White; Socks: White
**AWAY:** Shirts: Blue and Yellow halves;
Shorts: Blue; Socks: Yellow

**CLUB SPONSORS:** Packard Bell

**MANUFACTURERS:** Puma

## GROUND INFO

The ground looks quite impressive from the outside, but once in the away section you find that there are five pillars within a very short space, thus pretty much guaranteeing a restricted view wherever you sit. The East Stand has a shopping mall and plenty of eating and watering holes, the longest cantilever in Europe, and is a very good place to go if you're a neutral (or are suffering from laryngitis and won't be able to cheer your team on). If you stick to the Lower Tier, as it is a heck of a climb to the top, then you should note that this is a dedicated family enclosure.

Many of the fans feel that the developed stadium lacks the passion of the old ground and have rechristened it 'Bland Road'. This is true to a degree, but only to the extent that if you were a Christian in Roman times then getting thrown to five lions was better than getting chucked in with six. The club has said that it is looking at ways it can develop the 'audible aspects' of the matchday, but to be honest it sounded kind enough to me.

1997-8 saw Leeds cut down from a four category pricing structure to one where there were just two categories. One of these had the audacity to be called 'premier' — they're all Premier games, mate. If you want an accurate description try — in my opinion — 'extortionate' and 'even more extortionate'; £22.50 for away fans for a 'Premier' game is nothing more than a bad joke for a cramped corner of the ground.

**CAPACITY:** Stands: 40,000; Terrace: Nil

**AWAY FANS:** South East Corner: 1,800
The area allocated is dependent on the number of away supporters. On occasions both sections of the South Stand will be allocated — 3,900 spaces.

Bizarrely, as you go in you will be given a letter requesting that you stay behind after the game to allow the surrounding roads to be cleared. I'd have thought a tannoy announcement would have sufficed.

**DISABLED FACILITIES:** There are spaces for 40 wheelchair-bound supporters and 40 helpers along with 80 ambulant spaces in the West Stand Paddock. In the North Stand there are spaces for 25 wheelchair-bound supporters and helpers along with 58 ambulant spaces. The South West Corner offers accommodation for 34 wheelchair-bound supporters and helpers, 30 blind supporters and helpers and 13 ambulant. Radio coverage is available for the blind. Disabled supporters have access to their own lounge. Escort tickets cost £10.50 (both categories).

The good news is that disabled supporters are admitted free no matter what the category of match.

**PROGRAMME:** £2.00
Improved markedly in 1997-8. A bit of thought has been given to the away section and, apart from all the obvious bits and pieces, there are some nices touches, such as one page articles comparing one player from each side.

**FANZINES:**

| | |
|---|---|
| The Hanging Sheep | 60p |
| The Square Ball | £1.50 |
| Till The World Stops | 50p |
| We Are Leeds | £1 |
| To Ell & Back | £1 |

A fair bunch of fanzines, the pick of which is probably The Square Ball. This is a thoughtful and interesting read which manages to take the piss out of others in more original ways than most.

## TRAVEL

**NEAREST RAILWAY STATION:** Leeds City (0113 244 8133)

**BUS:** Swinegate bus station (0113 245 1601)

**BY CAR:**
**NORTH:** A58 or A61 into the city centre. Follow the signs for, then get onto, the M621. After 1.5 miles on the motorway leave at the junction with the A643, and take this road at the exit roundabout for Elland Road and the ground.
**SOUTH:** M1 to J47. At J47 take the M621. Continue for one mile to the junction with the A6110. Leave the motorway and take the A6110 for Elland Road.

**EAST:** A63 or A64 into the city centre. Pick up signs for the M621, then as north.

**WEST:** M60, M621 to junction with the A643, and then as north.

**PARKING:** There is parking for 1,000 vehicles opposite the ground in Wesley Street but this fills up very quickly on matchdays. As the attendants cram as many cars as they can in the available space, it can take ages to escape after the match. A second car park can be found at the bottom of Wesley Street by the shopping centre. The club says that, in conjunction with the council, they can offer 3,500 to 4,000 car parking spaces around the stadium at £2/car. If you want to get away from the ground either leave at half-time or forget it. It is as well to wait 20-25min to let the congestion clear. If you do join the mad scrum at the end of the game, then don't expect any of the local drivers to give way or pause a moment to let you through a gap.

NB: The good people of Yorkshire seem obsessed by certain names, and thus you get Noster Grove, Noster Hill, Noster Place etc, all adjacent to each other. So make sure you pay attention to the second part of the name of the street you park.

## FUTURE DEVELOPMENTS

No major projects, but the club has recently been awarded the contract by the council to build a sports and leisure arena on the stadium complex, likely to be integrated on the west side. Disruption should be minimal during rebuilding.

## OTHER INFORMATION

If you're a visitor it can be as well to avoid the Peacock which is just outside the ground, and instead make your way to the numerous pubs in the city centre that serve a hand-pulled pint of Tetleys. Alternatively, the Woodman which is out towards the M1/M60 about two miles from

the ground isn't bad. The United Fisheries just down the road from the Peacock does a fine fish and chips, but there are massive queues from about two hours before kick-off. Unless you are of Yorkshire descent or have a very strong stomach, avoid the local delicacy of pie and peas — the pie is pork, and served hot, which for some reason I find fairly appalling. If you don't care about your teeth, there is a mobile van which dispenses a fine array of sweeties near to the ground. Inside Elland Road the away catering facilities have been upgraded, and you can now get a beer with your grub.

It is fair to say that the stewards have one of the worse reputations in the country. I'm afraid in my experience it is easy to see why; their attitude towards away fans is deplorable, and if you've got a problem either put up with it, or sort it out yourself, because you won't get much help from these people.

It has to be said that a trip to Elland Road is slightly less daunting than a few years back, although it remains one of those away trip that tests your loyalty (and, at £22.50 a ticket, your wallet as well). The majority of the fans are OK and, while they may not welcome visiting supporters like long lost brothers, they adopt a live and let live attitude. However, this is not the case with everyone and caution is still recommended. The Munich 58 chants and merchandise still seem, incredibly, as popular as ever and although the club seeks to stop this, the way it goes about it is not always successful. A good example of this is that last season the Chairman 'pleaded for an end to the sickening anti-Manchester United airport song in the wake of Leeds United's miraculous escape at Stansted'. He should insist on an end to this, not because Leeds nearly had an accident themselves, but because it is simply not acceptable behaviour (and no, before you write in, I am not a Man Utd supporter, I am just a football fan).

*Total Football* **Experience Rating: 68**

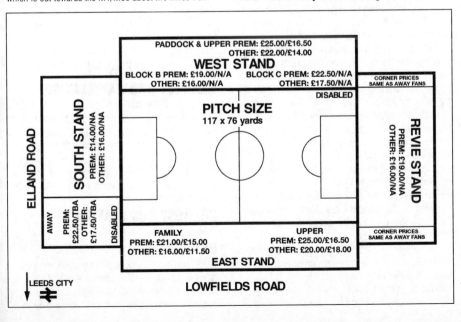

# LEICESTER CITY

**ADDRESS:** City Stadium
Filbert Street
Leicester LE2 7FL

**TELEPHONE No:** 0116 291 5000

**TICKET OFFICE:** 0116 291 5296

**FAX:** 0116 247 0585

**CLUBCALL:** 0891 12 11 85

**WEB SITE:** www.lcfc.co.uk

**NICKNAME:** The Foxes

**RECORD ATTENDANCE:**
47,298 v Spurs FA Cup 5th 18 February 1928 (L 0-3)

## CLUB COLOURS:
**HOME:** Shirts: Blue; Shorts: White; Socks: Blue
**AWAY:** Shirts: White; Shorts: Blue;
Socks: White

**KIT SPONSORS:** Walkers Crisps

**MANUFACTURERS:** Fox Leisure
This is the club's own brand and the range covers a variety of garments including a baseball cap which is popular amongst away fans. (Tell anyone you're going to the ground and the reaction tends to be 'Leicester? Wear the fox hat!?')

## GROUND INFO

Filbert Street is quite a weird ground with each stand being a different height. This means that although the stadium has been to a large extent redeveloped, there is still character about the place and fans can discover their 'own' area, ranging from the magnificent Carling Stand, to the North Stand which looks like the crossing bridge at a motorway service station with seats underneath.

Away fans go in the East Stand which is basically terracing with seats on it. Because the steps on which each row of seats are fixed are not very tall this does tend to mean you can spend a lot of time staring at the back of the neck of the person in front. The view is also not helped by the fact that the seats are low compared to the ground which means, in the first few rows, you are almost looking up at the action. There are pillars from row H backwards which add to the fun.

Still, at least the admission price of £15/£18 is amongst the cheapest you'll come across in the Premier League (as an away fan you'll come across much worse views than the East Stand at Filbert Street and probably be charged 50% more for the privilege) and the £7.50/£9 concession is second to none.

The home fans in the Shanks & McEwan South Stand will let you know they are there and sometimes can get a little over-excited, but at least the club has had the foresight to put a plastic sheet between the two stands with green netting at the top which prevents any clowns

from tossing their loose change at you.

**CAPACITY:** Stands: 20,000; Terrace: Nil

**AWAY FANS:** East Stand Block U: 892;
East Stand Block T: 1,209;
Total: 2,101

If there is sufficient demand from away supporters they will also be allocated 1,174 seats in the South Stand.

**DISABLED FACILITIES:** There are 62 spaces available at the ground, 34 in the Carling Stand, 20 in the Shanks & McEwan South Stand Lower Tier, and 17 in the East Stand Block T for away fans. The standards of all these facilities are pretty good. Admission is free for disabled supporters and £15.00 for helpers. The club requires you to pre-book. The club has now also introduced five headsets, which are available for the use of visually impaired fans. Car parking is only available at Filbert Street but only for members of Leicester City Disabled Association.

**PROGRAMME:** £2.00
Still the best in the league, 56 pages thick with a great visitors' section and plenty of general interest articles to keep you going. On the other side of the Leicester City pull out poster is even a visiting player for you to take home and stick on your wall... A copy of this should be sent to every Premier League ground in the country to prove what can be done if you want to.

## FANZINES:
| | |
|---|---|
| When You're Smiling | £1 |
| The Fox | £1 |
| Where's The Money Gone | £1 |
| Foxed Off | £1 |

*The Fox* was the only one I saw being sold on my last visit. It's a so-so read but, for visiting supporters, doesn't offer too much (it's mostly diary and adverts for old Leicester replica tops).

## TRAVEL
### NEAREST RAILWAY STATION:
Leicester (0116 248 1000)
Incredibly, when friends of mine arrived there on a normal service, all the blokes who got off (regardless of age or whether they were wearing colours) were lined up against a wall by the police and videoed, while they were given the gentle reminder 'Right we got you on tape now, any trouble and your nicked' (only with a lot more swear words in it). Dreadful.

### NEAREST BUS STATION:
St Margaret's bus station (0116 251 1411)

### BY CAR:
**NORTH:** A46 through Leicester city centre following the signs for Rugby. This will bring you onto Welford Road. (Don't be tricked into following fans who appear to be travelling in a different direction to you, as they are

likely to be going to see Leicester Rugby Union Club whose stadium is on Welford Road.) After a while you will see a cemetery on your left. Turn right by the cemetery into Almond Road, then right at the T-junction into Aylestone Road, and immediately left into Brazil Street. At the bottom of Brazil Street turn right into Burnmoor Street and the ground is on the left.

NB: If you are coming down the M1 leave at J22, follow the signs for Leicester City Centre and Rugby, then as above.

**EAST:** A47 into the city centre, follow the signs for Rugby, then as north.

**SOUTH:** M1 to J21, and pick up the A46 as you leave the motorway. After half a mile turn onto the A563 (signposted Aylestone). After two miles pick up the A426 which becomes the Aylestone Road, continue for about a mile and a half then turn left into Raw Dyke Road which leads onto Burnmoor Street and the ground.

**WEST:** M69. Follow the signs for Leicester City Centre and Rugby, then as north.

**PARKING:** There is loads of street parking around. Whilst, to be honest, the ground is not in the nicest part of the city, I've never had any hassle. The real problem comes with getting away from Leicester after the match. Expect serious congestion, which becomes nightmarish if Leicester RUFC have also been playing at home.

## FUTURE DEVELOPMENTS

The club has come to the conclusion that it has gone as far as it can with Filbert Street and is now looking to move to another ground (with, it appears, the general blessing of the fans). It is currently looking at five sites (including a free one offered by a local businessman and City fanatic) with the aim of building a 40,000 capacity ground which may be open for business by 2000-1 season.

## OTHER INFORMATION

For a club that rightly prides itself on having a very progressive and friendly attitude towards visiting fans, it has to be said that Leicester are let down in the extreme by the attitude of the police (and it must be said of some stewards). This attitude was among the worst I came across in 1997-8. Apart from the incident at the railway station mentioned earlier, on my last trip (where there was not even a hint that there might be problems) the policing was dreadful and inflammatory, fans weren't allowed to move freely around the ground and any attempts to get into pubs were met with threats of arrest.

The one advantage of this policy was that it did help me to discover a new pub a bit further from the ground, namely the Full Back & Firkin (as opposed to the Physio & Firkin by the Rugby Ground). If you park at the back of the ground, towards or off Bonner Street, you can't miss it. A big pub (which even takes Switch cards for your rounds and offers cashback), it does excellent beer and food in a relaxed football/rugby/home/away atmosphere.

The Wing Wah chip shop, which is just beyond the park and the Turnstile PH (a definite home affair), does very good chips (if you can persuade the local constabulary that you are not going to turn into a bottle wielding hoolie if allowed to pay it a visit). Inside the ground the food is OK — although the queues cause massive congestion along the East Stand — and the girls serving it all make the effort by wearing the visiting team's kit.

The Experience Rating is not meant to be a reflection on the club, which I reiterate does its best to make away fans welcome (and not poor), but rather on the hassle you may well experience is getting to the ground in the first place.

***Total Football* Experience Rating: 50**

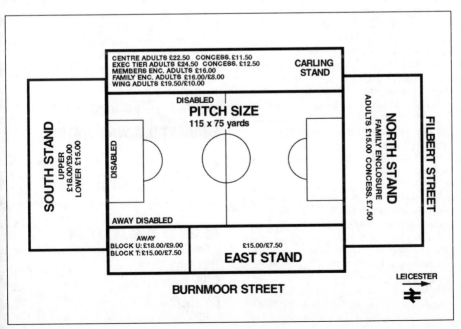

# LEYTON ORIENT

**ADDRESS:** Leyton Stadium
Brisbane Road, Leyton
London E10 5NE
**TELEPHONE No:** 0181 926 1111
**TICKET OFFICE:** 0181 926 1008
**FAX:** 0181 926 1110
**CLUBCALL:** 0891 12 11 50
**WEB SITE:**
www.matchroom.com/orient (official)
**NICKNAME:** The Os
**RECORD ATTENDANCE:** 34,345 v West
Ham FA Cup 4th 25 January 1964 (D 0-0)

## CLUB COLOURS:
**HOME:** Shirts: Red with White checks;
Shorts; Black; Socks: Red
**AWAY:** Shirts: Yellow with White front panel;
Shorts: White; Socks: Yellow

**KIT SPONSORS:** Marchpole
**MANUFACTURERS:** Olympic

## GROUND INFO

One of Barry Hearn's first undertaking was to give the ground a facelift and improve the offices which means that the East Stand looks a lot tidier (from the outside) than previously although Barry is perhaps being overly cautious with the amount of 'anti-climb' paint that has been daubed on the outside walls. The general level of facilities in the ground has also improved.

The South Terrace was pulled down a couple of seasons ago and replaced with a temporary (in the loosest sense of the word) car park. Expect this to remain for at least another season (although see Future Developments). This means that away fans are confined to the East Stand South Wing seats and the East Stand South Wing enclosure (or at least they are if they can manoeuvre through what must be one of the tightest turnstiles in the league). If you go in the seats expect to have some of the pitch obscured by a pillar. If you go in the back of the enclosure you can be fairly sure of staying dry when it rains.

You may find your attention wandering slightly due to a distinctly unpleasant aroma. This is one of the rare occasions when the cause is unlikely to be down to your neighbour's consumption of two burgers and half a dozen pints, but is more likely to be attributable to the 'Waste Disposal' works which are less than 0.25 mile away.

**CAPACITY:** Stands: 7,133; Terrace: 6,673;
Total: 13,842 (includes 36 spaces for disabled fans and helpers)

Note: this is prior to the opening of the South Stand which will add approximately 3,300 new seats at the ground.

**AWAY FANS:** East Stand: 932;
South Enclosure: 1,245;
Total: 2,177

**DISABLED FACILITIES:** There are covered spaces for 18 wheelchair-bound fans with 18 helpers at the front of the North Terrace on the East Stand side. There is no charge for disabled fans or their helpers, but you must pre-book.

Home fans should also note that the club offers a minibus pick-up service. Contact the club directly and speak to the Football in the Community Officer, regarding matchday commentaries. Parking facilities are available.

**PROGRAMME:** £1.50

You'll open this one with a fair sense of anticipation and for the first seven pages, you'll think it is going to be one of the best in the division as there is only one page of adverts and several good and interesting columns. However, you might as well stop here as the remaining 41 pages contained 24 full pages of adverts/sponsorship offers and what was left was generally filled with pictures and the banal.

## FANZINES:

| | |
|---|---|
| *The Leyton Orientear* | £1.00 |
| *Cheery O's* | 30p |
| *The O Zone* | 60p |
| *All Aboard the Wagon Train* | 50p |

The *Leyton Orientear* remains the O's fanzine to buy. Well over 100 issues have been produced and it shows no sign of slowing up. Moans and laughs aplenty, a good few general interest articles and even the match reports are a reasonable read. A definite buy. *Cheery O's* is a new fanzine which is produced by the people who do the web-Orient internet pages. A new one is produced for every home match (and includes team listings).

## TRAVEL

**NEAREST RAILWAY STATION:** Leyton
Midland Road (0171 928 5100)
The club is also supporting the proposal for a new local station on the Stratford-Richmond (North London Line) and Victoria Line. This would be by the West Stand and it is provisionally going to be called Orient (although it is unlikely to be open before late 1998).

**NEAREST TUBE STATION:** Leyton
(Central Line) — Turn right as you leave the tube station for the walk to the ground.

**BUS:** London Transport — 0171 222 1234

**BY CAR:**
**NORTH:** M11 into London. At the end of the M11 turn

right on to the A12 (signposted Wanstead). Continue for 1.25 miles, going straight over at the roundabout, then 0.25 mile later turn right into Church Lane. Turn left at the T-junction with Grove Green Road, bearing left after 200yd onto the one-way system (still Grove Green Road). After 0.75 mile turn right into Leyton High Road. Take the fifth left (Osborne Road) to the stadium.

**EAST:** A12 into London via Gidea Park and Wanstead. Then as north.

**SOUTH:** A23 to A205 (South Circular Road) turning right onto A205 (signposted Tulse Hill). Follow signs for Woolwich then turn left on to the A207 Shooters Hill Road. After 1.5 miles turn right onto the A102(M) and continue on this road through the Blackwall Tunnel. Once through the tunnel carry on for 1.5 miles then turn right onto the A11 (signposted Leytonstone). A quarter of a mile after Maryland station turn left into Chobham Road, and after a further 0.25 mile turn right into Major Road. A mile later turn left into Osborne Road at the bottom of which is the ground.

**WEST:** M40/A40 into London. Turn left onto the A406 North Circular Road (signposted Willesden/Hendon) and continue along the North Circular via Finchley, Wood Green, Edmonton and Woodford. Just after South Woodford turn right at the roundabout onto the A113 Chigwell Road (if you cross the M11 you've gone too far). After 1.75 miles you get to a major roundabout; take the third exit on to Leytonstone Road (A11) and 0.25 mile later turn right into Church Road. Then as north.

NB: The A12-M11 link road (due for completion in 1999) will make getting to and from the ground easier, but until this is complete expect some fairly major road upheavals.

**PARKING:** 100 spaces at the back of the old South Stand (£3 a throw!). When the South Stand is built a new 250+ car park will be opened on Oliver Road. Parking is available in some side streets near(ish) to the ground.

## FUTURE DEVELOPMENTS

The 3,000+ South Stand is planned to open in May 1999 although, when it first opens, it will not be fully used as some of the seats are too far away from the pitch. This is because after completion of the South Stand the club intend to rotate the pitch through 90 degrees to make this stand run along the pitch rather than behind the goal. The stand will then link up with new stands which are to be built along the other sides of the ground. The end result will be a 16,000+ all-seater stadium which is pencilled for completion around 2000. Once the South Stand is opened this will be used for home fans and the club will reassess where away fans should be sited.

## OTHER INFORMATION

The nearest pub to the ground is the Coach & Horses on Leyton High Road, which is good, but because it's the only one in the vicinity does tend to get packed.

The Atlanta Chip shop is OK but takes an age to serve you and the Royal Café does a brilliant all-day breakfast — plus a great bubble & squeak; these are both on the High Road and neither are too far away from the 'Kum TV' shop (which is named after the owner and nothing else). However, don't feel that you have to eat at either of these places because, despite what the Colman's Football Food Guide says — it ranked Orient as the worst food in the league — the stuff you get inside the ground is on the good side (and improving with every season with a new in-house caterer). The pies especially are hot and tasty — they're served on paper plates as well, very Hyacinth Bucket — and you can even add your own milk to your tea and coffee. The serving hatch is fairly small, but the people in it keep busy which does help to restrict queues. One minor grumble — it ain't cheap!

***Total Football* Experience Rating: 89**

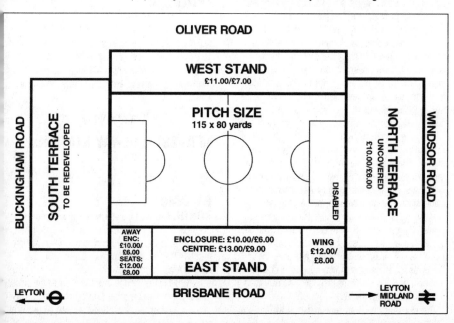

# LINCOLN CITY

**ADDRESS:** Sincil Bank Stadium
Lincoln LN5 8LD
**TELEPHONE No:** 01522 880011
**TICKET OFFICE:** 01522 880011
**FAX:** 01522 880020
**IMPSLINE:** 0930 55 59 00
**WEB SITE:**
http://isfa.com/server/web/lincoln
(official)
**NICKNAME:** The Red Imps
**RECORD ATTENDANCE:** 23,196 v Derby
Lge Cup 4th 15 November 1967 (L 0-3)

**CLUB COLOURS:**
**HOME:** Shirts: Red with Black & White stripes;
Shorts: Black; Socks: Red
**AWAY:** tba
**KIT SPONSORS:** Alstom
**MANUFACTURERS:** Super League

## GROUND INFO

Sincil Bank is a strange ground; for those who remember how bad it used to be, the vast majority of changes are welcome. It must be applauded that the club has redeveloped the ground without turning into something an eight year old with a Meccano set might construct. Having said that, the St Andrew's Stand runs along the side of the pitch but size wise would probably fit behind a goal without much trouble. This means that there is an empty space between it and the Stacey West Stand and there is a second stand built between it and the South Park Stand. This is the Family Stand which is much smaller than its neighbour and gives the whole of that side of the pitch the impression of not being quite right.

Visiting supporters are located in the south end of the Simons' Stand (previously the Linpave), which offers above average facilities and a good view of the game with fair leg room. If demand requires it, the South Park Stand can also be opened, but for the main part this remains shut, thus highlighting the problem that by insisting on ground redevelopment at all levels of the game, clubs were forced into a position whereby they either built small stadia which limited the potential for the future, or large grounds like Sincil Bank where, until the club achieves success, fans rattle around like peas in a pod, which does adversely affect the atmosphere. It should also be noted that at the end of last season the club also made the Stacey West End available to away supporters (and guess how popular that was with the Imps fans who had stood there for the whole of the season).

The club does offer away supporters concessions and

these weigh in at a whopping £2!! (No, juniors don't get in for £2, I do mean a £2 reduction from £10 to £8.) What is especially annoying about this is that every time I go to the ground there always seems to be a great scheme on for home fans. *Stop press:* For 1998 the reduction will be £5 but only because the adult price has gone up to £13!

Experiences of the stewarding fall into two camps, with fortunately the majority being very helpful. However, some of the more senior employees seem to have about as much idea of customer service as Sweeney Todd, and there is one in particular, with whom away fans may well come into contact, who spends the whole match barking orders at both visiting supporters and other stewards. This gets very, very irritating and sadly undoes all the good work of the other staff.

**CAPACITY:** Stands: 8,345; Terrace: 3,167;
Total: 111,512

**AWAY FANS:** Linpave Stand: 2,425 maximum
**DISABLED FACILITIES:** There are 80 spaces in the Simons' and South Park Stand, with away fans having their own section of 20 spaces in the Simons' Stand. Admission for disabled supporters is free of charge, with helpers paying £8. Due to the number of spaces available the club advises that you contact the Secretary, Clair Lait, to pre-book. Parking facilities are available at the ground (but are very limited in number), but there are no commentaries for the visually impaired.

**PROGRAMME:** £1.70
Excellent in both content and layout. This will fill the half-time break without any problems and is well worth the investment.

**FANZINES:**
| | |
|---|---|
| The Deranged Ferret | £1 |
| Yellow Belly | £1 |

*The Deranged Ferret* is an excellent read, though not too easy on the eye as it is (stoatily) crammed with small print. A good mix of moaning and supporting the club. A great read and (weasily) better than many you'll come across.

## TRAVEL
**NEAREST RAILWAY STATION:** Lincoln Central (01522 539502)

**BUS:** Central bus station (01522 525312)

**BY CAR:**
**NORTH:** A15 into Lincoln city centre until you cross the River Witham. About 250yd further on, turn right on to the A57. Continue until you pass the railway station then turn left onto the B1262 High Street (signposted Newark A46). Carry on until you pass the site of a now demolished railway bridge, then take the next left onto Scorer Street. Take the second right (not the first right into Sincil Bank) into Cross Street, and the ground is at

the bottom of this road.

**EAST:** A46 or A158 into Lincoln city centre following the signs for A46 Newark. This will bring you on to the High Street. Then as north.

**SOUTH:** A1, A46. Follow signs for Lincoln South and City Centre, this brings you onto the High Street. Continue until you see the Miller's Arms pub on your left (this is by a pelican crossing) and take the next right into Scorer Street. Then as north.

**WEST:** A46 into Lincoln. Go through the city centre following the signs for A46 Newark. This will bring you onto the High Street. Then as north.

**PARKING:** There is a car park in Cross Street next to the ground although at £2 it isn't cheap, as well as some street parking in the vicinity. For other car parks you need to go into the city centre, which is a bit of a walk, but doesn't get too clogged up at the end of matches.

## FUTURE DEVELOPMENTS

The opening in March 1995 of the £1 million Simons' Stand which seats 5,700 means that there is seating on all four sides of Sincil Bank. There is still a small area of terracing at the Stacey West End of the ground which could be transformed into seating easily enough, but expect the ground to stay as it is until such a time as the club reaches the higher echelons of the league.

## OTHER INFORMATION

Sincil Bank is definitely one of the grounds where it is better to eat inside than out. The nearest chip shop to the ground is on the corner of Scorer Street and Cross Street; directly opposite this is a pet shop, and both establishments sell fish. I just think maybe if they had a rush at the chippie one day, well... Besides, the pies and sausage rolls inside the ground are made by a local butchers and are excellent — hot, well filled and with a delicious pastry. What is more, they are served by a couple of charming old girls who treat every male customer under 40 like the prodigal son returning home from the wilderness! They make a terrific cup of tea as well.

The city centre has numerous good pubs. Nearer the ground you can enjoy a pint in either the Miller's Arms (John Smiths) or the George & Dragon; the latter is the bigger of the two, but the Miller's tends to have a better atmosphere. Both pubs are on the High Street just by the Scorer Street turning. A better bet though is to walk down Sincil Bank towards the town, at the end of which is the Portland Arms; this is a free house that serves an excellent pint in a good and relaxed ambience. If you can't be bothered walking then try the bar at the back of the South Park Stand — mind you, be warned: cheap it isn't!

The dug-outs at Lincoln are only really big enough for three, which often provides, especially on wet days, wonderful pre-match entertainment as the visiting team's substitutes realise this fact. There tends to follow:

• 1: A go-as-fast-as-you-can-without-breaking-into-a-run competition;

• 2: A jostle-your-neighbour-for-position competition;

• 3: An all-out race, elbows, fists, anything-goes type scrap for a place in the dry and warm.

A final thought. Elsewhere in this book I talk about the Bradford Fire being almost a forgotten disaster in English football, and perhaps this is best illustrated by the fact that when you ask the vast majority of fans who Bradford were playing on that terrible day, they will not be able to provide the answer. It was Lincoln. The club has not forgotten though and to ensure that this remains the case the first part of its own ground that was redeveloped was called the Stacey West Stand in memory of the two Lincoln fans who lost their lives in the tragedy.

*Total Football* **Experience Rating: 53**

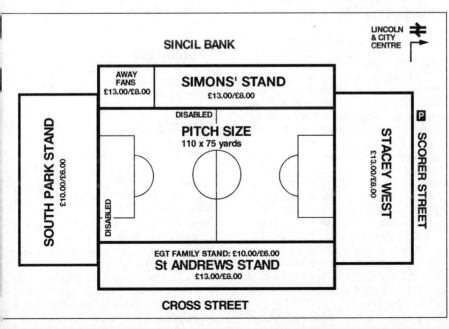

# LIVERPOOL

**ADDRESS:**  Anfield
Anfield Road
Liverpool L4 0TH

**TELEPHONE No:** 0151 263 2361

**TICKET OFFICE:** 0151 260 8680;
0151 260 9999

**FAX:** 0151 260 8813

**CLUBCALL:** 0891 12 11 84

The club does take credit card bookings on 0151 263 5727, and states that tickets can be booked up to 26 days in advance.

It is worth noting that the second of the numbers quoted under ticket office is a 24hr matchday information line, as the club is one of the few that doesn't charge at a premium rate for this service.

## WEB SITE:

http://anfield.merseyworld.com/ (unofficial)

**NICKNAME:** The Reds

**RECORD ATTENDANCE:** 61,905 v Wolves FA Cup 4th 2 February 1952 (W 2-1)

## CLUB COLOURS:

**HOME:** Shirts: Red; Shorts: Red; Socks: Red
**AWAY:** Shirts: Yellow;
Shorts: Black; Socks: Yellow

**KIT SPONSORS:** Carlsberg

**MANUFACTURERS:** Reebok

## GROUND INFO

Hats off to the builders of the redeveloped Anfield Road End. The construction was scheduled to take well into 1998 but was, in fact, open for business for Chelsea's visit on 5 November 1997. There can be no doubt that the new creation is a marked improvement on the previous incarnation and offers more leg room and a better view. Some things never change, though, and the family section next to the away supporters still appears to be packed full of 10-year-olds who prefer to spend their whole time questioning your parentage, sexuality and general sanity rather than watching the game; mind you, given that the option is watching David James or Brad Friedel marshalling the home side's defence, perhaps they are right to take the easy way out. On a serious note, although the abuse can be fairly irritating, it is as well to ignore it as if they illicit any response from you, you may well get an 'outraged' parent rushing to the stewards and demanding that you be chucked out for such disgraceful behaviour in front of kids.

Sadly, for a club which seems to promote the 'family'

ideals in football, I did not find that away fans were offered concessions although the club has said they are offered to visitors on a reciprocal basis.

If you can't get a ticket for the away end then anywhere is equally safe/risky. The touts around the ground tend to have tickets for the Kop, which I have to say isn't too bad providing that it isn't a big game and that you can keep a lid on it if you score (and remember this is the Liverpool of the 1990s not the 1980s we're talking about so this may well happen). Whilst obviously not being the single amorphous mass of humanity that it was when it was terracing, the Kop is still an intimidating sight and when they let rip with You'll Never Walk Alone, you'll know that seating has not dulled the passion.

Two points to consider if you do opt for a touted ticket: firstly, touting is against the law (so obviously I don't expect you to do it) and secondly, be careful! I have heard tales of fans being taken a little off the beaten track to buy a snide ticket and then having been on the receiving end of a kicking.

**CAPACITY:** Stands: 45,040; Terrace: Nil

**AWAY FANS:** Anfield Road End 3,023
The club advises that this is an 'average' allocation and can be revised up/downwards as appropriate.

**DISABLED FACILITIES:** There are 80 places available for disabled supporters in the Kop and Main Stand. Tickets are generally purchased on a season ticket basis; if you phone up the club you may be able to get a place but do not count on it. If you are to get a space, pre-booking is essential. There are match commentaries for the blind, and also disabled parking facilities at the ground. Once again pre-booking is required for these facilities. Should you be lucky enough to get a space expect to be charged £3 with helpers paying £20-£18.

**PROGRAMME:** £2.00
Went up 25% last season in price without any noticeable improvement in the quality of the content. You can buy it inside or outside the ground if you're desperate to add it to your collection.

## FANZINES:

| | |
|---|---|
| *Red All Over The Land* | £1 |
| *All Day and All of the Night* | £1 |
| *Another Vintage Liverpool Performance* | £1 |

*AVLP* was the only one of the above that I saw being sold around Anfield on my last visit and, on first look, you'd think it was one to avoid with its front cover formed of just two columns of print and one very small picture. If you are looking for style and fancy layouts, then this should be enough for you to leave well alone. If however, you don't mind what it looks like so long as it reads well *AVLP* will suit you quite well, although it must be said that amongst the gems there are one or two pieces that are as wide of the mark as a Karl Heinz Riedle volley. If you get a chance, have a chat with the sellers about the rumours surrounding the club. I got one very well-worn tale and a fantastic one of unbridled lust in a Liverpool hotel which I would love to repeat here but just can't...

## TRAVEL
### NEAREST RAILWAY STATIONS:
Kirkdale (0.75 miles)
Lime Street (four miles) (0151 709 9696)
Lime Street is the main city station. Once there, either take a local service to Kirkdale, bus it, grab a cheapish cab, or be prepared for a long walk.

**BUS:** Central bus station (0151 709 8600)
From Lime Street or the city centre, any 17 bus (17a, 17b etc) will take you to Utting Avenue which adjoins Anfield Road. To get back grab a bus from Utting Avenue.

### BY CAR:
**NORTH:** M6 to J28, then follow signs for A58 to Liverpool. Keep going until you hit Walton Hill Avenue. You will then pass Stanley Park, after which turn left into Anfield Road.

**SOUTH/EAST:** M6/M62 until you reach the end of the motorway. Turn right onto the A5058 (Queens Drive). After three miles take a left into Utting Avenue. One mile further on turn right at the Arkles PH into Anfield Road.

**WEST:** Go through Mersey Tunnel (toll) into city centre. Follow the signs for Preston (A580) this will take you into Walton Hall Avenue, and you will see Stanley Park in front of you. Just before you reach this, turn right into Anfield Road.

**PARKING:** There is a large car park by Stanley Park which takes an age to get out of and which is apparently for permit holders, although this never seems a great problem. Alternatively you can park by Everton FC on the other side of the park. Which weighs in at a none-too cheap £3.50!

## FUTURE DEVELOPMENTS
The opening of the 8,000 plus seat Anfield Road Stand marks the end of developments at the ground for the moment.

## OTHER INFORMATION
If you fancy a drink near the ground, there are two pubs which are always open on match days: the Albert (behind the Kop), and The Arkles (both on the Anfield Road). Of the two the Albert is probably the better bet as it serves a reasonable and cheap pint of Tetleys; The Arkles is on the route from the coach park to the ground. A little further afield are the Oakfield and the Clarencote Hotel. If you want food it's worth going to the Kop Snack Bar behind, naturally enough, the Kop Stand. Great chips but poor (mushroom) gravy. Once inside, the food is, in my opinion, on the bad side of awful, and the hot drinks are so hot that they can melt your cup/finger/clothing before you've had a chance to get to your seat.

People either love Liverpool or they hate it; there seems to be no in-between. Whatever camp you fall in, any trip to Anfield should incorporate a visit to, and some reflection at, the Hillsborough Memorial which is 50yd down Anfield Road from the visitors' entrance. The names on the wreath-bedecked shrine are those of ordinary football fans, men and women who went for a day at a football match and who never came back. Which one of us doesn't know in our heart of hearts that the tragedy could have easily occurred at any ground, and that it is only by the grace of God that the memorial isn't somewhere else with our own name upon it? We shall never forget.

*Total Football* **Experience Rating: 71**

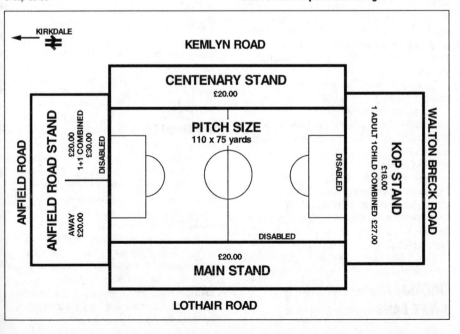

# LUTON TOWN

**ADDRESS:** Kenilworth Road
Stadium, 1 Maple Road
Luton LU4 8AW

**TELEPHONE No:** 01582 411622

**TICKET OFFICE:** 01582 416976

**FAX:** 01582 405070

**CLUBCALL:** 0891 12 11 23

**WEB SITE:**
http://www.btinternet.com/~ben.w/
(unofficial)

**NICKNAME:** The Hatters

**RECORD ATTENDANCE:** 30,069 v
Blackpool FA Cup 6th Rep 4 March 1959 (W 1-0)

## CLUB COLOURS:

**HOME:** Shirts: White with Blue shoulders/White trim;
Shorts: Blue with White side panel;
Socks: Blue and White

**AWAY:** Shirts: Orange with Blue sides, white trim;
Shorts: Orange with Blue sides;
Socks: Orange

**KIT SPONSORS:** Universal Salvage Auctions

**MANUFACTURERS:** Pony

## GROUND INFO

The remnants of Luton's ill-fated 'Members only' scheme are still prevalent. Tickets for the away sections of the ground are not on sale on the day of the match and are available from the visiting club's ticket office only. Membership schemes are still in place around the rest of the stadium although anyone can apparently buy tickets for Block E of Main Stand on matchdays (subject to availability).

Those supporters who wish to become members should apply direct to the Ticket Office.

Just to reiterate, inhabitants of Beds, Bucks, and Herts can become members without any problems. People from other areas may be refused; eg if you live in Wallsend don't apply for membership a fortnight before a cup-tie with Newcastle!

The away entrances in Oak Road are tucked in between two rows of terraced housing, and to get to this you may find yourself having to negotiate the 'atmospheric' alleyway Beech Hill Path. It is right in the middle of this alleyway that the entrance to the executive boxes is situated — lucky old box holders!

The Oak Road Stand is multi-pillared, so expect to get some kind of obstruction.

**CAPACITY:** Stands: 9,975; Terrace: Nil

**AWAY FANS:** Oak Road Stand: 2,257

**DISABLED FACILITIES:** There are 32 spaces for wheelchair-bound supporters, and admission to this area is free for disabled supporters and helpers. Pre-booking is essential, as it is for the match commentary facility. The club will try to assist with car parking if contacted early enough. Otherwise I was advised by the police that they don't mind disabled fans being dropped off outside. This of course is especially good news if you've driven yourself to the match as you can drop yourself off before getting back into the car and hunting for that elusive parking spot.

**PROGRAMME:** £1.60.
56 pages, lots (and lots) of adverts, but enough to keep you occupied for a while.

## FANZINES:

*Mad As A Hatter*                    50p

60 pages ranging from excellent articles to obvious page-fillers of newspaper cuttings — these tend to be more anti-Watford than pro-Luton — and out of date match reports. Still, it is well worth getting as it appears to be continuing to improve with age. Sellers abound and you can pick it up from the club shop.

## TRAVEL

### NEAREST RAILWAY STATION:
Luton (01582 27612)
Supporters arriving *en masse* can still expect to be met by the police who will take them by bus directly to the ground and put straight into the stadium. The same happens at the end of games (except obviously the other way round).

**BUS:** Luton & District Transport (01582 404074)
There are plenty of buses to the ground, and the best place to catch them is on Upper George Street (very handy for the Duke Of Clarence, see Other Information). Any Dunstable bus will do the trick, numbers include 20, 22, 23, 31, 37, 38, 68, 69... Dividend forecast is low.

### BY CAR:
**NORTH/WEST:** M1 to J11. Take the A505 (signposted Luton), this brings you onto a one-way system which you should go round following signs for Dunstable (ultimately you will find yourself travelling back in the direction you have come from, but on a different road). Turn left into Oak Road and the ground is on your left.

**SOUTH:** M1 to J10. Follow the signs for the town centre, then turn left onto the Inner Ring Road, and keep going straight until this becomes the Dunstable Road. Continue under the railway bridge and after about 0.25 mile turn left into Oak Road for the ground.

**EAST:** A505 following signs for Luton and town centre until you get to the Inner Ring Road; turn left onto this, then as south.

**PARKING:** There is a car park by the ground, but this is for permit holders only and almost impossible to talk your way into. There is a maze of roads around the ground where you can park, or try the Sainsbury's car park just off the Dunstable Road (it has a two-hour parking limit and is for customers only — NB: it is patrolled). There are further car parks by the Arndale Centre, but be prepared for a delay getting away after a match as the one-way system can get very congested.

## FUTURE DEVELOPMENTS

The long awaited Kohlerdome remains a long way away although the £30 million redevelopment (which is backed by Whitbread plc) is still not dead in the water. The move would create the country's first indoor stadium — this has been sanctioned by the FA and Football League — and would seat 20,000 fans. The site for this development is just off J10 of the M1 and there would be a new station (Luton Parkway) built as well as changes to the road infrastructure. You get the feeling that once the ball for this starts rolling it will gather momentum and be unstoppable. However, it is that first step which is proving to be the hardest. The club was talking about the construction of this stadium when this book first came out four seasons ago. There are signs that there is general unrest towards Mr Kohler by some factions within the club and this has spilled over into attacks on property in his home town of Radlett, which hardly seems the best way of getting someone to help you. Whatever the rights and wrongs, something needs to be down quickly as Kenilworth Road is fast becoming an eyesore.

## OTHER INFORMATION

There are no pubs in the vicinity of the ground. Nelson's Flagship is about the nearest and is tucked in the corner of Sainsbury's car park (about half-way between the town centre/station and the ground). This was previously a real home pub but is now a lot more ambivalent. A better bet is to go to the Duke of Clarence on Upper George Street: leave the Arndale Centre at the Burger King/C&A exit, head towards the statue and you can't miss it. This has the advantage of having a Ladbrokes right next to it for your fixed odds.

Inside the ground (very) cramped leg room is the order of the day. Sadly away fans do not get the benefit of using the public bars, one of which is named after the footballing legend that is Nick Owen (bizarrely there is also a turnstile that reads 'Press/Photographers/Matchday Staff/Nick Owen' — The man on the sofa with Anne Diamond is a demigod in Luton).

Inside Kenilworth Road the pies are very stodgy but with a nice meat filling. The tea comes in paper cups which fold in on themselves given the slightest pressure (ie trying to pick it up from the counter). One other very irritating habit is that if you ask for a chocolate bar and a cup of tea they tend to carry them in one hand which means you are faced with a mass of melted chocolate beneath the wrapper.

The away fans in block G of the Main Stand make themselves known to visitors (usually with some fairly inventive chanting). It's good for the atmosphere and never really threatens to spill over into anything nasty (there are always tons of police around and you get the feeling that the club has never fully got over the Millwall experience). If you are on that side of the Oak Road, you can engage in some friendly banter, though if you are on the opposite side you'll have to restrict yourself to chatting with the toffs in the exec boxes (all of which look like bottom of the range conservatories).

*Total Football* **Experience Rating: 58**

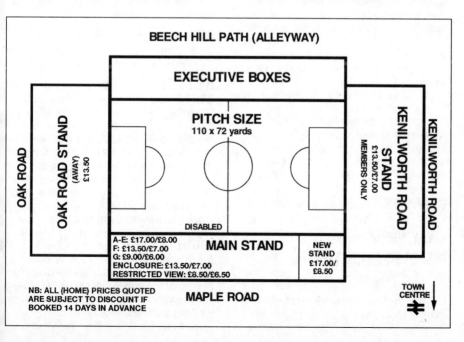

BEECH HILL PATH (ALLEYWAY)

EXECUTIVE BOXES

PITCH SIZE
110 x 72 yards

OAK ROAD

OAK ROAD STAND
(AWAY)
£13.50

KENILWORTH ROAD STAND
£13.50/£7.00
MEMBERS ONLY

KENILWORTH ROAD

DISABLED

A-E: £17.00/£8.00
F: £13.50/£7.00
G: £9.00/£6.00
ENCLOSURE: £13.50/£7.00
RESTRICTED VIEW: £8.50/£6.50

MAIN STAND

NEW STAND
£17.00/£8.50

NB: ALL (HOME) PRICES QUOTED
ARE SUBJECT TO DISCOUNT IF
BOOKED 14 DAYS IN ADVANCE

MAPLE ROAD

TOWN CENTRE

# MACCLESFIELD TOWN

**ADDRESS:** Moss Rose Ground
London Road
Macclesfield
SK11 7SP

**TELEPHONE No:** 01625 264686

**TICKET OFFICE:** 01625 264686

**FAX:** 01625 264692

**BLUES LINE:** 0930 55 58 35

**WEB SITE:** http://www.mtfc.co.uk/

**NICKNAME:** The Silkmen

**RECORD ATTENDANCE:**
9,003 v Winsford Athletic Cheshire Senior Cup 2nd R
4 February 1948 (W 2-1)

**CLUB COLOURS:**
**HOME:** Shirts: Blue; Shorts: White; Socks: Blue
**AWAY:** Shirts: White; Shorts: White; Socks: White

**KIT SPONSORS:** Zeneca Pharmaceuticals

**MANUFACTURERS:** Super League

## GROUND INFO

To be honest Moss Rose only offers the very basic of amenities, although this is in some way compensated for by the good stewarding and friendly attitude of those associated with the club. Following a few problems at the start of last season, when both the capacity for away supporters was frequently insufficient and also away fans were trying to get into home sections where admission prices where slightly cheaper, the club both standardised its prices and also moved visiting fans onto the Silkman End Terrace. This had the effect of doubling capacity but, on the negative side, taking away the roof which was available on the Estate Terrace.

Given the restricted capacity at the ground and the fact that the club seems to be moving through the leagues like a dose of salts, it is highly likely that the vast majority of games next season will be all ticket. However, given that the club is still failing to attract the levels of support that it so richly deserves, it should still be possible to get in at the majority of matches if you plan ahead slightly.

**CAPACITY:** Stands: 2,665; Terrace: 3,835;
Total: 6,500

**AWAY FANS:** Silkman End:1,679

**DISABLED FACILITIES:** There are 10 spaces for disabled supporters and helpers in the Main Stand just to the left of the players' tunnel. Admission is £5.00 each. Pre-booking is required at which time the club will sort out a car parking pass if requested. No commentaries for the visually impared are available.

**PROGRAMME:** £1.70
Without doubt the most improved programme in the league in 1997-8, although much of the reason behind this is the fact that the club's effort whilst in the Vauxhall conference was truly abysmal. The away section is so-so, but this tends to be made up for by a couple of very readable pieces elsewhere.

**FANZINES:**
*Hang 'Em Up*                    50p
I didn't see any copies of this being sold on my last visit.

## TRAVEL

**NEAREST RAILWAY STATION:**
Macclesfield (0161 832 8353 — Manchester Enquiries)
Excellent rail links with the rest of the country... providing you are going to a match on a Saturday and you don't live too far north. If you are going to an evening kick-off, the last train southbound leaves at about 8pm and instead you will have to travel across to Manchester Piccadilly and connect from there.

The best thing about going by rail to Macclesfield is that you don't have much of a problem finding a decent pub to enjoy a pint in. Immediately opposite the station there is 108s (Vaux), the Old Millstone (Marstons), the Nags Head (Robinsons) or the Queens Hotel (Joseph Holt Manchester Ales). One of these is bound to meet your requirements. Be warned. It is a fair trek to the ground from the station (it'll take about half an hour). If you do decide to yomp it, then turn left as you leave the station (right as you leave the pubs) to the main set of traffic lights (not just pelican crossing). Turn left, walk down Mill Lane/London Road for the ground.

**BUS:** Macclesfield bus station (01625 348508)
The bus station is near the railway station. Either a 9, 14, 16 or a 201 will take you from the town to the ground.

**BY CAR:**
**NORTH:** M6 to J19. Take the A556 (signposted Macclesfield). Turn left at the junction of the A556 and the A537 onto the A537 and follow this road through Knutsford and into Macclesfield. Once you hit Macc, carry straight on down A537 (Chester Road) then turn left at the roundabout, following signs for town centre. Continue down Cumberland Street, until you go down a hill to a large roundabout. Turn right here onto the A523; this is initially called The Silk Road and then becomes London Road (signposted Leek). Moss Rose is 1.5 miles on your right.
**SOUTH:** M6 to J17. Take the A534 (signposted Congleton) and continue until you get to the A536 (signposted Macclesfield). Follow this road into the town till you get to the junction with Moss Lane (this turning is immediately after a Texaco garage into Moss Lane which will lead you to the ground).
Alternatively pick up the A54 from the A534 and

continue to the junction with the A523. Turn left onto the A523 (signposted Macclesfield) and continue for approx four miles till you see the ground on your left (this route is longer but, depending on traffic, may be faster.)

**EAST/WEST:** Take the A537 into Macclesfield to the junction with the A523. Turn onto the A523 (signposted Leek) and continue for 1.5 miles for the ground.

## PARKING:
There is no parking available at the ground and the nearest off-street car park is probably in the town centre (25min walk). However, if you turn into Moss Lane this will lead to many side streets which you can park in, although these can (and do) get fairly crowded quite early.

## FUTURE DEVELOPMENTS

An area of some confusion. It was announced in the national press that the club would be building a new 1,500-seat stand during 1998-9 (although apparently this would only add about 500 places on the terracing it replaced). However, when I phoned the club for more details it denied that any changes were going to happen... Stop press: This is now going up where the estate Terrace is.

## OTHER INFORMATION

There are a few pubs in the immediate vicinity of the ground and all of them welcome visiting supporters. The nearest of these is the Silkman, which is right on the corner of Moss Rose. It serves its own Silkman's Bitter, which I have never seen before or since, which went down a treat. Alternatively, if you walk two minutes up London Road — heading away from Macclesfield — you come across the Star Inn, where the only problem is the fact that it is fairly small, so, if there's any more than two men and a dog in it, it is packed. I was tipped off to go to

the Flower Pot (Robinsons) and have to say that it is probably the best of the bunch (although a good 10min walk away). To get to it, you have to go to the end of Moss Lane and bear right. It is a cavern of a pub with a decent garden and very friendly landlord and bar staff (when I was there I also got about three offers of a lift down to the ground if I wanted to stay for another beer).

If none of these tickle your fancy — and at this stage I'd think you're getting a bit picky, to be honest — then the town centre has a great selection of pubs (see 'Nearest Railway Station' for a ready made session). It also has the added advantage of having quite a lot of places where you can get a decent bite to eat. If you do take this option then a cab to the ground (which is a good mile and a half away) will only set you back about £1.

Nearer to the ground the options for food are less numerous and the only place of note (or should that be existence) is Bonds the Bakers, which does some storming fresh pies. Once inside the ground, Moss Rose gives me the unusual opportunity to say that I would really recommend the burgers, which are cooked to perfection, and are very juicy and tasty (which is just as well because there weren't any pies on sale). Hot drinks are also reasonable. Depending on what part of the ground you are in, the more silver-tongued among you may be able to charm your way into the supporters' club bar for half-time refreshment (although unless you get in there early then expect to queue for at least 15min).

A trip to Moss Rose offers little in terms of refinement but much in terms of the way you are treated. To be honest, I don't know whether I would want to put up with the chances of getting a soaking every Saturday of the season, but it's a good trip to make once in a while just so you remember what being a supporter is all about.

*Total Football* **Experience Rating: 68**

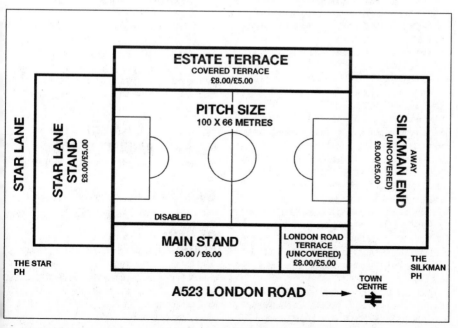

STAR LANE

STAR LANE STAND
£8.00/£5.00

ESTATE TERRACE
COVERED TERRACE
£8.00/£5.00

PITCH SIZE
100 X 66 METRES

SILKMAN END
AWAY
(UNCOVERED)
£8.00/£5.00

DISABLED

MAIN STAND
£9.00 / £6.00

LONDON ROAD TERRACE
(UNCOVERED)
£8.00/£5.00

THE STAR PH

THE SILKMAN PH

A523 LONDON ROAD →

TOWN CENTRE

# MANCHESTER CITY

**ADDRESS:** Maine Road
Moss Side
Manchester M14 7WN
**TELEPHONE No:** 0161 224 5000
**TICKET OFFICE:** 0161 226 2224
**FAX:** 0161 248 8449
**CLUBCALL:** 0891 12 11 91
**WEBSITE:** http://www.mcfc.co.uk
**E-MAIL:** citynet@www.mcfc.co.uk
**NICKNAME:** The Citizens
**RECORD ATTENDANCE:**
84,569 v Stoke FA Cup 6th 3 March 1934 (W 1-0)
**CLUB COLOURS:**
**HOME:** Shirts: 'Laser' Blue (presumably the traditional
name of sky-blue being far too uncool for
those hep cats at Kappa)
Shorts: White with Navy trim; Socks: Navy
**AWAY:** Shirts:Navy with Citrus Yellow & Navy stripes;
Shorts: Navy with Yellow & Laser Blue trim;
Socks: tba
**KIT SPONSORS:** Brother
**MANUFACTURERS:** Kappa

## GROUND INFO

The Kippax and Platt Lane Stands are very impressive from the outside, although the second of these is a bit of a monstrosity once in the ground. If you are a supporter who prefers grounds to be uniform then you may find Maine Road to be a disappointment. However, by apparently designing each stand as a separate entity the club have managed to retain some degree of varying personality between each of the constructions. Whatever your standpoint, it is harder to work out the purpose of the corrugated metal between the executive boxes and the main structure.

The away seats in the North Stand are OK although don't expect to be able to lounge about as the leg room seems tight. 1,000 spaces are in the uncovered section and are £1 cheaper. One downer is the fact that City have introduced a three-category pricing system. the club states this system is due to increased policing/ stewarding costs at some matches.

Not everything has changed at Maine Road; 'Big Helen' the bell-ringer who sits in the corner of the North Stand, remains omnipresent. To the visitor the bell seems like an amusing and novel way of rallying the troops, but spare a thought for the person who sits in front of her week in, week out.

Take note, City run a membership scheme which you may need to be a member of if you want to buy tickets. Membership costs £5 (£3.00 renewals) but cannot be obtained on the day of a game. Games are only usually made members-only if the visiting club sells its entire allocation. However, If you can't get a ticket for the away end then it is worth contacting the club, which it must be said are always very helpful, to ensure that you are going to be able to get in.

**CAPACITY:** Stands: 33,148; Terrace: Nil
**AWAY FANS:** North Stand Blocks S,T,U: 3,200
The club may extend this to 4,000 spaces, again all within the North Stand, in the future.

**DISABLED FACILITIES:** There are places for 88 disabled supporters at Maine Road. These are sited in the Platt Lane and Kippax Stands. Disabled supporters are admitted free of charge, with helpers paying £5. Match commentaries are also available for the visually impaired. Places/commentaries must be pre-booked at least seven days in advance. There are no parking facilities available, but despite this, the club can be rightly proud of its facilities in this area, with good clean accessible toilets and staff with an attitude that means if you want to travel on your own and you need a hand, then you should have no problems.

**PROGRAMME:** £1.70
Minuscule print and a really cramped layout that may have you putting it in the back pocket before you've really given it a chance. Persevere as it is actually a very good read. It is also one of the few programmes which has given space to supporters who it appears can disagree with the official club viewpoint.

**FANZINES:**

| | |
|---|---|
| *Bert Trautmann's Helmet* | £1 |
| *King of the Kippax* | £1 |
| *This Charming Fan* | £1 |
| *Are you Blue or Are You Blind?* | £1 |

*King of the Kippax* is without doubt the top City fanzine and manages to be able to laugh as well as rage at the position that City find themselves in; it also keeps the obvious anti-United stuff down to acceptable levels.

## TRAVEL

**NEAREST RAILWAY STATION:**
Manchester Piccadilly (0161 832 8353 or local enquiries: 0345 484950)

**BUS:** Chorlton Street bus station (0161 228 7811)
A 99 and a 111 drop off on Lloyd Street South which is 2min walk from the ground.
**BY CAR:**
**NORTH:** M61, M63 to J9. Take the A5103 Princess Road (signposted Manchester) and after 3 miles you will reach the junction with Wilbraham Road (the ground is signposted). Turn right down Wilbraham Road, after 0.25 mile, turn left down Lloyd Street. Continue for 0.5 mile and the ground is on your right.

**EAST:** M62 to J17. Take the A56 Bury New Road into Manchester. Follow signs for the airport. Then turn left onto the A57(M), following signs for Birmingham. Turn left onto the A5103 Princess Road and continue for 1.5 miles. Turn left into Claremont Road. Continue for 0.5 mile, and Maine Road is on your right.

**SOUTH:** M6 to J19. Follow the A556 to Stockport till you pick up the M56. Continue to J3, then take the A5103 (signposted Manchester), then as north.

**WEST:** M62/M63, then as north. Alternatively M56, then as south.

**PARKING:** There is some parking around Platt Lane and Platt Fields Park. To get to them continue past Maine Road and instead turn into Yew Tree Lane. At the first major crossroads turn left onto Platt Lane for the park. There is also on-street parking. Finally, many local schools open their gates to cars (at a price).

## FUTURE DEVELOPMENTS

There was talk about giving the ground a more cohesive look by further building work at the North and Platt Lane stands as well as between the Kippax and North Stands. This would add another 9,000 seats to the capacity. However City's fall from grace has meant that the initial target date for this of 1999 is very unlikely to be realised. Recently a further option has arisen, namely for City to move into the new Millennium Stadium which is being built in Manchester for the Commonwealth Games. The club have stated that they will let the fans decide which path they takes. However, how this show of democracy will be conducted has yet to be announced.

## OTHER INFORMATION

Given the area the ground is in, most visitors will find it a more rewarding experience to go to the city centre, rather than try to find food and drink locally, although the Parkside on Lloyd Street South isn't too bad (provided

you can get in) and opposite is a good chip shop. A far better bet though is the Sherwood on Claremont Road which is one of those genuine football pubs where home and away fans can mix, enjoy a beer or two and swap tales of current woe and past glories.

For food, if you like either Chinese or Indian grub, then you are in for a treat as Manchester not only houses the largest population of Chinese people in Europe — and the quality of the food in all the places I have ever eaten in has been superb — but also, about a mile or so away from the ground on Wilmslow Road, are literally hundreds of Indian eat-in/take aways. Once inside Maine Road the food is OK but nothing more; still, at least the service is reasonably quick.

I always find the club and its fans to be friendly on my visits, although I would not necessarily recommend walking round some of the streets in the area wearing a visiting team's replica top. There is undoubtedly a great dislike for their rivals from Stretford but, given that the two clubs are an ocean apart, at the moment, some of the venom behind this has dissipated (which is no bad thing). Certainly you can but admire the supporters' loyalty and it would be rude not to join in with the almost inevitable cries to sack the chairman/board/manager that are likely to ring round the ground on a visit.

Finally, on a trip to Maine Road, you won't fail to notice the hundreds of items of merchandise with 'Oasis' style lettering on them, but what is worth taking a second look at is the new club badge, which seems to have appeared from nowhere and resembles something that you feel should be worn by the German national side. In case you're interested, the wording underneath reads 'Superbia in Proelio' or Pride/Passion in Battle, which means that, while the fans have got every right to wear it, some of the players may be misleading you.

*Total Football* **Experience Rating: 80**

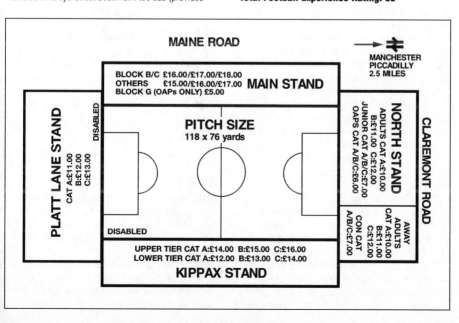

# MANCHESTER UNITED

**ADDRESS:** Old Trafford
Sir Matt Busby Way
Manchester
M16 0RA

**TELEPHONE No:** 0161 872 1661
**TICKET OFFICE:** 0161 872 0199
**FAX:** 0161 876 5502
**CLUBCALL:** 0891 12 11 61
**WEB SITE:**
www.sky.co.uk/sports/manu (official)
**NICKNAME:** The Red Devils
**RECORD ATTENDANCE:**
76,962 Wolves v Grimsby FA Cup Semi 25 March 1939
(L 2-1)

## CLUB COLOURS:
**HOME:** Shirts: Red; Shorts: White; Socks: Black
**AWAY:** Shirts: White; Shorts: White; Socks: White
**THIRD:** Shirts: Blue with Black markings;
Shorts: Blue; Socks: Blue/Black

**KIT SPONSORS:** Sharp
**MANUFACTURERS:** Umbro

## GROUND INFO

Welcome to the 'Theatre of Dreams' (possibly so called because dreaming is about as close as many kids from Stretford will actually get to watching their heroes).
It cannot be denied, Old Trafford is a magnificent stadium, although from the outside it always seems to have an air of being slightly run down. Once inside though, the stadium is breathtaking (even if the roof does look like it has been made out of the same kind of stuff they make Scalextrix track out of). The jewel in the Old Trafford crown is the North Stand, a huge and magnificent creation. If you do get tickets in here, let me tell you that from the back it is almost impossible to distinguish the players and the rake of the stand is incredible and makes you feel as though you are almost falling forward. Certainly it isn't a place to visit if you suffer from vertigo. The club also advises that access to the third tier involves climbing over 170 steps via 10 levels.

Unless you have a ticket, then your chances of getting in are slim. There are 10,000 tickets available for each match but these are for members on a first come first served basis. Furthermore there are over 100,000 members (and new applications are being accepted).

A big issue this year has been the 'standing' threat that the local authority may close the ground if bums don't remain on seats (apparently due to breaches of safety regs). This has led to not only many a visiting fan

being ejected but also home fans having season tickets confiscated etc. Things have got fairly heated with the stewards and as a gesture of goodwill the club did have a one match amnesty when you could stand if you wanted and not be ejected.

**CAPACITY:** Stands: 55,300; Terrace: Nil
**AWAY FANS:** Stand L: 1,850; Stand K: 600;
South Stand: 600; Total: 3,050

**DISABLED FACILITIES:** These are sited at the front of the South East Stand and for 1998-9 the number of spaces on offer have increased to 253. There is no charge for either disabled supporters or helpers. Places tend to be pre-booked via a season ticket, and you must contact the club in advance. Manchester United Radio (1413 AM) provides a match commentary.

**PROGRAMME:** £1.80
Went up 20% in 1997-8, but it's easy to see why. After all the cost of producing all those adverts can't be cheap.

## FANZINES:
| | |
|---|---|
| *Red Issue* | £1 |
| *Red News* | £1 |
| *United We Stand* | £1 |

*Red Issue* is the country's biggest selling fanzine, though WSC still won't include it in its listings as a result of the vitriolic nature of some of *RI's* attacks on other fans. I've got to say that I enjoy getting a copy of *RI* about once a season; it's funny, angry and knows where to point the finger. *UWS* started appearing in WHS last year; strangely this did not seem adversely to affect the writing style at all and it still remains an excellent read.

## TRAVEL

### NEAREST RAILWAY STATION:
Old Trafford (0161 832 8353)
The station is behind the South Stand, and can be got to via Oxford Road in the city centre. Apparently there is talk (though at this stage no more than talk) of a new Metro station being opened at the ground in the next couple of years.

**BUS:** Aytown Street (0161 228 7811)
Grab any bus in the city centre which is bound for Stretford.

### BY CAR:
**NORTH:** M61, M63 to J4. On leaving the motorway take the A5081 (signposted Manchester). Continue on the A5081 for 2.5 miles, then turn right into Sir Matt Busby Way (formerly Warwick Road), and first right into United Road.
**SOUTH:** M6 to J19, then follow the signs for A556 Stockport. This will lead you onto the A56 to Altrincham. When in Altrincham continue to follow the signs for A56 Manchester for six miles, then turn left into Sir Matt

Busby Way, and after 0.5 mile left again into United Road.

**EAST:** M62 to J17, then take the A56 Bury New Road (signposted Prestwick/Manchester Airport/Manchester) into Manchester, following the signs for 'South' and then Chester. When the road becomes Chester Road (still A56) continue for two miles then turn right into Sir Matt Busby Way and left 0.5 mile later into United Road.

NB: This route takes you through Manchester city centre. If you'd prefer to avoid this, continue along the M62 to the M63, then as north.

**WEST:** M62 to M63, then as north.

NB: the major development continues apace which means that as the road infrastructure is laid there may well be delays/diversions as you approach the ground, so allow yourself plenty of time.

**PARKING:** There are loads of 'private car parks' at which to leave your car around Old Trafford. Expect to pay about £3 and to be surrounded by BMWs, Mercs etc. There have been a lot of road improvements in the area, which means that getting away can be a bit of a nightmare, although this should come to an end in 1998-9 and make going home a bit easier.

## FUTURE DEVELOPMENTS

Well, the pitch is being relaid in the summer and the club museum relocated into the North Stand but, apart from that, nothing. There is talk of making every stand the size of the North Stand (which would give the ground an 85,000 capacity) but the club may wait to see what the impact of pay per view TV has before undertaking such a project.

## OTHER INFORMATION

Following the club's lead, the majority of pubs around the ground are either members only or expect patrons to buy a football lottery ticket before going in (funnily enough these never seem to be drawn while I've been still in the pub). If this doesn't put you off try either the Gorse Hill Hotel or the Trafford on Warwick Road. A much better choice is the nearby Railway Club where you can be signed in as a guest, and you can enjoy a pint for just over £1 together with a decent bite to eat. Away fans are welcomed (within reason) but the place does get packed out from about 1.45pm onwards. There are loads of chippies in the area and I have to say that it is better getting your fill before you go inside because I found the food in the ground is all a bit bland. You can also get lager in the away section at £2 a pint.

Whatever you do, it is difficult to escape the blasting PA, which seems to spend about an hour before the match playing United 'classics' such as Sing Up For The Champions (OK If you insist... 'Come on Arsenal!') and the revamped United's Calypso (a song so abysmal that even United Fred the Red Mascot looks embarrassed when it is played).

A trip to Old Trafford will probably bring out a number of emotions in you: awe at the sheer scale of the place; jealousy; and, perhaps sadness or anger, in that you can't ever kid yourself that as a fan (away or home) you will ever mean anything to the club. It is probably best to accept it for what it is — a big corporation earning money. At least you get a decent view and the club does offer away fans concessions.

Finally a word of warning. Although it didn't receive much publicity, there were quite a few problems between rival sets of supporters last season and, on more than one occasion, the forecourt was turned in to a battleground. I would say that generally you can avoid any flare ups, but it is as well to keep your wits about you.

*Total Football* **Experience Rating: 86**

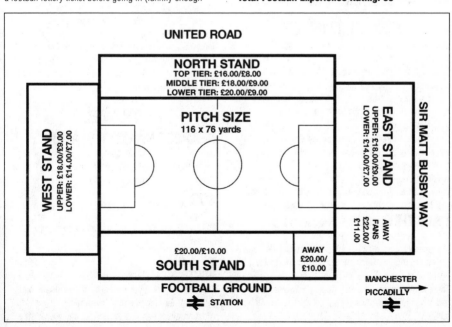

UNITED ROAD

**NORTH STAND**
TOP TIER: £16.00/£8.00
MIDDLE TIER: £18.00/£9.00
LOWER TIER: £20.00/£9.00

**PITCH SIZE**
116 x 76 yards

**WEST STAND**
UPPER: £18.00/£9.00
LOWER: £14.00/£7.00

**EAST STAND**
UPPER: £18.00/£9.00
LOWER: £14.00/£7.00

AWAY FANS £22.00/£11.00

SIR MATT BUSBY WAY

£20.00/£10.00
**SOUTH STAND**

AWAY £20.00/£10.00

**FOOTBALL GROUND** ⇌ STATION

MANCHESTER PICCADILLY ⇌

# MANSFIELD TOWN

**ADDRESS:** Field Mill, Quarry Lane
Mansfield
Notts NG18 5DA

**TELEPHONE No:** 01623 23567

**TICKET OFFICE:** 01623 23567

**FAX:** 01623 25014

**CLUBCALL:** 0891 12 13 11

**WEB SITE:**
http://web.jet.es/roe/mtfc/main.htm
(unofficial)

**NICKNAME:** The Stags

**RECORD ATTENDANCE:**
24,467 v Nottingham Forest FA Cup 3rd 10 January
1953 (L 0-1)

**CLUB COLOURS:**
**HOME:** Shirts: Amber with Royal Blue side stripe;
Shorts: Amber with Royal Blue side stripe;
Socks: Royal Blue with Amber trim
**AWAY:** Shirts: White with Blue pinstripe;
Shorts: White with Blue pinstripe; Socks: White
**THIRD:** Shirts: Chocolate and Light Blue stripes;
Shorts: Light Blue; Socks: Light Blue
Home fans will be pleased to know that the third kit is not
merely another way of squeezing a few pennies out of
supporters but a 'celebration' of the club's centenary.

**KIT SPONSORS:** Mansfield Brewery

**MANUFACTURERS:** Beaver International

## GROUND INFO

The ground has a real run-down feel to it from the
vandalised programme booth near the car park to the
boarded hut by the away end, and the club shop is
perhaps the saddest in the league. Still, at least Field Mill
has some unique aspects about it; after all there aren't
many away ends which fans get to share with an
electricity sub-station.

The stewarding at the ground is good without having
any airs or graces. The police adopt a fairly no nonsense
approach, which some may feel spills over into bloody-
mindedness but, in truth, they will only mess fans around
if the fans are perceived as causing problems, otherwise
you'll be left pretty much to your own devices.

**CAPACITY:** Stands: 2,695; Terrace: 4,027;
Total: 6,905
This actually totals 6,722, but the club has included an
extra 183 Directors, Disabled, Press and Sponsors in its
final total of 6,905. These are as for 1997-8, but see also
future developments. The first stage of redevelopment
has started and capacity at the start of the season will be
5,289.

**AWAY FANS:** Quarry Lane End Uncovered
Terrace: 1,464;
Bishop Street Stand 563;
Total: 2,027
While some may grumble that the terracing at Field Mill
is a bit pricey for adults, and that it is unfair to charge
away fans the same as home fans as the home terracing
is covered, at least Mansfield do offer the visitors
concessions, and what concessions they are! £3 for a
child is excellent and deserves to be praised. If the
weather is bad then it is as well to try out the Bishop
Street or West Stand, which at a £2 premium for adults
and children can be worth it.

**DISABLED FACILITIES:** There are 40
spaces for disabled fans in the Bishop Street Stand.
Admission for disabled supporters is free, and it is £5 for
helpers. It is worth noting that there is a concessionary
price of £3 for helpers. Pre-booking is not required.
Although there are no specific disabled parking facilities
at the ground, I have heard that if you phone them up
before your visit, they may be able to work something
out, as the car park can get a bit cramped and is not the
easiest place around which to manoeuvre a wheelchair.
Matchday commentaries are available for the visually
impaired.

**PROGRAMME:** £1.50
'It's cheap' and 'it tries hard' are probably the nicest
things that I could say about it.

**FANZINES:**
>*Follow The Yellow Brick Road*    £1
>*Iffy Haircut*    40p

I actually managed to get hold of a copy of *FTYBR* last
year and well worth the wait it was too. This is not
printed very frequently (four or so a season apparently)
which means that if you are towards the end of a run they
can be a little dated. *Iffy* is a fanzine/journal that has
appeared in the WSC listings for a couple of years, but I
have never seen a copy.

## TRAVEL

### NEAREST RAILWAY STATION:
MANSFIELD !! (01302 340222 — Doncaster Enquiries)
Yes in 1995 it finally happened, Mansfield strode into the
19th century by getting a train station.

**BUS:** Rosemary Street bus station (Mansfield) (01494
211007)
Either an 8 or a 54 will drop you off by the A60 for the
ground.

### BY CAR:
**NORTH:** M1 to J29, then take the A617 to Mansfield.
After about 6.5 miles you will see the civic theatre on
your right. Take the next right into Rosemary Street (if
you drive all the way past the civic centre, you've gone

too far), and follow Rosemary Street past the bus station where it becomes Belvedere Road, and then Portland Street (A60). After 0.5 mile, turn right into Quarry Lane and the ground is 300yd on the right.

**EAST:** A617 into Mansfield until the road is intersected by St Peters Way (dual carriageway). Turn left into St Peters Way and continue to the bottom of the road, then left again into Portland Street. Take the third right into Quarry Lane and the ground is 300yd on the right.

**SOUTH/WEST:** M1 to J28, then follow the A38 (Sutton Road) into Mansfield. As you approach the town centre you will pass the Victoria Hospital. Take the third right after this into Belvedere Road, then as north.

**PARKING:** There is a large car park by the ground which appears to be a bit of a free-for-all.

## FUTURE DEVELOPMENTS

In 1997/98 it was announced that the possible move to a new ground at Portland Sidings would be shelved and Field Mill redeveloped. In March 1998 it was stated that it was virtually certain that this work would start in the summer with the first stage of the work being the construction of a 5,500-seat West Stand, which apparently will utilise the current foundations (and roof). If this does go ahead the seating currently available for visiting supporters in the Bishop Street Stand may be reduced/discontinued as home supporters' requirements are met. There are, however, still some questions which remain unresolved as this book goes to print regarding the financing of this stand — the fact that on occasions the players' wages weren't paid on time for a start — and I would not be altogether surprised if the old stand remained in place at the start of 1998-9. If all does go to plan, there will be further work in 1999-2000 in rebuilding the North Stand and Quarry Lane terrace into 2,500-seat stands, with the Bishop Street Stand being the

final area of development. This will give Field Mill a 15,000 all-seated capacity. Note: latest news is that the Quarry Lane Terrace and North Stand may be the first areas on which work is started.

## OTHER INFORMATION

Before the game, try what must be the expert summariser's dream, the Early Doors, which is about 200yd away. Be warned though this themed American diner is not the cheapest place in town at which you can have a pint, and a better bet can be the Plough (next to Safeways) or the Victoria in the town centre.

The food inside the ground is OK, though the pies crumble to the touch (still, if you don't have anything to eat or drink then you won't have to use the toilets which are very grim). Outside Field Mill other than a KFC, you need to take a 15min walk into the town centre for nourishment. If you do decide to stretch your legs, then check out Pie's Plaice for some rather tasty chips with gravy.

The corner flags at the Mill have the word's 'Good'ay Sport' written on them — sadly, a reference to the fact that they are sponsored by a local shop rather than a greeting from the club to supporters. Finally it should be noted that 1997-8 saw the introduction of an official club mascot, which, unsurprisingly given the club's nickname, is supposedly a stag (though it looks more like a moose to me). Whilst generally this is very much a run of the (Field) Mill character, it does offer away fans the potential of some amusement by having a head which — even by mascot standards — is too big for its body. This means that during periods of high winds (October to April), the creature can be seen trying not to let itself be decapitated and thus traumatise the kids it is trying to amuse.

*Total Football* **Experience Rating: 61**

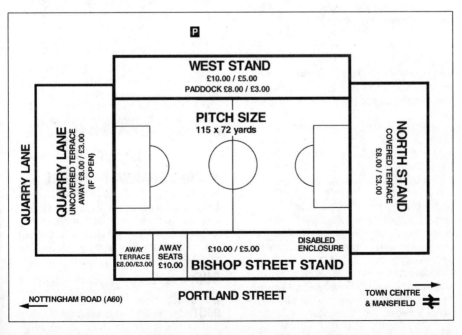

# MIDDLESBROUGH

**ADDRESS:** Cellnet Riverside
Stadium
Middlesbrough
TS3 6RS

**TELEPHONE No:** 01642 877700
**TICKET OFFICE:** 01642 877745
**FAX:** 01642 877840
**LIVEWIRE:** 0891 42 42 00
**WEB SITE:**
www.geocities.com/Colosseum/1088/
(unofficial)
**NICKNAME:** Boro
**RECORD ATTENDANCE:**
Riverside Stadium: 30,228 v Oxford United Div 1
3 May 1998 (W 4-1)

**CLUB COLOURS:**
**HOME:** Shirts: Red; Shorts: White; Socks: Red
**AWAY:** tba

**KIT SPONSORS:** Cellnet
**MANUFACTURERS:** Errea

## GROUND INFO

'The ground that was named by the fans' is how the stadium was announced, and quite rightly, after all it was from a supporters' poll that the club came up with the name The Riverside Stadium, and so it stayed for... oh a good couple of weeks until Cellnet offered a wad of cash to have their moniker stuck at the front of it.

The ground is in the middle of nowhere and all that surround it are piles of rubble (this may sound like an exaggeration but is true), which means that if you want to live on the wild side (you know, buy a newspaper or the like) then you will have to do so in the town centre. This being the case allow yourself a good 20min to walk to the ground.

Surprisingly, given the inclemency of the local weather, one of the things that those involved with the construction of the stadium were keen to promote was the fact that they undertook a 'sun study' which involved establishing the latitude and longitude of the ground and daily sun paths generated, which led to translucent panels being introduced into the roof on the South and West Stands. Hopefully this will see an end to those dreadful November days when you can hardly see to drive your car home having spent 90min squinting into the ferociously hot sun.

Be aware that the vast majority of seats are sold on a season ticket basis and that if you haven't got a space in the away section, you may be in for a long fruitless journey as there is a distinct lack of touts around. The

lads from *FMTTM* may be able to point you in the right direction if they know of any spares but they DO NOT deal in touting tickets.

**CAPACITY:** Stands: 34,600; Terrace: Nil
(Post completion of infilling of corners.)

**AWAY FANS:** South Stand: 2,700
The South Stand provides good leg room and a fine view.

**DISABLED FACILITIES:** The club's attitude towards disabled supporters is second to none and, rather than just grand words and empty gestures, it practices what it preaches when it states its objective is 'Integration Not Discrimination'. Scandalously because other clubs do not share this enlightened vision, many wheelchair-bound Boro fans who hold season tickets with the club have missed out on the big occasions because they cannot be accommodated in the numbers required. There are over 300 spaces in total available, of which 24 are designated for visiting fans. Contact the club to pre-book a seat and a parking space. Cost of admission is £15 for a joint ticket for one disabled fan and one helper. One of the best — if not the best — trips in English football.

**PROGRAMME:** £2.00
A very good programme for home fans that has won a number of awards over the last two years, well put together with plenty of information stats and good overall readability.

**FANZINES:**

| | |
|---|---|
| Fly Me To The Moon | £1 |
| The Boys From Brazil | 80p |

Last season *Fly Me To The Moon* became the first fanzine to break the 200 issue mark. This is a remarkable feat in itself, as is the fact that there is a new one produced for every game at the Cellnet. However, what is really incredible is the standard that is maintained within the pages; these are consistently funny and incisive, providing a real view as to what is going on in the club rather than half a page of waffle from a club official. The latter is all you'll get in the official publication. Buy it instead of a programme and expect it — although it is considerably slimmer — to last at least twice as long.

## TRAVEL

### NEAREST RAILWAY STATION:
Middlesbrough (0191 232 6262 — Newcastle Enquiries)
Middlesbrough station is one of the nearest buildings to the ground. In fact, when you leave the ground you may just be able see it on the horizon (well, OK that was a bit of an exaggeration). Allow yourself a good 15min to get to the ground from here.

**BUS:** Middlesbrough bus station (01642 244166)
**BY CAR:**
**SOUTH:** A19 to A66. Head towards Middlesbrough on

the A66 (M'boro By-Pass) exit the A66 for St Hildes and take the first left exit off the roundabout. Follow this road through the tram lights and into Dock Street, and then Scott's Road off which is the ground.

**WEST:** A66, then as south.

**NORTH:** Either — A19, A1032 (cross river by Tees Bridge), then left onto the A66. Take the first exit at the next major roundabout and bear right into Bridge Street, then as south.

Or — A178/A1046, cross the Tees by the Transporter Bridge. Take the second left onto Commercial Street which leads to Scott's Road and the ground.

**PARKING:** There are 1,320 parking spaces at the ground, but these are all taken up by permit holders.

## FUTURE DEVELOPMENTS

Not ones to let the grass grow under their feet, Boro are infilling the two corners that would join the West Stand to the rest of the stadium thus adding approximately 4,000 to the capacity. This should be completed for the start of the 1998-9 season.

## OTHER INFORMATION

If you are looking for a pre-match pint a quick word of warning: there is a pub by the station which you may think about popping into. This is a real home pub and I've heard countless tales of away supporters getting grief in there, so it's probably best to steer clear.

A question: what is the most irksome sound in footie? Graham Kelly? The whoosh before a replay on Sky Sports? Possibly, but up there amongst them must be the Boro tannoy announcer (apparently an ex-Radio 1 DJ, which I think supports the case). His pre-match announcements and 'entertainment' appear to consist of

shouting 'Woo!' a lot and trying to break the 'record' of Mexican waves around the ground (a feat which no away fans should ever participate in). The Boro fans aren't too enamoured with him either, especially since he stopped playing the 'Power Game' when the players ran out; he now plays Pig Bag's 'Stand Tall' at Bryan (man of the people) Robson's request! This chap is an ideal excuse to stay in the pub until two minutes before kick-off (or at least would be if there were any pubs around).

The food inside the ground is good but fairly pricey; a couple of cheeseburgers and chips is going to set you back well over a fiver, tea is about £1 and beer and lager are around the standard £2 a pint mark. Given this, it is quite easy to rattle up a fairly big bill, which makes it all the more irritating that you almost have to plead with the girls behind the counter (who do a fine line in surly) to take a £20 note — or maybe I just struck them as being the dishonest type.

I have been asked to mention that the wine that is served at the club apparently won the best in the Premiership award last season (Oh really, how super, come on Cressida, we must go down to the Cellnet for a glass of vino and a spot of soccer). Actually I prefer the comment of the Boro fan who admitted to me that he had tried it once (but only when his mates weren't there) and said that he had enjoyed it because it got him pissed quite quickly (now if they marketed it using that slogan I'm sure sales would rise). Any 'interesting fact' fans will no doubt be fascinated to know that the first ever half-time scoreboard was introduced by Boro in 1902, and the first ever score that was shown on it was when the crowd at a reserve match were informed that the first team were leading in their away match. Zzzzzz...

*Total Football* **Experience Rating: 68**

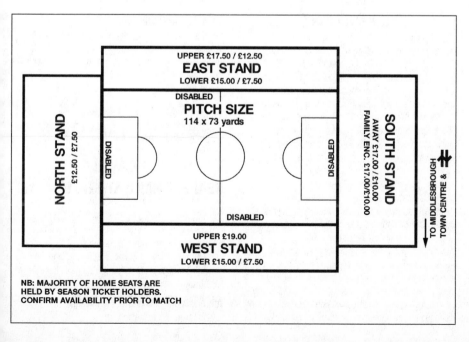

**EAST STAND**
UPPER £17.50 / £12.50
LOWER £15.00 / £7.50

DISABLED

**PITCH SIZE**
114 x 73 yards

DISABLED

**NORTH STAND**
£12.50 / £7.50

DISABLED

DISABLED

**SOUTH STAND**
AWAY £17.00 / £10.00
FAMILY ENC. £17.00/£10.00

DISABLED

**WEST STAND**
UPPER £19.00
LOWER £15.00 / £7.50

TO MIDDLESBROUGH TOWN CENTRE &

**NB: MAJORITY OF HOME SEATS ARE HELD BY SEASON TICKET HOLDERS. CONFIRM AVAILABILITY PRIOR TO MATCH**

# MILLWALL

**ADDRESS:** The Den
Zampa Road
London SE16 3LN
**TELEPHONE No:** 0171 232 1222
**TICKET OFFICE:** 0171 231 9999
**FAX:** 0171 231 3663
**CLUBCALL:** 0891 400 300
**WEB SITE:** www.millwallfc.co.uk
(official)
There is an unofficial site at freespace.virgin/angela.
grice/millwall.html but there isn't a lot there.

**NICKNAME:** The Lions

**RECORD ATTENDANCE:**
48,672 v Derby FA Cup 5th 20 February 1937 (W 2-1)
At The New Den: 20,093 v Arsenal FA Cup 3rd
10 January 1994 (L 0-1)

**CLUB COLOURS:**
**HOME:** Shirts: Blue; Shorts: Silver; Socks: Blue
**AWAY:** Shirts: White; Shorts: Black; Socks: White
How times have changed!!! Forget about all-seater stadia,
the New Den etc; who could have believed Millwall would
have ever turned out in 'silver' shorts. 'Arry Cripps would
have ripped your throat out for even suggesting it.

**KIT SPONSORS:** Live-TV (the Weather In
Norwegian)

**MANUFACTURERS:** Asics

## GROUND INFO

The ground appears to have been modelled on Ibrox, and
is a very impressive stadium with facilities to match.
Prior to the game, at half-time, and again at full-time, you
can have a beer and watch TV. In fact the club are aiming
for a situation whereby fans turn up at 11am and go
home at 7pm (except for evening matches naturally) and
thereby ease the congestion that occurs at many grounds.
(The extra income the club earns from the fans has
nothing to do with it then?) Brilliant concessions are
available for all fans. The only minor criticism is that it is
slightly cramped for leg room.

Don't be fooled into thinking that the nice new
stadium means nice new fans. True, some of the
supporters feel somewhat out of place having been used
to the comforts of the old Den, but when you come down
to it, the atmosphere can be just as hostile and
intimidating; and incidentally, unlike the old ground
where you had a fair idea of where you were most likely
to avoid grief, in the new ground there isn't that kind of
identity! (My first visit there was straight from work with
me in a suit with a briefcase, and I ended up in a different
section to the one I thought I was going in. I blended in

like a chameleon on a kilt — a very relaxing night that
was!) Stick to your own sections in all but the most
important of circumstances.

Note, due to some of the problems that the club is
encountering, certain parts of the ground may be closed
on matchdays if it is considered that there is unlikely to
be sufficient demand (I don't know why but seeing
swathes of empty seats brings on a feeling of melancholy
and can take the edge off the day — though obviously
not as much as it takes the edge off the club's day). You
tend to find that, again based on reputation, there is quite
a high police presence in and around the ground. This
tends to be fairly unobtrusive and the officers have
obviously been briefed that fans like to have a sing, shout
and may occasionally blaspheme (gasp! how shocking!).
If you get out of hand you will be dealt with, but you will
not be expected to behave like monks.

**CAPACITY:** Stands: 20,146; Terrace: Nil

**AWAY FANS:** North Stand Upper: 2,458;
North Stand Lower: 1,924;
Total: 4,382
Also available are up to 250 seats in the executive area
and boxes. It should be noted that the North Stand can be
sub-divided according to the level of away support.

**DISABLED FACILITIES:** There are 200
places in the West Stand Lower Tier, with one helper
admitted per disabled fan. Disabled fans are admitted free
of charge, with helpers paying £10.

Matchday commentaries are available. If you wish to
avail yourself of the facilities pre-book, though this is not
compulsory, when you can also sort yourself out a
parking space.

**PROGRAMME:** £1.70
Last season's stood out as a good 2nd Division effort
although, if you want a copy, then buy it early as it is
worth knowing that on my last visit there were none on
sale inside the ground.

**FANZINES:**

| | |
|---|---|
| *The Lion Roars* | £1 |
| *No-One Likes Us* | £1 |
| *Tales From Senegal Fields* | £1 |

## TRAVEL

**NEAREST RAILWAY STATION:** South
Bermondsey (0171 928 5100)
This is about 0.5 mile away from the ground and has a
fairly decent service to/from London Bridge. The first
couple of trains after a match do tend to get very packed
and a bit silly. If you are going to a game with young
children it is sensible to dally a while before attempting to
head back.

**NEAREST TUBE STATION:**
Surrey Quays (East London Line).

## BUS:
London Transport (0171 222 1234)
The tube station is about 10min walk from the stadium, and the trip takes you under some very spooky railway arches around which seems to hang a permanent fog. As such, BR is probably the best choice of public transport. Alternatively go to Elephant & Castle (Northern Line) and get a 53 bus from the bus stop on the opposite side of the road to the cinema. Ask for Ilderton Road and, rather than show your ignorance by asking the driver to tell you when you're there, just follow the crowd.

## BY CAR:
**NORTH:** Leave the M1 at J2 and follow the City/A1 signs then pick up signs first for Shoreditch, Whitechapel, and finally Ring Road. Continue over Tower Bridge and take the first exit at the roundabout onto the A2. Follow the A2 Old Kent Road and after four miles turn left at the Canterbury Arms pub into Ilderton Road, then follow Surrey Canal Road into Zampa Road for the ground.

**SOUTH:** A20, A21 into London. At New Cross follow the signs for City/Westminster into Kender Street, then first left, right at traffic lights into Ilderton Road, then as north.

**WEST:** From M4 follow the South Circular (A205) following signs for Clapham, City, A3, then Camberwell, New Cross, Rochester until you get to the junction with Kender Street (which is on the left). Turn into Kender Street, then as south.

**EAST:** A2 to New Cross, then as south.

**PARKING:** Street parking only at present.

## FUTURE DEVELOPMENTS
Nothing other than survival.

## OTHER INFORMATION
There's an excellent choice of food at the ground and there is also a bar (just in case you need that little bit of Dutch courage!!!) It isn't cheap but there aren't that many other places around the ground that you can use as an alternative — the Cliftonville is probably the closest, and relatively safe; none-the-less I'd think twice about going in there with an away replica top on. If you don't fancy pricey beer and the luxury of watching the Lions' last match on the TV then it is probably as well to stick to the City (where you can drink expensive beer but you don't have to watch old Millwall matches), although make sure you leave yourself enough time for the deceptively long trip to the ground.

One good thing about the food in the ground is that, unlike the song which heralds the entrance of the teams by suggesting that you should have 'jellied eels with a nice glass of beer', there are no apodes (wobbly or otherwise) on the menu.

As you head towards the ground there is a sign proclaiming it to be the 'New Den' (and you've got to wonder how many times the painter had to do that before the club were satisfied; somewhere there has got to be a pile of signs welcoming you to Zampa Road, The New London Stadium, etc). Given that the ground is only a few years old what is curious is that the sign appears to have been done in the late 1890s and is already peeling and flaking like nobody's business, which is perhaps a sad reflection on the dire financial straits that the club found itself in last year.

Without wanting to sound hackneyed and clichéd, the club has done a lot of work in promoting its role in the community, and a family spirit amongst the fans. To a degree this has worked: everybody seems to know everybody else, and it can be argued that this is what a football club should be all about, local people supporting their local team.

***Total Football* Experience Rating: 71**

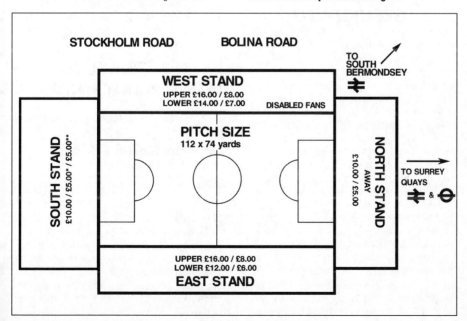

# NEWCASTLE UNITED

**ADDRESS:** St James' Park
Newcastle upon Tyne
NE1 4ST
**TELEPHONE No:** 0191 201 8400
**TICKET OFFICE:** 0191 261 1571
**FAX:** 0191 201 8600
**CLUBCALL:** 0891 12 11 90
**WEBSITE:** www.nufc.co.uk
**NICKNAME:** The Magpies
## RECORD ATTENDANCE:
68,386 v Chelsea Div 1 3 September 1930 (W 1-0)
The club holds the record for the highest attendance for
an abandoned match — 63,480 v Swansea in the FA Cup
in 1953, which was halted after 8min play. And if you
think you've got a bad job, just imagine being the poor
guy who had to tell that lot no refunds.

## CLUB COLOURS:
**HOME:** Shirts: Black and White stripes; Shorts: Black;
Socks: Black with White hooped top
**AWAY:** Shirts: 'Italian' Blue with Yellow markings;
Shorts: 'Italian' Blue with yellow markings;
Socks: 'Italian' blue with three Yellow stripes
The club also offers a limited edition home shirt with the
words 'FA Cup Final Wembley 1998' under the badge.
Worth every penny of £39.99 surely?

**KIT SPONSORS:** Newcastle Brown Ale —
Scottish and Newcastle Breweries
**MANUFACTURERS:** Adidas

## GROUND INFO
Last season, once again, well over 90% of the available
spaces went to season ticket holders, and as these were
naturally on offer initially to existing holders, it has
become somewhat of an 'inheritance' to have a relative
with a season ticket. For the most part, expect it to be a
struggle to gain admission. Your best bet of getting in is
to have one of your own club's season tickets and hope
that you get lucky with one of the fairly small away
allocation. Credit to the club for making some (about
1,000ish) tickets available to the general public for some
matches (sold mid-week before a match) although the
fact that the queues for these started forming at about
5am means that only the most dedicated got their hands
on one. It should be noted that the maximum per person
is two (but not necessarily together).
   The transformation of St James' Park is staggering
when you think of what it was like just a few years ago,
but on my last visit I have to say that I began to wonder
at what cost. Stewarding was very picky and such
heinous crimes as standing up when the teams emerged,
brought rebukes — not because it could spoil the view
but because 'the cameras can't pick out the advertising

108

hoardings if you do'.

**CAPACITY:** Stands: 36,610; Terrace: Nil
**AWAY FANS:** Sir John Hall Stand
East Corner: 1,876
On my last visit to the ground I witnessed the spectacular
sight of someone sliding down the banister which runs
from the top to the bottom of the away end. This
spectacular feat of derring do — which I have to point
out is very dangerous and should not be tried — was
accompanied by rhythmic clapping from both home and
away supporters. Sadly, the stewards at the bottom failed
to see the funny side and ejected the fan in question at
the bottom of his run.

**DISABLED FACILITIES:** There are spaces
for 116 disabled fans. Admission is half the standard
price for wheelchair-bound supporters and full price for
helpers. However, the majority are allocated on a
seasonal basis, but you can always contact the club to try
and obtain a place. Match commentaries for the visually
impaired are also available on Magpie Radio (1413AM).

**PROGRAMME:** £2.00
A fairly poor and dull effort, in my opinion.

## FANZINES:
| | |
|---|---|
| *The Mag* | £1.40 |
| *The Number Nine* | £1 |
| *Talk Of The Toon* | £1.20 |

Two great efforts in *The Mag* — the only problem with
which is its unhandy A4 size — and which broke
through the 100 issues barrier last year — and *The
Number Nine*. For me, *The Mag* shades it; it's a brilliant
mix of defending and attacking the club (and even the
club's supporters if that is warranted) interspersed with
some large dollops of humour. As a visiting fan, you may
find some of the (slightly fawning) interviews a bit dull,
but get it anyway.

## TRAVEL
**NEAREST RAILWAY STATION:** Central
station (0191 232 6262)
From here either get on the Metro to St James' or walk up
Grainger Street which will take 10-20min.

**NEAREST METRO STATION:**
St James' (behind Gallowgate)

**BUS:** Gallowgate or Haymarket bus stations (0191 232
4211)

## BY CAR:
**SOUTH:** Take A1, A68 and then A6127, go over the
Tyne Bridge and at the roundabout take first exit into
Mosley Street. You then enter a one-way system, keep to
the left-hand lane for Neville Street and at the bottom of
this turn left into Leazes Park Road — another one-way
system — and left then right into St James' Street for the
ground.

**NORTH:** A1 into Newcastle and follow the signs for Hexham until you get to Percy Street. Turn right into Leazes Park Road and right again into Strawberry Place.

**WEST:** A69 into Newcastle leading onto the West Road, continue until you reach Newcastle General Hospital. Immediately after the hospital there are some traffic lights; turn left at these into Brighton Grove, then right after 0.25 mile into Studley Terrace. After a further 0.25 mile this merges with Barrack Road. Left at next roundabout (still called Barrack Road) and the ground is on the left.

**EAST:** A189 to A193 (signposted Newcastle City Centre). After you cross the motorway (A6127) turn left into Haymarket (by the metro station). This becomes Percy Street, then as north.

If you are coming up the A1 you can't fail to notice the 'Angel of The North' sculpture (although it didn't seem as big as I imagined it would be).

**PARKING:** There are several car parks around the ground, including on Barrack Road and one just by St James' metro station which is directly outside the stadium. Be warned though that these are all murder to get away from and you should allow at least 20-30min before expecting to hit a (moderately) free road.

## FUTURE DEVELOPMENTS

It now appears that the idea of a new ground at Castle Leazes has been shelved and the club is going to spend an awful lot of money increasing the capacity at St James' to just over 50,000. The plans for realising this are being finalised and work is expected to start at the end of the 1998-9 season.

## OTHER INFORMATION

The nearest pub to the ground is the Strawberry. However, like the majority in the immediate vicinity, it gets packed about two minutes after opening its doors and it is has a real home feel about it. (So much so that at many pubs unless you have a Newcastle season ticket you won't get over the threshold.) A good away pub is the Akenside Trader; this is just after you have gone under the very tall bridge in Dean Street which is off from Grey Street and fairly near the Bigg Market. This is about a 15min walk from the ground.

Inside the ground the food has improved massively over the years I have been going. Mind you, taste has come at a price, with burgers hitting the £2 plus barrier. A better and more reasonable bet is the Mag Pie (groan) — hot and tasty, it will help to keep out the bitter wind that still invades the stadium.

Many people said to me that they felt that the atmosphere at SJP was dying on its feet, but on my visit I found that stories about the demise of the fans' passion had been greatly exaggerated, although, unlike previous years, I did hear boos mixed among the cheers when some of the home team's names were read out.

If you get the opportunity, stay overnight in the city as the place is buzzing and you can see just how inaccurate Hall and Sheppard were when they called the local girls 'dogs'. I do have to say that the club seems these days to take its fans for granted. There are numerous instances of this I could quote, but for sheer mean spiritedness perhaps the award should go to the story that it banned two fans from releasing an unofficial cup final song claiming it was illegal because it included the words 'Toon Army', on which the club owns the copyright. I've got to say, if I was a T**n (presumably how I have to write it) fan, the words would stick in my throat next time I was chanting them to try and encourage the team through another uninspiring Premier League match.

***Total Football* Experience Rating: 88**

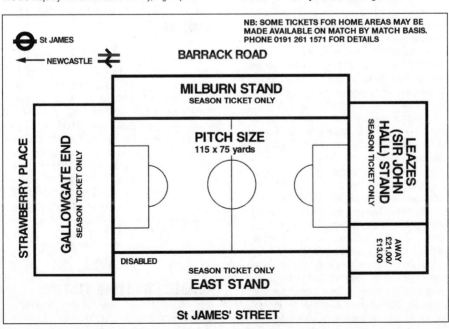

# NORTHAMPTON TOWN

**ADDRESS:** Sixfields Stadium
Upton Way
Northampton NN5 5QA
**TELEPHONE No:** 01604 757773
**TICKET OFFICE:** 01604 588338
**FAX:** 01604 751613
**COBBLERS CLUBCALL:**
0930 55 59 70
**WEB SITE:**
http://web.ukonline.co.uk/ntfc/
(unofficial)
**NICKNAME:** The Cobblers
**RECORD ATTENDANCE:**
24,523 v Fulham Div 1 23 April 1966 (L 2-4)
At Sixfields — 7,501 v Bristol Rovers Div 2 13 May
1998 (W3-0)
**CLUB COLOURS:**
**HOME:** Shirts: Claret with White vertical stripes;
Shorts: White; Socks: White
**AWAY:** Shirts: White with single Claret hoop;
Shorts: Black; Socks: Black
**SHIRT SPONSORS:** Nationwide
**MANUFACTURERS:** Pro-Star

## GROUND INFO

Sixfields is a good stadium and, despite the fact that it is out of town, since the area is fairly well developed around it, there is still quite a lot of character and feel to the place. Away fans get given the South Stand, in which you are assured a decent view no matter where you go, although the leg room could be a little more generous. The club offers concessions which, whilst not being earth shattering in their generosity, are at least fair in that they are the same as those offered to home supporters. One minor irritation which it is worth noting is that you are expected to use the toilets by the West Stand, and if you happen to be sitting in the east side of the stand, you will have to walk all the way across to the other side of the ground rather than use the ones 20ft away by the corner of the East and South Stand, and quite right too. Good honest hard-working home supporters don't want you polluting their urinals, you never know what they might catch! The club's policy is to encourage better use of its family enclosures in the East and West Stands and away fans are also welcome to take advantage of the concessions available in these areas. The prices for the West Stand family enclosure are: Tandem (ie adult and one child) £16; Tricycle (ie adult and two children) £20.50; and Quad (ie two adults and two children) £28. These tickets must be booked (tel: 01604 588 338).

There are now two family enclosures, one in both the East and West Stands.

One thing guaranteed to get on your nerves (although I have been told that this is not the club's decision but the local authority's) is the ridiculous ticketing system which means there are no cash turnstiles. Instead you have to track down the portakabin selling tickets for the area you want to go in, which in itself is a chore as these aren't brilliantly signposted, then you have to queue up to get your ticket and then you have to queue up again to get into the ground. This seems totally pointless, and all it seems to achieve is that countless away fans (the home fans have got it sussed by now) miss the start of matches. Get there 15min early to sort yourself out.

**CAPACITY:** Stands: 7,653; Terrace: Nil
**AWAY FANS:** South Stand: 944; East Stand: 333
**DISABLED FACILITIES:** There are 77 places for disabled fans and 78 for carers — who is the lucky person who gets to sit with two of their mates I wonder? — which are sited in all parts of the ground. The cost of admission is £6 each for both wheelchair-bound supporters and helpers. Pre-booking is not required. There are matchday commentaries available for the visually impaired, and designated parking facilities.

**PROGRAMME:** £1.50
Excellent value for a 48-page programme, or so you'd think. However, there were over 26 pages of adverts and sponsorship opportunities in the last one I saw. The visitors' section was basically pen pics (but without the pics). Other than that there was a one page divisional round-up and one page on European football which would keep you occupied, but after that very little at all.

**FANZINES:**
*What A Load Of Cobblers* £1
The issues that were produced last season were easily the best of this fanzine's 10-year history. You get all the normal fanzine stuff; the majority of the criticism seems to be aimed not at the club, board or players, but at the fans who are accused — unjustly in my experience — of being passionless, dull and unworthy of the team. There was a programme profile which (maybe coincidentally) looked at old programmes which had been produced for previous encounters between the day's opponents (and which in doing so showed more initiative than not only the Northampton programme, but half of the ones in the league) as well as a couple of excellent pieces by 'The Olney Cobbler'. However, one disturbing thing was the bloke who sold my copy to me had a wild-eyed staring look about him, which made me very nervous!!

## TRAVEL

**NEAREST RAILWAY STATION:** Castle station: (01908 370883 — Milton Keynes Enquiries)
**BUS:** Northampton Transport (01604 755155)

A 100 starts off at the County Ground and goes via the bus station (Bay 14) to Sixfields in about 20min. Alternatively you can get a 27 or 28 from the bus station to the ground (10min).

## BY CAR:

**NORTH/WEST:** M1 to J16. Take A45 (signposted Northampton/Duston). After roughly 3.25 miles there is a roundabout; take the fourth exit onto Upton Way for the ground.

**SOUTH:** M1 to J15a, then A43 (signposted Northampton) to A45 Northampton Ring Road. Bear left (signposted Daventry) at the second roundabout, then take the first exit into Upton Way and the ground is immediately on the left.

**EAST:** Either A43 or A428 to A45. Once on the A45, follow signs for Daventry until you pass the Rugby Ground (Franklin Gardens). At the second roundabout after this, take the first exit into Upton Way for the ground.

No matter which direction you are coming from, the ground is very well signposted.

**PARKING:** There is free on-site parking at Sixfields with six overflow car parks to take the strain on busy days.

This a major step forward from the club's County Ground days when fans were forced to use the maze of nearby streets, and better still, the club appears to have avoided the problems encountered at other purpose-built stadiums such as Walsall, where the lack of exit roads means at least a half-hour wait before getting away.

## FUTURE DEVELOPMENTS

The club does advise that the capacity at Sixfields can be extended to 15,000 if required 'without too much of a problem'.

## OTHER INFORMATION

There are a couple of bars around the Sixfields complex but I would urge caution as, on my last two visits to one of these, the Washington Square, I saw fights flare up over nothing at all. If you want a quiet beer then you are better off catching a bus or getting a cab into town. If you decide to save a few pennies and walk it, be warned as it is a good couple of miles and there is only about one — not very good — pub, Big Hand Mo's, on the way (although you will see a shop which combines a reptile house and a poodle parlour!?). If you do walk in to the centre there is a reasonable chip shop, The Rainbow, but you have got the choice of Burger King, Little Chef, Pizza Hut etc at the complex.

Inside Sixfields, the food was pretty good; the sausage rolls are worthy of mention as is the fact that they had HP brown sauce rather than the unlabelled sump oil you find at some places. Service was a bit slow — it took three people to serve me with a sausage roll and a cup of tea — and there wasn't any chocolate on offer.

Music obviously doesn't play a big part in the lives of those who work at the ground as the sides emerge to a mixture of Fanfare For The Common Man and The Leader of The Gang. Even more irksome is that when the Cobblers score you get a quick burst of the CanCan (cranked up to full volume, and very distorted just what you need to calm the nerves after your defence has let you down again). Still, it is worth getting to the ground early because behind the North Stand is a huge grass bank which if, for whatever reason, you can't get into the ground itself, offers a decent free view of most of the pitch. However, where it really comes into its own is during the 10min period 2.55-3.05 when late-arriving fans have the opportunity to use it as a shortcut to the ground. Inevitably, a large proportion of those who go for it end up somersaulting, bouncing and sliding down its muddy sides… splendid entertainment.

*Total Football* **Experience Rating: 85**

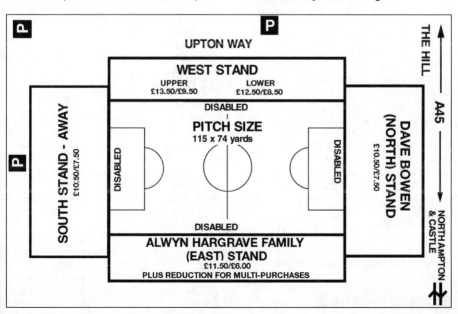

# NORWICH CITY

**ADDRESS:** Carrow Road
Norwich
Norfolk NR1 1JE
**TELEPHONE No:** 01603 760760
**TICKET OFFICE:** 01603 761661
**FAX:** 01603 613886
**CLUB CALL:** 0891 12 11 44
**WEB SITE:** www.ecn.co.uk/ncfc
(official)
**E-MAIL:** ncfc@ecn.co.uk
**NICKNAME:** The Canaries
**RECORD ATTENDANCE:**
43,984 v Leicester FA Cup 6th 30 March 1963 (L 0-2)

**CLUB COLOURS:**
**HOME:** Shirts: Yellow; Shorts: Yellow; Socks: Yellow
**AWAY:** Shirts: Green; Shorts: Green; Socks: Green
Designed by Bruce Oldfield, no less.

**KIT SPONSORS:** Colmans
**MANUFACTURERS:** Pony

## GROUND INFO

Three quarters of Carrow Road is a neat and tidy ground with impressive stands, which still retain some character. Not that it will bother away fans too much as they are in the South Stand, which makes up the other quarter. Actually, if you look beyond the South Stand's lived-in exterior, you find it's not that bad. Firstly you get an along-the-side view of the action, for which you pay only as much as non-members at each end of the ground. Secondly, there seem to be fewer pillars blocking your view in this stand than there are in some of the newer constructions. In particular there are places between the Main Stand and River End which only offer a view of about half the pitch and any attempts to stand and peer round pillars are only likely to bring the wrath of stewards and fellow supporters on your head.

Norwich do offer concessions for both home and away supporters (although the £5 reduction isn't that generous). However, the club is another of those who think it is fair to punish supporters of popular visiting sides by having a two-category pricing system.

**CAPACITY:** Stands: 21,994; Terrace: Nil
**AWAY FANS:** South Stand F Block: 334; South Stand G Block: 692; South Stand H Block: 715; Total: 1,741
This can be increased to 4,080 South Stand seats as required.

**DISABLED FACILITIES:** There is a purpose-built area in the South Stand which can accommodate up to 115 fans (40 wheelchair-bound supporters, 40 helpers and 35 others); admission is free for disabled supporters, with helpers paying concessionary rates (£9 grade 'A', £5 grade 'B'). The club requests that you pre-book. Match commentaries for the visually impaired are provided (via Radio Norfolk 95.1FM) but parking is only available on a seasonal basis.

**PROGRAMME:** £2.00
Some people I know think it's excellent and I believe it has won awards in the past, but I just can't see what the fuss is all about.

**FANZINES:**

| | |
|---|---|
| *Cheap Shot* | 50p |
| *Liverpool Are On The Tele Again* | 60p |
| *Ferry Cross The Wensum* | £1 |
| *I Can Drive A Tractor* | 50p |
| *Love Shaq* | £1 |

You'll only tend to see one or at most two of these around on a match day. *LAOTTA* packs an awful lot into its pages, and tends to throw up some amazing articles about what is going on at the club which can leave you slack jawed with shock. Of the others which I have seen, they tend to be a fairly middling bunch.

## TRAVEL

**NEAREST RAILWAY STATION:**
Norwich (0.5 mile) (01603 632055)

**BUS:**
Eastern Counties Omnibus Co Ltd (01603 788890)
Your trip to Carrow Road can be fairly dire if you are relying on public transport, especially for night matches when the vast majority of 'last trains to' are before 9pm. Equally, there are no buses that drop off outside the ground, although this is apparently under review.

**BY CAR:**
**NORTH:** A140. Turn left onto the A47 Outer Ring Road (signposted Yarmouth). Whilst on the A47 the road changes names as follows — Mile Cross Lane, Chartwell Road, Mousehold Lane, Heartease Lane and Harvey Lane. At the bottom of Harvey Lane turn right into Thorpe Road. After 0.3 mile turn left into Carrow Road. Cross the railway and continue along Carrow Road as it bears right, and the ground is on the left.
**SOUTH:** A11. Turn right onto the A140 and continue for one mile until you get to the junction with the A146 at which you should turn left (signposted Norwich). Continue for a further mile then turn onto the A1054. After 0.25 mile you will see Carrow Road, into which you should turn, the ground being 0.25 mile further on.
**WEST:** A47 Outer Ring Road (signposted Yarmouth) and continue along this road until it becomes Martineau Lane. At the roundabout with the A146 take the second

exit into Bracondale, then first right into King Street and the second right into Carrow Road. Go over Carrow Bridge (crossing the River Wensum) and the ground is on the right.

**EAST:** A47 into Norwich, then as north.

Actually finding Carrow Road can be one of life's great frustrations. In my experience, if you ask a passer-by for directions they will either look at you very blankly, as if the very fact that Norwich had a football team had escaped them, or, and I'm positive this is part of some mean-spirited plot hatched by the people of Norfolk that is designed to keep the city free of visiting supporters, they will send you in the exact opposite direction to the one you want. To make matters worse, there is a McDonalds that everyone uses as a point of reference in their instructions, but which I'm sure must be on castors because no matter which way you are facing the first phrase that you'll always hear is 'No, my booty, you want to be on the other side of the road, then carry on till you see the McDonalds...'. After about the 10th attempt I can only suggest you abandon your vehicle and get a cab!

**PARKING:** Nearest car park to the ground is the Riverside which is opposite the City Stand, but it can be tricky to get out of. A better bet can be found off Thorpe Road towards the city centre — once you've crossed the Wensum, take the second left into Mountergate, and there is a multi-storey with 750 spaces on your right.

## FUTURE DEVELOPMENTS
Nothing of any significance.

## OTHER INFORMATION
If you are looking for watering holes, or places of worship, then Norwich is for you with its claim of having a different pub for every day of the year, and a different church for every Sunday. The nearest pubs are the Clarence Harbour (which is by a decent chip shop) on Kerrison Road, and the Kingsway on the corner of Carrow

Road. The Clarence in particular is very popular with away fans, although if there are more than a handful, you'll soon end up feeling like a sardine (and the local constabulary are not overly keen on you taking your drinks and standing outside). If this doesn't appeal there are some slightly further afield. One of my favourites is the Jubilee on St Leonards Road which has a good selection of beer and lager as well as doing some cracking home made food.

There are plenty of stewards and police around the ground, the majority of whom are laid back and helpful.

Inside the ground away fans have the benefit of what can be best described as a train waiting room. This comprises a food serving area and a couple of TVs. Whilst not being fantastic it is a hell of a lot more than you get at some places. The pies in the ground are in the running for the tastiest you will come across, being deep and well-filled with meat. The only trouble is that the club never seems to have them heated enough. The hot drinks are average in both heat and taste.

Apparently City director Delia Smith is going to do the catering in 1998-9 which presumably should signify even better grub so presumably come a bleak January evening you may soon be able to look forward to 'viande pomme de terres en croûte' (that's a meat and potato pie to you and me) or possibly quail and venison served in a raspberry coulis.

Since the departure of the unlamented Mr Chase the club seems a lot more positive about making a visit even more enjoyable. Last season it even commissioned a survey to find out what people thought about how the club operated which covered all aspects of matchdays. It will be interesting to see how or if the results of this review will be implemented during the 1998-9 season. Fans were apparently paid £30 for their thoughts (so I'll expect a cheque from the club through the post any day now then...).

*Total Football* **Experience Rating: 75**

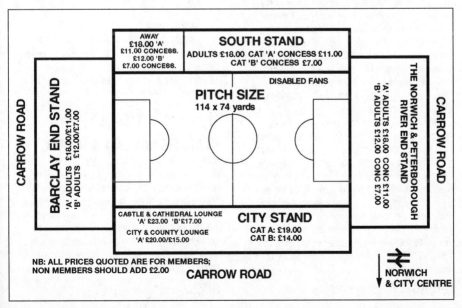

| AWAY £18.00 'A' £11.00 CONCESS. £12.00 'B' £7.00 CONCESS. | SOUTH STAND ADULTS £18.00 CAT 'A' CONCESS £11.00 CAT 'B' CONCESS £7.00 |

**CARROW ROAD**

**BARCLAY END STAND**
'A' ADULTS £18.00/£11.00
'B' ADULTS £12.00/£7.00

DISABLED FANS

**PITCH SIZE**
114 x 74 yards

**THE NORWICH & PETERBOROUGH RIVER END STAND**
'A' ADULTS £18.00 CONC £11.00
'B' ADULTS £12.00 CONC £7.00

**CARROW ROAD**

CASTLE & CATHEDRAL LOUNGE
'A' £23.00  'B' £17.00

CITY & COUNTY LOUNGE
'A' £20.00/£15.00

**CITY STAND**
CAT A: £19.00
CAT B: £14.00

NB: ALL PRICES QUOTED ARE FOR MEMBERS;
NON MEMBERS SHOULD ADD £2.00

**CARROW ROAD**

NORWICH & CITY CENTRE

# NOTTINGHAM FOREST

**ADDRESS:** The City Ground
Nottingham
NG2 5FJ

**TELEPHONE No:** 0115 982 4444
**TICKET OFFICE:** 0115 982 4445
**FAX:** 0115 982 4455
**CLUBCALL:** 0891 12 11 74
0115 982 4446

The second of these numbers gives match and ticket news, and is available at standard rates, as opposed to the 39/49p a minute premium rate.

**WEB SITE:**
http://www.nottinghamforest.co.uk

**NICKNAME:** The Reds, Forest

**RECORD ATTENDANCE:**
49,945 v Man United Div 1 28 October 1967 (W 3-1)

**CLUB COLOURS:**
**HOME:** Shirts: Red with Black trim;
Shorts: White; Socks: Red
**AWAY:** Shirts: Blue; Shorts: Blue; Socks: Blue

**KIT SPONSORS:** Pinnacle Insurance
**MANUFACTURERS:** Umbro

## GROUND INFO

Last season the City Ground was the most expensive ground for away fans to go to in the First Divison and, while the Bridgford Lower Stand is OK (reasonable leg room and unrestricted views), I certainly couldn't say it was worth the £20 that was being charged. If you're looking for compensation then all I can offer is that Forest fans who were paying on the day were charged the same amount — although the club does sell a lot of discounted season tickets. Funnily enough, Forest threatened to take legal action when other clubs suggested that they may raise their prices to these levels when Forest came to play them.

More bad news is that the some of the home fans in the Upper Bridgford seem to think that is their job/right to give you a hard time; expect anything from insults to spit via hot drinks and half-eaten pies to fall like stars from the sky (especially if your side has the temerity to score a goal). If you're thinking of complaining to the police or stewards you'd be as well saving your breath because, in my experience, they are not going to be interested. If you are walking to the city after a match it is as well to walk round via the Colwick Road rather than opting for the pathway behind the Trent Stand which can get very congested.

**CAPACITY:** Stands: 30,602; Terrace: Nil

**AWAY FANS:** Bridgford Stand Lower
Tier: 4,750

This is the maximum allocation in this stand, which may be sectioned if there is not sufficient demand (with the allocation being 3,000). You can't complain about the allocation, although for some matches there do appear to be difficulties getting through the turnstiles which don't always seem to be plentiful enough, and if you're not careful you can end up missing the first five minutes. NB: Away tickets can be purchased from the outlets by the Executive Stand, but once again expect to queue.

**DISABLED FACILITIES:** Forest were one of the first clubs to recognise that just because a fan is in a wheelchair, they do not necessarily want to be dumped *en masse* with the 'enemy', and this forward thinking attitude is still reflected in current facilities. There are 22 visitor spaces in the Bridgford Lower, home fans being sited in the Bridgford Upper (15 places), Trent Lower (16 places) and Trent Upper (14 places). Disabled supporters are admitted free of charge, with helpers paying the relevant amount for the part of the ground they are in. Match commentaries are available and there are parking facilities at the ground. These, along with your seat, should be reserved 14 days in advance.

**PROGRAMME:** £1.60
This continues to plod along at its own pace; there's a reasonable away section and the manager's column (or should that be rantings) is always entertaining. Generally very average though.

**FANZINES:**

| | |
|---|---|
| *The Tricky Tree* | 50p |
| *The Almighty Brian* | 70p |
| *Forest Forever* | £1 |
| *Garibaldi* | £1 |

The *Almighty Pierre* might be a better title for all the Forest fanzines, given have much they been smitten by their Dutchman. Despite having less to moan about in 1997/98 than the previous years, the top three of these are all worthwhile publications.

## TRAVEL

**NEAREST RAILWAY STATION:**
Nottingham Midland (01332 257000 — Derby Enquiries)
When leaving the ground you will see a massive sign apparently pointing the way to the station. Ignore this as it is directing you in the exact opposite way to the one which you want to be going in. Presumably the sign is there to persuade away fans that the route march that the Nottinghamshire Police are about to take them on is really in their interest (and if you want to see the back streets of Nottingham then they're right, it is!).

**BUS:** Victoria Centre bus station (0115 924 0000)

## BY CAR:

**NORTH:** M1 to J26, then the A610 into Nottingham until you see signs for Melton Mowbray and Trent Bridge. Follow these signs onto the A606 and continue until you cross the river. Then take the second left into Radcliffe Road and the second left again for Colwick Road.

**EAST:** A52 Radcliffe Road into Nottingham following the signs for Trent Bridge. As you approach the City/Trent Bridge there is an intersection of six roads; bear left (still Radcliffe Road), then take the next right for Colwick Road.

**SOUTH:** M1 to J24. Take the A453 (signposted Nottingham South) and continue into Nottingham following signs for Trent Bridge (do not cross the river by Clifton Bridge). As you enter Nottingham the A453 (Wilford Lane) is crossed by the A60 Loughborough Road; turn left onto the A60 (signposted Trent Bridge). Just before Trent Bridge turn right onto Radcliffe Road then left on to Colwick Road.

**WEST:** A52 into Nottingham, then follow signs for Melton Mowbray and Trent Bridge (A606). Cross the river, then as north.

There are plenty of signs in Nottingham saying 'Football Grounds' which take you within about 0.5 mile of both Forest and County. However, when you get this close, instead of detailing how to get to each ground they disappear completely, leaving you to your own devices.

**PARKING:** There is a decent car park at the ground behind the Executive (East) Stand, and on-street parking about. Alternatively, take the Radcliffe Road (heading eastwards away from Trent Bridge) for 200yd to a large intersection, go straight across into Holme Road and there is parking on the left.

## FUTURE DEVELOPMENTS

The completion of the Trent Stand was the final stage of the rejuvenation of the City Ground. There are rumours (but no more) that the club may at some point in the future implement a proposed plan to develop a three-tier Main Stand which would add 3-5,000 to the capacity.

## OTHER INFORMATION

If you're looking for food and drink, then the closest place to the ground is the 'world famous' Trent Bridge Inn, although a better bet is the Aviary, which is just by Trent Bridge. What I would suggest though is going over the bridge and checking out the Cattle Market Tavern and Café or the Navigation (read the Notts County entry for more details). If you do do this then allow 20min to get back to the City Ground (and that is if you don't dawdle). Alternatively go into the city centre and see for yourself whether the story about there being 'eight beautiful women for every ugly bloke' is true.

The chip shops in the area around the City Ground are all fairly dire so that if you want a snack I would suggest popping into the McDonalds which is only five minutes away. If you want to go a bit more up-market, then you could try the Trent Bridge café and bistro. This looks very nice — although I have never actually eaten in there — but it always seems — in football terms — to me the sort of place you'd go before sitting with your corporate chums and saying how marvellous 'soccer' is.

The food on offer inside the ground has got a little better over the last couple of years. However, it is still not a patch on what is available at Meadow Lane (perhaps in the spirit of brotherly love, County could give Forest the address of their pie suppliers), and the club still has to understand that wrapping dodgy food in paper emblazoned with the club colours does not improve its taste.

*Total Football* **Experience Rating: 63**

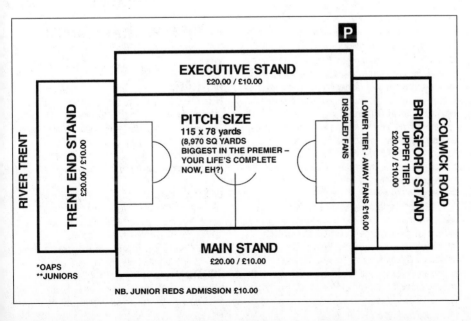

EXECUTIVE STAND
£20.00 / £10.00

PITCH SIZE
115 x 78 yards
(8,970 SQ YARDS
BIGGEST IN THE PREMIER –
YOUR LIFE'S COMPLETE
NOW, EH?)

RIVER TRENT

TRENT END STAND
£20.00 / £10.00

DISABLED FANS

LOWER TIER · AWAY FANS £16.00

BRIDGFORD STAND
UPPER TIER
£20.00 / £10.00

COLWICK ROAD

MAIN STAND
£20.00 / £10.00

*OAPS
**JUNIORS

NB. JUNIOR REDS ADMISSION £10.00

# NOTTS COUNTY

**ADDRESS:** Meadow Lane
Nottingham
NG2 3HJ

**TELEPHONE No:** 0115 952 9000
**TICKET OFFICE:** 0115 955 7210
**FAX:** 0115 955 3994
**CLUBCALL:** 0891 88 86 84
**WEB SITE:**
http://www.nbs.ntu.ac.uk/staff/baylidj/
ncfc.htm (unofficial)
**NICKNAME:** The Magpies
**RECORD ATTENDANCE:**
47,310 v York City FA Cup 6th 12 March 1955 (L 0-1)

**CLUB COLOURS:**
**HOME**: Shirts: Black and White stripes;
Shorts: Black; Socks: Black
**AWAY**: Shirts: Denim Blue; Shorts: White;
Socks: White

**KIT SPONSORS:** Sapa
**MANUFACTURERS:** Avec

## GROUND INFO

If you haven't been down to Meadow Lane for a while then you're in for a big surprise. It has been completely transformed from the dump it once was into a really tasty stadium with excellent facilities. What's more, they even started the work before the Taylor Report was issued!

There is plenty of leg room, and although there are a couple of pillars in the Kop Stand, you'll be mighty unlucky if you get a bad view. Plenty of toilet facilities are available for both sexes, and the food counters are manned by staff who aren't averse to speaking to people and don't even mind selling food! If you add that to the generally friendly and helpful stewards and office staff, it all makes for a very pleasant day out (even if the majority of these people do mention as an aside that they are really Forest fans!). County offer visiting fans concessions and what is excellent to report is that these are exactly the same as those that home fans get and are genuine 'half-price' tickets rather than the £2 reductions that some clubs offer. In terms of facilities and admission prices for visiting fans this makes Meadow Lane one of the best value stadia in England and Wales.

The atmosphere improved immensely last season (it wasn't hostile before, just lifeless). However, the point remains that 7,000 crowds in a 20,000 stadium means a lot of empty spaces and sometimes games can just seem to happen without you getting properly into them. Hopefully more people will be attracted to the ground to see Second Division football and this situation will improve further.

The Meadow Lane Stand is a family stand and is strictly out of bounds to away fans. If you go in and are sussed, you will be asked to leave (well actually not so much asked, more ordered).

**CAPACITY:** Stands: 20,300; Terrace: Nil
**AWAY FANS:** Kop Stand: 5,438; Total: 5,438
**DISABLED FACILITIES:** There are spaces for up to 100 disabled fans and these are sited in the Family Stand, the Derek Pavis Stand the Jimmy Sirrel Stand and the Kop Stand. The club does ask that you pre-book your place, and whilst on the phone you should also be able to sort out a parking space as well.

Admission is free for disabled supporters, with helpers paying £10. There are no matchday commentaries for the visually impaired.

**PROGRAMME:** £1.50
This looks nice enough but, apart from one or two exceptions, is a deadly dull read. It will be in your back pocket within five minutes.

**FANZINES:**
| | |
|---|---|
| *The Pie* | 50p |
| *No More Pie In The Sky* | 50p |
| *The Better Half* | 50p |

*The Pie* remains a very classy fanzine and well worth the (increased) cost. However, it always seems a bit of a struggle to get your hands on a copy, unlike *NMPITS* which is available on the corner of Meadow Lane and County Road. WSC states this is a joint Notts County and Stockport County fanzine, but the only reference to the chaps from Edgeley Park was a single line on how 'our buddies' did in the cup. Hardly separated at birth!!

## TRAVEL

**NEAREST RAILWAY STATION:**
Nottingham Midland (01332 257000 — Derby Enquiries)

**BUS:** Victoria Centre bus station (0115 924 0000)

**BY CAR:**
**NORTH:** M1 to J26. Take the A610 into Nottingham until you see signs for Melton Mowbray and Trent Bridge. Two hundred yards before the river, turn left into Meadow Lane (if you miss this turning, take next left into Quayside Close — again before the river — and turn back onto the London Road). The ground is 200yd on the left.

**EAST:** A52 Radcliffe Road into Nottingham, following the signs for Trent Bridge. As you approach the city centre, there is a large intersection; bear left (still Radcliffe Road). Shortly after this there is a T-junction; turn right (signposted Trent Bridge) and cross the river. The second left is Meadow Lane.

**SOUTH:** M1 to J24. Take the A453 (signposted Nottingham South) and continue towards the city following signs for Trent Bridge (do not cross the river by

Clifton Bridge). As you enter Nottingham, the A453 Wilford Lane is crossed by the A60 Loughborough Road; turn left onto the A60 (signposted Trent Bridge), cross the river and take the second left into Meadow Lane.

**WEST:** A52 into Nottingham picking up signs for Melton Mowbray and Trent Bridge (A606). Then as north.

**PARKING:** There is a car park in Cattle Market Road (turn left just past the ground, and then next right), and also some on-street parking in the area. However, a third option which is especially good for those coming from the south and east is to park by Forest's ground and walk across the Trent Bridge to Meadow Lane.

## FUTURE DEVELOPMENTS
None.

## OTHER INFORMATION
There are quite a few reasonable pubs around. You might like to try the Trent Bridge Inn (over the bridge and closer to Forest's ground) or the Aviary (on the river). Nearer to the ground is the Navigation, but my own favourite is the Cattle Market Inn & Tavern (down Meadow Lane away from the ground and turn left into the Cattle Market after about 300yd). This has the advantage of combining an excellent greasy spoon (the all-day breakfasts are spot on) with a bar that serves a good pint (you can sit in the café if you would prefer just a cup of tea). To be honest these look like the sort of places that you'd normally cross the road to avoid (though I've never had any trouble here) but you don't go in here for the décor, you go in for the food and drink. If you feel that this might not be your cup of tea, why not try the Trip To Jerusalem in the city centre which is more touristy/pleasant. The club bar is for members only.

You can get a drink inside the away section but, at £2 a can of lager, make sure you've got plenty of cash on you. As for food, the pies at County are probably some of the tastiest I've ever eaten, but — and this is a big but — they never really seem hot; in fact last season they were struggling to get to tepid, which does not do them any favours at all.

The PA at the ground is loud, booming and manned by someone who, whether he is damning the Football League for not awarding Sam Allardyce the Manager of the Month award or beseeching fans to behave well ('I beg you, please don't blow your whistles, just put them away and we'll have a bit of fun' — ooooer) is nothing if not passionate.

It is as well to know that the atmosphere in Meadow Lane can get pretty tense at times and if you are easily intimidated you may find it better to stay away rather than hear the Magpies sing in harmony.... 'I had a wheelbarrow, its wheel fell off, I had a wheelbarrow, its wheel fell off.' The story behind this brilliant chant (Come on chaps, they're singing the wheelbarrow song, I know we can pull those four goals back) is rather confused; some say that it originates with Jimmy Sirrel, who once complained that running the club was like trying to push a wheelbarrow up a hill after the wheel had fallen off (surely an understatement), whilst others insist that it came about after one of the players was caught indulging in carnal activities with a young lady on a wheelbarrow (???). Either way, it is a classic.

*Total Football* Experience Rating: 91

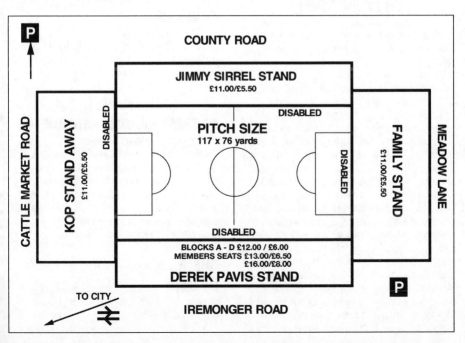

# OLDHAM ATHLETIC

**ADDRESS:** Boundary Park
Oldham
OL1 2PA
**TELEPHONE No:** 0161 627 1802
**TICKET OFFICE:** 0161 624 4972
**FAX:** 0161 652 6501
**CLUBCALL:** 0891 12 11 42
**CLUBCALL:** www.u-net.com/latics/
**E-MAIL:** paul@backbeat.u-net
Note this is a form address for responses to a
questionnaire about the E-mail site.
**NICKNAME:** The Latics
**RECORD ATTENDANCE:**
47,671 v Sheffield Wednesday FA Cup 4th
25 January 1930 (L 3-4)
**CLUB COLOURS:**
**HOME:** Shirts: Blue; Shorts: Blue; Socks: Blue
**AWAY:** Shirt: White/Claret/Navy; Shorts: Claret/Navy;
Socks: Claret/Navy

**KIT SPONSORS:** Slumberland
I don't know who came up with the idea of teaming up
the Latics with something that will help you get a good
night's sleep, but I do know they have never been sued
for misrepresentation!!!
**MANUFACTURERS:** Pony

## GROUND INFO

The Lookers Stand and the George Hill Stand have
'members-only' sections which means if you can't get a
ticket for the away end, you are limited to where you can
go.

Those of you who haven't visited Boundary Park for a
while may have stayed away as a result of your previous
visit! You probably parked in the muddy car park,
climbed and slipped your way up the muddy hill to the
ground, where you paid through the nose to stand on an
uncovered mud heap watching the players wallow around
in the mud. How times have changed! True the car park is
still dire, and Boundary Park is still not the cheapest of
grounds to get into (although the £5 concessions for all
supporters can only be applauded), but at least now away
fans get to sit in the cantilevered Rochdale Road Stand
which is far and away the best part of the stadium,
offering decent views of the pitch, reasonable facilities,
and, most importantly given the inclemencies of the
weather in Oldham, a roof. It also contains a little
paddock at the front of it where you can dance a jig of joy
when your team score (you just want to be on the end-of-
season video don't you, you sad person). Having said
that, the last activity is probably not recommended, as
some of the stewards at the ground (who are probably a

bit fed up with it now) can be a little bit overzealous if
you do.

In general, paddock dancing excepted, the police and
stewards operate a softly softly approach, and although
they will act if they perceive an individual is becoming
overly rowdy, they manage to do so without acting in an
inflammatory manner. It is also worth noting that they
don't expect away fans to behave like monks, and
chanting and cheering is not frowned or acted upon.
**CAPACITY:** Stands: 13,559; Terrace: Nil
**AWAY FANS:** Ellen Group (Rochdale Road)
Stand: 1,843
A special mention must be made to the way the club
deals with queries from away fans — by mail, phone and
in person on match days — which, it has to be said, is
probably one of, if not the, best I came across this
season in my research.

**DISABLED FACILITIES:** There are 52
spaces in the Rochdale Road and Seton Stands. Disabled
fans are admitted free of charge, with helpers paying £12.
Pre-booking is required. There are car parking facilities at
the ground, which are well used. This is located close to
the entrance on a tarmacadamed surface in an area
patrolled by the police. Ramps are laid for access to this
area. The club no longer has match commentaries for the
visually impaired because when it did have the service
'no one took advantage'.

**PROGRAMME:** £1.60
Very run of the mill. One of those that you buy because
you always buy a programme, and will have stuck in your
back pocket after checking the teams.

**FANZINES:**
Beyond the Boundary                    80p
Produced by a bloke from Lincoln. Once again I couldn't
get hold of a copy on my visit. The last one I saw (three
seasons ago) was OK, if that's any help.

## TRAVEL

**NEAREST RAILWAY STATION:**
Oldham WERNETH (0161 832 8353)
The railway station is about 1.5 miles from the ground,
which is a long enough walk in itself, especially as by
some quirk of nature, it doesn't seem to matter what
direction you are walking in, you always seem to be
going uphill. However, this will appear to be a mere stroll
in the park if by some mistake you end up going to
Oldham MUMPS which is about three days by foot from
Boundary Park.

**BUS:** West Street bus station (0161 228 7811)

**BY CAR:** From everywhere (all roads lead to
Oldham!): M62 to J20, then take A627(M). Then,
dependent on how the traffic is moving, either:
• continue along this road for 2.5 miles to a large

roundabout, at which you should take the first exit onto A633 Broadway; then first right off the Broadway into Hilbre Avenue. The ground is at the bottom of this road. Or:

• at the roundabout, take the second exit on to Chadderton Way; after 0.5 mile turn left into Boundary Park for the ground.

**PARKING:** The Lookers Stand car park at the bottom of Hilbre Avenue has space for 1,000 cars. There is some off-street parking in the vicinity of the ground, but if you want alternative off-street parking then you really need to travel into Oldham town centre, which is a fair trek and also difficult to get away from after the match. At the club car park watch out for the stewards who say you will not be blocked in and then as soon as you are out of sight guide the next car about 3cm in front of you. There is also a car park with 125 spaces situated 100yd behind the Rochdale Road End with a charge of £1.

## FUTURE DEVELOPMENTS

The club has abandoned plans for the new Lookers Stand in favour of a scheme to build a new 20,000 all-seater stadium adjacent to the existing ground. this is due to open in August 2000.

## OTHER INFORMATION

For pre-match refreshment try the White Hart and the Old Grey Mare on the Rochdale Road, where away fans are welcome. Not so at the Clayton next to the ground, which is members only. The chip shops seem to close at 1.30 on matchdays, but there are plenty of mobile snack bars around the ground, which, like the facilities inside the stadium, serve edible if not exactly tasty or exciting fare.

There seems to be a bit of a depression hanging over Boundary Park and it feels like a million light years ago that they were in the top flight and seconds away from a cup final appearance. Do not mention the words 'Mark Hughes' unless you want to get the locals frothing at the mouth as they feel it was his last gasp equaliser in the FA Cup semi-final that was the start of all the club's woes. Horribly (given the way you are likely to be treated), you leave the ground thinking that this decline may be terminal unless something happens very quickly.

Oldham is but a few physical miles from Old Trafford but in other areas it is light years away. For a start, they don't tend to say 'Hiya' at Man Utd when you go in the ground, but also where United have got their Mega-Super-Fab stores, Ath's club shop which is called Latique (very continental eh?) also combines a trophy shop for those handy moments when there isn't an FA Cup handy, and a travel agents (presumably after each match fans can decide whether they want to buy a ticket for the following game or if they'd prefer a week somewhere away from it all).

If you have never been to Boundary Park before, dress not to impress, but for arctic survival. Don't let the idea that you are going up in August or April mislead you into thinking that there will be anything but a bitter wind and horizontal rain.

In fact, the only way I can emphasise how cold this place really is, is by pointing out that I once saw a Geordie slip on a second T-shirt when watching a game here!

Finally while there is plenty to like about Oldham, one thing they should be roundly condemned for is the group of fans who released a record last year which included the lyrics 'meat pie, sausage roll, come on Oldham, Gi'us a goal'. This truly awful effort has been rightly ignored by the fans and you should avoid listening to it for fear that, like me, it will get into your head and you will never be able to forget it.

***Total Football* Experience Rating: 68**

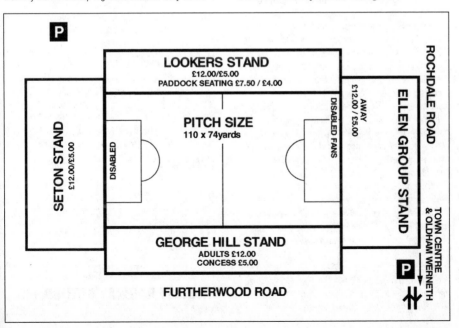

# OXFORD UNITED

**ADDRESS:** The Manor Ground
London Road
Headington
Oxford
OX3 7RS

**TELEPHONE No:** 01865 761503
**TICKET OFFICE:** 01865 761503
**FAX:** 01865 741820
**CLUBLINE:** 0891 44 00 55
**WEB SITE:** www.oufc.co.uk
**E-MAIL:** Oxford_united@msn.com
**NICKNAME:** The U's
**RECORD ATTENDANCE:** 22,730 v Preston
FA Cup 6th 29 February 1964 (L 1-2)

**CLUB COLOURS:**
**HOME:** Shirts: Yellow;
Shorts: Navy; Socks: Navy
**AWAY:** Shirts: White;
Shorts: White; Socks: White

**KIT SPONSORS:** Unipart
**MANUFACTURERS:** Manor Leisure

## GROUND INFO

For anyone who bought the third edition of this book I can only offer my heartfelt apologies. Not, I hasten to add, for providing information about the new Minchery Farm ground into which the club was supposed to move during 1997-8 — that was unfortunate — (how could I guess that the contractors were going to stop work two days after we had gone to print due to non-payment?). What I do apologise for is falling for the guff that someone at the club fed me about being more responsive to the needs of visiting fans, for the Manor remains, in my experience, the worst away trip that you can endure, and the message in the programme/on the hoardings of 'Welcome to the Manor Ground' is possibly the biggest lie in football.

Where do I start? Well, as we are in 'Ground Info', feast your eyes on the following:

• There is fencing for away fans at both the terracing (over 6ft high) and the seated part of the ground (less high but still an obstruction if you are towards the bottom of the stand);

• There is a video camera mounted on a tall (12 ft approx) girder in between the Cuckoo Lane Terrace and the goal which results in more obstructions;

• The away terrace is uncovered. However, for the

pleasure of standing on it, you will pay the same price as home supporters do for a covered terrace;

• The ground is over-populated with stewards who seem to think that every away fan is a potential terrorist: over excessive body searches combined with occasional confiscation of bizarre items. I had a plastic coke bottle taken off me as I went in. This would be fair enough, if the club didn't sell exactly the same thing inside the ground, which it seemed perfectly happy for me to have in my possession;

• The police still see fit (although not for every match now) to video visiting supporters as they arrive at the ground.

If you're looking for bright points, then I would say that the club does offer concessions and it appears to have dropped the categorisation of matches.

**CAPACITY:** Terrace: 6,769; Stand: 2,803;
Total: 9,572

**AWAY FANS:** Cuckoo Lane Terrace: 2,107;
Stands: 542; Total: 2,649

The entrance for the terrace and the seats are at the same point. If you go into the seats, you will be given a ticket which you have to show at a gate to gain access to the stand. However, there are no food facilities in the stand so you have to return to the terrace when you want to feed.

**DISABLED FACILITIES:** There are approximately 20 places for wheelchair-bound supporters in the corner of the ground between the Cuckoo Lane end and the Main Stand. I was unable to obtain pricing details from the club, but I believe that a nominal charge is levied on disabled supporters, with helpers paying normal terrace prices. Places should be pre-booked. There are no match commentaries for the visually impaired, nor any special parking facilities.

**PROGRAMME:** £1.50

I have to say (grudgingly) that this is a very good read, well thought out and put together, although I had to laugh at the audacity of one column which bemoaned the lack of facilities at Swindon Town. While it is true that the County Ground is neither cheap nor luxurious, the attitude of the staff there is, at least, not prehistoric.

**FANZINES:**

| | |
|---|---|
| *Rage On!* | £1 |
| *Yellow Fever* | £1 |

The latter is a new guise for the popular old fanzine *Raging Bull*. As I understand it, the name was changed to try and break the association the fanzine had with ex-editor Ed Horton.

## TRAVEL

**NEAREST RAILWAY STATION:** Oxford
(01865 722333)

**BUS:** Oxford (01865 785400)

From the city centre take any bus — of which there are many — which stops at Headington. It's between a 10 to 30min ride depending on just how bad the traffic is.

## BY CAR:

**NORTH/EAST:** M40 to J8. Take the A40 (signposted Oxford and Headington) and continue to the roundabout with the A420 London Road. After 0.75 turn right into Ostler Road. Cuckoo Lane and the ground are on the left.

**WEST:** A40. Shortly after you pass Barton there is a roundabout with the A420 and the A4142. Take the third exit signposted Headington then as north/east.
If you get lost, just look for signs for Headington and you can't miss the ground.

**SOUTH:** Either M40 to J8 and then as north/east or A34 towards Oxford until you get to the A423 southern by-pass onto which you should turn right. At the second large roundabout take the first exit onto the A4142 eastern by-pass. Continue for four miles until you get to a roundabout with the A40/A420 and take the first exit on to the A420, then as north/east.

**PARKING:** There is a dearth of street parking around the ground — lots of residents-only areas — but if you seek hard enough from about 0.25 miles away you can be lucky. The best bet is to drive along the A420 and, if you are heading away from the city, turn right at the Barclays Bank into Old High Street (obviously turn left here if you are heading towards Oxford). About 150yd on the right is the entrance to a pay-and-display car park (£1 for four hours) which, although small, I have always managed to get a space in. Note: when you leave this car park for the ground, instead of turning left towards London Road turn right and about 30yd on the left there is a passage way which will take you right to the Cuckoo Lane Entrance.

## FUTURE DEVELOPMENTS

Sadly, it looks as if away supporters will have to endure at least another season (and possibly two) before the Minchery Farm stadium is completed, after which it will be a move to this 15,000 all-seater stadium by Blackbird Leys.

## OTHER INFORMATION

Be careful not to tar the whole of Oxford with the same brush as that which you will undoubtedly wish to use on the club. There are two good pubs on the London Road — the Britannia and the Royal Standard — in both of which you can enjoy a decent pie, a chat and a laugh with the locals. For food you can do worse than the Mediterranean Chip Shop, which is right at the end of the parade of shops in Headington as you go away from Oxford. The Kebab House is very different from the place that you'd normally get your kebabs from and a little pricey, but the food is good quality.

Inside the ground the club is ready to heap more indignity upon you. There are two serving hatches and, as you queue up, you might wonder why you keep seeing purple-faced fans moving from one queue to the other. The reason for this is simple... The serving hatch that serves hot food does not do hot drinks and vice versa!! (I kid you not.) Which means that you get to queue up twice for your half-time refreshments. Any attempts to say surely you can get me a cup of tea with my pie, will be met by exasperated sighs and the phrase 'read the signs'. Once you do eventually get your food (or should that be 'Providing' as on my visit they had run out of meat and potato pies at 2.15pm) the steak & kidney pie is excellent although scalding hot. My cup of tea had a lot of UFOs in it and was not pleasant at all.

*Total Football* **Experience Rating: 35**

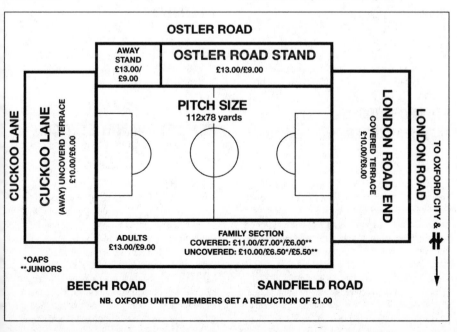

OSTLER ROAD

| AWAY STAND £13.00/ £9.00 | OSTLER ROAD STAND £13.00/£9.00 |

CUCKOO LANE

CUCKOO LANE (AWAY) UNCOVERD TERRACE £10.00/£6.00

**PITCH SIZE**
112x78 yards

LONDON ROAD END

COVERED TERRACE £10.00/£6.00

LONDON ROAD

TO OXFORD CITY &

| ADULTS £13.00/£9.00 | FAMILY SECTION COVERED: £11.00/£7.00*/£6.00** UNCOVERED: £10.00/£6.50*/£5.50** |

*OAPS
**JUNIORS

**BEECH ROAD**          **SANDFIELD ROAD**

NB. OXFORD UNITED MEMBERS GET A REDUCTION OF £1.00

# PETERBOROUGH UNITED

**ADDRESS:** London Road Ground
Peterborough
Cambridgeshire
PE2 8AL

**TELEPHONE No:** 01733 563947

**TICKET OFFICE:** 01733 563947

**FAX:** 01733 557210

**CLUBCALL:** 0891 121654

**WEB SITE:** http://freespace.virgin.
net/mick.bratley/POW/posh.htm

Note: the far quicker www.posh.net will also get you to this rather tasty unofficial site run by 'Posh Out West'.

**OFFICIAL WEB SITE:**

http://come.to/pufc

**NICKNAME:** Posh

**RECORD ATTENDANCE:**

30,096 v Swansea Town FA Cup 5th 20 February 1965 (D 0-0)

Those of you who like conspiracy theories can't fail to notice that civil rights leader and closet Posh fanatic Malcolm X was assassinated on this day. Coincidence or something else? Spike Lee was unavailable for comment.

**CLUB COLOURS:**

**HOME:** Shirts: Royal Blue; Shorts: White;
Socks: Royal Blue with White hoops

**AWAY:** Shirts: Red with White sleeves; Shorts: Red
Socks: Red

**THIRD:** Shirts: White; Shorts: White;
Socks: White with Blue hoops

The silly old sausage who (kindly) filled in the questionnaire I sent the club forgot to mention that they had a third kit. Did he think I'd complain that they were ripping the fans off? Surely not? If they have three kits I'm sure they need them!!

**KIT SPONSORS:** Thomas Cook Group Ltd

**MANUFACTURERS:** Patrick (UK)

## GROUND INFO

Apart from the Freemans Stand — apparently Posh are paying for 48 easy instalments, and if they didn't like it they could have returned it to the constructors with no questions asked — London Road is beginning to look a little run down, although given some of the club's recent problems, survival and not ceramically-tiled toilets has rightly been the priority.

Slightly less understandable is the fact that visiting supporters do not get concessions on the Moys Terrace (home fans get great ones everywhere) and the fact that Barry Fry's *joie de vivre* has failed to rub off on the

stewards, who, on my visit, are as humourless a bunch as you could expect to meet; on a recent visit a lad was thrown out for playing with a pre-match ball that had been — deliberately — kicked into the crowd.

The away facilities are basic but not actually that bad — things keep getting a lick of paint etc — although, if you are towards the back of the seated area, there is a pillar that can get in the way and you will probably have to wander the terrace for a bit before you can find an unobstructed view (but on the plus side you are covered which makes it great for singing — and keeping dry!).

The home supporters also take advantage of their covering to create quite a noise, but what always surprises is the fact that one of the London Road End's favourite chants is 'We're the middle, we're the middle, we're the middle of the road'; every time you hear this you always hope that if this is really the case they will follow it up by doing a couple a verses of 'Chirpy Chirpy Cheep Cheep' but sadly they never do.

**CAPACITY:** Stands: 9,614; Terrace: 5,700;
Total: 15,314;

**AWAY FANS:** Moys Terrace: 3,900;
A Stand: 800; Total: 4,700

**DISABLED FACILITIES:** There are 40 spaces available to disabled supporters in D Wing of the Freemans Stand and the Enclosure of the Old (Main) Stand. Admission is £3 for both disabled fans and their helpers. There is no need to book. Parking facilities are available at the ground, but there are no match commentaries for the visually impaired.

**PROGRAMME:** £1.50

**FANZINES:**

*The Peterborough Effect* £1

The only complaint about *The Peterborough Effect* is that it doesn't come out regularly enough, so check that you're not buying something that is over a month old before you part with your money.

## TRAVEL

**NEAREST RAILWAY STATION:**

Peterborough (0345 484950 — Leicester Enquiries)

**BUS:** Peterborough bus station (01733 54571)

**BY CAR:**

**NORTH/WEST:** A1, then take the A47 towards the city centre. Turn right at the roundabout onto the A1260, and then take the second turning to the left onto the A605 Oundle Road. Continue for just under two miles until you get to a roundabout; take the third exit onto London Road, and the ground is on the left.

**SOUTH:** A1 to the roundabout with the A15. Take the London Road (signposted Peterborough A15) going under the flyover and over two railway bridges. You then get to a large intersection at which you should turn left (continuing along London Road) and the ground is immediately on the right.

**EAST:** A47 through Eye, and pick up signs for Peterborough City Centre. Once in the city centre follow signs for Whittlesey (A605); this will take you across the River Nene and onto London Road. Continue along London Road and the ground is on the left. There is good signposting for 'Football car parks' around the city, which although they end up taking you around the houses a bit, do at least get you there.

One of the best things about the new stand from an away fan's perspective (being that we aren't allowed to sully its beauty with our presence) is that it dominates the surrounding area and provides a good landmark to get you to the ground.

**PARKING:** There is the club's own car park at the ground, and also a car park on the Oundle Road (left at the roundabout as you are driving towards the ground) which is only about 300yd away. Alternatively, there is ample parking in the city centre.

## FUTURE DEVELOPMENTS

The club is apparently getting the architects who designed Stamford Bridge to give London Road the once over with the aim of building a new Main Stand and then constructing stands — at first the Moys and then the London Road ends with (eventually) wraparounds built in the corners. The club states that it is committed to keeping terraces as long as possible. Even if plans are submitted quickly, it is unlikely that much (if anything) will be started before the end of the 1998-9 season.

## OTHER INFORMATION

There are quite a few pubs around the ground; the Bridge pub has crash barriers outside and tends to be used by visiting supporters. Be warned, though (or tipped off, depending on your preferences), on non-matchdays this is a gay pub. To be honest, I prefer the Peacock (ex-Wag & Bone), which serves a decent pint in a good atmosphere or the Charters Cafe Bar which is a large bar moored on the Nene by the Bridge as you walk into town and is about five minutes from the ground (this is not as bad as the term cafe/bar suggests and in fact it won the Camra Pub of the Year competition a few years back). Inside the ground the food took a spiralling nosedive last season, in my opinion, and, I think, some of the caterers may have misunderstood the club's motto of 'On This Rock' as being an instruction as to the consistency that the pies should have. Horrible. The Bovril remains an insult to dead cows everywhere and I'd really consider staying hungry/thirsty as a viable option.

Last season the club got in the news for sponsoring an art show — but that will serve Barry right for asking the board that more Monet be made available to him. To be honest, however, there are a million things that the cash spent here could have been better used for and it perhaps illustrates that, at the moment, some of those at Peterborough have not got their focus quite right.

For food, Foley's Fish & Chips by the ground is OK; they do a reduced price special of chips and curry sauce for footie fans, which is a nice thought. However, the chips I had were a bit cold and I think they microwave their gravy! Wherever you go, it can be worth staying for a few minutes extra, if just to miss the cavorting of 'Mr Posh' and the Post Horn Gallop that is played as the teams run out.

Finally, remember, if you ever get to speak to a Posh fan do NOT ask him to sing the Pompey chimes as that is a different club altogether (mind you, you'd have to be a complete non-footballing arse to make this mistake and certainly not the sort of chap who gets paid lots of money to host a Saturday evening phone-in show... Wouldn't you?).

*Total Football* **Experience Rating: 65**

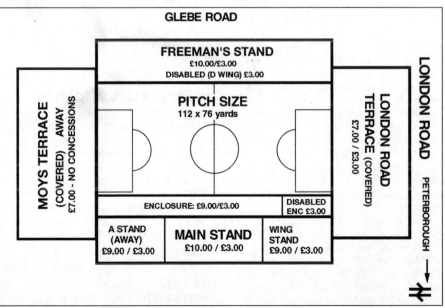

GLEBE ROAD

FREEMAN'S STAND
£10.00/£3.00
DISABLED (D WING) £3.00

PITCH SIZE
112 x 76 yards

MOYS TERRACE
(COVERED) AWAY
£7.00 - NO CONCESSIONS

LONDON ROAD TERRACE (COVERED)
£7.00 / £3.00

LONDON ROAD

PETERBOROUGH

ENCLOSURE: £9.00/£3.00

DISABLED
ENC £3.00

A STAND
(AWAY)
£9.00 / £3.00

MAIN STAND
£10.00 / £3.00

WING
STAND
£9.00 / £3.00

# PLYMOUTH ARGYLE

**ADDRESS:** Home Park
Plymouth
Devon PL2 3DQ

**TELEPHONE No:** 01752 562561

**TICKET OFFICE:** 01752 562561

**FAX:** 01752 606167

**PILGRIMLINE:** 0839 44 22 70

**WEB SITE:** www.argyle.org.uk

**NICKNAME:** The Pilgrims

**RECORD ATTENDANCE:**
43,596 v Aston Villa Div 2 10 October 1936 (D 2-2)

**CLUB COLOURS:**
**HOME:** Shirts: Green, White & Black stripes;
Shorts: White; Socks: Green
**AWAY:** Shirts: Champagne with Green trim;
Shorts: Black; Socks: Champagne

**KIT SPONSORS:** Rotolok

**MANUFACTURERS:** Errea

## GROUND INFO

To stand at the away (Barn Park) end at Home Park means exposing yourself to the elements as there is no cover, although there is a marvellous aesthetic quality about the place — as you leave the ground the banking has been made into a little rockery. If the weather is inclement and you're not into 'Gardeners' Question Time' and the marvellous world of herbaceous borders, go into the Grandstand. Price-wise a trip to Home Park is not the cheapest you'll make during the season. Last season the club introduced a three-level categorisation system — presumably based on whether the opposition were better, exceedingly better or absolutely streets ahead of the team that Argyle fans loyally shelled out to see every other week. Still, at least the club decided to make it a bit easier for visiting supporters to work out how much they were going to have to pay by not offering concessions at the Barn Park End — thanks. To be honest, the whole concession system is something of a joke at the club because, other than in the family enclosure, kids who weren't part of the Junior Green scheme only got between a £1.50 (standing) or £2 (seating) reduction. Somewhat strangely, OAPs were not given concessions in the family enclosure (presumably grandparents don't take kids to matches in Devon).

One bright spot was that I know for a fact that, on a couple of occasions last season, when the weather was dreadful and there weren't too many away fans, the stewards transferred them to the Barn Park Wing of the Grandstand. And, it has to be added, to the credit of the Argyle fans, no-one seemed to complain about the fact that the poor bedraggled creatures who now sat among

them had paid nearly a fiver less for the privilege.

The Lyndhurst Stand is popular for home supporters and offers very good leg room. It is also acoustically impressive and the fans certainly can (and do) get some noise going from this area, which due to the lack of away cover (and the fact that you may feel like you've travelled half-way round the globe to get to what is not only the most southerly but also the most westerly ground in Britain) can make your efforts sound rather feeble.

**CAPACITY:** Stands: 8,800; Terrace: 11,180;
Total: 19,980

**AWAY FANS:** Barn Park End: 2,640;
Total: 2,640

**DISABLED FACILITIES:** There are 15 spaces for wheelchair-bound supporters and 33 designated seats in the Devonport End of the ground. Disabled fans are admitted free of charge, with helpers paying £7.50, £8 or £8.50 dependent on the category of the match. Spaces should be pre-booked. The club does offer match commentaries for the visually impaired (these are provided in the Grandstand) and there are car parking facilities available. Again, contact the club in advance to discuss your requirements.

**PROGRAMME:** £1.50
Stayed the same price in 1997-8 but the content improved somewhat. On the inside of the first page, where you would normally find the manager's column, there is an article by a fan and throughout the 40 pages there are plenty of general interest items.

**FANZINES:**

| | |
|---|---|
| *Rub Of The Greens* | 50p |
| *Way Out West* | £1 |
| *Hoof* | 80p |

None of these seemed to be on sale during my last visit. I have seen *ROTG* and *WOW* before and both were reasonable enough reads.

## TRAVEL

### NEAREST RAILWAY STATION:
Plymouth North Road (01752 221300)
If you want to walk to the ground — be warned: although you'll spot it fairly quickly, it's a good two miles plus — turn right out of the station, keep heading straight till you see the floodlights in front of you and you should be able to see the ground from there (you can take a bit of a short cut across the park). Alternatives are to turn right as you leave the station and get in a cab which is only 10yd away and which will set you back £3ish, or to grab a bus (look for those going to Milehouse).

**BUS:** Bretonside bus station (01752 222221)
Buses 20F, 42F and 37F stop directly outside Home Park.

### BY CAR:
**NORTH/EAST:** M5 to J31 (final junction), then take

the A38. Turn left onto the A386 (Tavistock Road) — this road branches into two, keep to the left (signposted Plymouth). Just over a mile on the left is the ground's car park which has space for 1,000 cars.

**WEST:** Take the A38, turn right onto the A386 (Tavistock Road), then as north/east.

**PARKING:** As stated earlier, there is a large car park adjacent to Home Park, which is ideal only if you have got the rest of the weekend to fritter away. The cars are parked nose-to-tail and inevitably you will be parked around people who amble across to the vehicles 20min after the match. This will then mean that you get badly clogged up in the local traffic.

There is some street parking around, but even this is no guarantee that you will be speedily on your way home.

## FUTURE DEVELOPMENTS

A bit of a weird one here with the City Council saying it wants to build a new 23,000 all-seater stadium (possibly in the Central Park area) and Dan McCauley, the club's owner (at least he was when this book went to print), threatening to build supermarkets on the land. All very strange. No doubt, when the ownership of the club is sorted out then progress can be made, although, while some sources are touting a date of 1999 for moving into a new stadium, to be honest, I'd be very surprised if it was before the 2000/01 season. The club had been talking about installing temporary seating on the Barn Park Terrace, but, given the fact that they have just been relegated and so this is not a requirement, I would expect no changes at Home Park in the short term.

## OTHER INFORMATION

You'll be lucky to get into the supporters' club bar in the ground and it is as well to take the 10min drive into the busy city centre to find a decent watering-hole.

Inside Home Park itself the pasties are above average as is the tea and Bovril, so you've got no excuse for not stocking up on those carbohydrates.

Everything Argyle sells now seems to have the club's mascot, Pilgrim Pete, stuck on it and of course there is a Styrofoam PP who lumbers around the ground before matches, taking the occasional dodgy penalty. The club say PP is a great character and the fans love him, but to the more discerning eye the question must be 'why is Bugs Bunny's arch enemy Yosemite Sam cavorting round Home Park in a strange outfit?' Given PP's resemblance to the cartoon character one can only hope that somebody will find a job lot of acme dynamite and give it to the irritating blighter to hold.

Occasionally, when compiling this book, I get to hear stories of unsung football heroes. One of these people is the PA announcer at Argyle who gives the half-time scores out. 'Nothing unusual about that' you may cry and I would be forced to agree with you IF the chap hadn't on one occasion substituted managers names for their teams (so that's Eddie May 2 Graham Taylor 0) and on other occasions swapped team names with club sponsors (and why the hell couldn't he have been doing it a few years back when Virgin would have met Nobo?). As I understand it, the club were not overly pleased with this break from tradition, but the fans loved his cryptic quiz.

The club were in a bit of turmoil last season; they were up for sale, had an owner who said he would close the club if a buyer wasn't found and then banned some members of the local press from the ground because they dared to criticise the club (magnificently, rather than meekly accept this or go back cap-in-hand and apologise the journos hired a bucket crane which they parked outside the ground and then extended so they could look at what was going on inside).

Still, a trip to Home Park remains a good one.

*Total Football* **Experience Rating: 64**

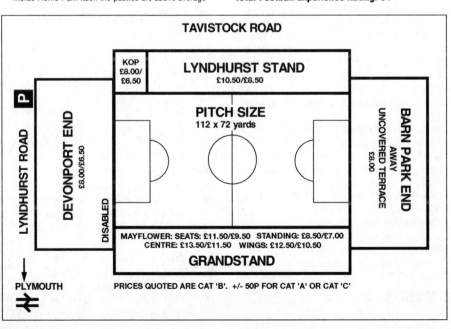

TAVISTOCK ROAD

KOP £8.00/£6.50

LYNDHURST STAND £10.50/£8.50

PITCH SIZE 112 x 72 yards

LYNDHURST ROAD

P

DEVONPORT END £8.00/£6.50

DISABLED

BARN PARK END AWAY UNCOVERED TERRACE £8.00

MAYFLOWER: SEATS: £11.50/£9.50 STANDING: £8.50/£7.00
CENTRE: £13.50/£11.50 WINGS: £12.50/£10.50

GRANDSTAND

PLYMOUTH

PRICES QUOTED ARE CAT 'B'. +/- 50P FOR CAT 'A' OR CAT 'C'

# PORT VALE

**ADDRESS:** Vale Park
Burslem
Stoke-on-Trent
ST6 1AW
**TELEPHONE No:** 01782 814134
**TICKET OFFICE:** 01782 814134
**FAX:** 01782 834 981
**CLUBCALL:** 0891 12 16 36
**WEBSITE:** http://www.port-vale.co.uk
**E-MAIL:** pvfc@port-vale.co.uk
**NICKNAME:** The Valiants
**RECORD ATTENDANCE:** 50,000 v Aston
Villa FA Cup 5th 20 February 1960 (L 1-2)

**CLUB COLOURS:**
**HOME:** Shirts: White with Black trim; Shorts: Black;
Socks: Black with White hoops
**AWAY:** Shirts: Yellow & Black;
Shorts: Yellow; Socks: Yellow

**KIT SPONSORS:** Tunstall Assurance
**MANUFACTURERS:** Mizuno

## GROUND INFO

First the good news, Port Vale do offer away fans concessions in the Hamil Road Stand. Perhaps less pleasing is the fact that they only reduce prices by £4 for juniors and OAPs to £9 which still makes Vale Park a pricey day out if there are a few of you going. Even more annoying is the fact that the concessions elsewhere in the ground are excellent (juniors opposite you in the Bycars Stand pay only £6.00). You get to pay £15 for a 'behind the goals' view whereas home fans in the Main Stand pay £1.50p less for an excellent position on the half-way line. You explain the logic (or fairness) in that if you can (oh, and by the way, adult home fans sitting down opposite you will have paid £3 less for their seats).

There isn't much leg room and getting into and out of your seat — you are expected to go into your allocated seat no matter what the size of the crowd — isn't the easiest thing in the world. One of the good things about the away end is that the roof is one of those that seems to amplify chants and it doesn't take much effort to get a cracking atmosphere going.

Away supporters should also note that Vale have desegregated the Family Stand which offers better reductions, although not necessarily enough for fans to choose to isolate themselves and go there rather than the Hamil Road End.

**CAPACITY:** Stands: 22,616; Terrace: Nil;
Total: 22,616

This is post completion of work on the Lorne Street Stand. 1997/98 capacity was: 17,616 seats; 4,740 terrace; Total 22,356.

**AWAY FANS:** Hamil Road Stand: 4,550

**DISABLED FACILITIES:** There are 72 places available in the Tunstall Assurance Specialist Stand. Admission is £5 if you use a wheelchair but £6 if you want to sit on a bench. Helpers are charged £10 (whether they sit on a bench, on the floor or stand on one leg with their arms crossed). Matchday commentaries for the visually impaired are available as are parking facilities at the ground. All must be pre-booked. Other than the bizarre distinction between wheelchair users and those who can (or want to) sit on benches, it has to be said that Vale appear to have this area sewn up and a trip to Vale Park should be one of the easier one in a season.

**PROGRAMME:** £1.50
The price remained static last year but an already good programme got even more readable. A good section on the visitors, together with lots of general interest articles — a good proportion of which seem to be written by genuine fans rather than club officials.

**FANZINES:**
*The Memoirs of Seth Bottomley*  £1
In the last edition of this book I had the unfortunate job of announcing the demise of this fantastic (if exceedingly unhandy A4-sized) fanzine. Happily, I have heard reports from Vale that *Seth* has risen from the grave in a couple of specials and one-offs.

## TRAVEL

**NEAREST RAILWAY STATION:**
Longport (0345 484950)
Longport is a couple of miles from the ground and hardly anything stops here, so you are more likely to end up at Stoke. This is a not very walkable five miles away, so either grab a cab (£6.50ish) or take a 24 bus to Burslem (not the fastest mode of transport you'll encounter), get off in the town centre and it is about a five minute walk, or a 25 bus to Kidsgrove via City Centre, Newchapel, which stops at the top end of Hamil Rd on High Lane. The ground is 200yd away.

**BUS:** Potteries Motor Transport (01782 747000)
Sometimes abbreviations work, and sometimes they don't. Plastering PMT all over your buses and bus stops most definitely falls into the second category.
If you decide to risk it, a 452 will drop you off on Hamil Road by the stadium.

**BY CAR:**
**NORTH:** M6 to J16 and follow the signs for Stoke (A500). Turn left when you see the signpost for Tunstall (A527). This brings you to a roundabout; take the second exit into Newcastle Street which later becomes Market

Place. Go through the traffic lights and take the second left into Hamil Road. The ground is on the left.

**SOUTH/WEST:** M6 to J15, then take the A500 (signposted Stoke). Follow this road for approximately 4.5 miles then turn right onto the A527 (signposted Tunstall), then as north.

**EAST:** A52 into Stoke. Follow the signs into Burslem, this will bring you on to Waterloo Road (A50). Turn right at the lights, then as north.

**PARKING:** There is parking by the away end in Hamil Road. Alternatively, just after you go through the major crossroads there is a car park on the left which is about 600yd from the ground.

## FUTURE DEVELOPMENTS

Last season the club announced the forthcoming construction of the 'Premier Stand' where the Lorne Street Terrace now stands. This will incorporate 14 boxes, a new club restaurant and 5,000 seats, and will, as I understand it, have a very steep rake between each row of seats so that you don't end up with a perfect view of the bloke in front's bald patch and nothing else. Scheduled to be completed 'in 1998', the stand will also contain access points for disabled and visually impaired supporters.

## OTHER INFORMATION

In the last edition of the book I suggested that the club got its name as follows: the Port comes from all the canal ports from which pottery was transported, and the Vale comes from the Vale Inn pub side out of which the club was founded. However, I received a veritable sack of mail (well, two letters) informing me I was a chump and the way the club got its name was:

• That the club was formed at a meeting place called Port Vale House and was named after this (minus the house bit);

• That the club took its name from a wharf on the

Burslem Canal. Oh well, that clears that one up then...

For a pre-match pint, if you can't resist going into pubs with silly sounding names then the Sagger Makers Bottom Knocker will be right up your alley, but if you prefer going into pubs for the beer then try the Vine on Hamil Road, which is excellent, or Lloyds Tavern. I have been told that for big matches (ie Stoke) things can get somewhat tense, but on every visit I've made I've had no hassle at all. The reopened Club pub is meant to be for home fans only.

For food, check out the local delicacy of oatcakes (like a pancake although made — perhaps not surprisingly — with oats) stuffed with assorted bits and pieces at Hamil Oatcakes (which, although you might not guess from the name, sells oatcakes and is, believe it or not, on Hamil Road). There is the lack of a decent chip shop near the ground — this was one of the few occasions last season where I was forced into a KFC — which is a shame because once inside Vale Park the food was fairly poor on my last visit. The club has, however, taken over the catering for the 1998-9 season in an effort to improve things.

One small point of irritation is that thwgb bfhry dof sheyfg... I said, it's bloody impossible to understand a word that's coming out of the PA system. Truly dreadful!

Don't be fooled into thinking that you can buy a ticket from the ticket office (that would be madness) — this is for matchday complimentaries and away match sales only.

Finally, perhaps a trip to Vale Park was best summed up by Vale's own manager who is quoted as saying 'I've been here 16 years, even the Great Train Robbers didn't get that long!'. OK, so it will never be an Old Trafford, or Anfield, but somehow there is something about the place that makes for a good time.

*Total Football* Experience Rating: 78

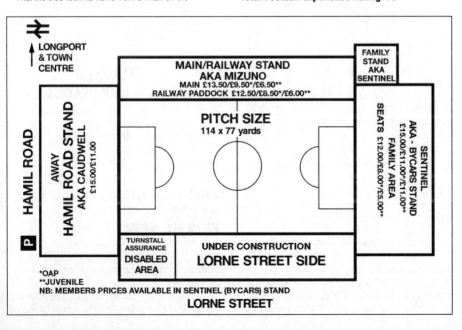

LONGPORT & TOWN CENTRE

FAMILY STAND AKA SENTINEL

**MAIN/RAILWAY STAND**
**AKA MIZUNO**
MAIN £13.50/£9.50*/£6.50**
RAILWAY PADDOCK £12.50/£8.50*/£6.00**

**PITCH SIZE**
114 x 77 yards

HAMIL ROAD

AWAY
HAMIL ROAD STAND
AKA CAUDWELL
£15.00/£11.00

SEATS £12.00/£8.00*/£5.00**

SENTINEL AKA - BYCARS STAND £15.00/£11.00*/£11.00** FAMILY AREA

TURNSTALL ASSURANCE DISABLED AREA

**UNDER CONSTRUCTION**
**LORNE STREET SIDE**

*OAP
**JUVENILE
NB: MEMBERS PRICES AVAILABLE IN SENTINEL (BYCARS) STAND

**LORNE STREET**

# PORTSMOUTH

**ADDRESS:** Fratton Park
57 Frogmore Road
Portsmouth
Hampshire PO4 8RA

... and site of England's first ever floodlit footie match when Pompey played Newcastle in 1956.

**TELEPHONE No:** 01705 731204
**TICKET OFFICE:** 01705 618777
or 01705 750825 (24hr)
**FAX:** 01705 734129
**CLUBCALL:** 0891 12 11 82
**WEB SITE:** www.pompeyfc.co.uk
**E-MAIL:**
jbaker@portsmouthfc.bdx.co.uk
**NICKNAME:** Pompey
**RECORD ATTENDANCE:**
51,385 v Derby FA Cup 6th 26 February 1949 (W 2-1)

**CLUB COLOURS:**
**HOME:** Shirts: Blue; Shorts: White; Socks: Red
**AWAY:** Shirts: Yellows;
Shorts: Blue; Socks: Yellow

**KIT SPONSORS:** KJC
**MANUFACTURERS:** Admiral

## GROUND INFO

1997-8 saw a massive change at Pompey with the opening of the new KJC Stand (where the old Fratton End used to be). It has been taken immediately to the hearts of the Pompey fans (who presumably see a £1 price rise as a pittance to pay to avoid sitting exposed to the elements) and the volume of noise that gets produced from there is incredible. This has also had the effect of revitalising the rest of Fratton Park, and despite the club's (on the whole) poor performance last season, there is a real buzz and expectancy around the place which is good to see.

Visiting fans (and some home ones) still get the privilege of sitting on seats laid on old terracing, which are open to the elements. Leg room is minimal and keep your fingers crossed that you'll have an empty seat on one or other side of you so you can spread out to occupy more room than a cramped sardine. The club offers excellent concessions for both home and visiting fans.

Away fans are separated from home fans by a bit of black netting, and the atmosphere at the ground can on occasion go from the intense to the outright hostile. However, the stewards at the club are excellent (and look incredibly mean) and, although they are happy for people to sing and chant what they want, if the line gets crossed

they are more than willing to ensure no one (bar the offender) gets hurt. Last season I saw a Pompey fan run on to the pitch after they had scored a goal and I've got to say he was brought down like a gazelle by a pack of lions. The message is: enjoy yourself but don't break the law.

**CAPACITY:** Stands: 19,214; Terrace: Nil
**AWAY FANS:** Milton Stand: 3,104
Note: this is the maximum capacity (FA Cup matches etc) and normally approximately 800 seats are allocated.

**DISABLED FACILITIES:** There are spaces for 35 disabled supporters at the front of the Fratton Road End. Both disabled fans and their helpers pay concessionary rates. There are (very) limited parking spaces at the ground for disabled fans. Contact the club in advance to pre-book. No match commentaries for the visually impaired are available.

**PROGRAMME:** £2.00
Up 33% in 1997/98 but it still seemed to be very much the programme that was produced for £1.50 the previous year.

**FANZINES:**

| | |
|---|---|
| Pisces | £1 |
| January 3rd 88 | £1 |
| Frattonise | 50p |
| Blue and Wight | £1.00 |
| True Blue | £1 |

I don't know if *Frattonise* is still going; if it is, it used to be worth a read (though not if you are easily offended). There's some great stuff in *Jan 3rd* although, at 24 pages, it is a bit pricey for what it is. *True Blue* is the organ of the official supporters' club, but although it does tend to toe the party line it will speak out if it feels it has to. The other two were not available on my last trip.

## TRAVEL

**NEAREST RAILWAY STATION:** Fratton
(01703 229393 — Southampton Enquiries)
To avoid getting lost if you come by rail (easily done) walk down Goldsmith Avenue when you leave the station. You will see a large park (Milton Park) in front of you, take a left just before you reach the park, which will take you to the ground.

**BUS:** Red and Blue Admiral (01705 650967)

**BY CAR:**
**FROM ALL PARTS:** Please note: this is a new route that was given to me last year and which I tested out and found to be about 10 times better than the one previously given. Apologies for any inconvenience the old route caused.

M3 to M27. Do not take the M275 but instead keep going as the M27 becomes the A27. Continue till you see the exit for Southsea (A2030). As you go onto the slip road stay in the right-hand lane. At the exit roundabout take the A2030 (which for 99% of the way is dual carriageway) Note: there are a couple of fairly innocuous pubs (Harvester etc) along here where you can stop for a quiet pint. Continue till you reach a roundabout at the end of Velder Avenue and the ground is straight ahead.

Note: for the St Mary's Hospital car park turn right at this roundabout and it is 0.25 mile on your left (with a very missable entrance).

## PARKING:

There is a bit of disused ground about 200yd away from the club which acts as a lorry/car park (at £2.50 a throw), but a better bet is to use the pay-and-display at St Mary's Hospital on Milton Road which is not only £1.50 cheaper but also makes for a quicker post-match getaway (although you should still allow yourself a good 20min to get out of the city).

## FUTURE DEVELOPMENTS

At some point in the not too distant future it is considered likely that the Milton Stand will be converted to something like the KJC Stand opposite it. Hopefully work may start during the tail end of 1998-9 (in which case away fans may be moved into part of the South Stand and Enclosure). However, this is yet to be confirmed.

## OTHER INFORMATION

I quite like Portsmouth, in that, unlike its neighbour Southampton, there doesn't seem to be any pretence about the place. However, it should be pointed out that it can be a bit rough at times and some of the pubs can get a little hairy of a Friday and Saturday. Probably the nearest pub to the ground is the Shepherd's Crook, but you're probably best heading down Milton Road where you will find the Brewers Arms, Travellers Joy, Mr

Pickwick and the Miltons Arms in close proximity. A better bet for a quieter drink is to carry on walking till you get to the White House pub. About 50yd further down the road from this, and on the opposite side of the road, is Barnacles, which is an excellent fish and chip shop (although do note that the bloke who owned it retired at the end of the 1997/98 season so the new fryer is as yet untested). There is also a Lloyds Bank, which doesn't normally warrant a mention but does on this occasion as it is about the only cashpoint I can think of in about a two-mile radius of Fratton Park.

Inside the ground I have to say I found the food disgusting in terms of cost and taste. They had sold out of pies by half-time and the insides of the pasties were like baby food. The burger was overcooked and the hot dogs were of the skinned European variety (and a shocking shade of pink inside). The girl serving me mistook my order of a cup of tea for coffee and I couldn't tell by looking at it but only after about three horribly bland sips.

The PA at the ground seems to work with the sort of time delay normally associated with a satellite link to America. Still it manages to blast out Mike Oldfield's 'Portsmouth' loud enough when the teams make their entrance.

On the mascot front, it has to be reported that (happily) the foamy headed Terry Venables effort seems to have departed along with its mentor, but there is still a chap in an ill-fitting sailor's outfit who wanders around looking embarrassed holding a billboard proclaiming 'Play up Pompey'. He is sponsored by the local paper, the *News*, which, it must be said, has to be applauded for continuing to put money into the club; surely, however, there could be a better way of doing it than by the ritual stripping of some poor sod's dignity.

*Total Football* **Experience Rating: 72**

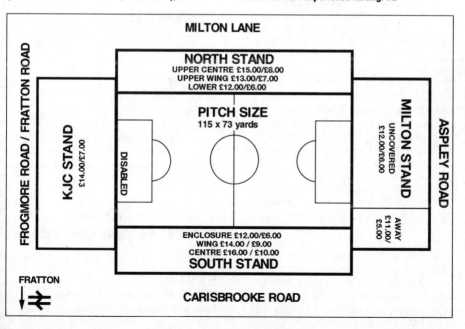

MILTON LANE

**NORTH STAND**
UPPER CENTRE £15.00/£8.00
UPPER WING £13.00/£7.00
LOWER £12.00/£6.00

**PITCH SIZE**
115 x 73 yards

FROGMORE ROAD / FRATTON ROAD

**KJC STAND**
£14.00/£7.00

DISABLED

**MILTON STAND**
UNCOVERED
£12.00/£6.00

ASPLEY ROAD

AWAY
£11.00/
£5.00

ENCLOSURE £12.00/£6.00
WING £14.00 / £9.00
CENTRE £16.00 / £10.00
**SOUTH STAND**

FRATTON

CARISBROOKE ROAD

129

# PRESTON NORTH END

**ADDRESS:** Sir Tom Finney Way
Deepdale
Preston PR1 6RU

**TELEPHONE No:** 01772 902020

**TICKET OFFICE:** 01772 902000

**FAX:** 01772 653266

**CLUBCALL:** 0891 660 220

**WEB SITE:**
http://www.prestonnorthend.co.uk/
(Official)

**NICKNAME:** The Lilywhites

**RECORD ATTENDANCE:**
42,684 v Arsenal Div 1 23 April 1938 (L 1-3)

**CLUB COLOURS:**
**HOME:** Shirts: White;
Shorts: Navy; Socks: White
**AWAY:** Shirts: Royal Blue with fluorescent trim;
Shorts: Navy Blue;
Socks: Royal Blue with fluorescent Yellow
stripes on turnover
**THIRD:** Shirts: Red with Navy sleeves;
Shorts: Red; Socks: Red & Navy hoops

**KIT SPONSORS:** Baxi

**MANUFACTURERS:** Kit by North End (own brand)

## GROUND INFO

Initially Deepdale looks like a real one stand ground as the Tom Finney Stand dominates not only the ground but the surrounding countryside. Once you get inside you find that the club has got itself really clued up and each section of the ground has its own unique atmosphere.

The redeveloped Kop Stand (rechristened the Bill Shankly Stand in memory of the ex-Preston player) should be open for business in August 1998. This will abut the Tom Finney Stand, and will further illuminate the difference between the 'old' Deepdale and the new creation that is rising from the ashes. The TF and Bill Shankly Stands are as good as anything you will see in the league (the TF Stand won a design and innovation award from the Football League) housing 8,000 and 6,000 fans respectively and with enormous floodlights that you can see from just outside Blackpool.

Funnily enough, before the TF Stand was built there used to be the West Stand; this was a bigger monstrosity than the Pav (which grandiosely, and frankly unbelievably, has an executive area).

The Town End is developing into one of the best 'Ends' in English football; there always seems to be something going on in it (and no, I don't mean a small group of little kids with horrible high-pitched chanting)

and by 2pm the place is jumping (as it remains throughout the entire match).

The club also advises that it offers Family and Student memberships which may be of interest/benefit to home fans.

**CAPACITY:** Stands: 15,131; Terrace: 6,164;
Total: 21,295
NB: These figures are pre-development of the Kop End.

**AWAY FANS:** Pavilion Paddock North: 667;
Pavilion Paddock South: 2,000;
Total: 2,667
NB: The Bill Shankly Kop (New North Stand) should be open for 1998-9 and will accommodate up to 4,000 away fans.

**DISABLED FACILITIES:** There are 48 spaces for disabled supporters in the Tom Finney Stand and this number is due to increase with the opening of the Bill Shankly Stand in August 1998. Whilst a good number of these are taken up by home supporters season ticket holders, there are normally few problems in getting a place. However, these should be pre-booked from two weeks in advance to be on the safe side.

Match commentaries for the visually impaired are available, as are designated parking spaces and again these should be pre-booked. The club states that they are keen to encourage disabled fans to visit Deepdale. Well, this is the theory. However, in practice the club leaves a little to be desired and one visually impaired supporter I spoke to told me that when she arrived at the ground she was asked 'Couldn't you leave the (guide) dog in the car?'. Hm, sensitive.

**PROGRAMME:** £1.80
Has improved immensely since it dropped the horizontal layout used in 1996-7. The focus is now much more on readability rather than style.

**FANZINES:**
Pie Muncher      £1
Silence of the Lamb      50p
Pie Muncher is undoubtedly the pick of the two and is loved by fans and players alike, although it doesn't let its popularity with the club get in the way of saying what has to be said. Latest information is that the club has taken over its publication from August 1998 and will re-launch under a new name.

## TRAVEL

**NEAREST RAILWAY STATION:** Preston
(Info Line 01772 556618)
**BUS:** Preston bus station (01772 263333)
**BY CAR:**
**NORTH:** M6 to J32, M55 to J1. Take A6 (signposted Fulwood and Preston) and continue until you pass the Royal Preston Hospital and Moor Park. Immediately after

you have passed Moor Park, turn left onto St Thomas's Road (if you miss this the next left into St George's Street is as good). At the T-junction turn left into Deepdale Road, and the ground is on your right.

NB: New junction 31A on the M6 is nearer the ground.

**EAST:** A59 towards Preston, and as you approach the town take the second exit at the roundabout into Blackpool Road. Continue for 1.5 miles until you get to the crossroads with the A6063 Deepdale Road; turn left on to this road for the ground.

**SOUTH:** M6 to J31, then take the A59 towards Preston. After one mile take the second exit at the roundabout into Blackpool Road, then as east.

**WEST:** M55 to J1, then as north.

**PARKING:** The club car park is generally for season ticket holders only but you can park opposite by Moor Park or in the school yard which is a hundred or so yards up the road. There is plenty of on-street parking available in side streets.

## FUTURE DEVELOPMENTS

The club intends fully to redevelop Deepdale in line with the two stands already constructed. However, after the building of the TF Stand there was a delay of one season before work commenced on the Bill Shankly Stand and this may be the case again. Due to the popularity of the Town End, it is likely that the Pavilion Stand will be the next to be transformed. In the event that this does occur during the 1998-9 season, away fans are likely to be allocated a section in the Bill Shankly Stand.

## OTHER INFORMATION

For grub you can do a lot worse than wandering up Deepdale Road slightly — opposite side of the road to the ground, walking away from the ground towards town — and visiting Clare's Pantry where they serve a brilliant meat and potato pie (definitely one of the top ones you'll come across). Inside the ground (where the club has recently taken over the catering) there are Ashworth Pies, which are OK (though the potato in mine was a bit hard). A bit of advice is to avoid the hot drinks as they are served in cups which for some reason really taint the taste and leave you feeling as if you've chewed on a bit of polystyrene. If you do opt for the TF Stand, you will be a lot better off sticking to the Thwaites Bitter which is a fine pint.

It's worth getting to Deepdale a bit early, not only for the antics of the Town End — given that some grounds are very sterile, it's refreshing to see a crowd who are so into it — but also for the club mascot, not the official 'Deepdale Duck' but rather the unofficial Kanga Man who appears occasionally in a well-dodgy brown fuzzy felt kangaroo outfit and maniacally hops around the pitch and then scarpers again — fine entertainment. Also pin back your ears at about 2.55pm and you will hear what sounds like a very poor Country & Western record; keep listening, though, and you will find that it is actually a C&W footie record — 'Who are you? Watch Out for the PNE'. It goes so far beyond the boundaries of awfulness that it is brilliant and it is only a shame that the club cuts it off just before the teams actually emerge and replaces it with the triumphal march from Aida.

There are a couple of good pubs around Deepdale (the Garrison possibly shading it over the Summers Arms opposite) although Legends, which is right by the ground and incorporates a night-club and a pool hall, is not the most hospitable of places for visiting fans. The County Arms on the corner of Deepdale Road and Ribbleton Road looks rough but isn't too bad, and the Hesketh Arms on the way in from J31 is always worth a visit.

*Total Football* **Experience Rating: 86**

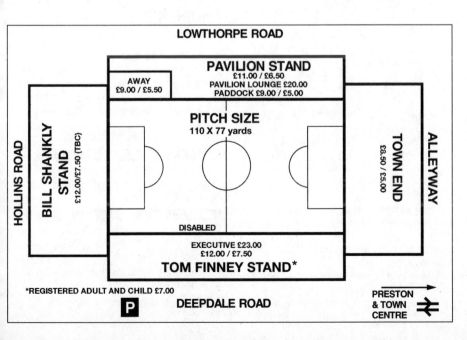

**LOWTHORPE ROAD**

**PAVILION STAND**
£11.00 / £6.50
PAVILION LOUNGE £20.00
PADDOCK £9.00 / £5.00

AWAY
£9.00 / £5.50

**PITCH SIZE**
110 X 77 yards

**BILL SHANKLY STAND**
£12.00/£7.50 (TBC)

HOLLINS ROAD

**TOWN END**
£8.50 / £5.00

ALLEYWAY

DISABLED

EXECUTIVE £23.00
£12.00 / £7.50

**TOM FINNEY STAND***

*REGISTERED ADULT AND CHILD £7.00

**P**

**DEEPDALE ROAD**

PRESTON & TOWN CENTRE

# QUEENS PARK RANGERS

**ADDRESS:** Rangers Stadium
South Africa Road
Shepherds Bush
London W12 7PA

**TELEPHONE No:** 0181 743 2575

**TICKET OFFICE:** 0181 740 0610

**24-HR INFO LINE:** 0181 740 0503

**FAX:** 0181 749 0994

**CLUBCALL:** 0891 12 11 62

**WEB SITE:** www.qpr.co.uk

**NICKNAME:** The R's, Superhoops

**RECORD ATTENDANCE:**
35,353 v Leeds Div 1 27 April 1974 (L 0-1)

## CLUB COLOURS:
**HOME:** Shirts: Blue and White hoops;
Shorts: White with Blue trim; Socks: White
**AWAY:** Shirts: Red and Black hoops;
Shorts: Red with Black side panel; Socks: Red
**THIRD:** Shirts: Yellow; Shorts: Yellow; Socks: Yellow
The yellow kit was unveiled at the end of the 1997-8 season and if anyone can explain to me when Rangers will need to wear it, I'll be very impressed.

**KIT SPONSORS:** Ericsson
**MANUFACTURERS:** Le Coq Sportif

## GROUND INFO

Lesson number 842 in translating commentator-speak into real English is the expression 'Loftus Road is a compact little ground'. What this actually means is that you can find yourself crammed sardine-like into your seat, spending 90min with your knees up by your ears.

The view from the Upper Tier of the School End is reasonable, and although the Lower Tier isn't brilliant, the low roof does have good acoustic qualities, which means a good singsong is always in order. The club operates a twin-category pricing system and if you go to a 'B' category match you'll probably be fairly OK with the price you pay; somehow, the 'A' prices, although only a couple of quid more, seem extortionate and can cause much unhappiness. Still, at least away fans are offered concessions.

It can be worth going into the Ellerslie Road Stand, which is mixed but as safe as houses. You are still terribly cramped, but as you are along the pitch rather than behind the goals, the view is a bit better (although still far from being perfect).

Certainly one of the best things about the ground is the fact that the club treats visiting supporters like normal human beings and the stewards genuinely try to help. It's difficult to think of many other grounds where the home club makes announcements (and sounds as if it means them) over the tannoy that if there is any assistance that supporters need, please let the stewards know because they are there to help.

Finally, given that a few years ago Loftus Road was one of those pitches that seemed to turn into a swamp in about October, it is surprising to report that, even with Wasps Rugby Union club in residence, the ground held up well last year.

**CAPACITY:** Stands: 19,074; Terrace: Nil

**AWAY FANS:** School End: 3,100
NB: If required, the club may make available a section of the Ellerslie Road Stand (capacity about 480) and part of the old West Paddock in the South Africa Road Stand (capacity about 750) for away fans.

**DISABLED FACILITIES:** There are 20 places for wheelchair-bound supporters; seven of these are given to QPR season ticket holders and the remaining 13 are up for grabs — get in quickly. The season ticket holders go in Block A of the West Paddock of the South Africa Road Stand, and visiting supporters are in Block X of the Ellerslie Road Stand. Admission is free of charge for disabled supporters and their helpers. There are match commentaries for the visually impaired. Good news on the parking front is that the club has advised that cars with disabled badges on them can park in Ellerslie Road on matchdays.

**PROGRAMME:** £2.00
This went up 20% in 1997-8. It's a fairly reasonable mix of news and articles, although its graphics and layout are probably better than the writing.

## FANZINES:
| | |
|---|---|
| In The Loft | £1 |
| A Kick Up The R's | £1.50 |
| Beat About The Bush | £1 |
| All Quiet on The Western Avenue | £1 |

All of these are excellent reads. Probably the best two are *AKUTR* and *AQOTWA* (the latter produced from that well-known Superhoop stronghold of Nuneaton).

## TRAVEL

**NEAREST RAILWAY STATION:**
Paddington (0171 262 6767 — Paddington Enquiries)
This is miles away from the ground, but you can pick up the tube from here.

**NEAREST TUBE STATION:** White City (Central Line). Take a right, then first left when you leave the station for the ground. Alternatively, Shepherds Bush (Hammersmith & City Line) is also easily walkable. Leave the station and turn right; walk till you see Loftus Road, take a right here for the ground.

**BUS:** London Transport: 0171 222 1234
A 72, 95 or 220 will take you to White City Underground

which is a five-minute walk from the ground. Alternatively take a 283 to Bloemfontein Road, which is where you'll find the away end.

## BY CAR:
**NORTH:** M1, then turn right onto the A406 (signposted Neasden). After three miles turn left oto the A404 (signposted Harlesden). 1.75 miles later bear right into Scrubs Lane, and after a further 1.25 miles you will see White City. Take the first right after White City into White City Road (if you go past BBC TV you have gone too far), and then first left into South Africa Road. The ground is 0.25 mile on the left.

**EAST:** A12, A406, then A503. At the end of the A503 follow signs for Oxford to bring yourself on to the A40(M). After two miles, branch left off the A40(M) to join the M41 (signposted The West). At the roundabout take the third exit for the A40, then left onto the A4020 Uxbridge Road (signposted Acton). 0.25 mile later turn right into Loftus Road.

**SOUTH:** A3, and turn left by reservoirs at Putney Heath onto the A219 Tibbets Ride/Putney Hill. Continue along this road for 1.5 miles (crossing Putney Bridge) then bear left for Fulham Palace Road, still the A219, signposted Hammersmith. Once in Hammersmith, follow the one-way system until you turn left on to the A219 Shepherds Bush Road. (If you go past a big hotel on your left, you have gone too far and will need to follow the one-way system round again.) Continue for 0.75 mile then turn left onto the A4020 Uxbridge Road (signposted Acton) and 0.25 mile later turn right into Loftus Road.

**WEST:** M4 into Chiswick, then continue along the A4. At Hogarth roundabout take the first exit still following the A4 Great West Road (signposted Hammersmith). Follow the one-way system, then as south.

**PARKING:** Good news! You can now park at the BBC TV Centre in White City. Bad news! It'll cost you a fiver if you want to do so. There is also an NCP at White City which you will pass if coming from the north (instead of turning into Uxbridge Road, continue past BBC TV and it's on your left).

## FUTURE DEVELOPMENTS
To be honest, Loftus Road is looking a bit past its sell-by date. However, numerous factors (not least of all lack of space) mean that it would be difficult to redevelop the ground and there has been talk about the club upping sticks and moving to a new site, but expect everything to stay as it is for at least this season.

## OTHER INFORMATION
The only pub in close proximity to the ground is the Springbok which, true to the QPR experience, is a place where home and away fans can mingle. The pub is not that big, and the police don't seem to object to people taking their drinks into the square outside. A little further afield is the Grasshopper which is another popular port of call for away fans.

The square by the Springbok also houses a bookies and an above average chip shop. I'd recommend you visit the second of these as once in the ground there are massive slow-moving queues for food. There has been a bit of improvement in the grub since the club got new caterers — for example, no longer is it compulsory to serve everything cold — but there is still a tendency to smother everything in strong raw onion. In the past I have even found a piece in a tea I ordered.

Given the categorising of matches, the below average facilities, etc, I always feel that I should dislike QPR, but somehow I always leave Loftus Road in a good frame of mind. The key thing is perhaps that, as previously mentioned, everyone associated with Rangers who you'll meet on a matchday is friendly and tries to be helpful.

*Total Football* **Experience Rating: 81**

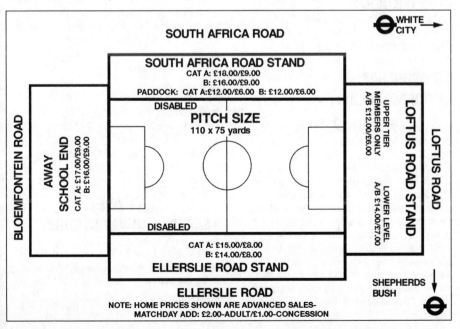

SOUTH AFRICA ROAD

WHITE CITY

SOUTH AFRICA ROAD STAND
CAT A: £18.00/£9.00
B: £16.00/£9.00
PADDOCK: CAT A:£12.00/£6.00 B: £12.00/£6.00

DISABLED

PITCH SIZE
110 x 75 yards

DISABLED

CAT A: £15.00/£8.00
B: £14.00/£8.00
ELLERSLIE ROAD STAND

BLOEMFONTEIN ROAD

AWAY
SCHOOL END
CAT A: £17.00/£9.00
B: £16.00/£9.00

LOFTUS ROAD STAND
UPPER TIER
MEMBERS ONLY
A/B £12.00/£6.00

LOWER LEVEL
A/B £14.00/£7.00

LOFTUS ROAD

ELLERSLIE ROAD

SHEPHERDS BUSH

NOTE: HOME PRICES SHOWN ARE ADVANCED SALES-
MATCHDAY ADD: £2.00-ADULT/£1.00-CONCESSION

# READING

**ADDRESS:** The Madejski Stadium
Bennett Road
Reading
RG2 0PL

**TELEPHONE No:** 0118 968 1100
**TICKET OFFICE:** 0118 968 1000
**FAX:** 0118 968 1101
**CLUBCALL:** 0891 12 1000
**WEB SITE:**

www.readingfc.co.uk (official)
http://www.i-way.co.uk/readingfc
(unofficial).

This is the site of 'Hob Nob Anybody' which is as near to an electronic fanzine as anything I've come across. It also has tons of information and is well worth a visit.

**E-MAIL:** readingfc@i-way.co.uk

This is the E-Mail of Graham Loader, webmaster at Hob Nob. If you have a question about anything to do with the club then he's the man to get in touch with (this bloke is such a good egg that he actually gave me his phone number which, after deliberation, I have not included here as I'm sure he can do without loads of abusive calls from Swindon and Oxford fans).

**NICKNAME:** The Royals

**RECORD ATTENDANCE:** 33,042 v

Brentford FA Cup 5th 19 February 1927 (W 1-0)

**CLUB COLOURS:**
**HOME:** Shirts: Blue and White hoops;
        Shorts: White; Socks: White and Blue hoops
**AWAY:** Shirts: Red with White sleeves;
        Shorts: Red; Socks: Red

**KIT SPONSORS:** Auto Trader
**MANUFACTURERS:** Mizuno

## GROUND INFO

Half of me wants to launch into a tirade about Mr Madejski calling the new ground after himself (and hopefully having a large turnstile put in to get his ego through). However, the point remains that this is a man who has put a lot of cash into what cannot really be considered a fashionable club. He has saved away fans from the toilets with ivy growing in them and the uncovered terraces that were on offer at Elm Park and — equally gratifying — built a stadium which is still (just about) walkable from the town centre and all the amenities it offers, but at the same time is only a mile and a bit away from the M4 and a quick getaway after the match. So I guess it is hats off to Mr M and his stadium offspring.

Potted information about what you should find in the ground is as follows: there will be 24,200 unobstructed and covered seats built over four floors. All areas will have bars and TVs. Already in the process of being built are a restaurant, conference centre, exhibition area, training pitch and an indoor running track/leisure centre. However, there still remains a considerable amount (over 80,000sq ft) land which can be redeveloped according to demands/requirements so the total development is unlikely to be completed for a long time.

It should be noted that the stadium is near a sewage purification works and when I paid it a visit — the ground, not the works — there was a definite niff in the air reminiscent of the one you normally only encounter an hour or so after eating a football van burger.

A retractable roof on the ground and video screen in the East Stand originally proposed have been scrapped due to excessive costs.

**CAPACITY**: Stands: 24,200; Terrace: Nil

**AWAY FANS:** South Stand: up to 4,000
This capacity may be adjusted on a match-by-match basis according to demand. It should be noted that the club state that visiting supporters will (continue to) receive the same concessions as those offered to home fans at the new stadium.

**DISABLED FACILITIES:** 128 designated spaces on all sides of the ground have been set aside for use by wheelchair-bound supporters. Prices for 1998-9 are £6 (all areas) pre-purchased tickets and £7 for those bought on the day. At Elm Park the charge for disabled fans used to include the cost of admission for one helper. However — although this has yet to be confirmed — it is thought that at the new stadium helpers will not be charged. There will be parking facilities at the ground on a first come first served basis and 12 places with match day commentaries for the visually impaired will also be available. Pre-booking is not necessary.

**PROGRAMME:** £2.00
**FANZINES:**
  *Heaven 11*                 75p
  *Taking The Biscuit*        £1
I still haven't seen a copy of *TTB* (although this is I believe its third year of existence) so I'll reserve judgement.

## TRAVEL

**NEAREST RAILWAY STATION:**
Reading (0118 959 5911)
This is a good 2.5 miles from the new ground. The club is apparently discussing with the rail companies about getting a new station built to serve the stadium itself.

**BUS:** Reading bus station (0118 959 4000)
The 7, 9 and 11 all go from the centre along the

Basingstoke Road (A33) and past the ground. There will be specials running from various points of the town to the ground on matchdays.

## BY CAR:

**NORTH:** Either M25 to M4 then as east/west or A34 to M4 J13. Follow the M4 to J11 then as east/west.

**EAST/WEST:** M4 to J11. Take the A33 (Basingstoke Road) towards Reading. Go over the first roundabout then the next left after Acre Road — Bennet Road — and then first right into Commercial Road and then on to the stadium. This diversion is in place during construction.

**SOUTH:** M3 J6. Follow the A33 towards Reading crossing the M4 at J11. Then as east/west.

It should be noted that one of the conditions of the stadium's planning permission was that the club should contribute to the construction of a relief road to the A33 which will take traffic from the M4 J11 roundabout directly to the stadium. There remains work to be done on this road, but it is hoped that it will be open for business in December 1998/January 1999.

**PARKING:** There is to be parking for 1,800 vehicles at the ground and this is being designed so that, when the relief road is built, all vehicles will be able to leave the area within 30min (although being somewhat of a cynic, I will only say that I'll believe that when I see it). If you don't fancy this, then there are plenty of dropping-off points around the Worton Grange Industrial Estate (signposted as you approach Reading from the M4) which is about a 10min walk from the ground.

## FUTURE DEVELOPMENTS

There will be, for some considerable period of time, work carried on around the site as the supporting amenities to the stadium are constructed.

## OTHER INFORMATION

If you don't fancy having a beer at one of the ground's 50+ bars, you will probably be as well going into the town centre. The nearest pub to the ground is a Harvester on the Basingstoke Road which is about a 5-6min walk away. For food there is the Seagull Fish Bar which is near the pub, but a better bet is to go along the A33 heading away from Reading until you get to the roundabout leading to the Worton Grange IE. On the left there is a little parade of shops which includes The Chippy. This has posters outside proclaiming it was voted Reading's best chip shop (hooray)... in 1993 (oh). Fortunately, while a trip to watch the Royals is a very different thing to that five years ago, I am happy to report that the fish and chips produced here are still right on button.

Hopefully the food inside the ground will match the club's new palatial surroundings because, if you tasted the burgers at Elm Park, you were always left with the feeling that although they might be fit for human consumption, they were not much better than that.

One thing that may not come as a pleasant surprise to home fans is that one of the builders of their new ground was a very big Manchester City fan (there was a poster proudly displayed in one of the site buildings). One of his mates told me that he had planted a Manchester City shirt in the foundations so that the ground would always be a City stronghold. Before Royals' fans get too irate, it is worth pointing out that apparently the ground was built on tons of rubbish which was not removed from the site, so they can argue that at least the shirt will feel at home.

*Total Football* **Experience Rating: 65**

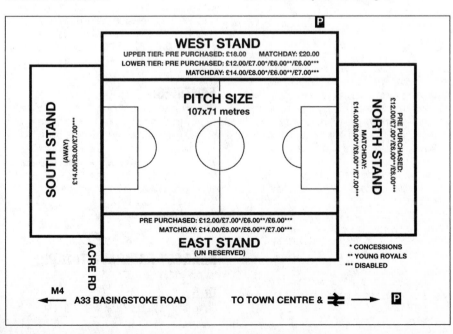

**WEST STAND**
UPPER TIER: PRE PURCHASED: £18.00    MATCHDAY: £20.00
LOWER TIER: PRE PURCHASED: £12.00/£7.00*/£6.00**/£6.00***
MATCHDAY: £14.00/£8.00*/£6.00**/£7.00***

**PITCH SIZE**
107x71 metres

**SOUTH STAND**
(AWAY)
£14.00/£8.00/£7.00***

**NORTH STAND**
PRE PURCHASED:
£12.00/£7.00*/£6.00**/£6.00***
MATCHDAY:
£14.00/£8.00*/£6.00**/£7.00***

PRE PURCHASED: £12.00/£7.00*/£6.00**/£6.00***
MATCHDAY: £14.00/£8.00*/£6.00**/£7.00***
**EAST STAND**
(UN RESERVED)

**ACRE RD**

M4 ◄— **A33 BASINGSTOKE ROAD**

* CONCESSIONS
** YOUNG ROYALS
*** DISABLED

**TO TOWN CENTRE &** 🚉 —►

# ROCHDALE

**ADDRESS:** Sandy Lane
Spotland
Rochdale
OL11 5DS
**TELEPHONE No:** 01706 644648
**TICKET OFFICE:** 01706 644648
**FAX:** 01706 648466
**DALE NEWSLINE:** 0891 555 858
**WEB SITE:** http://www.rochdale-football-club.co.uk/
**E-MAIL:** club@rochdale-football-club.co.uk
**NICKNAME:** The Dale
**RECORD ATTENDANCE:** 24,231 v Notts County FA Cup 2nd 10 December 1949 (L 1-2)
**CLUB COLOURS:**
**HOME:** Shirts: Blue; Shorts: White; Socks: Blue
**AWAY:** Shirts: Yellow; Shorts: Black; Socks: Black
**KIT SPONSORS:** Carcraft
**MANUFACTURERS:** uhlsport

## GROUND INFO

Spotland is one of those grounds where you can always be assured of a warm welcome. Previously a little run down, the ground too is getting a face-lift and this is a real must away day. The new WMG Stand eventually opened in 1997-8; apparently part of the problem with the delays in getting it built was that Rochdale Hornets RLFC — with whom the club ground shares — refused to contribute to it, saying the capacity of the ground suited them as it was and they didn't see the need for the development. It took a little time for Dale to dig deeper into their pockets, although I am happy to say that, after the stand was built and the rugby club expressed an interest in using it, they told them there was no chance.

Away fans are sited on the Willbutts Lane Terrace (but see 'Future Developments'), which is a bizarre construction, the steps of the terracing actually starting about 10yd back from the side of the pitch, with a huge concrete walkway in between (which you are more than welcome to stand in if you want to get close to the action). There is a roof on the terrace but, on my last visit, it was snowing and the flakes seemed to have no difficulty getting through the roof. Still, it does at least provide some protection against the biting wind (although this is to no avail if you want to go to the toilets or get some food as these facilities are on an open section of terracing).

Away fans who travel with children are welcome to make use of the new WMG Stand Family Enclosure, which admits up to two kids for £1 each with each adults. There is also the option of using the Pearl Street (WMG) End of the Main Stand for £10 (£5 concessions). Normally I would moan heartily about the fact that there are no concessions on the terracing, but the reductions that the club offers visiting fans in other parts of the ground mean that the cry of 'unfair' is quelled in my throat.

If there is one disappointment with the ground, it is that the new stand still has pillars supporting the roof (as do all the areas of the ground) which result in some restriction of view. The club has sorted out previous problems with the PA and have installed a brand new scoreboard.

**CAPACITY:** Stands: 4,686; Terrace: 4,509; Total: 9,195

**AWAY FANS:** Main Stand: 275; Willbutts Lane Terrace: 2,044; Family Area WMG Stand: 100; Total: 2,419

**DISABLED FACILITIES:** There are 14 places for wheelchair-bound supporters (and helpers). Disabled supporters are admitted free of charge, but helpers pay £8. These facilities are sited in the Main Stand. Match commentaries for the blind are available, and there are special parking facilities at the ground. Contact the club in advance to pre-book your place.

**PROGRAMME:** £1.60
No increase in price last year, but it did seem to get a little more meat on the bones and is worth buying. There is a fairly good section on the visiting team and a couple of decent general interest articles. Standing head and shoulders above all of these are Ian Bailey's columns, which bring to the attention information such as the fact that Salisbury Town have offered Fareham Town a toilet block in exchange for their star striker.

**FANZINES:**
*Exceedingly Good Pies* £1
*EGP* is a great example of not only what a fanzine should be about (laughing at yourself/your rivals, getting angry when needed and being resigned at all other times) but also of how practice makes perfect. When it originally started, it was more miss than hit but, with every season, the quality of the writing seems to improve and it becomes a better read, although latest news is that it is temporarily out of production again.

## TRAVEL

**NEAREST RAILWAY STATION:**
Rochdale (0161 832 8353)
**BUS:**
Baillie/Smith Street bus station (0161 228 7811)

The station is quite a way from the ground, with the bus station about half-way between the two. If you don't fancy walking, take one of the following buses — 443, 444, 459, 460 or 461 — to Spotland.

## BY CAR:

**FROM ALL DIRECTIONS:** M62 to J20, turn left onto the A627(M) and take the second exit at the second roundabout into Roch Valley Way. A mile later turn right into Willbutts Lane.

**PARKING:** Last season the club introduced pay parking at the ground (at the back of the WMG Stand [£2]). Alternatively there are plenty of side streets around. Perhaps the best place to park is Denehurst Park. When you drive to the ground turn left at traffic lights into Edenfield Road. Continue for 300yd where you can park in the Denehurst Park car park or on any of the side streets there, or indeed on Edenfield Road itself.

## FUTURE DEVELOPMENTS

Although the club responded that there was nothing scheduled for the next 12 months in the questionnaire I sent them, when I was at Spotland there was much talk of the Willbutts Lane Terrace being demolished and a new 4,000 seat stand being built (to which, I was assured, the rugby club would contribute). When this happens (and some people even suggested that it might be as early as the summer), it is likely that the away allocation in the Main and WMG Stands will be increased during construction. After the stand is finished it is considered likely that a section of this will be allocated to away support and that the current away seating in the Main Stand will be discontinued.

There is also a new supporters' bar (Studds) by the WMG Stand to which — in typical Dale fashion — everyone is welcome.

## OTHER INFORMATION

If you fancy a pre-match pint, the Ratcliffe Arms is on the corner of the ground and is fairly welcoming (though not the cheapest place you'll ever imbibe at). Mind you, if the signboard is an accurate depiction of ex-Dale chairman Fred Radcliffe, I reckon he could have given John Merrick a run for his money! You can take your drinks outside if you want and if you do there are normally a bunch of lads sat on the wall who are happy to chat about life, the universe and everything over a beer. Also worth a call is the Cemetery Hotel on Bury Road which has an excellent selection of beer, and the Church which is just behind the Pearl Street End. There are also plenty of good pubs in the town centre which are very welcoming.

As far as food is concerned, Cockleys fish and chip shop outside the ground on Willbutts Lane is good but a bit small and thus you can have a fair queue for your food. The food in the ground — prepared and served by the wonderful 'Chelle and Baz (who's not Ryan Giggs' sister no matter what she says) — is above average, although the pies could be just that bit hotter. Excellent hot drinks.

In fact, other than the fact that the club has employed a mascot — one 'Desmond dragon', who is not content with wandering around the pitch during the kick about but also goes into the stands and shakes hands with kids during a match (which led to the wonderful complaint from one Dale fan that he had missed goals through getting pies/going to the toilet/arriving late before, but this season was the first time he'd missed one because he had a dragon's arse in his face) — the only problem with Rochdale is that, unless you are a home fan, you get to go there only once a season.

***Total Football* Experience Rating: 93**

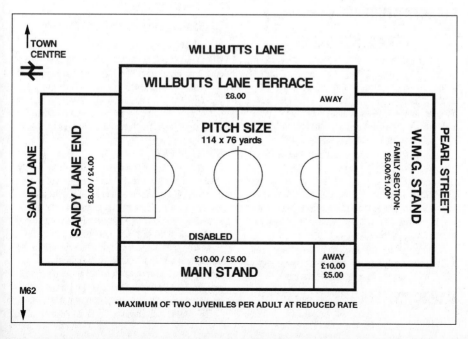

# ROTHERHAM UNITED

**ADDRESS:** Millmoor Ground
Millmoor
Rotherham S60 1HR

**TELEPHONE No:** 01709 512434

**TICKET OFFICE:** 01709 512434

**FAX:** 01709 512762

**MILLERS CHATTERBOX LINE:** 0891 12 16 37

**WEB SITE:** www.rotherhamufc.u-net.com/ — official but not very good or interesting at all. Instead I'd recommend the much longer established (but totally unofficial) Millers on-line site at www2.krisalis.co.uk/wwwneil/index.html

**NICKNAME:** The Merry Millers

**RECORD ATTENDANCE:** 25,149 v
Sheffield Wednesday Div 2 26 January 1952 (D 3-3) The club programme states the biggest crowd is 25,000 for the above match and a match in December 1952 against Sheffield United, but what do they know!

**CLUB COLOURS:**
**HOME:** Shirts: Red with White sleeves;
Shorts: White; Socks: Red
**AWAY:** Shirts White, Red and Black trim;
Shorts: Black; Socks: Black

**KIT SPONSORS:** One-2-One

**MANUFACTURERS:** Bodyline Sportswear

## GROUND INFO

The entrance to the away sections is via Millmoor Lane which is very narrow and strewn with dog mess. There is a sign warning fans to walk slowly and carefully and it is as well to observe the second part of it unless you want to end up with an unpleasant aroma in the car on your way home. As for the first part you don't have much of an option as it can get fairly packed and congested.

Once inside the ground, the roof gives excellent resonance to chanting and you can get a good atmosphere going quite easily. It's fair to say that for the prices charged, the facilities are more than basic and Millmoor plays host to some of the worst toilets in the league (uncovered troughs *circa* 1523); still, at least you get reasonable concessions.

If you are feeling very skint then (apparently) you can wait till half-time and get in for £3, which I have heard that some supporters do on a fairly regular basis.

**CAPACITY:** Stands: 4,442; Terrace: 7,047;
Total: 11,489

**AWAY FANS:** Railway End Terrace: 3,125;
Millmoor Lane Stand: 1,094;
Total: 4,219

**DISABLED FACILITIES:** There are 13 places in the Millmoor Lane Stand family section. There is no cost for disabled supporters, but helpers pay £5. The club does stipulate that this is true only if there is one helper per disabled fan, so if you were planning on organising a coach trip and aiming on making a few bob by claiming that everyone was with you, then I'm afraid your devious plans have been thwarted. There is disabled parking at the ground, which together with your place should be pre-booked. Match commentaries are available and again should be pre-booked.

**PROGRAMME:** £1.60
The price stayed static again last year and, from being an expensive programme, this is now at the bottom of the range price-wise. Perversely it seems to have become a slightly better read each year over the last three seasons.

**FANZINES:**
*Moulin Rouge* £1
This is one that is steadily getting better and brilliantly captures the 'always say die' spirit that surrounds the club with moaning a plenty. There is always underlying wit (and desperation) behind the articles and you'll probably find yourself nodding in agreement with a lot of what's in there even if you are not a fan of the Merry Millers.

## TRAVEL

**NEAREST RAILWAY STATION:**
Rotherham Central (0114 272 6411)

**BUS:** Rotherham bus station (01114 276 8688)

**BY CAR:**
**NORTH/WEST:** M1 to J34. Take the A6109 Meadow Bank Road (signposted Rotherham) and continue for just over a mile until you get to a roundabout with the A629. Turn right at this roundabout onto the Wortley Road (A629), then take a right at the next roundabout onto Masbrough Street. The fourth left is Millmoor Lane and the ground is on your left.

**SOUTH/WEST:** (Yes! Yes! I know it says west above as well, but I couldn't decide which route you were likely to take so I decided to put both down and let you take your pick!) M1 to J33. Turn on to the A630 (signposted Rotherham) then left at the next roundabout onto Bawtry Road (A631). Straight over the next roundabout and you will be back on the A630 Canklow Road (signposted Rotherham and Canklow). 1.5 miles later, turn left (by the White Rose) onto Old Sheffield Road. Turn left again at the end of this (short) road, then right at the roundabout onto the A630 Centenary Way. Left at the next roundabout onto Masbrough Street, then as north/west.

NB: Meadowhall Shopping Centre is situated at J33

of the M1 so if the game coincides with a busy shopping period it can be better to go to J34 and follow the directions from the north.

**EAST:** (But definitely not west). A631 into Rotherham until you get to a roundabout with the A6021 Wichersley Road. Take the A6021 and go straight over the next roundabout. A mile later turn left into Hollowgate; this becomes Alma Road, at the bottom of which you should turn left onto the A630 Canklow Road and then immediately right onto Old Sheffield Road, then as south (and, dammit, west as well!).

**PARKING:** You can park at the club car park, but it is a bit of a shenanigans to get into it. You are not allowed to drive in the front entrance (that would be far too easy) as only players and directors are allowed to use this. Instead, turn away from the ground (opposite the car park entrance) and follow the small side road by the bridge. Turn left through the railway arches and this brings you into the tradesmen's entrance. There is also some street parking around.

However, if you do park outside somebody's house you may get an angry resident belting out of their front door and asking the question 'How would you like it if I parked outside your house when I went to watch Rotherham?' Note, the smartarse reply of 'It doesn't bother me mate, but as I've just driven a hundred and forty miles to get here you're going to have a pretty long walk to the ground' is probably best kept to yourself (if only I'd listen to my own advice).

## FUTURE DEVELOPMENTS

There was talk of the Rugby Union club building a new super stadium (20,000 capacity), but strangely the football club did not seem to be included in the plans. I say strangely because, with the best will in the world, you can't imagine either the RU club filling it (even if the

football club played there on the same day you'd be struggling) or Rotherham needing two stadia. Expect either the two to get together or for everything to stay pretty much the same.

## OTHER INFORMATION

Away fans are welcome at the cavernous Tivoli which is by the ground, but a better bet is to wander down Masbrough Street to the Moulders Arms. Don't be put off by the two blokes who are semi-blocking the doorway because inside you'll find a decent pub with friendly staff and, more importantly, an excellent pint. The pub also does B&B for £12.50 for any fan who may fall in love with the town (???) and wish to stay for a night (or even the week). A reasonable alternative to the Moulders is the Queens which is just opposite.

For food, avoid the Millmoor fisheries (unless you like expensive lukewarm chips served with a surly 'yer what' attitude); Julia's Café is better, but is only worth going into if you have got a good 20min to spare, as the service always seems fairly slow. It's probably as well to wait until you get inside the ground to have one of the steak and kidney or beef and potato pies. These are very tasty but unbelievably hot and unless you give it a good five minutes after you've bought it before tucking in, the odds are you will burn the inside of your mouth. The tea is drinkable.

One thing that you can't fail to be impressed by at Millmoor is the state of the pitch, which always seems to be in absolutely first-class condition (so that's one line of excuse gone if you get stuffed 3-0 up there). Apparently the groundsman, Mr Corby won an award for his work last season (my, won't he be happy if the rugby and football teams end up sharing the same turf!!).

*Total Football* Experience Rating: 64

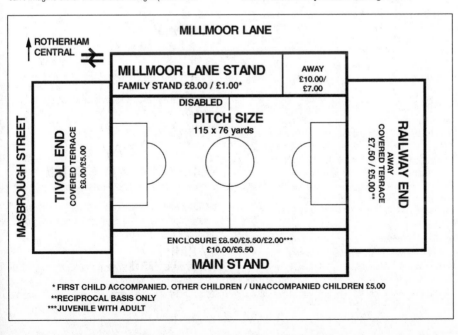

**MILLMOOR LANE**

ROTHERHAM CENTRAL

**MILLMOOR LANE STAND**
FAMILY STAND £8.00 / £1.00*

AWAY £10.00/ £7.00

DISABLED

**PITCH SIZE**
115 x 76 yards

MASBROUGH STREET

TIVOLI END
COVERED TERRACE
£8.00/£5.00

RAILWAY END
AWAY
COVERED TERRACE
£7.50 / £5.00**

ENCLOSURE £8.50/£5.50/£2.00***
£10.00/£6.50

**MAIN STAND**

\* FIRST CHILD ACCOMPANIED. OTHER CHILDREN / UNACCOMPANIED CHILDREN £5.00
\*\*RECIPROCAL BASIS ONLY
\*\*\*JUVENILE WITH ADULT

# SCARBOROUGH

**ADDRESS:** The McCain Stadium
Seamer Road
Scarborough
North Yorkshire
YO12 4HF

**TELEPHONE No:** 01723 375094

**TICKET OFFICE:** 01723 375094

**FAX:** 01723 378733

**CLUBCALL:** 0891 12 16 50

**WEB SITE:** http://www.
yorkshirecoast.co.uk/scarbrofc/

**E-MAIL:**
scarbrofc@yorkshirecoast.co.uk

**NICKNAME:** Boro or Seadogs

**RECORD ATTENDANCE:**
11,162 v Luton FA Cup 3rd 8 January 1938 (D 1-1)

**CLUB COLOURS:**
**HOME**: Shirts: White with Red/Green trim;
Shorts: White; Socks: White/Red
**AWAY:** Shirts: Flourescent Green with Black trim;
Shorts: Black; Socks: Green/Black hoops

**KIT SPONSORS:** Errea

**MANUFACTURERS:** Errea

## GROUND INFO

If you are making your first visit to the McCain Stadium, don't expect a brand-new ground à la Huddersfield, Scunthorpe or Walsall; the McCain Stadium is simply the Athletic Ground at which the club has always played, but with a bit of sponsorship.

However, the ground has improved beyond belief over the last few years (this, it must be said, is in no small part down to the club's chairman John Russell who has really galvanized the place). There are two new stands which whilst not huge, offer decent leg room and a good view as well as cover from the wind which the locals refer to as bracing, but for which the word bitter is more accurate.

One good thing with the new stands is that, despite their relatively small size, they do not give the ground a 'legoland' nor a 'warehouse' feel about it and The McCain Stadium is still very much a football club's home rather than a leisure facility.

One thing inside the ground which is slightly disturbing is the number of memorial plaques which appear to be attached to anything and everything, and to be honest, if you've just had a long drive up to Scarborough and watched a dodgy game of football in the wind and rain, then the last thing you want to be reminded of is your own mortality.

Excellent concessions are available for both home and visiting fans. Home supporters pay the same for either a seat in the stand or a place on the open terrace, and it is a bit surprising how many opt for the latter no matter what the conditions.

On the odd occasion you'll hear a small band of fans desperately trying to put the words of the club's motto ('No Battle No Victory') to some kind of rhythm. This is an impossible task as the words have no kind of natural cadence. This always peters out after about three goes and for some bizarre reason leaves you feeling a bit depressed about the whole affair.

**CAPACITY:** Stands: 3,516; Terrace: 2,037;
Total: 5,553

**AWAY FANS:** West (Edgehill Road) Stand: 1,352;
Main Stand Seats: 286;
Terracing (West): 390; Total: 2,028

**DISABLED FACILITIES:** There are spaces for a total of 20 wheelchair-bound supporters in the East (Seamer Road) and Main Stands. Each supporter can have one helper directly by them. Admission costs are £4.00 for disabled fans and standard admission for helpers. Pre-booking is required and this can be made from one month prior to a fixture. Unfortunately, there are neither match commentaries for the visually impaired nor special parking facilities. From reports received it appears that the club is very clued up to the needs of wheelchair supporters, and assistance is readily and happily given.

**PROGRAMME:** £1.50
It continues to stutter along, improving bit by bit with every season yet somehow remaining fairly dull and uninspiring.

**FANZINES:**
*The Seadog Bites Back* £1
The main problem with this fanzine (now entering its third season) is its general lack of availability round the ground (I got an old copy from a Boro fan who I was chatting to and who summed it up by saying 'Oh, I sometimes see the bloke who writes this; he might have a newer one on him').

## TRAVEL

**NEAREST RAILWAY STATION:**
Scarborough Central (01482 26033 — Hull Enquiries)

**BUS:** Scarborough and District (01723 375463)
A number 843 bus will drop you off at the ground from the town.

**BY CAR:**
**FROM ALL PARTS:** Take the A64 main York to Scarborough Road. As you approach the town you will see a number of superstores (B&Q, Halfords, etc) and the ground is directly opposite the Do-It-All. The approach to

the town takes you through some really remote areas, ideal for making you think about how far you would have to walk if your car broke down, especially at night. This invariably leads to panic (is the engine misfiring?) and thoughts of such fine cinematic feasts as 'American Werewolf in London'.

**PARKING:** As you approach the town you will see a number of superstores... Alternatively drive past the ground and take the next left into Barry's Lane, by the school. Initially this is coned as no parking, but about half-way up the hill the restriction is lifted and there is plenty of street parking available. The attitude of some of the locals may go some way to explaining why it is unlikely that the club is ever going to be a major force in English football. One of the last times I went to the ground I parked up here, and as I was getting out, a local asked me what I was doing. I said that I was off to the football, but rather than the expected tirade of 'Well, you can't park here', I simply got asked the question 'Where?'. At 2.30pm on a Saturday afternoon, this is not good news for the club.

## FUTURE DEVELOPMENTS

There is some safety work going on regarding the uncovered terracing, which will increase the capacity to over the 6,000 mark. However, apart from this, there are not any major projects planned for the near future although this can and will be revisited as or if league requirements demand.

## OTHER INFORMATION

If you fancy a drink then you can go inside the ground to the Main Stand where, to the shame of the club, there is actually a price differential if you want to go in the club on a day pass as an away fan (£1.00) compared to the charge if you are a home fan (50p), (perhaps the only instance of discrimination against away fans that you'll come across). For this reason alone I would recommend you wander towards North Shore and try the Scarborough Flyer (next to the organ exchange shop) which serves a good pint and doesn't charge anything extra for the privilege. Elsewhere the Tap and Spile is also worth popping in.

If you are looking for food, be warned that the chip shops tend to shut at about 1.30. Inside the ground, if you opt to go into the West Stand then you will miss out on the rare treat of mushy peas, which are brewing in a giant cauldron in the Main Stand — excellent with pies (which are also cheap and tasty). Given the sponsors of the ground, it is a bit disappointing to report that on my last visit they had run out of chips before the end of the half-time interval. If you fancy a drink then I'd recommend that you stick with the traditional tea or Bovvie and not opt for one of the soft drinks which are named after players, Somehow the thought of sipping at Ian Ironside's Iron Brew or Jason Rockett's Rockett Fuel (which must be non-premium given the pace he seemed to go at in the second half of the match I saw) does not fill me with culinary delight.

The club managed to get itself in the papers last season when it presented one of the supporters with a life-time membership. The supporter in question was an eight-year-old lurcher called Honey, which Eric, a Boro fan, brings to all the home matches. Honey actually is a replacement for Eric's previous dog, which had spent its Saturdays in a similar manner before it went to the great lamppost in the sky.

Finally, one point of discord to note is that not only does the club wish fans happy birthday at half-time, it also plays a horrible version of the song over the tannoy. Fortunately, the fans resist all attempts to get them to sing along with this.

*Total Football* **Experience Rating: 90**

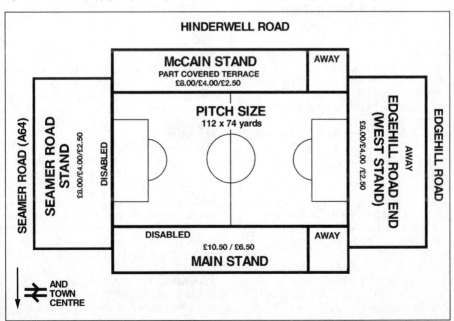

HINDERWELL ROAD

McCAIN STAND
PART COVERED TERRACE
£8.00/£4.00/£2.50

AWAY

PITCH SIZE
112 x 74 yards

SEAMER ROAD (A64)

SEAMER ROAD STAND
£8.00/£4.00/£2.50

DISABLED

EDGEHILL ROAD END
(WEST STAND)
£8.00/£4.00 /£2.50

AWAY

EDGEHILL ROAD

DISABLED

AWAY

£10.50 / £6.50

MAIN STAND

AND TOWN CENTRE

# SCUNTHORPE UNITED

**ADDRESS:** Glanford Park
Doncaster Road
Scunthorpe
North Lincolnshire
DN15 8TD

**TELEPHONE No:** 01724 848077
**TICKET OFFICE:** 01724 848077
**FAX:** 01724 857986
**CLUBCALL:** 0891 12 16 52
**WEB SITE:** http://www.isfa.com/
isfa/lists/scunthorpe/

(Mailing List Only)

**NICKNAME:** The Irons
**RECORD ATTENDANCE:**
23,935 v Portsmouth FA Cup 4th 15 January 1954
(D 1-1). At Glanford Park: 8,775 v Rotherham Div 4
1 May 1989 (D 0-0)

**CLUB COLOURS:**
**HOME:** Shirts: Claret and Blue; Shorts: White;
Socks: White
**AWAY:** Shirts: Yellow with Navy trim; Shorts: Navy;
Socks: Yellow

**KIT SPONSORS:** Motek
**MANUFACTURERS:** Loki (Mizuno)

## GROUND INFO

The pricing policy at Glanford Park is excellent and a far cry from the days when visiting supporters got no concessions. Home fans do have the benefit of still being able to go on terracing and the combined cost for one adult and child for this would be just over a tenner, which is reasonable by anybody's standard.

The ground itself is fairly functional although you may find yourself wondering how come a stadium built less than 10 years ago still manages to have pillars in every stand. These can be a real bind for some of the seats in the Caparo (Away) Stand, although, to be honest, rare is the occasion that you will not be able to get up and find yourself a better spot. This is even more true when you consider the fact that (incredibly) the Old Showground was the first in the Britain to have a cantilever stand.

Away fans views of Glanford Park tend to fall into one of two categories. Either they feel it is a soulless warehouse or — and a few people have expressed this view to me — now that it has been up for almost a decade it has a feeling of being more lived in and is developing a bit of a personality. Whichever of these two views you end up with it's an odds on cert that, unless you go at the height of summer, you'll agree that it's cold.

**CAPACITY:** Stands: 6,410; Terrace: 2,773; Total: 9,183

**AWAY FANS:** South Stand: 1,678
**DISABLED FACILITIES:** There are 16 spaces for wheelchairs at the ground, in the GMB Stand, and six headsets for the blind. Disabled supporters are admitted free, with helpers paying £9.00. There are decent toilet and parking facilities for supporters at the ground. Pre-booking is required. The club does seem fairly receptive and geared up towards supporters' needs, which means a trip to Scunthorpe will be one of your easier away days during the season.

**PROGRAMME:** £1.70
Available inside the ground. I've got to say that this did improve last season, although the use of claret printing gives it a strangely 1950s look. The visitors' section is OK and there is also an excellent 'third degree' column which looks at what is happening in the whole of the division. The whole thing is put together in a nicely pessimistic way; for example, the 'Next At Glanford Park' column I saw, read 'We could be in for a real battering from a vastly improved Barnet outfit'.

**FANZINES:**
*Son Of A Ref* £1
The club itself sent me a copy to review, and I've got to say this is probably the only way you'll get hold of one as there never seem to be any sellers around.

## TRAVEL

**NEAREST RAILWAY STATION:**
Scunthorpe (two miles) (01302 340222 — Doncaster Enquiries)

**BUS:**
Scunthorpe bus station (two miles) (01724 842233) There are no buses direct from the station to the ground. Instead, go to the town centre bus station (about 10min walk) and get either a 341 or a 335 to the stadium. These leave every quarter of an hour.

**BY CAR:**
**NORTH/SOUTH/WEST:** M180 to J3, then M181. At the end of the M181 turn right onto the A18 Doncaster Road. After 200yd, turn right into the approach to the ground and car park.
**EAST:** M180 to J4. Take the A18 (signposted Town Centre), continue to the roundabout with the A159 Ashby Road and take the second exit into Kingsway. At the next roundabout (again with the A159) take the second exit into Doncaster Road, and the approach to the ground is 300yd on the left.
**PARKING:** There is parking for over 600 vehicles by the ground which costs £1. If you are looking for a quick getaway have a word with one of the (very helpful) attendants who will guide you to a decent spot.

# FUTURE DEVELOPMENTS

There has been talk of pulling down the Evening Telegraph Stand and building a new two-tier construction. Certainly this seems a little way off becoming reality, but it may be just what the ground needs to help give it a better atmosphere and break up the sameness of the stadium.

# OTHER INFORMATION

Glanford Park is about two miles from the centre of Scunthorpe, although this fact has become a little less irritating since the opening of the Old Farmhouse pub right by the ground. This includes Uncle Tom's Playbarn, which isn't as sleazy as it sounds but rather a good place to park the kids while you have a beer. Alternatively you may be able to get yourself into the charmingly named 'Iron Bar' at the ground, although don't bank on it. The food outlet in the British Steel Stand also opens up to feed fans who are outside the ground. The menu is fairly impressive, although when I was there, they had run out of the first four things I asked for. The chip butties are excellent — really fat succulent chips, and the pies are also well worth trying, piping hot with plenty of meat in them. Go for tea rather than the bovvie, as the latter was a bit bland. They didn't have any spoons for sugar but there were stacks of blue forks on the side which, after a bit of debate between the servers, it was agreed could be used for stirring purposes.

If you don't fancy hanging around the ground, there are plenty of decent pubs and chippies in the town centre. If you do wander down that way then the Safeway that you see on your left, as you approach the town, is the site of the old ground. All that remains is a small plaque which has been liberally daubed with graffiti. If you are looking for a watering hole in the town, The Mint or the Royal Hotel are OK, and the Hungry Fisherman is a good chip shop with plenty of tables. If you fancy sticking something up your nose, the newsagent's by the Hungry Fisherman boasts a large selection of snuff.

On my visit, the ground was virtually empty until kick-off time, with seemingly everyone opting for the warmth of their cars and the radio previews until about 2.55.

The stewards at the club are both chatty and helpful, and dole out useful advice about getting into town etc, but will also talk about the forthcoming game — although they tend to find it hard not to express their surprise that anyone should want to travel any distance to see their team.

Scunthorpe have got a lot going for them. They treat away fans exceptionally well in terms of both attitudes and prices. It is easy to get to and away from and there is plenty of parking available at the ground, and the facilities, whilst nothing spectacular, are probably above average for the division. It is difficult to understand then why a visit to Glanford Park always feels like a chore rather than a pleasure. The only conclusion I can draw is that it seems to be a place which is devoid of great passion, and this can easily rub off onto visiting fans. This means, instead of having a sing and a laugh and getting a good atmosphere going (which the acoustics in the ground make it fairly easy to do), you end up sitting in an almost eerie semi-silence where you can clearly make out what the players are shouting (or more usually swearing) at each other on the pitch. It is difficult to see what more the club itself can do about this it so it would be wrong not to give the club a reasonable 'score'. However, because this score reflects the total experience of going to a ground, it stays fairly low.

***Total Football*** **Experience Rating: 69**

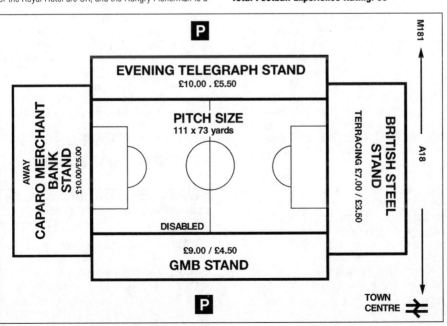

# SHEFFIELD UNITED

**ADDRESS:** Bramall Lane
Sheffield
S2 4SU

**TELEPHONE No:** 0114 221 5757

**TICKET OFFICE:** 0114 221 1889

**FAX:** 0114 272 3030

**CLUBCALL:** 0891 888 650

**WEB SITE:** http://www.sufc.co.uk (official)

**SITE:** info@sufc.co.uk

**NICKNAME:** The Blades

**RECORD ATTENDANCE:** 68,287 v Leeds Utd FA Cup 5th 15 February 1936 (W 3-1)

**CLUB COLOURS:**
**HOME:** Shirts: Red and White stripes;
Shorts: Black; Socks: Black
**AWAY:** Shirts: White; Shorts: White; Socks: White

**KIT SPONSORS:** Ward's

**MANUFACTURERS:** Le Coq Sportif

## GROUND INFO

Bramall Lane has been fully restored to four-sided glory with the opening of the John Street Stand, an impressive if somewhat overdue one-tier structure. Less impressive is the Bramall Lane Stand, which is a bit of a concrete monstrosity with some restricted views and a lower tier which is only partially covered. To be fair, the club recognises this and does print warnings on tickets which are, if anything, a little too doom laden — I was in row Q which is deemed an uncovered area, but stayed dry when it rained, although people from about row O forward were not as lucky. Whichever row you sit in, leg room is at a premium.

The club does offer concessions to away fans and although a 30% discount isn't the most generous you'll come across, the £10 adult charge is very reasonable. Home supporters at the Kop End receive the same level of concession.

The variety of facilities on offer in the away end are good (there is a bookies in the ground), but there always seems to be quite a lot of congestion under the stand and the food sellers are incredibly slow. The toilets have traffic flow which helps speed your journey through them; this is just as well because they're a bit grim.

Good news (for some), though, is that the club does on occasion make seats available for visitors in the family section of the John Street Stand. Admission is £11 with a £5 concession. No 'unaccompanied' adults are admitted to this section.

**CAPACITY:** Stands: 30,370; Terrace: Nil

**AWAY FANS:** Bramall Lane Stand Lower Tier: 2,063

The away allocation can be increased to the whole of the Bramall Lane Stand (total 4, 563) if demand is sufficient.

**DISABLED FACILITIES:** There are 106 spaces for wheelchair-bound supporters in the Westfield Enclosure of the John Street Stand; note: this is also the area where matchday commentaries for the visually impaired are available. These places must be pre-booked at least two weeks in advance. The good news is that admission for wheelchair-bound supporters is free, with any adult helpers having to pay £5 (concessions free). The bad news is that if you go with more than one mate then you will end up being split up. The club only allows one helper per wheelchair, with everyone else being directed to the Bramall Lane End (my word, can people in wheelchairs have more than one mate? How extraordinary...).

When you are pre-booking your space, let the club know whether you want a car parking space (there are only a limited number of car park passes available for the ground).

**PROGRAMME:** £1.50

On the plus side it is not too expensive. On the debit side it is dull, dull, dull for visiting supporters. If this gets you all the way through half-time, you are a slow reader.

**FANZINES:**
| | |
|---|---|
| *The Red and White Wizaaards* | 50p |
| *The Flashing Blade* | 50p |
| *The Greasy Chip Buttie* (video) | £4.99 |

*The Greasy Chip Buttie* gets its name from the fans' version of 'Annie's Song': 'You fill up my senses, like a night out in Sheffield, like a greasy chip buttie, like a good pinch of snuff' and they say that Yorkshiremen can't express their emotions!

*The Flashing Blade* is still one of the best fanzines available. Angry, incisive and (very) funny in large portions — no trip to the Lane is complete without one.

## TRAVEL

**NEAREST RAILWAY STATION:**
Sheffield Midland (0114 270 0237)

**NEAREST BUS STATION:** Pond Street bus station (opposite BR Station) (0114 276 8688)

**BY CAR:**
**NORTH:** M1 to J34. On leaving the motorway take the A6109 Meadow Hall Road (signposted Sheffield). Continue for three miles until this road merges with the A6135, then bear right into the seductive sounding Blonk Street. Take the fourth exit at the roundabout onto the A61. Go past Sheffield station and then take the first exit

at the next roundabout, keeping in the left-hand lane for Suffolk Road. Once on Suffolk Road take the fifth exit at the next roundabout into St Mary's Road (signposted Bakewell), and left at the next roundabout into Bramall Lane. The ground is 200yd on the left.

**SOUTH/EAST:** M1 to either J31 or J33. From J31 take the A57 and from J33 take the A630, until the two roads merge. Continue along the A57 into Sheffield; take the third exit at the roundabout onto the A61, then as north.

**WEST:** A57 into Sheffield. Just after the University there is a roundabout. Take the fourth exit into Upper Hanover Street. Turn right at the second roundabout into Bramall Lane and the ground is 200yd on the right.

## PARKING:
Plenty of street parking. Alternatively for those coming from the north/south/east there is a car park by Sheffield station, and for those coming from the west there is a car park by the roundabout at the bottom of Upper Hanover Street. The car park at the ground is for permit holders only.

# FUTURE DEVELOPMENTS
None planned.

# OTHER INFORMATION
Bramall Lane is a great place for beer and food; the best pub for visitors is the Golden Lion Hotel which is about five minutes from the ground. It's not massive, but the landlord welcomes away supporters and actually encourages them to phone up in advance so he can have things ready for you. A definite one not too miss (0114 258 1640). To get there, go up Bramall Lane (ground on

left, Railway PH on the right), turn right into Woodhead Road then after about two minutes, walking turn left into Alderson Road for the pub).

The food inside the ground is OK but not a patch on the surrounding streets. Try either Munchies on Shoreham Street, where a hot pie (magnificently tasty) will set you back the whole of 35p, or Shoreham Fisheries (also on Shoreham Street) where, if you fancy something different, you can have a spot-on chicken madras and chips for £1.50. Also on Shoreham Street is a second-hand book shop which amongst its wares offers would-be buyers a choice of slightly used 'adult' magazines. I don't know if I'm being over-sensitive, but the more I thought about this concept the worse I felt!

The PA at the ground is a bit strange; for example, the 'ping pong' sound, which elsewhere indicates a testing of the alarms, was followed by a sombre announcement 'This is a control room message, the bars will close in five minutes'. However, my own favourite was the fact that, with about five minutes to go, the announcement is made to away fans that they should 'please leave the ground by the exits indicated' — God, and there was I about to run across the pitch and scale a wall!

Finally, I have to mention the cheerleaders at the ground — The Bladettes — not for any apparent dancing skill but rather for the fact they transfixed the away fans when I was last there on a bleak February afternoon by the fact that they were still only wearing vest tops — now that is hard!!!

*Total Football* **Experience Rating: 88**

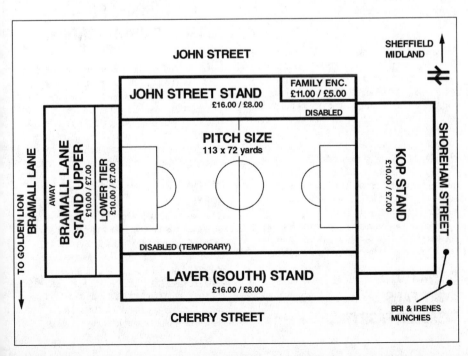

# SHEFFIELD WEDNESDAY

**ADDRESS:** Hillsborough
Sheffield
S6 1SW

**TELEPHONE No:** 0114 221 2121

**TICKET OFFICE:** 0114 221 2400

**FAX:** 0114 221 2122

**CLUBCALL:** 0891 12 11 86

**WEB SITE:** http://swfc.co.uk

**NICKNAME:** The Owls

**RECORD ATTENDANCE:** 72,841 v Man City FA Cup 5th 17 February 1934 (L 2-4)

## CLUB COLOURS:

**HOME:** Shirts: Blue and White stripes;
Shorts: Black; Socks: Black

**AWAY**: Shirts: Yellow with Navy & White stripe on front; Shorts: Navy; Socks: Navy

Perhaps the club does deserve praise for introducing a scheme whereby shirts purchased at the club shop could be signed by either one player or the whole team (and in the case of a Kevin Pressman top probably by the whole of Yorkshire) at no extra cost.

**KIT SPONSORS:** Sanderson Electronics

**MANUFACTURERS:** Puma

## GROUND INFO

Although you can never really go to Hillsborough without recalling the tragic events of 1985, it has to be said that it is a magnificent ground. The huge South Stand is truly one of football's great sights (or should that be sites?). For away fans though, looking is all you can do, as you will be stuck in the West Stand (which, to my chagrin, seemed to have had the wooden seats removed from it). You do, however, have the advantage of being in the upper tier of this construction, which means that you at least avoid the rain of spit, tea, pies etc when your team has the audacity to score.

There is some good news (and quite a lot of bad news) about the pricing at Wednesday. On the negative side they operate a two-tier pricing system. In addition to this you might like to ponder awhile as to how come the fans opposite you pay up to £3 less for a similar (if not better) view than you.

The good news that you were promised? Well the club does offer visiting fans concessions (but guess what — they're not as good as the ones the home fans get).

**CAPACITY:** Stands: 39,814; Terrace: Nil

**AWAY FANS:** West Stand Upper: 3,900

**DISABLED FACILITIES:** There are 100 places available for disabled supporters in the North and West Lower Stands. One helper can accompany a disabled supporter, with no admission charge being made for either. The majority of the places are allocated as season tickets to home fans, with any remaining places on a first come first served basis (pre-book from four weeks in advance). Match commentaries are also available. However, the club advises that there are now no disabled parking facilities other than for season ticket holders.

## PROGRAMME: £2.00

A very average Premier League programme with all the stuff you'd expect, but no real initiative or innovation. Strangely, the match tickets have the warning on them that match programmes 'can only be bought from official sellers', which is obviously a very useful tip if you were thinking about going into a chip shop to try and get one.

## FANZINES:

| | |
|---|---|
| *Cheat!* | 50p |
| *Boddle — Taking The Wednesday* | |
| *Into Insanity* | 80p |
| *War Of The Monster Trucks* | £1 |
| *The Blue and White Wizard* | £1 |
| *Spitting Feathers* | £1 |

A real good range of fanzines, although you can easily go to a game without seeing one. *War Of The Monster Trucks* is (or at least certainly was when I last got hold of a copy) a great fanzine which is more than just a weird title. My own favourite though is *Spitting Feathers*, which comes out with quite a bit of stuff about the visiting team.

## TRAVEL

### NEAREST RAILWAY STATION:
Sheffield Midland (0114 270 0237)

**BUS:** Pond Street bus station (0114 276 8688) Pond Street is opposite the railway station, and as the ground is about four miles away is probably worth a visit. After the match, away fans tend to be herded straight onto buses, the drivers of which seem to take vicarious pleasure in transforming their vehicles into one of the slowest moving objects known to man. Given the general congestion, it can take ages to get back to the station.

### BY CAR:
**NORTH:** M1 to J34. Take the A6109 Meadow Hall Road towards Sheffield. After 1.5 miles there is a roundabout; take the third exit onto the A6102 Upwell Street and just over three miles later take a left into Herries Road South (B6395). This brings you onto the A61 and the ground is directly in front of you.

**SOUTH/EAST:** M1 to J31 or J33. From J31 take the A57 and from J33 take the A630, until these two roads merge. Continue along the A57 to the next major roundabout at which you should turn right onto the

A6102 Prince of Wales Road. Carry on until the road is intersected by the A6178 Attercliffe Road, at which point turn left. After about 100yd turn right into Janson Street, this becomes Upwell Street (A6102), then as north.

**WEST:** A57 towards Sheffield. As you approach Sheffield the road splits in two; take the left fork onto the A6101 Rivelin Valley Road (if you miss the fork take the next left into Rails Road and about 0.25 mile later turn right onto the A6101). Continue for 3.75 miles turn right into Holme Lane which becomes Bradfield Road. At the junction with the A46/Penistone Lane turn left.

Sheer volume of traffic, and a seemingly endless desire to dig up stretches of the road, can make Hillsborough a nightmare to drive to. You get to stages of almost absolute gridlock so count on up to 90min between leaving the motorway and parking up (a distance of about four miles), especially for night matches.

**PARKING:** There is some street parking around Hillsborough. Alternatively, those coming from the north/south/east can continue down Penistone Road (those coming from the west turn right onto Penistone Road) and there is a car park just past Bamforth Street, albeit a good 1.5 miles from the ground.

## FUTURE DEVELOPMENTS
None planned.

## OTHER INFORMATION
The nearest pub to the ground is the Travellers but, as with many around the ground, it is a bit inhospitable for away fans. I would actually recommend going to the Golden Lion (see Sheff Utd), but again be warned: the two grounds are about five miles apart and so it will take

a good time to get between them, so you may be better off sticking to the city centre.

Inside Hillsborough, the food is on the bland side of average. The pick of a fairly poor bunch are probably the pies (don't worry about what type you ask for as they all taste the same). In honour of the club's most famous fan (about whom more later) the club does sell Tango, although at over a quid a shot they are more than welcome to keep it.

No mention of the club would be complete without mention of the Sheffield Wednesday band. I've got to say I initially thought it would be just another passing phase (a sort of noisy inflatable if you will), but it seems to get bigger every time I go to the ground. I bumped into the musicians last year at the ground and the thing that impressed me most was that they seemed to be both a genuine bunch of footie fans and also that they had a good sense of humour/banter. If you do have the good fortune to meet them, try and persuade them to go for a beer and tell you some of their stories, or at least have the good grace to laugh when they come up with an off the cuff piece of music after they spot your away shirt. Another Wednesday legend is, of course, Tango Man (to whom we all owe a debt of gratitude, if only because it stopped the name Roy Hattersley being used whenever Wednesday and celebrity fans were being discussed). Last season there was a horrible rumour going round that he was going to emulate the Sheffield chaps' other claim to fame and do a 'Full Monty'. Thankfully I don't think the incident ever happened; be warned: it may still be on the cards for 1998. Lock up your children and avert your eyes!!

*Total Football* **Experience Rating: 72**

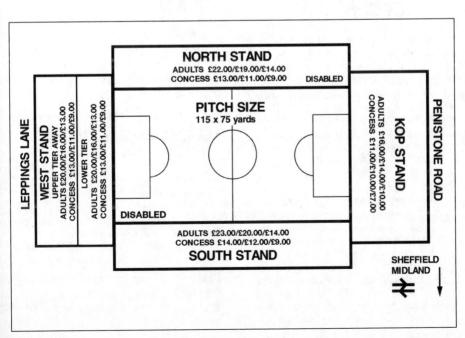

**NORTH STAND**
ADULTS £22.00/£19.00/£14.00
CONCESS £13.00/£11.00/£9.00    DISABLED

**PITCH SIZE**
115 x 75 yards

LEPPINGS LANE

WEST STAND
UPPER TIER AWAY
ADULTS £20.00/£16.00/£13.00
CONCESS £13.00/£11.00/£9.00

LOWER TIER
ADULTS £20.00/£16.00/£13.00
CONCESS £13.00/£11.00/£9.00

KOP STAND
ADULTS £16.00/£14.00/£10.00
CONCESS £11.00/£10.00/£7.00

PENISTONE ROAD

DISABLED

ADULTS £23.00/£20.00/£14.00
CONCESS £14.00/£12.00/£9.00
**SOUTH STAND**

SHEFFIELD MIDLAND

# SHREWSBURY TOWN

**ADDRESS:** Gay Meadow
Shrewsbury
Shropshire
SY2 6AB

**TELEPHONE No:** 01743 360111
**TICKET OFFICE:** 01743 360111
**FAX:** 01743 236384
**TOWN TALK:** 0891 121194
**WEB SITE:**
www.shrewsburytown.co.uk (official)
**NICKNAME:** The Town
**RECORD ATTENDANCE:**
18,917 v Walsall Div 3 26 April 1961 (L 1-2)
Shrewsbury hold the unique distinction of having news of their record attendance share the same newspaper page as the news of Sierra Leone gaining independence. Naturally, the Third Division match, which meant promotion for the visitors, was the lead story.

**CLUB COLOURS:**
**HOME:** Shirts: Blue with White shoulder trim;
Shorts: White; Socks: Blue with White trim
**AWAY:** Shirts: Yellow with Blue trim;
Shorts: Yellow; Socks: Yellow and Blue trim

**KIT SPONSORS:** Tern Hill Communications
**MANUFACTURERS:** Patrick

## GROUND INFO

The word picturesque to describe football grounds always sounds a bit twee, but there is no other term that adequately describes Gay Meadow with its small stand and terraces, with the River Severn running alongside.

The facilities for away fans are fairly basic: the Station End is a part-covered Terrace behind the goal. For a while the club offered no concessions to visiting fans, but happily this situation has been rectified (although you still don't get concessions if you choose to sit down).

The Station Stand is overpriced at £12 (although the club says this is under review) and, despite being built less than 20 years ago, has a very old and run-down feeling to it.

You know that you are not in for the plushest of surroundings when you discover that one of the turnstiles through which you will make your way into the ground dates back to the late 19th century. It is the club's proud (???) boast that it is still in working order, although it does tend to open it up only if the number of away supporters warrants every available entry point being used. The food at the Station End is pretty bog standard (which is more than can be said for the bogs which are dank, dingy, roofless and generally not pleasant)

although, on my last couple of visits, there has been a lot of stuff sold out before half-time (classic conversation of last season: Me: 'What hot food have you got, please?' Server: 'Pasties and Pies.' Me: 'I'll have a meat pie please.' Server: 'Sorry we've sold out of pies.' Me: 'Give us a pastie then.' 'Sorry the man before you bought the last one.').

The club still insists occasionally on keeping away fans locked in till the final whistle has gone which, when you're cold, wet and have just seen your side lose heavily, is the last thing you want to happen.

It should be noted that the Wakeman Stand is named after a local school and not dodgy 1970s rock geezer Rick.

**CAPACITY:** Stands: 3,600; Terrace: 4,400;
Total: 8,000

**AWAY FANS:** Station End Terrace: 1,500;
Main (Station) Stand: 500;
Total: 2,000

**DISABLED FACILITIES:** Spaces are available for home fans in the Main Stand Wakeman Wing, and for away fans in front of the Station Wing. Each section holds about 10, with helpers in adjacent seats. There is no charge for disabled supporters, and helpers pay £5; places should be pre-booked (phone: 01743 356316).

The disabled facilities are a bit open to the elements, and there is room for improvement. A toilet for the disabled is available.

**PROGRAMME:** £1.50
**FANZINES:**

| | |
|---|---|
| *A Large Scotch* | 50p |
| *The Mighty Shrew* | 60p |

I finally managed to get hold of a copy of *The Mighty Shrew* last season and well worth the effort it was too. Because it is produced fairly infrequently it does run the risk of being a little dated.

## TRAVEL

**NEAREST RAILWAY STATION:**
Shrewsbury (01743 364041)
If you are a bit pressed for time, then there is a short cut to the ground from the station. Leave the station, turn left and go up the path round the back of the station (it actually takes you seemingly back into the station). This leads you down a disused platform and to Gay Meadow. If you have more time, turn left and follow the road up the hill which goes past the castle, and then follow the traffic towards English Bridge over the Severn to the ground.

**BUS:**
Riverside Shopping Centre bus station (0345 056785)
Buses 1, 11, 8 and 81 run from the bus station to the ground.

## BY CAR:

**NORTH:** A49 into Shrewsbury. When you actually hit Shrewsbury this road is first called Battlefield Road and then Whitchurch Road. In Whitchurch Road there is a major roundabout, take the second exit into Telford Way (A49). Cross the River Severn, then at the second roundabout, take the third exit (in effect turning right) into Monkmoor Road. Follow the road to its end, at which you should turn right into Abbey Foregate, and the ground is 0.5 mile on the right.

**SOUTH:** A49 into Shrewsbury. As you approach the centre of town the road is called Coleham Head. At the T-junction turn right into Abbey Foregate and the ground is immediately on the left.

**WEST:** A458, the A5 (Roman Road). As you travel down the A5 you will see a playing field on your left, and about 0.5 mile further on there is a roundabout. Take the first exit into Longden Road. When the road comes to a T-junction turn left into Coleham Head, then as south.

**EAST:** A458 (or A5) into Shrewsbury. Go straight over the roundabout by Lord Hill's Column (who?) into Abbey Foregate. Continue for 1.5 miles, to the ground.

**PARKING:** Loads! There is a car park next to the ground, and if you continue along Abbey Foregate across the river, there is a car park on your right; and finally, just before the stadium there is a small left turn off Abbey Foregate which leads to another car park.

## FUTURE DEVELOPMENTS

There has been plenty of talk of either moving to a different site — the Meole Brace site was mentioned (however, residents objected and this was eventually turned into a retail park) — or redeveloping the ground. Negotiations are apparently under way to shift the ground slightly towards the away end, and build new stands at first the Wakeman End, then the Riverside Terrace and finally the Station End. The end result being an 18,000 all-seated capacity. However, little actually appears to be coming to fruition and the only definite improvement that has been made over the last two seasons was the revamping of the press box. Watch this space.

## OTHER INFORMATION

The Crown Inn is the nearest to the ground, but you'll have a much wider choice if you walk five minutes into the town centre. The Nags Head serves a good pint and is welcoming. For food try the pies and the hot dogs at the Dropped Scone (opposite the Abbey Foregate car park). Alternatively the Vestry does a wide choice of vegey food.

The club probably knows that it is up against it when the local 'football superstore' advertises that they stock 'Man Utd and England kits, plus other teams!'

Following the death of the legendary coracle man in 1994, several have tried to save the club the cost of lost balls floating down the Severn, but none have successfully replaced the local hero whose own personal record was 12 balls in a day (and who apparently was slightly short-sighted and once tried to get a swan in his boat thinking it was a Mitre size 5). Now the spectacle is reduced to a couple of blokes with nets on long poles trying to fish balls out of the river before they get sucked into the weir (which, I hasten to add, coracle man always used to end up rowing against); now where's the fun in that?

There is something very nice about Shrewsbury; OK so it is not the most convenient place to get to, but the locals are friendly and there are some good pubs/food places around the town. It does have the potential for being a great away day, but somehow fails to live up to this billing. My own opinion for this is that there are some at the club who don't seem to appreciate that football has moved on since the bad old days of the mid-1980s, and away fans can (and should) be treated in the same manner as home supporters. This is all the more irritating, since whenever I have had call to ask the club questions about things — either anonymously or for this book — the staff have been unfailingly helpful.

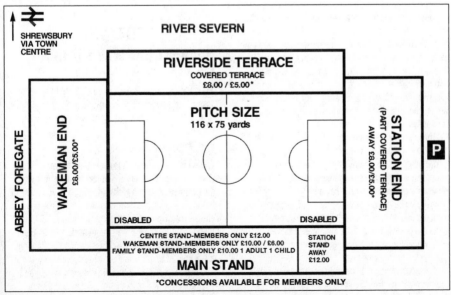

**RIVER SEVERN**

SHREWSBURY VIA TOWN CENTRE

**RIVERSIDE TERRACE**
COVERED TERRACE
£8.00 / £5.00*

**PITCH SIZE**
116 x 75 yards

**WAKEMAN END**
£8.00/£5.00*

**ABBEY FOREGATE**

**STATION END**
(PART COVERED TERRACE)
AWAY £8.00/£5.00*

P

DISABLED          DISABLED

CENTRE STAND-MEMBERS ONLY £12.00
WAKEMAN STAND-MEMBERS ONLY £10.00 / £6.00
FAMILY STAND-MEMBERS ONLY £10.00 1 ADULT 1 CHILD

STATION STAND AWAY £12.00

**MAIN STAND**

*CONCESSIONS AVAILABLE FOR MEMBERS ONLY

# SOUTHAMPTON

**ADDRESS:** The Dell
Milton Road
Southampton SO15 2XH

**TELEPHONE No:** 01703 220505

**TICKET OFFICE:** 01703 228575 / 01703 337171

The first of these numbers is the recorded information line which will tell you those matches which are currently sold out (all of them). The second one is for booking tickets should you be lucky enough to locate them.

**FAX:** 01703 330360

**CLUBCALL:** 0891 12 11 78

**E-MAIL:** sfc@tcp.co.uk

**WEB SITE:** www.soton.ac.uk/~saints/

**NICKNAME:** The Saints

**RECORD ATTENDANCE:** 31,044 v Manchester United Div 1 8 October 1969 (L 0-3)

**CLUB COLOURS:**
**HOME:** Shirts: Red and White stripes;
Shorts: Black; Socks: Red/White
**AWAY:** Shirts: Yellow with Blue trim;
Shorts: Blue with Yellow trim; Socks: Yellow

**KIT SPONSORS:** Sanderson

**MANUFACTURERS:** Pony

## GROUND INFO

Since the Dell went all-seater, away fans have been moved from the Archers Road Stand into the East Stand. This is compact to say the least and because you are stuck in a corner you have to twist and crane your neck to see what's going on. Watch out also as there are joists aplenty and these are placed just right for you to bang your head on (although to be fair to the club, it does seem to have invested in a job lot of warning signs). Even weirder is that there always appears to be a few phantom seats so that you invariably get some poor person wandering around aimlessly before and during a match trying to track down where they should actually be sitting.

The more vocal element of the Saints' support has migrated from the Milton Road Stand to the Archers Road End. This brings them fairly close to the visiting supporters and they do seem to enjoy swapping the occasional pleasantry during the game.

It should be noted that last season ALL league matches were designated all-ticket due to the low capacity of the ground (I believe that in some instances tickets could be obtained on the day, but if you go down without one and can't get in, don't blame me).

It is worth noting that there are not an abundance of touts about either, which means that there are always

some people who make the trip and who are disappointed.

Finally, given the club's nickname, it comes as no surprise that there is a church at the corner of the ground (St Mark's), which you can pop in to pray for some divine intervention if your defence has been looking a bit wobbly.

**CAPACITY:** Stands: 15,250; Terrace: Nil

**AWAY FANS:** Upper East Stand — Archers Road End: 720; Lower East Stand — Blocks J to L: 745; Total: 1,465

There are no concessions for away supporters.

**DISABLED FACILITIES:** There are places for 18 wheelchair-bound supporters plus 10 helpers 'Under West Stand'. Disabled fans are admitted free, with helpers paying £15. Pre-booking is required (and can be done by phone), at which time you can also organise a parking place. However, due to the limited number of spaces, away fans should consider themselves fortunate if they can secure themselves a spot.

Matchday commentaries for the visually impaired are available; these are provided just behind the manager's dug-out.

**PROGRAMME:** £2.00

A fairly disappointing and lacklustre affair. You'll feel you've seen it all before (many, many times).

**FANZINES:**
*The Ugly Inside* £1

I didn't see copies of *The Ugly Inside* being sold on my last trip (and you can't normally miss it as it comes in a big unhandy A4 size). To be honest, I preferred *Red Stripe*, but this has now folded.

## TRAVEL

**NEAREST RAILWAY STATION:**
Southampton Central (01703 229393)

**BUS:** Southampton Citybus (01703 553011)
Take either a number 5 to Archers Road, a 25 to Hill Lane or a 22/22a to Milton Road, all of which are two minutes from the ground.

## BY CAR:

**NORTH:** M3, then A33 towards the city centre. Continue into The Avenue, and take the first right after the Cowherds pub into Northlands Road (if you miss this turning, continue down The Avenue which becomes in effect a massive oval roundabout, drive round 360° and try again). Turn right at the bottom of Northlands Road into Archers Road, and the ground is 50yd on the right.

**EAST:** M27 to J7. Take the A334 (signposted Southampton, A3024, then follow signs for 'The West'. This will bring you onto Commercial Road. Once on

Commercial Road you will see a car park; turn right here into Hill Lane, then take the second right into Archers Road, and the ground is 100yd on the left.

**WEST:** M27, M271. At the end of the M271 take the A3024 (signposted Southampton). After 1.75 miles you will see Millbrook station on your right; turn left immediately after this into Paynes Road and continue across Shirley Road (A3057) after which the road becomes Howard Road. Go straight across at the next crossroads (over Hill Lane) into Archers Road and the ground is 100yd further on.

**PARKING:** There is some street parking available, and one of the best places to try is on Northlands Road. Alternatively for those coming from the north there is a park by the Cowherds where you can leave your car (take the first right after you turn into Northlands Road). There are plenty of car parks within a mile of the ground, but watch out for the short stay ones with a maximum waiting time of two hours.

## FUTURE DEVELOPMENTS

Southampton has announced plans to build a 25,000 all-seater stadium at Stoneham. To be honest, this is much needed as, with every passing year, the Dell is looking less and less like something that belongs in the top echelon of English Football (unlike the club). The move seems to have some support from local MPs and the local authority, but previous plans have been thwarted. If the scheme is given the go-ahead it should be open for business for 2000-1.

## OTHER INFORMATION

If you're looking for a pub, the Cowherds is fairly good, but closer to the ground are the Winston and the Gateway (OK for away fans, but use the side entrance). Keep a special eye out though for the Corner Post; it stands out with its mosaic-patterned outside walls and massive net curtains, but check out the sign; now is it me, or is the person taking the corner the ex-bubble head and now greying KK?

The pubs in the city centre aren't bad and it's worth popping into the city for some food as there isn't much around the Dell, although the cheeseburgers and coffee from the burger bar behind Milton Road are A1. However, once you are inside the Dell, the choice appears to be bland, bland or bland.

Somewhere, something seems to be going wrong at Southampton for the visiting supporters. One cannot really blame the club for the lack of spaces, but where you can and do get rightly annoyed is with the stewards, whose attitude is on occasion, in my experience, overbearing and potentially inflammatory. Then you hear stories about fans with tickets not being allowed into the ground because they are on crutches and also that the club barred the Sheffield Wednesday 'band' from taking their instruments into the ground and you wonder what the club is thinking about (presumably that we don't want a return to the dreadful days of the early 1980s when crutch-wielding trumpeters were besmirching the good name of football up and down the country).

If you want to extend your stay for the weekend then there are quite a few guest houses around the ground. To be honest though, more and more you get the feeling that the club (though not the fans) seems to be giving itself airs and graces. This means that this away day is becoming something of a trial and you'll probably be looking forward to getting home as soon as you can.

*Total Football* **Experience Rating: 51**

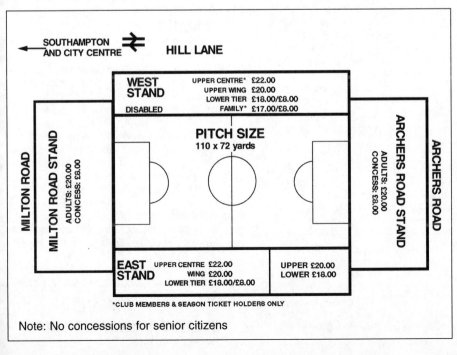

SOUTHAMPTON AND CITY CENTRE

HILL LANE

**WEST STAND**
DISABLED

UPPER CENTRE* £22.00
UPPER WING £20.00
LOWER TIER £18.00/£8.00
FAMILY* £17.00/£8.00

**PITCH SIZE**
110 x 72 yards

**MILTON ROAD**

**MILTON ROAD STAND**
ADULTS: £20.00
CONCESS: £8.00

**ARCHERS ROAD STAND**
ADULTS: £20.00
CONCESS: £8.00

**ARCHERS ROAD**

**EAST STAND**
UPPER CENTRE £22.00
WING £20.00
LOWER TIER £18.00/£8.00

UPPER £20.00
LOWER £18.00

*CLUB MEMBERS & SEASON TICKET HOLDERS ONLY

Note: No concessions for senior citizens

# SOUTHEND UNITED

**ADDRESS:** Roots Hall
Victoria Avenue
Southend-on-Sea
Essex SS2 6NQ

**TELEPHONE No:** 01702 304050

**TICKET OFFICE:** 01702 304090

**FAX:** 01702 330164

**SOCCERLINE:** 0839 66 44 44

**WEB SITE:** http://homepages.
enterprise.net/tonycowell/sufc/
(unofficial)

**NICKNAME:** The Shrimpers

**RECORD ATTENDANCE:** 31,033 v
Liverpool FA Cup 3rd 10 January 1979 (D 0-0)

## CLUB COLOURS:

**HOME:** Shirts: Blue with Black collar, White panel on
right & Black/Gray detail;
Shorts: White; Socks: White

**AWAY:** Shirts: Red; Shorts: Red; Socks: Red

**KIT SPONSORS**: Progressive Primbug (UK) Ltd

**MANUFACTURERS:** Olympic Sportswear

## GROUND INFO

If you like to arrive at a ground early then you may have to spend some time picking your way through the market that is held on the club car park every Saturday, but visiting supporters generally do not go through this area.

If you've ever wondered what happened to those old World War 2 air raid shelters, a trip to Roots Hall will provide the answer, as they appear to have been used to provide the roofing at the ground. Not the most attractive of covering at the best of times, they also have the problem of really magnifying the sound of any rainfall until it sounds like you've got a steel band suspended above you.

For away fans there are no on-the-day concessions available and the North Stand is simply the old terracing with seats bolted onto it. Once you are seated you are practically at sub-pitch level (a situation which is exacerbated by the fact that the club has not taken down the perimeter fencing). Anyway, the club operates a strict policy of sitting where your ticket identifies, and, as there are nine pillars holding up the roof then you have to get very lucky not to have some part of the pitch blocked from your view. Roots Hall is one of the grounds where for away supporters my experience is the introduction of the all-seater regulations has resulted in a significant deterioration in facilities offered. However, for those who remember the state of the toilets in the North Stand, the good news is that these have been replaced.

**CAPACITY:** Stands: 12,306; Terrace: Nil

**AWAY FANS:** North (Universal) Stand: 2,233
North West Enclosure: 728; Total: 2,961
Good news for visitors is that they now get to use the Northwest Enclosure. The stand is nothing special, but the costs of admission — £8/£4 — do help make a trip to Roots Hall slightly more affordable. Please note, though, that concessions are only available on a reciprocal basis and these tickets must be bought in advance.

**DISABLED FACILITIES:** There are 20 spaces at the front of the West Stand for wheelchair-bound supporters, with adjacent seating for helpers. Disabled fans are charged £5, whilst helpers pay £10 (£5 concessions). Pre-booking is not always required, but fans are advised to err on the side of caution. Parking facilities are also available, but they must be arranged in advanced. There are matchday commentaries available 'for blind seats' and again the club states that pre-booking is advisable. Admission is free for visually impaired fans and £10/£5 for helpers.

**PROGRAMME:** £1.60
Despite having spent its second season at £1.60, still no-one at the club seems to have twigged that they need to supply the sellers with moderate amounts of change; three of the people I tried to buy a copy off last year could not break the £5 I offered them. The programme itself is well laid out and, although there seem to be pages of adverts, it is thick enough to mean that even after these have been discounted you have still got some reasonable reading matter.

## FANZINES:

| | |
|---|---|
| *Shrimp Season* | £1 |
| *Roots Hall Roar* | 50p |
| *What's The Story, Southend Glory!* | 50p |

The lads producing these seem to have got themselves sorted out enough that a new edition of one of the fanzines comes out for every home game, but they do try not to clash with each other. When I went it was *WTS(SG)'s* turn — a fanzine that deserves a mention for its blindly optimistic title if nothing else. I also managed to get hold of a copy of *Shrimp Season*. Both of these were good enough reads, although, given what the club went through last year, they were — perhaps not surprisingly — a bit on the gloomy side. The focus of most vitriol does not seem to be the team's abilities (or lack of them) but the fact that the board seems to be taking the club relentlessly towards becoming a nursery club for West Ham.

It is also worth knowing that *WTS(SG)* and *SS* both have their own web sites on which you can sample their wares.

## TRAVEL

**NEAREST RAILWAY STATION:**
Prittlewell (01702 611811)

Southend Victoria is about 10-15min walk away (heading towards the town), with Southend Central a further five minutes.

**BUS:** London Road (01702 434444)
Numerous buses run from the town centre to the ground, ie 7, 7a, 8, 8a, 12, 12a and 29.

## BY CAR:

**NORTH/WEST:** A127 London-Southend arterial road into Southend. When you get to a large roundabout, take the third exit into Victoria Avenue (A127). Take the third right into Fairfax Drive and the ground is on the left.

**SOUTH:** A13 into Southend. When you get to Southend there are thousands upon thousands of turnings, especially to the left. Ignore these — this is a lot harder to do than it sounds as you inevitably start to think 'I should turn left here' after about half a mile — until you see a large turning to the left which almost appears to 'fork' the road. Take this and you will turn into West Road. After about half a mile turn left into Shakespeare Drive and the ground is on your right.

**PARKING:** Car parking at the ground is for season ticket holders only, and controls have recently been tightened up. There is loads of on-street parking, although with there being so many roads by the ground it is well worth making a note of the one you leave your car in. If you want to park on the main road by the ground you'll need to get there early and watch out for very small parking restriction signs.

## FUTURE DEVELOPMENTS

Numerous stories still abound about the 'Hall'; a plan to relocate fell foul of the apparently less than supportive council. The council and club are currently in negotiation but the Frank Walton Stand — where the old South (grass) Bank used to be — possibly shows the way

ahead; it is not massive, but its two-tier structure offers a decent view, fair facilities, and importantly meets the club's and the fans' needs. Work has also been undertaken in the Northwest corner of the ground.

## OTHER INFORMATION

In previous years I have always had a pint at the Spread Eagle or the Golden Lion, although last season when I tried to get in at the first of these, the bloke on the door told me to... well, the second word was 'off'. I backtracked to the Bell (you'll see this as you drive towards the ground), which welcomed away supporters. Alternatively there are plenty of pubs in the town centre and on the sea front, the vast majority of which are only too happy to take your cash for a couple of hours.

In previous years away fans had a bar at the ground. However, this is now for use of home supporters.

For food you really can't do any better than the Fish House on East Street. Inside the ground the away servers have got an awful lot better over the last 12 months. The bacon rolls get a thumbs up, though the burgers are only for the very hungry.

Southend's score has gone up this season, although it has to be said that the facilities on offer are still fairly dire. However, the pricing at the club has stabilised and the fact that some concessions are available is a big plus, added to which the club does seem to be trying to make the effort. It still has a long way to go, but at least it's heading in the right direction. Policing arrangements are determined according to criteria agreed between the police and the club and this can mean, on occasions, an apparent lack of police. Hopefully, the new security firm the club uses will keep up the tradition at Southend of using people who are actually prepared to help if they can — and point you in the right direction if they can't.

*Total Football* **Experience Rating: 55**

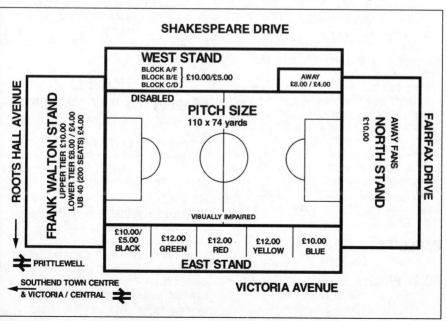

SHAKESPEARE DRIVE

WEST STAND
BLOCK A/F
BLOCK B/E  £10.00/£5.00
BLOCK C/D
AWAY £8.00 / £4.00
DISABLED

ROOTS HALL AVENUE
FRANK WALTON STAND
UPPER TIER £10.00
LOWER TIER £8.00 / £4.00
UB 40 (200 SEATS) £4.00

PITCH SIZE
110 x 74 yards

VISUALLY IMPAIRED

NORTH STAND £10.00
AWAY FANS
FAIRFAX DRIVE

| £10.00/ £5.00 BLACK | £12.00 GREEN | £12.00 RED | £12.00 YELLOW | £10.00 BLUE |
|---|---|---|---|---|

EAST STAND

PRITTLEWELL

SOUTHEND TOWN CENTRE & VICTORIA / CENTRAL

VICTORIA AVENUE

# STOCKPORT COUNTY

**ADDRESS:** Edgeley Park
Hardcastle Road
Edgeley
Stockport SK3 9DD

**TELEPHONE No:** 0161 2868888

**TICKET OFFICE:** 0161 2868888

**FAX:** 0161 286 8900

**CLUBCALL:** 0891 12 16 38

**WEB SITE:**
http://www.stockportmbc.gov.uk/county/

**NICKNAME:** The Hatters

**RECORD ATTENDANCE:** 27,833 v
Liverpool FA Cup 5th 11 February 1950 (L 1-2)

**CLUB COLOURS:**
**HOME:** Shirts: Royal Blue with White stripes;
Shorts: Blue with White trim;
Socks: Blue with White trim
**AWAY:** Shirts: Yellow with Green trim;
Shorts: Green; Socks: Green

**KIT SPONSORS:** Robinson Best Bitter

**MANUFACTURERS:** Adidas

## GROUND INFO

Away fans are sited on the Railway End Terrace. This lacks the facilities in the new Cheadle Stand — ie bar, numerous food outlets, although a new toilet block is to be built for the new season.

In the past the club has, on occasions put away supporters in two blocks of the Vernon Stand. Note, if you do end up in the Vernon Stand, watch out for the pillars which totally obscure one of the goals from some seats.

Despite the fact that the Vernon Stand is the same price as the Cheadle Stand, fans do tend to have stuck to the latter (probably because even though the leg room is minimal at least you can definitely see both goals). This means that the VS is not perhaps the no go (or go but keep very quiet) area that it once was. If it's raining and you can't get a place in the Main Stand then consider this as a viable option to pneumonia.

Away fans will be offered concessions at Edgeley Park, though this may be retracted if a reciprocal agreement is not reached.

**CAPACITY:** Stands: 9,110; Terrace: 2,651;
Total: 11,761

**AWAY FANS:** Main Stand Blocks E and F: 650;
Railway Terrace: 2,651;
Total: 3,301

**DISABLED FACILITIES:** There are 12 spaces for wheelchair-bound fans in the Main Stand. Disabled fans are admitted free of charge, with their helpers paying £10. Visitors are welcome, but pre-booking is essential. County is pioneering a new facility for visually impaired supporters which allows the fan to sit anywhere in the ground and listen to a match commentary via headphones, the signal coming from a transmitter in the commentator's pocket. An excellent idea that will hopefully catch on; telephone the club to book your headset.

**PROGRAMME:** £1.70
County's programme has been the best in whichever division they have played for the last good few seasons. Last season was the club's first in Division One and once again its programme was streets ahead of anything else produced (and probably is only beaten — and then only just — by Leicester's in the Premier). 56 pages long with so many good articles (for both home and away fans) that even if you arrive an hour before kick-off, you won't have finished it before the match starts.

**FANZINES:**
| | |
|---|---|
| *The Tea Party* | £1 |
| *I.O County* | £1 |

Not satisfied with having one of the best programmes in Britain, County also have one of the greatest fanzines in *The Tea Party*. This fanzine is packed with everything from trivial County facts, that will keep any County stattos that read it happy, to lots of general interest articles that provide loads of reading for home and away fans. The editor of *The Tea Party*, Dave Epsley, has also had a book published last season called *Saturday Night and Thursday Morning*, which any fan of a lower league team will be able to relate to and will enjoy. *I.O County* would be a decent enough fanzine at most other clubs, but at Edgeley Park it does suffer in comparison with *TTP* and the programme.

## TRAVEL

### NEAREST RAILWAY STATION:
Stockport Edgeley (0161 228 7811)

**BUS:** Mersey Square bus station (0161 228 7811) There is a wide selection of buses which pass the ground, amongst which are the 9, 10 and 11. The railway station is a five minute walk away.

### BY CAR:
**NORTH/SOUTH/WEST:** M63 to J11. When you leave the M63 take the A560 towards Stockport. After half a mile turn right into Edgeley Road. Continue for one mile then turn right into Caroline Street for Edgeley Park.
**EAST:** A6 towards Stockport town centre. As you approach the town centre there is a cemetery on your right-hand side; about 350yd after this turn left into Longshut Lane West. At the end of this road bear right

into Shaw Heath, take the first exit at the roundabout into Mercian Way and then the third left into Caroline Street. The ground is at the bottom of Caroline Street.

Whichever direction you come from, a trip to the ground became a lot easier from 1997-8 as signposts were put up guiding you to it.

**PARKING:** This can be a bit of a nuisance, as quite a few streets around the ground are either festooned with police bollards or double yellow lines. There is a smallish pay-and-display opposite the ground which at 10p for two hours or 50p all day won't break the bank; otherwise it's hunt the on-street space.

## FUTURE DEVELOPMENTS

There was some work done last season with improved facilities at the corner of the Main Stand and Railway End and a new restaurant opened in the Cheadle Stand.

At some point in time the Railway End is going to be developed. However, this still appears to be at the drawing board stage and it is unlikely that anything will be done until 1999 at the earliest. When work is carried out expect away fans to be given an allocation in the Vernon Stand.

## OTHER INFORMATION

Edgeley town centre has a variety of pubs ranging from the good (the Royal Oak) to the OK (the Robert Peel) to the very indifferent (the Jolly Crofter — who is so Jolly that there are signs on the door proclaiming a list of various 'no's which cannot cross its hallowed portals. There are also numerous chippies, my favourite being the Friary which is by the Royal Oak (the portions of chips and gravy there seem to get bigger and tastier with each passing season). There is a national bookmakers on the street for your fixed odds although this is at the other end to the Royal Oak.

An alternative to going into the town is to turn right (with the Main Stand at your back) and walk down the road to the junction where there is another raft of pubs. From my (increasingly scrawled) notes I remember going into the Bluebell, the Armoury, The Swan, the Florist and the Comfortable Gill (it was a very good day and someone else was driving!), none of which where brilliant but all of which were more than acceptable. Inside the ground the food was not too impressive at all and seems to have gone on a bit of a decline from the previous season (there was a large lump of gristle/muscle in my pie which came from some part of an animal that was definitely best left uneaten). At least the tea was hot and strong to wash it down with though.

The PA system at Edgeley has (apparently) been improved, but remains capable of giving out bursts of white noise, as does the announcer who gives out the Stockport County half-time score when they are winning (what a card!). One thing to be aware of is the testing of alarm systems when the ground first opens. The club seems to have about 20 different sirens and noises that it runs through and if you're not expecting it, you may think war has broken out.

Apparently the scoreboard at Edgeley Park is one of Blackburn's rejects, a tragic case of the old, old story of manager sees scoreboard, manager falls in love with scoreboard, manager pays through nose for scoreboard only to realise that the scoreboard isn't what he hoped it would be.

Edgeley Park is a bit on the pricey side for the facilities on offer. However, the people who work there and the home fans seem friendly enough (a far cry from when County used to play on Friday nights and a trip there could be an eye-opening experience). There is decent (out of the ground) food and drink and a good football atmosphere inside EP, all of which makes for a better than average day out.

*Total Football* **Experience Rating: 87**

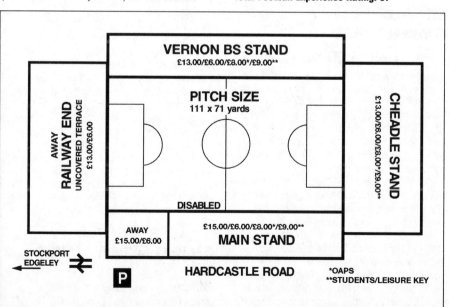

VERNON BS STAND
£13.00/£6.00/£8.00*/£9.00**

PITCH SIZE
111 x 71 yards

AWAY
RAILWAY END
UNCOVERED TERRACE
£13.00/£6.00

CHEADLE STAND
£13.00/£6.00/£8.00*/£9.00**

DISABLED

AWAY
£15.00/£6.00

£15.00/£6.00/£8.00*/£9.00**
MAIN STAND

STOCKPORT
EDGELEY

P

HARDCASTLE ROAD

*OAPS
**STUDENTS/LEISURE KEY

# STOKE CITY

**ADDRESS:** Britannia Stadium
Stanley Matthews Way
Stoke-on-Trent
ST4 4EG

**TELEPHONE No:** 01782 592222
**TICKET OFFICE:** 01782 592211
**FAX:** 01782 592221

Initially the road that leads to the stadium was to be called 'SIR Stanley Matthews Way', but the original 'Stan the Man' said he'd prefer it without the title as he was just plain Stanley Matthews when he was playing at the club. (I'm sure that if any of the current crop of Premiership players ever get knighted, their egos would also be strong enough to make such a decision.)

**CLUBCALL:** 0891 12 10 40

**WEB SITE:**
www.geocities.com/yosemite/9185/
(unofficial)

**NICKNAME:** The Potters

**RECORD ATTENDANCE:**
51,380 v Arsenal Div 1 17 February 1968 (D 1-1).
At the Britannia Stadium: 28,000 v Man City Nationwide League Div 1 3 May 1998 (L 2-5)

**CLUB COLOURS:**
**HOME:** Shirts: Red and White stripes;
Shorts: White; Socks: White
**AWAY:** Shirts: White with Teal shoulders;
Shorts: Blue; Socks: Blue and White

**KIT SPONSORS:** Britannia

**MANUFACTURERS:** Asics

## GROUND INFO

The Britannia Stadium is very much like Pride Park just down the A50 (or should that be the other way round?). It is very impressive (especially at night when it is illuminated and you can see it for miles as it stands on a hill above the city) with very decent facilities for both home and away supporters. It is also a couple of miles out of town, which means that there is very little else on offer around the stadium.

The club's pricing strategy should be praised as away fans are offered very reasonable concessions, although you could probably do without the unpleasant smells that waft through from the nearby incineration plant.

Tradition does live on in the shape (or rather sound) of 'Delilah' (one of the weirdest things about this is how well the fans get the long pauses between each of the 'woahs' synchronised), and the City fans have shown that they can make as much noise in their nice new seats as they did on the old Boothen End. The Britannia Stadium

was also one of the increasingly rare grounds at which a huge flag could be spotted last season, although sadly the gaps in the crowd tended to mean it wasn't passed properly and ended up in an untidy heap (usually upside down) in some corner of the stadium.

Note: there are no cash turnstiles for home supporters.

**CAPACITY:** Stands: 28,000

**AWAY FANS:** Signal Radio (South) Stand: 5,000
This is the maximum that will be allocated to visiting teams. The South Stand can be sub-divided into three equal(ish) parts which means that this figure may be reduced to either 1,500 or 3,000 as required.

The club is offering concessions for visiting fans — reciprocal basis only — oddly the age limit on this is 17.

**DISABLED FACILITIES:** There are 160 disabled places at the Britannia Stadium. These are sited in all parts of the ground, including the Signal Radio Stand. Admission for all parts of the ground will be £5 with 'Escorts paying prevailing prices' (better go in your BMW then). The club requests that these are pre-booked. Match commentaries are available for the visually impaired.

**PROGRAMME:** £1.80
Very poor. The visitors' section consists of incredibly tiny print pen pics, info and a couple of paragraphs about the club. Of the 48 pages, 17 are adverts/sponsorship opportunities and another eight are full-page pictures. What little writing there is, is dull and will not detain away fans for more than two minutes.

**FANZINES:**
| | |
|---|---|
| *The Oatcake* | 80p |
| *The Victoria Voice* | £1 |

Thank God for *The Oatcake*!! Less than half the price of the programme, it is also just half the size, but there the comparison stops because just the editorial offers more interesting reading than the whole of the official publication and every page is packed with excellent stuff. There is one produced for every home match, but the quality never varies; it is always top drawer. Never one to shirk issues, when Stoke fans invaded the pitch during the 7-0 embarrassment at home to Birmingham, the following issue's 'day of shame' column was aimed not at those who went on the pitch but those at the club who managed to produce such a poor performance to result in this action. *TVV* is rumoured to have ceased publication.

## TRAVEL

**NEAREST RAILWAY STATION:** Stoke-on-Trent (01782 411411)

**BUS:** Hanley bus station (01782 744744)
Potteries Midland Transport: 01782 747000

A shuttle service runs from Stoke and the other pottery towns. Away fans who don't fancy a taxi (my recommendation) can join the locals on a 574 or a 518 which drop off on Stanley Matthews Way by the Sentinel Stand.

## BY CAR:

**NORTH/SOUTH/WEST:** M6 to J15. Take the A500 signposted Stoke-on-Trent. After a couple of miles the road splits into five lanes, the far left lane takes you to the incinerator and the city centre. The two right lanes are the A500 and bypass the city. However, you need to take either the second left or middle lane. These are both signposted A50 Derby/Uttoxeter. As you go up the A50 (dual carriageway) you will see the stadium on the opposite side of the road. There is talk of building a link road. However, until that day arrives you will need to go on about 0.75 mile past the stadium to the next exit and do a 180° turn to get to the ground.

**EAST:** A50 toward Stoke till you see the ground (not overly hard really).

## PARKING:
There is parking at the ground for 650 cars plus 1,600 further spaces to the south of the ground, but this is likely to be 'all-ticket' this season. If you don't fancy coughing up for this, park in one of the side streets near the Michelin Works (about 10-15min walk). I've been told that you can park at the works themselves, but when I went I was told that I couldn't come in unless I was 'A Michelin man' and as I maintain I'm just pleasantly plump, I had no chance.

## FUTURE DEVELOPMENTS
With completion of new ground, none planned.

## OTHER INFORMATION
Once you get to the ground you have got the choice of what Stoke offer, you or nothing at all. This isn't as bad as it may appear as there are bars in all sections of the stadium and the food, while nothing to write home about, is better than some you will come across. For those of you who are looking for a bit more from your day out, it is best to stick to the city centre, although be warned, there are quite a few pubs around that don't take kindly to outsiders (and if you have travelled from further than Longton you are an outsider); stick to either the Plough Hotel or the Gardeners Retreat though, and you should be fairly confident of not only being put up with, but welcomed.

One place that you must visit is the Hog Roast van which is just before the bridge that will connect you with the stadium as you walk from the Michelin area. This serves absolutely magnificent roast pork and crackling in a roll, and apart from being different from your typical football fare, is as good as anything I had from a 'mobile' last season. If you are looking for a bit more cholesterol then try the mammoth burger that you can get just before it which at £4 for 1lb of meat should satisfy even the most demanding palate.

A trip to the new Britannia Stadium is good, yet seems to lack something that the Victoria Ground had — (character?). Certainly the club seems friendly enough towards away fans (even if the same cannot be said for all the home supporters) yet when you walk away, I doubt you will be eagerly awaiting your next visit. Perhaps the fact that the team had such a dreadful season last year meant that the new stadium could not properly find its feet (or more importantly its heart).

Finally, apparently there is a degree of annoyance amongst some Stokies that the ground does not provide the community facilities that was hoped for (to such an extent that I have been told of one supporter who phones the club each week to try and book a [non existent] badminton court...) Just goes to prove that you can't please all of the people all of the time.

*Total Football* **Experience Rating: 66**

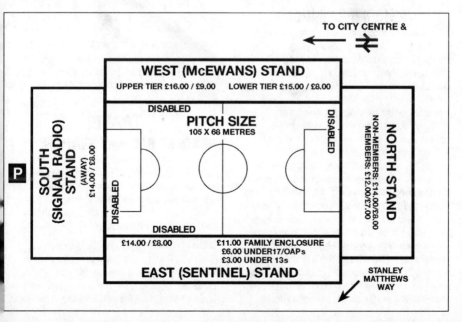

# SUNDERLAND

**ADDRESS:** The Stadium of Light
Stadium Park
Sunderland
SR5 1BT

**TELEPHONE No:** 0191 551 5000

**TICKET OFFICE:** 0191 551 5151

**FAX:** 0191 551 1234

**WEBSITE:** www.sunderland-afc.com

**CLUBCALL:** 0891 12 11 40

**NICKNAME:** A point of some query: it used to be the Rokerites, but since the move this is not really applicable. Likewise, the second choice of the 'Black Cats' can't be used as the cat does not appear on the redesigned club crest. The club suggest THE LADS or 'perhaps even' THE WEARSIDERS.

**RECORD ATTENDANCE:** 75,118 v Derby FA Cup 6th Rep 8 March 1933 (L 0-1 aet).
At the Stadium of Light: 41,214 v Stoke City Nationwide League Div 1 25 April 1998 (W 3-0)

**CLUB COLOURS:**
**HOME:** Shirts: Red and White Stripes;
Shorts: Black; Socks: Red
**AWAY:** Shirts: Navy with Red & White horizontal band
Shorts: Navy with Red & White vertical side bands;
Socks: Navy with Red & White horizontal band

**KIT SPONSORS:** Lambtons

**MANUFACTURERS:** Asics

## GROUND INFO

In the previous edition of this book I suggested that, with the passing of Roker Park, something was going to be lost from Sunderland and that the noise and passion of the fans would be the casualty. I was right in a way; what Sunderland have lost is a crumbling wreck of a ground that was not fit for human habitation and now they've got a fantastic stadium that is closer to the city centre than Roker Park. As for my comments about a reduction in passion; well, all I can say is that I talk a load of crap sometimes and I beg Sunderland to forgive me.

The SOL is simply magnificent and the pricing for visiting fans is reasonable (the concessions issue is being reviewed). Once you get in, you have all the normal facilities you'd expect from a new ground, but it is when you go to take your seat that it really hits you. Because the inner concourse is on an upper level, as you go to your seats you find yourself walking out level with the scoreboard in the North Stand. This is disconcerting but wonderful, and as you step up the ground almost unfolds around you and you are left spellbound by its size (and if you are turning up after 2.30pm, its noise as well).

Every seat in the away section — in the ground actually — has an unrestricted view an, because the pitch is slightly sunk down, it means that even if you are in the front row you still get to look down on the action.

Presumably as a tribute to Roker Park, although the ground is fully enclosed, you still get a wicked wind whistling around especially at the back of the stands.

**CAPACITY:** Stands: 41,600

**AWAY FANS:** Metro FM: 3,000
The club has given visiting supporters a section (but fortunately not a 'corner') behind the goal on the western side of the Metro FM Stand. For cup games the whole of the Metro FM Stand can be made available (6,000).

**DISABLED FACILITIES:** There are up to 300 vantage points in all parts of the ground, with away fans having the choice of a lower or upper position. Cost of admission is £11 for disabled supporters and standard prices for helpers. Match commentaries are available and these, together with all facilities, should be pre-booked. Parking is available at the ground contact the club two weeks in advance to make sure that you get a place.

**PROGRAMME:** *Red 'N' White Review* £1.70
Went up just over 10% in price last season, but the increased cost has also seen a massive improvement in this programme. Excellent visitors' section and, while naturally there is very much a home bias in the rest of it, there are also a couple of very good general interest items.

**FANZINES:**

| | |
|---|---|
| *A Love Supreme* | 80p |
| *The Black Cat* | £1 |
| *Sunderland Fanatic* | 50p |
| *It's the Hope I Can't Stand!* | 50p |

*ALS* is the Sunderland fanzine, although I seem to swing between loving and hating it. On the positive side, it's very well written and its style and layout are second to none, but it is expensive and does seem to have more than its fair share of adverts. Possibly you could argue that the truly great fanzines cover a bit of a broader range of topics.

## TRAVEL

**NEAREST RAILWAY STATION:**
Sunderland (0191 232 6262)
Sunderland station is about a mile from the ground. Much closer, but not currently used, is Monkwearmouth station. This is currently a railway museum, but it is planned that it will reopen under the guise of a Metro station within the next three to four years.

**BUS:** Central bus station (0191 232 5325 — Sunderland Busway). It is proposed that there will be shuttles running to the ground on matchdays, although regular services 2, 4, 5, 100, 104 all stop outside the DSS from where it is a five-minute walk up to the ground.

## BY CAR:

**NORTH:** A1018 into the city centre. At the large roundabout with a clock on it turn right onto the B1289 (signposted Alexandra Bridge, Sheepfold). Take the first left into Black Road, and then right into Millennium Way.

**SOUTH:** A1(M) to Carrville, then take the A690 (signposted Houghton-Le-Spring) following the signs for Sunderland and city centre. Pick up signs for South Shields (A1018). Once on the A1018 continue for 0.75 mile until you cross the Wearmouth Bridge. KEEP IN THE LEFT LANE on the bridge. Take the second left after you have crossed the bridge (NB: this is only about 50m after the end of the bridge) into Easington Street. Take the first right (Hay Street) for the stadium.

NB: If you miss the Easington Street turning, continue to the large roundabout by the clock and turn left into the B1289 (signposted Alexandra Bridge) and take the next left for the ground).

**WEST:** A1(M) to J65. Take the A1231 (Sunderland Highway/Wessington Way). Follow the signs for the city centre until you pick up the B1289 (Queens Road). After about 1-mile — the road is now called Southwick Road — you will see the Colliers Arms on your left, turn right into Black Road then right into Millennium Way

## PARKING: Possibly the only black spot about the ground. There is some parking off Hay Street around the ground, which is fine if you can get there early enough. Otherwise try the city centre car parks or the Park and Ride to the ground from just off the A19 Hylton Bridge. The real problem is getting away after the match; it took me 45min to get out of the congestion and I have heard that even two hours after games it can be a bit clogged.

## FUTURE DEVELOPMENTS

There is talk of extending the seating to allow another 5,000 souls to enter the hallowed portals.

## OTHER INFORMATION

Outside the ground there are a whole host of pubs within about one mile. Obviously these are of a predominantly home variety, but I didn't have any problems in any of the ones that I went into. The Halfway House, as you come in from the A19, is worth a visit or alternatively try to get someone to sign you in at the Sunderland's Companions Club on North Street. For food either go for the belting all-day breakfast with Tommy at the Roker Café (turn right on North Street into Roker Avenue and its 200yd on the left — be warned: it's take aways only from 1.45pm) or try Joan's Café which is right by the ground and near the 'A Love Supreme' Stand/shop. They serve bacon in a warm roll for £1.20 which is almost of Cambridge United class.

Once inside the ground, you can get lager (£2) or bitter (£1.80) in the away end and the food is fairly reasonable.

A lot has been said about the fact that the club belts out Prokofiev followed by Republica as the teams take the pitch, and I know it sounds like hype, but when you are there I swear it will make the hairs on the back of your neck rise and this, combined with the roar of the crowd (which I have to say is so much louder than anything I ever heard at Roker), is one of the great footballing experiences. Less pleasurable perhaps is the quick burst of 'I Feel Good' that they play whenever Sunderland - but not the opposition — score (James Brown is so cool though, you can almost forgive them that).

I've got to say that I left the Stadium of Light completely and utterly converted. The great thing is that with the new ground seems to have come a new and better attitude in both the club and the fans. If you only go to one football ground this season, make it this one. Different Class!!

***Total Football* Experience Rating: 94**

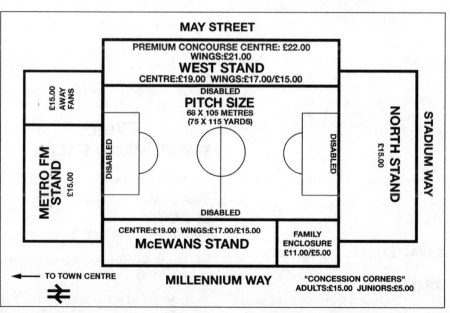

# SWANSEA CITY

**ADDRESS:** Vetch Field
Swansea
West Glamorgan
SA1 3SU

**TELEPHONE No:** 01792 474114
**TICKET OFFICE:** 01792 462584
**FAX:** 01792 464120
**CLUBCALL:** 0891 12 16 39
**WEB SITE:**
www.connect.co.uk/swansfc (official)
http://www2.prestel.co.uk/gmartin/ind
ex.html (unofficial)
**NICKNAME:** The Swans
**RECORD ATTENDANCE:**
32,796 v Arsenal FA Cup 4th 17 February 1968 (L 0-1)

**CLUB COLOURS:**
**HOME:** Shirts: White; Shorts: White; Socks: White
**AWAY:** Shirts: Maroon and White; Shorts: White;
Socks: White
**KIT SPONSORS:** South Wales Evening Post
**MANUFACTURERS:** New Balance (UK) Ltd

## GROUND INFO

When you know that a match got called off at the Vetch last season because the licensing authority placed a prohibition order on allowing fans in the ground, you get the idea that you are not going to be in the plushest of surroundings. To be fair, this order was placed due to the emergency power generator being defective, which from a fan's perspective is hardly going to impact on a normal trip to the football. The Vetch is very run down and with each passing season looks tattier and more decrepit. The move to Morfa can't really come quick enough.

The club adopts a non-segregation policy in the seated sections of the ground. My own advice would be to go into the East Stand (being careful to avoid the 150 or so restricted view seats), which tends to be used more by families and is thus a bit calmer. The away terrace, on which there are very good concessions, is covered with a bizarre upturned-boat-shaped roof and is fairly basic. There is still a large fence at the front of it, which means you need to go back a bit to get a decent view (although not too far back or you will find you have a pillar in your line of vision).

**CAPACITY:** Stands: 2,500; Terrace: 9,400;
Total: 11,900 (inc executive areas)

**AWAY FANS:** West Terrace: 1,541
Once you're in the ground, then you can feel safe enough (even the derby with Cardiff, which scaremongers were

predicting would be a war, saw only 11 arrests) — although your ears could be in for a fair assaulting — and it has to be said that the club has received numerous commendations by the police for the way it segregates and looks after crowds. However, around and about Swansea (which the club can do nothing about), I would recommend extreme caution as although the vast majority of Swans' fans are good for a laugh, chat and beer, there still remains a significant number who seem to be stuck in the mid-1980s and determined to give visiting supporters a hard time. Maybe I'm just unlucky, but for the last three seasons when I've been down to the Vetch, I have seen away fans given hassle by locals.

If you have any problems or questions then speak to one of the stewards as they are generally very helpful and will go out of their way to see you right.

**DISABLED FACILITIES:** There are 15 disabled spaces in front of the Wing Stand and visiting fans are welcome, although it is suggested that you book in advance (not compulsory). Disabled supporters are admitted free, with helpers paying £5 each. There are no matchday commentaries for the blind, nor are there any parking facilities at the ground.

**PROGRAMME:** £1.70
Generally a typical run-of-the-mill affair, it is considerably improved by a column which is produced by the lads who run the unofficial Internet page. The issue I saw dealt with the question of racism amongst the fans, didn't pull any punches and was head and shoulders above the rest of the writing. 1998-9 will see an increase in pages from 32 to 40.

**FANZINES:**
| | |
|---|---|
| Jackanory | 50p |
| Mag Rag | 50p |

1998-9 sees *Jackanory* start its third season of existence and certainly the copy I saw in 1997-8 was an improvement on the previous season. It's a bit predictable, but is good enough to fill a half-time and a good bit of the journey home. The first issue of *Mag Rag* came out last season. What there was of it was good, but at just 12 pages it isn't *War and Peace*.

## TRAVEL
**NEAREST RAILWAY STATION:**
High Street (01792 467777)
About 10min from the ground

**BUS:** Quadrant (01792 580580)

**BY CAR:**
**NORTH/EAST:** M4 to J42, then A48 Peniel Green Road. At second roundabout take first exit onto A4067 Neath Road. Go straight over at the next two roundabouts and follow the A4067 towards the city centre and turn right onto Alexandria Road (A4118). This becomes Mansel Street, then Walter Road. Turn left into Page Street (if you miss this turn, either of the next three lefts

— Nicholl Street, George Street and Henrietta Street — will bring you onto the same road). At the bottom of Page Street turn right into St Helens Road, then second left into Richardson Street. The ground is at the bottom of Richardson Street.

NB: The trick is to follow the signs for the City Centre and the Mumbles when you leave the motorway. Once in Swansea keep following the signs for the Mumbles and you will see the prison on your right. The Vetch is at the back of this — you can't miss the floodlights.

**WEST:** M4 to J45, take the A4067 towards the city centre, then as north.

**PARKING:** The car park at the ground is for permit holders only, and the one behind the East Stand belongs to the prison. You can either park on-street, or a better bet is to park at the Quadrant or by the Marina. When driving to the ground, the signs for the latter are opposite the road you turn into for the pub, and it's a brisk five minute walk at most.

## FUTURE DEVELOPMENTS

The clubs owners (Silver Shield) and Swansea City Council are going ahead with a £75 million project to build a 25,000 all-seater stadium at Morfa. This is two miles away from the Vetch and the development will include numerous facilities for other sports. The club expects that it will be playing home matches at this venue from August 1999.

## OTHER INFORMATION

There are plenty of pubs around the ground, with the nearest being a Welsh Brewers' house The Tafarn Clarence (Clarence Arms) in which visiting fans are welcome. The Singleton Arms on the corner of West Way and Western Avenue isn't too bad, but rather than use the chip shop next door, try the Argyle on the corner of

Argyle Street and Richardson Way. If you are nervous then head out of the city toward the Mumbles, where there is a greater choice and a more relaxed atmosphere. Be warned though, something that you may come across in the pubs are friendly locals who are not only happy to chat about footie, life and the universe, but are also prepared to teach you a few words of Welsh to help you feel at home. However, it's probably as well to know that *Twll dyn pob Saes* (pronounced 'twchh dean pobe sise') does not mean 'I'll have a lager.'

If you are in the centre and caught short, it is worth while noting the signs up by the public conveniences which state 'No alcohol in the toilet' — just in case you were thinking of putting your head down the pan and checking to see whether they flush with gin or vodka in South Wales!!!!!!

Inside the ground there aren't any pies on sale, but the pasties are fairly decent. If you want to enjoy them more it is probably as well not to look inside them as the colour of the meat I saw had me worrying about the quantity of 'E' numbers I was likely to be consuming. The club, however, has said that it will use new caterers for 1998-9 with refurbished kiosks and a range of new products.

The club also says that the toilets have been refurbished. Hopefully, that will mean you don't have to suffer the dark, dingy and pungent abomination I encountered that they call the toilets. A trip to the Vetch remains something to be endured rather than enjoyed and it is likely that you'll feel a lot happier when you come home after the match than when you set off for it. The club does do its best and in other circumstances this could be a great day but, with the archaic facilities, the attitude of some supporters, and lack of decent food and drink this isn't too much fun.

*Total Football* Experience Rating: 55

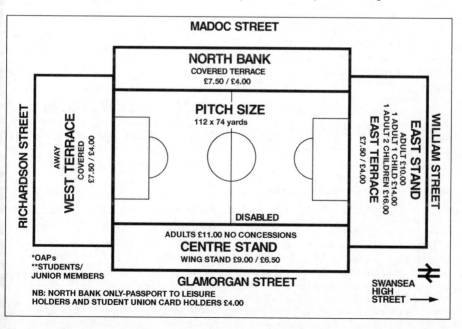

# SWINDON TOWN

**ADDRESS:** The County Ground
County Road
Swindon SN1 2ED

**TELEPHONE No:** 01793 430430
**TICKET OFFICE:** 01793 529000
**FAX:** 01793 536170
**CLUBCALL:** 0891 12 16 40
**WEB SITE:**
http://www.swindon-fc.demon.co.uk
**NICKNAME:** The Robins
**RECORD ATTENDANCE:**
32,000 v Arsenal FA Cup 3rd 15 January 1972 (L 0-2)
**CLUB COLOURS:**
**HOME:** Shirts: Red; Shorts: Red; Socks: Red
**AWAY:** Shirts: Blue/Black halves; Shorts: Blue;
Socks: Blue

**MAIN SPONSORS:** Nationwide
**MANUFACTURERS:** Mizuno

## GROUND INFO

Well, it is difficult to know where to start here. First things first, tickets prices. Prior to the 1997-8 season Robins' manager Steve MacMahon promised home fans that if the team did not get into the play-offs, the club would refund the increase in season ticket prices between 1995-6 and 1997-8. They didn't and he was true to his word. However, in March 1998 the club summarily whacked £2.50 on all ticket prices in an attempt to clear some of its debts.

Away fans sit in the Stratton Bank Stand. Actually Stand is too grand a word for it, as it consists of seats bolted onto the Stratton Bank Terrace. This is uncovered (but what can you expect for £14 Luxury?). The club does offer visiting fans concessions but this is only on tickets bought in advance.

One of the worst things about the Stratton Bank Stand is not the fact that you get soaked and stung. Nor the fact that there are some of the local constabulary who seem to think it acceptable to throw out fans who stand up (these people are not rioting, they are trying to stave off hypothermia). It is not even that the people opposite you had the luxury of a new roof being built over them last season (the old one seemed perfectly good to me), or that the fans on your left pay from only 50p more for a seat in the club's newest stand. No, what really sticks in your throat as the rain trickles down the back of your coat is the fact there are so many bloody empty spaces elsewhere in the ground and — while it is accepted that this would not be possible for big matches — you have got to think that it wouldn't be impossible for the club to allocate a space under cover for those fans who travel to Wiltshire to watch a football game.

Finally (and to try and end this section on a brighter note) it has to be said that the stewarding at the ground seems to have come on in leaps and bounds. This is an opinion that appears to be borne out by other fans I have spoken to, even nearish rivals, and at least does remove some of the stress.

**CAPACITY:** Stands: 15,728; Terrace: Nil
**AWAY FANS:** Stratton Bank: 2,180
**DISABLED FACILITIES:** There are spaces for 49 disabled fans in the Family Stand and the South Stand. There is no need to book, just go to the designated window by the Family Stand ticket office to buy a ticket which used to weigh in at £5.50 for one wheelchair-bound supporter and one helper. The club did not mention this, but I believe that even these tickets were affected by the £2.50 price hike and that joint admission is now £8. There are both designated parking facilities and matchday commentaries for the visually impaired.

Swindon have really got themselves sorted out with regards to disabled supporters. There are large entrances and exits, and a lounge where you can enjoy a pre-match pint. The stewards are brilliant, and it is one of the few grounds that I believe disabled fans can go to on their own with complete peace of mind.

**PROGRAMME:** £2.00
Not a bad read, with enough on the visiting team and general interest articles to make it worth buying.

**FANZINES:**

| | |
|---|---|
| The 69'er | 50p |
| The Randy Robin | 50p |

The title of the first of these, I am assured, refers to the year Don Rogers et al did for Arsenal in the League Cup final. Not always on sale on matchdays, but worth buying if you see it.

## TRAVEL

**NEAREST RAILWAY STATION:**
Swindon (0.75 mile) (0117 929 4255 — Bristol Enquiries) Turn left as you leave the station and keep walking to the roundabout with County Road

**NEAREST BUS STATION:** Fleming Way (01793 523700 — Thamesdown buses)
The 1, 2, 13, 14, 66 and 67 all stop at the stadium end of Fleming Way.

**BY CAR:**
**NORTH:** A419 Cricklade Road (this becomes Cirencester Way). You then get to the Transfer Bridges roundabouts. Turn left at the first of these and straight over the second one. Keep going to a mini-roundabout and the County Ground is on your left.
**EAST:** M4 to J15. Turn right onto the A419, continuing for one mile till you reach a roundabout at which you

should turn left onto the A4259. Go straight over at the first roundabout, then left at the second onto the A345 (Queens Drive). The ground is 0.25 mile on the right.

**WEST:** M4 to J16. A420 (signposted Swindon), go straight over at the first roundabout, and right at the second into Wootton Bassett Road. After 0.75 mile turn left into Westcott Place. Go straight over the next roundabout into Faringdon Road, then after 0.5 mile turn right into Fleming Way. The ground is at the bottom of Fleming Way on your right.

**SOUTH:** A361 into Swindon for the A345 and the ground.

Whichever way you go into Swindon the ground is well signposted. However, whichever way you go into the town you will also have to deal with the MAGIC ROUNDABOUT which is right outside the ground. This abomination is one big roundabout with five mini-roundabouts and various little islands dotted around it. Strangely enough, when the road is busy it isn't too bad as sheer volume of numbers tends to sort everything out, but when it is not so packed you get to witness the full spectacle of traffic going round islands the wrong way and people getting motion sickness as they go into a frenzied dervish-like dance trying to manoeuvre themselves 50yd up the road.

**PARKING:** There is limited parking at the ground. Alternatively, in Shrivenham Road (just keep going round the roundabouts until you see an escape route which is marked as a no through road; this is the one you want) is Hulford Motors where you can park for a quid (though they do like to lock up early after a game). Some street parking is available amidst the residents' zones, and there are two large car parks on the town side of Fleming Way. Watch out for new resident parking zones and also the private clamping firm which operate and are not slow off the mark.

## FUTURE DEVELOPMENTS

The plans to build a casino at the club were shelved last season and so (hopefully) Swindon might turn their attention to building some sort of proper stand at the Stratton Bank End. However, before you get too excited, apparently some local residents are dead set against the idea and — possibly more significantly — the financial position at the club is such that any major work is unlikely to be undertaken during next season.

## OTHER INFORMATION

If you like a pre-match pint, the County Hotel by the ground is a bit dingy, but serves its purpose. Alternatively, wander into town (which although it has got a real 1960s precinct feel to it, somehow seems to be able to carry it off) and try out one of the many pubs there; the Mail Coach on Fleet Street is probably one of the better ones. The Red Lion opposite the ground does nice turkey sticks, and banana fritters in syrup, although the chips I had from there were disgusting. Once inside you can indulge yourself in Peter's Pies and Pasties, which taste very nice but, for me at least, kept returning throughout the match and journey home.

Two unanswered questions: just what is the point of having what appears to be a sign comprising a cucumber in a stetson on the North Stand, and why did my match ticket have printed in large letters across it 'Unauthorised possession is theft!'? Are Town perhaps trying to halt the perceived decline in the social environment?

*Total Football* **Experience Rating: 52**

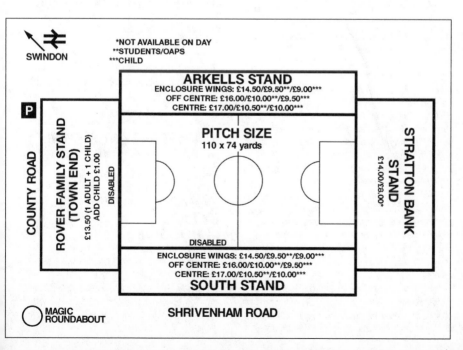

SWINDON

*NOT AVAILABLE ON DAY
**STUDENTS/OAPS
***CHILD

**ARKELLS STAND**
ENCLOSURE WINGS: £14.50/£9.50**/£9.00***
OFF CENTRE: £16.00/£10.00**/£9.50***
CENTRE: £17.00/£10.50**/£10.00***

**PITCH SIZE**
110 x 74 yards

P

COUNTY ROAD

**ROVER FAMILY STAND (TOWN END)**
£13.50 (1 ADULT + 1 CHILD)
ADD CHILD £1.00

DISABLED

**STRATTON BANK STAND**
£14.00/£8.00*

DISABLED

ENCLOSURE WINGS: £14.50/£9.50**/£9.00***
OFF CENTRE: £16.00/£10.00**/£9.50***
CENTRE: £17.00/£10.50**/£10.00***
**SOUTH STAND**

**MAGIC ROUNDABOUT**

**SHRIVENHAM ROAD**

# TORQUAY UNITED

**ADDRESS:** Plainmoor
Torquay
Devon TQ1 3PS

**TELEPHONE No:** 01803 328666

**TICKET OFFICE:** 01803 328666

**FAX:** 01803 323976

**WEB SITE:**
www.mervo.com/Torquay-united/
(unofficial)
Fairly sparse in itself, but with plenty of good links.

**NICKNAME:** The Gulls

**RECORD ATTENDANCE:** 21,908 v
Huddersfield FA Cup 4th 29 January 1955 (L 0-1)

**CLUB COLOURS:**
**HOME:** Shirts: Yellow and Navy stripes;
Shorts: Navy; Socks: Yellow
**AWAY:** Shirts: White;
Shorts: White; Socks: White

**KIT SPONSORS:** Westward Developments

**MANUFACTURERS:** Glory Years

## GROUND INFO

The club has an absolutely brilliant pricing system which is £8 for adults in the Pop Side (£5 OAPs/Students; £4 children) and £9 for anywhere else in the ground (£6 OAPs/Students; £4 children). Life would be a lot easier if other clubs took a leaf out of the Gulls' book. Almost incredibly, the local people failed to be attracted to the ground. No doubt they would all turn up in their droves if the club was about to fold or go out of the league, but that is not when they'll be needed.

In 1997-8 away fans had 1,000 uncovered terrace places at the Babbacombe End, together with 196 places in the Main Stand. With the proposed development of the Babbacombe End (see Future Developments), it is believed that away fans will stay in this part of the ground (although the capacity of 1,000 may be reduced if both the visiting team have insufficient support and adequate segregation can be introduced).

The potential development of the Babbacombe End means that there will no longer be the fear for visiting fans if on rainy days they left their seat to go to get a half-time cuppa that it would be claimed by another person (fans were free to transfer from terrace to stands as they wished) thus consigning them to 45min on the exposed open terrace.

The Family Stand (at the Warbro Road End) was the first area of the stadium to be developed and is not only a good place to watch the match from, but also allows for a quick getaway at the end of the match. This stand also houses the Directors Box making the Board at Torquay possibly the only one in England who enjoy a behind the goals view of the action (blimey, they'll be leading the chanting next!).

**CAPACITY:** Stands: 2,446; Terrace: 3,557;
Total: 6,003

**AWAY FANS:** Babbacombe End: 808;
Main Stand: 196; Total: 1,004

**DISABLED FACILITIES:** There are 15 spaces for wheelchair-bound supporters at the Ellacombe End of the ground, with disabled fans being admitted free of charge, and helpers charged £6. There is no need to pre-book, but the club advises you inform the in advance.

There are no general disabled parking facilities at Plainmoor, but if you phone before your visit then you might find that the club can work something out. Match commentaries are available, but they need to be pre-booked.

**PROGRAMME:** £1.50
The best thing about this is the front cover, a picture postcard scene of the English Riviera, which I believe was used every issue last season. Very little for the away fan here, however, except poor punctuation and grammar.

**FANZINES:**
*Bamber's Right Foot* £1.00
An excellent fanzine, which is now well established as a 'must buy'. It blends scathing attacks — at possible take-overs and the apathy of the 'missing gull' fans — with very large dollops of humour. Well worth the (modest) investment and likely to take a good hour to read on the way home. Or over a pint or three at 'Boots & Laces'. I believe that the editor, Hayden Jones (a man who can sum up magnificently in 100 words the pain and pleasure of being a footie fan) does a column in the local 'Weekender' which, if up to the standard of the stuff he produces here, makes this another publication worth buying.

## TRAVEL

**NEAREST RAILWAY STATION:**
Torre (01752 221300 — Plymouth Enquiries).

**BUS:** Torquay bus station (01803 613226)
Take a number 34 from Torquay town centre to the ground unless you fancy a very long walk.

**BY CAR:**
**NORTH/EAST:** M5 to J31 (final junction), then take the A38. Turn left onto the A380. When you get to Kingskerswell there is a roundabout, at which you should take the first exit, and about a mile later turn left (signposted Babbacombe A3022). After 0.75 mile turn left into Westhill Road. This becomes Warbro Road after 0.25 mile, and 200yd further on the right you will find the ground.

**WEST:** Follow the A380 into Torquay town centre. On Union Street turn right into Lymington Road (signposted Coach Station). Just past the coach station turn right into Upton Hill, and 500yd further on turn left into St Marychurch Road. After 0.5 mile turn at the crossroads into Warbro Road and the ground is 200yd on the right.

**PARKING:** Either street parking, or alternatively at the crossroads of Westhill Road, Warbro Road, St Marychurch Road and Manor Road, take Manor Road 0.25 mile down which you will find a car park.

If you are making a weekend of it, it is worth leaving your car in one of the many town car parks and walking to the ground. Depending on how invigorating you find the sea air, it should take 20-30min from Union Street (see route from west).

## FUTURE DEVELOPMENTS

The club is to redevelop the away (Babbacombe) end and replace it with an 1,800-seat stand in the near future. The completion date for this was due initially to be September 1995 but has been delayed several times and there are no plans to do this in the near future. It will represent the third stage in the redevelopment of Plainmoor and means that the ground is light years away from the dilapidated uncovered terraces (considered by many as being unfit for human habitation) of not so many years ago. The chairman and directors deserve a great deal of praise for having quietly brought about a mini-renaissance at the club, and a trip here gets better with each visit.

## OTHER INFORMATION

Sorry for the repetition from previous editions, but it has to be said (again) that Torquay once provided their fans with the greatest ever pre-match entertainment in the history of the beautiful game. This consisted of the wonderfully named Dave Beer, a local night-club bouncer, standing at one end of the pitch catching cannonballs which were fired at him from the other end of the ground. A millisecond after the moment of impact, Dave was lifted off his feet and about 20yd further back. (Hell of a guy though, he never let go!) This world class act used to be seen in the opening titles of 'Match Of The Day', when the BBC knew what football fans really wanted ('It's An FA Cup Final Knockout' etc), as opposed to nowadays when all we get is that silly yellow flag (and less than 15hrs coverage on Cup Final day).

There are quite a few pubs in Torquay and Babbacombe, but in all honesty they are not a patch on Boots & Laces, which is the Torquay FC pub. Visitors are more than welcome and it is a great place to go to enjoy a pint, chat about the game, watch 'Football Focus' and get your programme and fanzine. A lot of the locals reckon it is the only reason that they come to matches, and apparently it makes more money than the football club itself. Boots & Laces enjoys a great atmosphere and gives the lie to the idea that we are all animals who cannot enjoy each other's company while having a pint (not that you needed telling that anyway) — for my money, this is the best club-pub in the country.

Inside Plainmoor, when I visited, the food was less acceptable, and you are better off sampling the delicacies of one of the fish and chip shops near the ground, which surprisingly for 'Down South' serve chips and gravy as well.

One thing to be aware of is that there don't appear to be any national bookies in the area, so it can be as well to put your fixed odds on before you leave home.

All in all, despite it being likely to be a long away trip — the B&Bs are great and fairly cheap if you want to make a weekend of it — the way you are treated in all respects at Plainmoor means that this really is a great away trip and one you should try and do if it is possible.

*Total Football* **Experience Rating: 92**

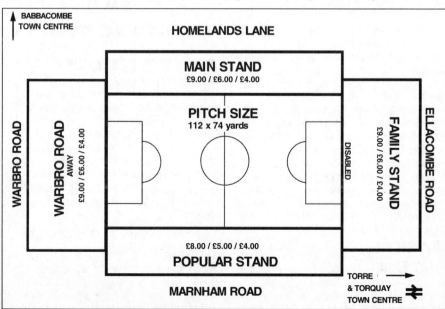

165

# TOTTENHAM HOTSPUR

**ADDRESS:** White Hart Lane
748 High Road
Tottenham
London N17 0AP

**TELEPHONE No:** 0181 365 5000
**TICKET OFFICE:** 0181 365 5100
**FAX:** 0181 365 5005
**SPURS LINE:** 0891 33 55 55
**WEB SITE:** www.spurs.co.uk
(official)
**NICKNAME:** Spurs
**RECORD ATTENDANCE:**
73,038 v Sunderland FA Cup 6th 5 March 1938 (L 0-1)
**CLUB COLOURS:**
**HOME:** Shirts: White; Shorts: Navy Blue;
Socks: White
**AWAY:** Shirts: Purple; Shorts: Purple;
Socks: Purple
**KIT SPONSORS:** Hewlett Packard
**MANUFACTURERS:** Pony

## GROUND INFO

For the majority, getting into White Hart Lane was almost an impossibility as there was a negligible allocation for away fans while the reconstruction of the North Stand was undertaken. Now building work has been completed, the only problem you'll face is not getting into the ground, but rather paying for the trip (although to be fair, there are other grounds in London that are more expensive).

That there are two categories of matches and no concessions for away supporters almost goes without saying. The view isn't too bad, but don't expect to be stretching your legs when you are sitting down. If you opt for either the West or the East Stand then the leg room is better, but the cost is astronomic, and unless you are a member you will not get concessions for juniors. One of the worst things about the Lane at present is that there is a complete lack of atmosphere about the place and, while I can accept that the team hasn't given the fans much to sing about, the same is true at other grounds yet the atmosphere at these is more fun and less funereal. Maybe it will improve now that there are more visiting supporters to share a bit of banter with, but, if it doesn't, then it remains one of the easiest Premiership grounds to out-sing the home support.

**CAPACITY:** Stands: 36,214; Terrace: Nil
**AWAY FANS:** South Stand: 4,000
Expect on average to get something like 2,067 seats, comprised of 833 South East Stand Lower Tier and 1,234 South East Stand Upper Tier.

**DISABLED FACILITIES:** There are facilities for 17 disabled fans plus helpers in the South Stand (to the right of the Park Lane goal) and 26 disabled fans plus helpers in the North Stand. In the past disabled fans have been admitted free, with helpers paying the price of a North Lower ticket. One thing that is worth noting is that in the past disabled supporters have HAD to be accompanied by a helper. Apply for spaces one calendar month in advance, and let the club know if you require a parking space at the ground.

The club also offers match commentaries for the blind.

**PROGRAMME:** £2.00
This is quite a decent publication of its kind, very glossy and bright with several decent bits and pieces amongst the hundreds of adverts to keep you going. Apparently it picked up an award in 1997-8 for being the best programme in London, although, considering some of the rivals it has for this title, the expression 'damned by faint praise' springs to mind.

**FANZINES:**
   *Spur Of The Moment*     £1
   *Cock A Doodle Doo*     £2
*CADD* seems to have taken over the mantle from *The Spur* as the club's most expensive fanzine, but unlike *TS* isn't worth it. I've said it before but if *CADD* is the nice cousin that your mum wants you to grow up like, *SOTM* is the lad who you play footie and have a laugh and a pint with. Capable of getting angry — and at the moment what is desperately lacking at White Hart Lane is passion — and being very funny; not perfect but well worth a quid.

## TRAVEL

**NEAREST RAILWAY STATION:** White Hart Lane (0171 928 5100 — Liverpool St Enquiries)

**NEAREST TUBE STATION:**
Seven Sisters (Victoria Line)
The distance between the station and the ground is enough to make Ffyona Campbell think twice before setting out to walk it.

If the idea of blistered feet does not appeal, then you can either get a bus from outside the tube station, or transfer to BR at Seven Sisters and take a train to either White Hart Lane or Bruce Grove. The latter is still a little walk from the ground, but does have the advantage of having some decent pubs round it.

**BUS:** London Transport (0171 222 1234)
Take either a 149, 259, 279 or 359 to the ground.

**BY CAR:**
**NORTH:** A10 through Enfield to the roundabout with the A406 North Circular Road and take the first exit (left) onto Sterling Way. After one mile turn right into Fore Street (A1010) which becomes High Road. 0.75 mile

down High Road take a left into Park Lane and the ground is on your left.

**SOUTH:** Cross the river at London Bridge and continue north via Gracechurch Street and Bishopsgate, following signs for A10 Cambridge. Continue for five miles until the A10 branches left into Bruce Grove; here you should bear right into High Road A1010 and turn right 0.5 mile later into Park Lane.

**EAST/WEST:** Take the A406 North Circular Road following signs for Edmonton. Turn right (if you're coming from the west) or left (from east) onto the A1010 Fore Street, then as north.

**PARKING:** Parking is a bit of a problem at White Hart Lane. As with their North London neighbours, there is much residents-only parking near the ground.

For those coming from north, east and west, it's as well to park in Edmonton and then either walk the mile or so to the ground or catch a train to White Hart Lane. Those coming from the south are advised to park in one of the side roads around Bruce Grove, again either walking about a mile or grabbing a train.

## FUTURE DEVELOPMENTS
None.

## OTHER INFORMATION
The nearest watering hole to the ground is the Corner Pin, which even if you can get in takes an age to get served. A better move is to wander down the High Road where there are plenty of other places. The Ship and the Elbow Room by Bruce Grove station are both worth a visit, and neither has a problem about serving away supporters.

There are reasonable facilities in the ground including

a bookies and a bar in the away section of the ground. The former serves drinkable beer and lager at around the £2.00 a pint mark. Whether it's a comment on how rough they think the patrons will be or just a very trendy attempt to recreate a typical 'Landan boozah' from years gone by, but there are liberal amounts of sawdust sprinkled on the floor — lahverley!

There are plenty of places to buy food in the area, and there is also a fairly decent choice in the ground itself, including excellent bagels (no, this is not a joke) and vegiburgers, although — and how surprised are you at this? — they are fairly pricey.

My last trip to Spurs can possibly be best summarised by someone I spoke to on the day, who said 'the trouble with Spurs is that they think they're a big club, but they're rubbish really. The team's rubbish, the fans are rubbish, Alan Sugar's rubbish and the ground ain't all that'. Worryingly for the club, this was said not by a rival supporter but by one of their own fans. The only thing he forgot to complain about was the stewarding which is officious to say the least.

A trip to Spurs used to be a great day out, but since the departure of Terry Venables, the club seems to have become both far less welcoming to visiting fans and apathetic to itself, and a trip down the Lane now hardly manages to stir any emotions in you (either good or bad) and is simply something that has to be done one Saturday per season.

Finally, hats off to Spurs in 'the rubbing their own noses in it stakes' for showing highlights of previous matches on the Jumbotron screen regardless of how many the team have recently lost by... very motivating!!

***Total Football* Experience Rating: 60**

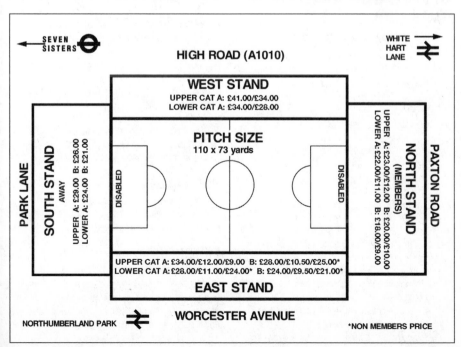

# TRANMERE ROVERS

**ADDRESS:** Prenton Park
Prenton Road West
Birkenhead
Wirral L42 9PN

**TELEPHONE No:** 0151 608 4194

**TICKET OFFICE:** 0151 609 0137

**FAX:** 0151 608 4385

**CLUBCALL:** 0891 12 16 46

**WEB SITE:**
http://www.merseyworld.com/rovers

**NICKNAME:** Rovers

**RECORD ATTENDANCE:** 24,424 v Stoke City FA Cup 4th 5 February 1972 (D 2-2)

**CLUB COLOURS:**
**HOME:** Shirts: White with slight Blue trim;
Shorts: Blue/White with Blue/Green trim;
Socks: Blue/White with Blue/Green trim

**AWAY FIRST:**
Shirts: Green with Orange & White trim;
Shorts: White with Orange & green trim;
Socks: Green with Orange & White trim

**AWAY SECOND:**
Shirts: Claret and Blue striped effect;
Shorts: Claret with Blue trim;
Socks: Sky Blue with Claret hoops

**KIT SPONSORS:** Wirral Borough Council

**MANUFACTURERS:** Mizuno

## GROUND INFO

Another ground where there appears to be definitely a case of one rule for the home fans and another for the visiting supporters. Before your shoulders drop in resignation, it is worth pointing out that it is the away fans who get treated by far the better and the home fans who get the stick. This seems to be especially true if you are taking a fairly decent following with you. On my last trip to Prenton Park I was talking to some (severely disgruntled) Rovers fans who were being kicked out of their normal seats to accommodate the visitors (and as the match wasn't a cup-tie there didn't really seem to be any real reason for this). Then during the match there was a fair bit of banter flying around from the away supporters, but as soon as the Tranmere fans gave it some back (and we are talking nothing excessive here) it was a case of 'out you go mate'. Bizarre! Sadly for 1998-9 Tranmere have introduced a three-category pricing structure (though if you are classified category C then you will actually pay £1 less in 1998-9 than you did in 1997-8). Concessions are apparently available if there was/is to be a reciprocal agreement.

Depending on your following, you'll get one, two or all of the sections of the Kop Stand. It fills up from the Main Stand side and, if there aren't many of you, then the first section used can be pretty dire (especially the first rows of seats which are almost subterranean; anything from row D is normally OK). The next block is probably the best to aim for (if you can) as you get a belting behind-the-goal view from about row K, though anywhere is OK. After that has been used, you start moving towards the corners again which, as previously mentioned, is so-so. Not masses of leg room. If you're feeling a bit flush then a couple of extra quid will get you into the Main Stand, although be warned: the atmosphere in here is like a library and, while you will never feel threatened, you are likely to get glares of disapproval if you start partaking in rowdy behaviour (clapping good moves, cheering when you score and the like).

The toilets in the stand are much better than those pre-development when they were open to the eyes of anyone passing by. The new models, whilst not massive, are clean, and have designated entrance and exit points which means that the half-time flow is unrestricted (figuratively speaking).

**CAPACITY:** Stands: 16,782; Terrace: Nil

**AWAY FANS:** Kop: 2,100
This can be extended to the whole of the Kop (5,842) if required. It should be noted that, despite requests from some Rovers fans that the visiting supporters should be given the (rather small) Borough Road Stand, the club has decided that the current arrangements will remain for at least the 1998-9 season.

**DISABLED FACILITIES:** There are 28 spaces for disabled fans at the front of the paddock. Admission for disabled supporters is free, but helpers pay standard prices. Away fans are welcome, although pre-booking is essential. Parking facilities are available at the ground (£3.50). It is worth noting that the enclosure is exposed to the elements so whack on your thermals and fill up the flask (although this is apparently being rectified)! Matchday commentaries were made available for the visually impaired in 1997-8 (four places). These are free of charge but should be pre-booked.

**PROGRAMME:** £1.60
Excellent, and very well worth the investment. There are a lot of general interest articles and it will keep you going well through half-time and beyond.

**FANZINES:**
*Give Us An R*                                    £1
*Give Us An R* improved again last season and is a good enough way to spend a passable 30min or so. It still isn't as good as the previous Rovers' fanzine, *White Love*, whose editors retired to the pub three years ago and have not yet re-emerged (in literary terms).

## TRAVEL
## NEAREST RAILWAY STATION:
Birkenhead Central or Rock Ferry (from Liverpool Lime Street) (0151 709 9696 — Lime Street)
Both stations are on the Chester line and trains leave every 15min from Liverpool. Each station is also about a mile from the ground, and you may find it easier to get off at Hamilton Square which, although further from Prenton Park, allows you to get straight onto a bus.

### BUS:
Central bus station (0151 236 7676)
Instead of taking the train you may wish to take the ferry across the Mersey. This will leave you in Woodside, from where a number 64 bus will take you to the ground.

## BY CAR:
**NORTH:** Go through the Mersey Tunnel (Kingsway) and once through, follow the signs for the M53. Take the M53 to J3, turning left at the exit roundabout onto the A552 Woodchurch Road. Follow this road for a mile and on the left there is a park; shortly after this the A553 is crossed by the B5151 Shoreton Road. Turn right onto this and then second left into Prenton Road West, where the ground is 0.25 mile on the right.

**SOUTH/EAST:** M6/M56 and M53 to J4. Take the fourth exit at the roundabout onto the B5151 Mount Road. Continue for about 2.5 miles (when Mount Road becomes Shoreton Road you have about 0.75 mile to go), and turn right into Prenton Road West; the ground is 0.25 mile on your right.

The police seal off a section of Borough Road on matchdays which only adds to the congestion.

### PARKING:
There is limited parking at the ground, but if you don't get a space then you have a real problem. Overflow parking is avaiable at Devonshire Park School car park (signed). Street parking (one of the side streets off Borough Road is probably the best choice), is a hard task among the broken yellow lines and residents-only bays, otherwise drive past the ground and onto Prenton

Road East. The third left takes you onto Church Road (B5148) and there is a car park 300yd on the right. If you have problems parking you may find it isn't worth asking a policeman for help, as the response I got to the question 'Is there anywhere round here to park?' was 'Yeah, if you can find a space'. (Thanks, I hadn't realised what was required.)

## FUTURE DEVELOPMENTS
None planned.

## OTHER INFORMATION
There are a couple of pubs right by the ground: the Prenton Park (a definite no-no for away fans) and the Mersey Clipper. I have heard some good reviews about the Clipper, but my own experience is that it remains a place where you can need to keep at least half an eye over your shoulder. A much better bet is to wander down Prenton Park away from the ground to the Sportsman's Arms. From the outside this place also looks as if it might be somewhere where you could get grief, but I ended up having a decent pint in a relaxed atmosphere with home and away fans who seemed more than happy in each other's company. A new arrival at Prenton Park is Aldo's; however, as it is members only (and apparently has its own entrance into the home section of the Kop) you are unlikely to be sampling its delights. For food, Chopsticks on Borough Road does a generous portion of chips with gravy. Inside the ground, the food is pretty bland, but the hot drinks are hot and come with lids so you don't end up spilling half of them on the way back to your seat. There is only one food bar though, so expect long waits for your grub.

A thing that may concern you on your visit is the sight of the 'Prenton Pups' clubhouse, which is a wooden hut done out like a kennel (and I thought the days of treating fans like animals were over). Children, apparently, love it!

*Total Football* Experience Rating: 67

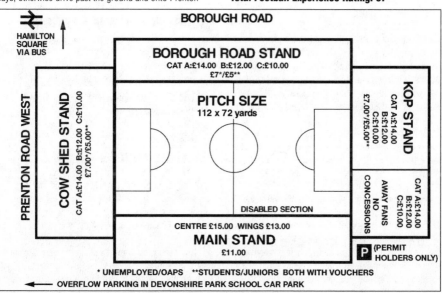

HAMILTON SQUARE VIA BUS

BOROUGH ROAD

BOROUGH ROAD STAND
CAT A:£14.00  B:£12.00  C:£10.00
£7*/£5**

PITCH SIZE
112 x 72 yards

PRENTON ROAD WEST

COW SHED STAND
CAT A:£14.00  B:£12.00  C:£10.00
£7.00*/£5.00**

KOP STAND
CAT A:£14.00
B:£12.00
C:£10.00
£7.00*/£5.00**

AWAY FANS
NO CONCESSIONS
CAT A:£14.00
B:£12.00
C:£10.00

DISABLED SECTION

CENTRE £15.00  WINGS £13.00
MAIN STAND
£11.00

**P** (PERMIT HOLDERS ONLY)

* UNEMPLOYED/OAPS  **STUDENTS/JUNIORS  BOTH WITH VOUCHERS
◄— OVERFLOW PARKING IN DEVONSHIRE PARK SCHOOL CAR PARK

# WALSALL

**ADDRESS:** The Bescot Stadium
Bescot Crescent
Walsall
WS1 4SA

**TELEPHONE No:** 01922 622791
**TICKET OFFICE:** 01922 651410
**FAX:** 01922 613202
**CLUBCALL:** 0891 855 800
**WEB SITE:**
http://www.saddlers.co.uk/ (official)
**E-MAIL:** wfc@saddlers.co.uk
**NICKNAME:** The Saddlers
**RECORD ATTENDANCE:**
25,343 v Newcastle Div 2 29 August 1961 (W 1-0)
At Bescot: 10,628 England B v Switzerland B 20 May 1991 (2-1)

**CLUB COLOURS:**
**HOME:** Shirts: Red and Black trim;
Shorts: Red and Black trim;
Socks: Red and Black turnover
**AWAY:** Shirts: Green with White trim;
Shorts: Green with White trim;
Socks: Green with White turnover

**KIT SPONSORS:** Banks's
**MANUFACTURERS:** Errea

## GROUND INFO

Prepare yourself for a treat because you are about to enter 'The most modern stadium in the country'. This, I have immediately to add, is the opinion stated on some of the club blurb I have seen and not necessarily — in fact make that definitely not — that of the author.

In truth, it doesn't matter where you go in the ground, you are likely to have a restricted view as, despite the fact that the Bescot was one of the country's first out-of-town stadia, it does not appear to have been built with the fans in mind as there are pillars everywhere and the leg room is fairly cramped.

On the bright side, admission is reasonable (for tickets bought on the day the away seats are the cheapest in the ground) and there are concessions available to all fans. Local fans should note that there are discounts of between 50p and £1 for tickets bought before the day of the match (this is not available in the visitors' section).

Perhaps it is even more surprising than normal that Walsall don't see away fans as a source of a quick buck when you consider the way they treated their own fans before last season's FA cup-ie at Old Trafford, when non-season ticket holders were allowed to jump the queue for tickets... providing that, in addition to buying the £19

ticket, they spent £25 in the club shop — nice touch eh!!!?!! If the visiting team has either a junior or family membership scheme and is prepared to offer a reciprocal arrangement to Walsall, then the club is happy to let them into the Family Stand. You will need your membership cards and adult males will not be admitted alone.

**CAPACITY:** Stands: 6,700; Terrace: 2,300;
Total: 9,000

**AWAY FANS:** William Sharp Stand: 1,916
In addition a further 1,100 seats may be made available in the Banks Stand.

**DISABLED FACILITIES:** There are 30 places for wheelchair-bound supporters in the Banks' Stand; both they and one adult helper are admitted free of charge. Pre-booking of this facility is required. The club has introduced specific parking facilities at the ground for disabled fans and your requirements should be sorted out when you book your ticket.

There are no matchday commentaries for the blind.

**PROGRAMME:** £1.80
This is a programme that keeps winning divisional awards for programme of the year, and it is easy to see why. Lots of general interest articles, and one of the few programmes that when reviewing past encounters between the teams sometimes includes defeats for the home team. There are occasional bizarre articles about 'Aynok and Ayli' which are written in quite incomprehensible Black Country dialect.

**FANZINES:**
Blazing Saddlers                    £1
Moving Swiftly On                   50p

## TRAVEL

**NEAREST RAILWAY STATION:** Bescot
(0121 643 2711 — Birmingham New Street Enquiries)
There is a fairly regular service from both New Street and Walsall to Bescot. Allow yourself half an hour from the former and about two minutes from the latter.

**BUS:** Central bus station (01922 25515 — West Midlands Travel Shop)
Routes 401,401E or 402

**BY CAR:**
**FROM ALL PARTS:** M6 to J9. When leaving the motorway take the A461 Bescot Road (signposted Walsall) keeping in the right-hand lane and after 0.25 mile bear right into the A4184 Wallows Lane; then turn right at the second set of traffic lights into Bescot Crescent. Follow this road for 400yd and the stadium is on the left-hand side.

If you are coming from the south and want to avoid some of the hell that is the M6 — and my isn't that sign at the ground which you can see from the motorway and which reads 'Duerrs Marmalade helps you beat the jams' amusing as you crawl along at the pace of an asthmatic snail? In fact, I was still laughing when I bought my next jar... of Robinson's marmalade — then you can exit at J7. Keep in the left-hand lane (trust me, I'm correct about this) and take the A34 to Walsall. After just over a mile turn left into Walstead Road — there is a pub here called the Bell which is not a bad port of call — and the ground is 1.4 miles further down the road.

## PARKING:
The stadium car park — away supporters have their own designated section — will add £2 to the cost of your trip although if you get there at a reasonable time, you will be able to find somewhere to park either at the Retail Park by the ground or in one of the roads off Bescot Crescent. Getting away can still be a bit of a grind, although the police do seem to have things slightly more under control. On a good day you can be snarled up in the M6 jams in five minutes, on a bad one it will take half an hour.

## FUTURE DEVELOPMENTS
Nothing planned at the moment and it is likely that the ground will remain the same until such time as League requirements dictate otherwise.

## OTHER INFORMATION
Whilst the name of Walsall may not conjure up the most seductive of images, the people from the town insist it is the jewel in the crown of the Black Country. However, if you are looking for a pie and a pint before the match then you are going to be struggling, and apart from the King George V on Wallows Lane (which has a decent chip shop next to it) and the New Fullbrook (keep going straight for about a mile and a quarter when you get to the right turn for the ground) on Broadway West which

also has a chip shop next to it, you are as well to stick to the town for pre-match entertainment. There is the Bescot Bar at the ground and also the Saddlers Club, which are members only but which for 'quiet' games you might be able to get into, but not if there are more than two of you and if you think you'll get in wearing an away replica top, well, in the words of the ground's other famous poster, 'That'll be the Daewoo'.

Fascinating fact number 13,187: a survey undertaken in 1997 came to the conclusion that people in Walsall are the fattest in Britain, with something like 1 in 5 being classified as grossly overweight. Much scientific head scratching went on to try and decide why this was the case, although a trip to the Bescot would have provided the answer. When you go to the ground, try the balti pie which is one of the true greats of English football. And which made its entry at The Bescot rather than Villa Park as some would have you believe. Hot (in more ways than one) and exceptionally tasty, a definite 'must eat' when you're on your travels. Though it's a shame to report that you'll have to wash it down with a mediocre cup of tea rather than a pint of lager which is probably what you'll really want after eating one.

Among the other attractions the town has to offer are the arboretum (a fancy Dan name for a park with trees in it) and a modern art gallery. It is also the home of Jabez Cliff & Co, which used to manufacturer leather caseys, the lace outline of which can still be seen firmly imprinted on some of the older locals' foreheads. Of course, if you do extend your stay then you'll have to visit the 'famous Bescot Stadium Sunday market' — what do you mean you've never heard of it? It's held at the most modern stadium in the country, everyone knows it!!

***Total Football* Experience Rating: 70**

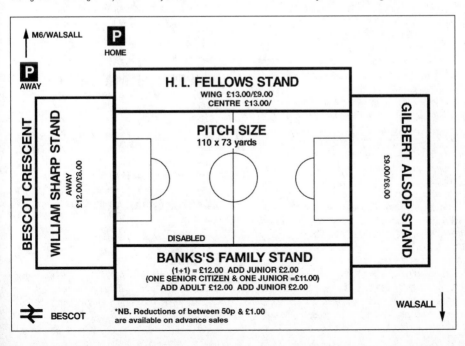

# WATFORD

**ADDRESS:** Vicarage Road Stadium
Vicarage Road
Watford WD1 8ER
**TELEPHONE No:** 01923 496000
**TICKET OFFICE:** 01923 496010
**FAX:** 01923 496001
**HORNET HOT LINE:** 0891 104104
**WEB SITE:** www.watfordfc.com
(official)
**NICKNAME:** The Hornets
**RECORD ATTENDANCE:**
34,099 v Man Utd FA Cup 4th 3 February 1969
**CLUB COLOURS:**
**HOME:** Shirts: Yellow with Red shoulders;
Shorts: Red; Socks: Red
**AWAY:** Shirts: Blue & Silver stripes;
Shorts: Blue; Socks: Blue

**KIT SPONSORS:** CTX Computer Products
**MANUFACTURERS:** Le Coq Sportif

## GROUND INFO

Away fans get the Rookery End and/or the Lower Tier of the Rous Stand depending on the number the club is likely to bring. Both offer a good view of the pitch, but neither offers much protection from the elements for the first half dozen or so rows.

Traditionally, the big problem with both stands is that to get to them, away fans have to take a long trek along Vicarage Road, down Occupation Road, round the back of the allotments (now guarded by a massive fence and gate for those who remember the 'potato runs') before heading back up a dirt track to get to the turnstiles which are about 100yd from where you started. If you want to avoid the same 10min journey on departure, find a kind-hearted steward who will let you nip through the Upper Tier of the Rous (the only thing being you will have to leave 5min early); the other alternative is to hang around after the match, until you are allowed out of the North exits, straight onto Vicarage Road (probably bumping into a ragged crocodile of fans who opted for the long walk). The club reports that on many occasions visiting supporters are now permitted access to the turnstiles via the Directors' car park, across the back of the Rookery End Stand, subject to police instructions.

1998-9 sees rather large price hikes and the introduction of categorisation in the Rous Upper Tier Stand — a nice thankyou for the fans who stuck by the club while it languished in the second division, don't you think? The club does offer concessions to visiting supporters, although the £4 discount on a £14 ticket is not what you would call massive.

**CAPACITY:** Stands: 22,763; Terrace: Nil
**AWAY FANS:** Rookery End: 6,936;
Total: 10,276

**DISABLED FACILITIES:** There are two enclosures for disabled supporters at the ground, one in the North Stand which has 16 spaces, and one in the Rookery End Stand which has 24 spaces. These cost £6 for disabled supporters and £14 for helpers. Pre-booking is not generally required. Parking spaces are not widely available at the ground, but if you phone the club it may be able to organise something.

There are no commentary facilities for the visually impaired.

**PROGRAMME:** £2
Another price rise for 1998-9 means this has gone up 33% in the last two seasons (although it has increased in size to 48 pages). Lots of snazzy computer-like borders and tabs on the pages. The content is actually fairly good as well, with lots of snippets and an excellent section on the visitors as well as a few general interest articles.

**FANZINES:**

| | |
|---|---|
| *Clap Your Hands And Stamp Your Feet* | £1 |
| *The Horn* | 50p |
| *Blind Stupid and Desperate* | £1 |

*BSaD* is actually an Internet fanzine, but last season I got hold of a 'luddite' edition on printed paper. Not too bad, although an unhandy A4 size and it was very much a 'best of' rather than a record of what was currently happening. I saw *CYHASYF* at an away game, and I'm not sure whether it has had a change of editor or what, but there has been a dramatic improvement in both the amount there was to read in it and the quality of the articles.

## TRAVEL

**NEAREST RAILWAY STATION:** Watford Halt, Watford High Street, Watford Junction (0171 387 7070)
A plethora of stations are available to the discerning traveller. Watford Halt is behind the ground and is on a direct line from Watford Junction. This operates for high profile matches only. Alternatively try the High Street which is walkable, and which offers a few more stopping-off points on the way to the stadium.

**NEAREST TUBE STATION:**
Watford (Metropolitan Line)

**BUS:** Network Watford (0345 788788)

**BY CAR:**
**NORTH:** Exit M1 at J5 and take the second exit off the roundabout onto the A41, signposted Harrow. Continue for a short distance to the next roundabout and take the third exit, Hartspring Lane. Follow this road through a set of traffic lights and continue straight ahead (along what is

now Aldenham Road) to another roundabout. Go straight over (second exit) still following Aldenham Road, to next traffic lights. When through the lights, move into the right-hand lane (marked Watford) and follow the one-way system around to Bushey station, then moving into the left-hand lane. Turn left under Bushey Arches into Eastbury Road. At traffic lights turn right into Deacons Hill and continue to next traffic lights, turning left into Cardiff Road for the visitors' entrance to the stadium/coach park.

**SOUTH:** M1 to J5 and take first exit off roundabout, then as north.

**EAST:** Exit M25 at J21A and join the M1 at J6. Exit at J5, then as north.

**WEST:** Exit M25 at J19 and take the third exit off the roundabout onto the A411 (Hempstead Road), signposted Watford. Continue for approximately two miles and at the roundabout go straight across (right-hand lane) to the next roundabout, then take the third exit into Rickmansworth Road. Take the second turning on the left into Cassio Road. Continue through traffic lights, to Merton Road and straight onto Wiggenhall Road. At traffic lights, turn right into Cardiff Road (as north).

**PARKING:** Matchday car parks are operated by Watford General Hospital (next to Vicarage Road Stadium) and by the Watford Girls' Grammar School (2min walk). Both make a small charge for parking. The meters outside the ground work at a rate of 10p for 12min, but before you start whipping out your calculators to work out how much you need, it should be noted that parking is restricted to a maximum of one hour.

## FUTURE DEVELOPMENTS

In response to my questionnaire the club stated 'That these were "Not really applicable for the 1998-9 season".'

The only real area of the ground that needs any work is the East Stand.

## OTHER INFORMATION

There aren't that many good pubs in the area (although the Red Lion on Vicarage Road isn't bad) and it's best to stick to the town centre. If you come in via Watford Junction, the Pennant just up the road is a popular port of call.

A little further afield is the Two Bridges by Croxley Green railway station, which serves a very decent pint. Otherwise try to the town centre, where there are any number of places to meet up. However, be careful you don't leave yourself short of time to get to the ground which is a reasonable distance away — after all, you wouldn't want to miss the teams' emergence to the strains of 'Z-Cars' and the dancing of Harry the Hornet would you?

Inside the ground the pies and pasties were hot and fairly tasty although the servers never risk breaking the speed limit getting them out to fans.

You should also note that the club does not accept £50 notes for either food or admission.

Watford is a good away day and the club is generally fairly welcoming to visitors — unlike Saracen's Rugby Union Club which shares the ground, and only appears to employ staff who can do a supercilious sneer — although the pricing structure does not reflect the happy family image that the club is keen to portray. Stewarding is fairly relaxed and you can enjoy a good singsong. A few more touches and this would be perfect, but sadly I can see it going the other way. Enjoy it while you can.

*Total Football* **Experience Rating: 82**

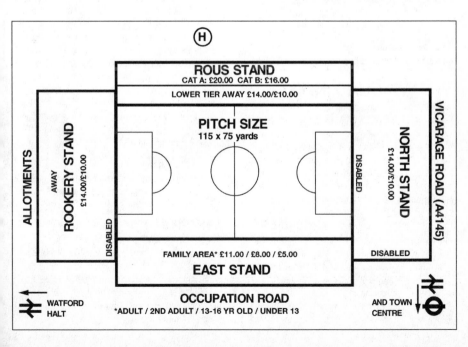

# WEST BROMWICH ALBION

**ADDRESS:** The Hawthorns
Halfords Lane
West Bromwich
B71 4LF
**TELEPHONE No:** 0121 525 8888
Commercial Dept: 0121 525 4714
**TICKET OFFICE:** 0121 553 5472
**FAX:** 0121 553 6634
Commercial Dept: 0121 553 4799
**WEB SITE:** www.wba.co.uk
**E-MAIL:** baggies@wba.co.uk
**CLUBCALL:** 0891 12 11 93
**NICKNAME:** The Baggies,
The Throstles
## RECORD ATTENDANCE:
64,815 v Arsenal FA Cup 6 March 1937 (W 3-1)
Interesting Fact Alert: The Hawthorns is the highest
ground above sea-level in England, and it is said that the
next thing a ball would hit on leaving the ground is the
Ural Mountains — sadly for the paying spectators,
Albion have in the past seemed quite intent on proving
this theory!

## CLUB COLOURS:
**HOME:** Shirts: Navy Blue and White stripes;
Shorts: White; Socks: White & Navy
**AWAY:** Shirts Red with Navy Blue sleeves;
Shorts: Navy with two White stripes;
Socks: Red and Blue hoops

**KIT SPONSORS:** West Bromwich BS
**MANUFACTURERS:** Patrick

## GROUND INFO

I know this may sound stupid, but going to the
Hawthorns is like going to a 'proper' football ground. As
you pull off the motorway, you soon see the 'bent arm'
floodlights which beckon you straight to the stadium. The
ground always seems buzzing, even early on matchdays,
and you get a real feeling of excitement as you wander
round — the ground is half perched on the top of a hill
which means as you walk round you suddenly have weird
inclines and descents to negotiate — and the stands,
while being all-seater, have retained a lot of character
from the old days. Visitors are sited in the Smethwick
Road End which offers reasonable enough leg room and
— generally — a decent view of the game (although try
to avoid the first couple of rows unless you want a
cricked neck from looking up at the action). The club
does offer good concessions in all parts of the ground. If
you are a neutral (or feeling a bit flush) then the Halfords

Stand is a good safe place to watch the game, although if
you do go in the wing section of this, it is probably as
well to go in at the Birmingham Road End rather than the
Smethwick Road End as around here there are a few boys
who like having a bit of banter (though I've never seen it
any worse than this) with the visiting supporters.

One thing you can't fail to be impressed with is the
way with which Albion have taken 'seatwriting' to their
hearts in the redeveloped ground. Not for them a plain
printed 'Albion' or 'WBA', instead they use nice joined up
writing with scarves and the like also embellishing the
seats.

Sadly, the improvement in the ground seems to have
lessened the passion and frequency of the legendary
'Boing Boing' (possibly as this is a far riskier movement
on a spring-loaded seat than it used to be on an open
terrace). However, what it has been replaced by is a
fantastic rendition of the 'The Lord's My Shepherd'. Again
you get to feel there is a logic in this move as, given the
last couple of seasons the Baggies have 'enjoyed', they
must be used to praying a lot more than celebrating.

## CAPACITY: Stands: 25,100; Terrace: Nil
## AWAY FANS: Smethwick Road End: 2,100
If required, the whole of the Smethwick Road End
(formerly known as the West Midlands Travel Stand) can
be allocated to visiting supporters, which increases the
capacity to 5,200.

## DISABLED FACILITIES: Wheelchair-bound
supporters are sited behind the goals at the Apollo 2000
and Travel West Midlands Community Stands and there
are approximately 150 spaces in total. To be truthful,
what with the advertising boards in front of you, and the
constant flow of traffic from people moving from various
points around the rest of the stand and walking directly in
front of this area, this is not one of the better grounds to
watch football from. Admission is free, with helpers
paying £13 (£7 Conc). The club prefers that you pre-
book, and for big matches this is essential. There are
also 12 seats which have headphone facilities (hospital
radio) for the visually impaired. Again these are free and
the club prefers them to be pre-booked. Parking is
available at the ground.

## PROGRAMME: £1.50
The best thing you can say about it is that it is one of the
cheapest in the division, but manages to fill 48 pages
without saying very much at all.

## FANZINES:
*The Grorty Dick*                                   90p
*The Grorty Dick* is a magnificent specimen of a fanzine,
thick and packed with brilliant articles which cover the
whole range of emotions of being a football player, from
anger at the club's ineptitude to the joy of having done
the double over your most bitter rivals, all of which is
liberally sprinkled with humour.

# TRAVEL

## NEAREST RAILWAY STATION:

The Hawthorns is about 300yd from the ground (0121 643 2711 — Birmingham New Street Enquiries).

**BUS:** Birmingham Central (0121 200 2700 — Centro Hotline) Any of the following will do the trick: 74, 77, 78, 79, 450.

## BY CAR:

**FROM ALL PARTS:** M5 to J1. When you leave the motorway, take the A41 Birmingham Road (signposted Handsworth, Birmingham). Follow the signs for the ground.

**PARKING:** Parking at the ground is mainly for season ticket holders only, although there are places available behind the Family Stand and off Halfords Lane at £3. Otherwise, continue down Halfords Lane as the road leads to an industrial area with plenty of opportunities for on-street parking. Halfords Lane itself can be a bit of a nightmare to get away from. The club has also introduced a Park and Ride scheme.

## FUTURE DEVELOPMENTS

There are provisional plans for a £10 million development of the WBBS Stand, although this is very much for the medium to long-term future.

## OTHER INFORMATION

The Hawthorns pub on the corner of Halfords Lane and Birmingham Road is members only, but you may be able to get in, especially if you arrive early. The Woodmans on Birmingham Road operates a closed door policy. Either go down Halfords Lane to the Waggon & Horses, or continue along the A41 towards West Bromwich for the Royal Oak.

If I tell you that you are best off eating at one of the mobiles outside the ground you will probably have a good idea of the quality of other eateries. The chippies in West Bromwich are very heavy on the grease, and don't seem capable of giving you chips 'open' without the paper unfolding when you are 2min up the road. Inside the ground the food improved a lot in 1998. If you do go in the Halfords Stand, you can even get your hands on a curry (and there's a vegetarian one on offer as well) although naturally this is not for us mere plebs in the Smethwick Road End, so instead try one of the meat pies which are hot and tasty. One thing that may stick in your throat, though, is the fact that the club still charges away fans more than home supporters for exactly the same menu items.

Note: the ground is policed by the West Midlands force. In the last couple of seasons I have noticed a marked improvement in the way fans are treated, although I still hear of fans who have had problems with theses chaps, so be a little cautious.

Finally, the Hawthorns does offer fans the chance to see how mature they really are, as the corner flags are about 6in away from the front row of seats which means that, whoever takes the kicks, will possibly be sitting in your lap if they want more than a half yard run up. If you are towards the front then consider yourself fairly grown-up if you don't give the opposition kicker abuse when he comes to take the kick, and very grown-up if you can resist the temptation to pat your own player on the back when he does likewise (unfortunately, so far this test has revealed everyone I know to be bloody childish).

*Total Football* **Experience Rating: 75**

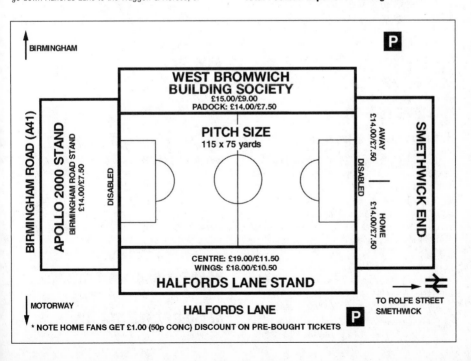

# WEST HAM UNITED

**ADDRESS:** Boleyn Ground
Green Street
Upton Park
London E13 9AZ

**TELEPHONE No:** 0181 548 2748

**TICKET OFFICE:** 0181 548 2700
Note: you can get recorded information on 0181 472 3322

**FAX:** 0181 548 2758

**CLUBCALL:** 0891 12 11 65

**WEB SITE:** http://www.whufc.co.uk/

**NICKNAME:** The Hammers,
The Irons

**RECORD ATTENDANCE:**
42,322 v Spurs Div 1 17 October 1970 (D 2-2)

**CLUB COLOURS:**
**HOME:** Shirts: Claret with Blue sleeves;
Shorts: White;
Socks: Light Blue with Claret hoops
**AWAY:** Shirts: Ecru and Blue; Shorts: Claret;
Socks: Ecru and Blue

**CLUB SPONSOR:** tba
The Hammers managed to go all through last season without a name on their chests; some said it was because the club wanted to hark back to the old traditions, others that the club couldn't agree on a figure with potential backers. I believe the impact on sales made the club step in and say that fans who bought the unsponsored shirt from the club shop would be able to bring it back and get the applicable name put on them if any deal was settled. Perhaps the strangest thing of all was, far from bringing a nostalgic glow when you saw the shirts, they just didn't really look right with nothing on the chest.

**MANUFACTURERS:** Pony

## GROUND INFO

The ground has now been fully developed, and whilst it is certainly more grand than it was, it has still retained a lot of its intimacy, fans are still very much on top of the play, and for fans who remember the old ground the 'chicken run' spirit still lives on. Amazingly the pitch still looks very small, although in terms of square yardage it is bigger than many grounds, including Tottenham and Newcastle.

Having experimented with putting away fans in the Bobby Moore Stand when it initially opened, the club has now decided to site them in the Centenary (ex-North) Stand, which is a bit of a shame as I thought the Bobby Moore Stand was the better of the two. One thing that is true regardless of which stand you are in, is that it very expensive for what you get. The Hammers operate a two category system in which the cheapest price for an away fan is £20 and the most expensive is £24. In trying to offer some word of comfort, at least away fans are offered concessions. Perhaps worst of all, is that if the visiting team does not take its full allocation, then tickets are made available to home supporters at prices which are, I have been told, £2 cheaper for exactly the same type of seat. To be honest, home fans are also charged high prices though they can obtain reductions if they join the club's membership scheme (at £20 a season).

Stewarding at the club is OK, though it tends to err on the strict side. It is also one of those grounds where 'backchat' can easily lead to you being chucked out.

**CAPACITY:** Stands: 26,014; Terrace: Nil

**AWAY FANS:** Centenary (North) Lower Stand:
Max 3,687.
The entire Lower Stand will be allocated if there is sufficient demand; otherwise a minimum allocation of 2,290 will be made.

**DISABLED FACILITIES:** There are 117 places for disabled supporters — who are admitted free of charge — at the ground; these are sited in the West Lower, Bobby Moore and Centenary Stands. Helpers pay £14. Places must be pre-booked, and there is no parking available at the ground. Contact the club to pre-book, matchday commentaries are also available for the blind.

**PROGRAMME:** £2.00
Chock-a-block with pictures of birthday Hammers, long-range Hammers, and the ever popular Hello-I'm-two-weeks-old-this-is-a-picture-of-me-lying-on-my-West-Ham-scarf Hammers. A great programme for home supporters, but less so for visitors.

**FANZINES:**

| | |
|---|---|
| The Water in Majorca | £1 |
| The Ultimate Dream | £1 |
| On The Terraces | £1.50 |
| On A Mission | £1.50 |
| Over Land And Sea | £2 |

£2 is an awful lot to pay for a fanzine, but if you are prepared to do so then I can recommend Over Land and Sea unreservedly. Each issue has 20 pages in the middle which act as an unofficial programme for the game in question. This is funny, angry, joyous and nostalgic and one of, if not the best, in the Premier League. The other fanzines on offer could probably be classified as above averaget.

## TRAVEL

**NEAREST RAILWAY STATION:** Barking
(0171 928 5100 — Liverpool St Enquiries)

**NEAREST TUBE STATION:**
Upton Park (District Line)

As with Crystal Palace, avoid the temptation to get out at the stop bearing the club's name.

**BUS:** London Transport (0171 222 1234) Any of the following buses will take you to the ground: 5, 15, 15B, 58, 58A, 104, 147, 162, 238.

## BY CAR:

**NORTH:** M11 into London, at the end of which turn right onto the A12 (signposted Wanstead/Leytonstone). After one mile turn left into Blake Hall Road. Just under 0.75 mile later the road forks left towards East Ham Memorial Hospital; at this point continue straight into Centre Road. At the T-junction turn left, then take the fourth right into Green Street, and the ground is one mile on the left.

**EAST:** A13 into London. Turn right at the crossroads with the A117 and left after one mile into Barking Road (A124). Continue for 0.75 mile, then turn right into Green Street and the ground is immediately on the right.

**SOUTH:** Pick up the A206 in London, and cross the river via the Blackwall Tunnel. Once through the tunnel, turn right onto the A13 (signposted Canning Town). After 0.5 mile there is a roundabout; take the second exit onto the A124 Barking Road (signposted Plaistow). 1.5 miles later turn left into Green Street and the ground is immediately on the right.

**WEST:** M40, A40, A40(M). At the end of the A40(M) pick up the A501 and continue on this road past Euston and King's Cross, then follow the signs for Shoreditch and Whitechapel. When in Whitechapel take the A13 (signposted Limehouse and Canning Town), then at the roundabout in Canning Town take the second exit onto the A124 Barking Road (signposted Plaistow), then as south.

**PARKING:** Street parking. Alternatively there is a small car park off Green Street in Queens Road, near Upton Park tube station.

## FUTURE DEVELOPMENTS

Last year the club indicated that it intended to build a new West Stand (which would take the capacity to 36,000) but the plans are at an early stage and the only thing that will be changing in the closed season is that the club will be installing undersoil heating for the pitch.

## OTHER INFORMATION

If you fancy a pint before the match The Queen's, the Duke of Edinburgh and the Anne Boleyn are all definite home pubs. It has been suggested that the Boleyn Tavern is OK for visitors, but it is hardly a relaxing place.

For grub there is only one place to go — the Cassettaris Café on the Barking Road — top dollar fry ups (albeit a little pricey) but it is the place where all the West Ham old boys used to go and plot the downfall of West Germany in 1966. If you want jellied eels, pie & mash and the like then try Nathan's, although expect to queue.

Inside the ground, food is served by a bunch of friendly people. The food can probably best be described as being inoffensive; typical of the whole day, though it isn't that cheap.

Finally after the dancing hammer mascot and the electronic scoreboard with its surreal messages, West Ham are proud occasionally to offer for your delight and delectation 'The Hammerettes' — a cheerleading group which manages not only to fail to lead any cheers but rather seems to make the home fans take a sudden interest in their shoes/programme/that little bit of dirt they've got under their fingernails.

*Total Football* **Experience Rating: 60**

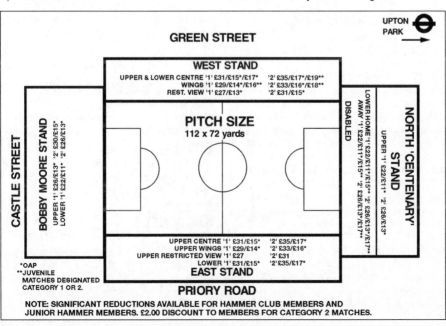

NOTE: SIGNIFICANT REDUCTIONS AVAILABLE FOR HAMMER CLUB MEMBERS AND JUNIOR HAMMER MEMBERS. £2.00 DISCOUNT TO MEMBERS FOR CATEGORY 2 MATCHES.

# WIGAN ATHLETIC

**ADDRESS:** Springfield Park
Wigan
Lancashire WN6 7BA

**TELEPHONE No:** 01942 244433
**TICKET OFFICE:** 01942 244433
**FAX:** 01942 494654
**CLUBCALL:** 0891 12 16 55
**WEB SITE:**
http://home.clara.net/ajhudson/
(unofficial)
**NICKNAME:** Latics
**RECORD ATTENDANCE:**
27,500 v Hereford United
FA Cup 2nd 12 December 1951 (D 1-1)
And for the collectors of footballing trivia amongst you,
Wigan were, in 1978, the last team to be elected to the
league rather than be promoted.

**CLUB COLOURS:**
**HOME:** Shirts: Blue with White side panels;
Shorts: Blue with White trim;
Socks: Blue with White stripes
**AWAY:** Shirts: White with Blue side panels;
Shorts: Blue with White side panels;
Socks: Blue with three White stripes

**KIT SPONSORS:** JJB Sports
**MANUFACTURERS:** Adidas

## GROUND INFO

To be honest, along with Bloomfield Road, Springfield
Park is probably the most dilapidated stadium in the
country, and perhaps the only one to have fencing at the
back of the terraces rather than the front. The terraces
loop in a semi-circle away from the pitch and are open to
the elements. As the ground is at the top of a hill, this
tends to mean that you have a Siberian wind whipping
around you even in mid-August. On all other days,
however, it is worth considering paying a little bit extra
and claiming one of the seats in the Phoenix Stand which
offers respite from the weather, and the opportunity for
any sadists to have a particularly good view of their
fellow supporters suffering. In truth the Phoenix Stand is
not brilliant, although the club has recently spent money
on it. In the toilets (which are just as you imagine them
to be) there is a sign that they are protected by Pier
Security Limited, although quite what there is in them
that warrants such attention is difficult to ascertain. Away
fans are also welcomed in the Cable Northwest family
stand (space in which can either be pre-booked or
obtained on the day). The club offers absolutely excellent
concessions in all parts of the ground (so there's no
excuse for you not to make your children suffer as well).
Having made various adverse comments about the
ground, I do have to say that I'll miss it when it goes, and
while the JJB Stadium is without doubt a massive leap
forward for a club that appears to be going places, if you
haven't been to Springfield Park then make sure you visit
in 1998-9 and say goodbye to 100 years of tradition.

**CAPACITY:** Stands: 1,128; Terrace: 6,338;
Total: 7,466

**AWAY FANS:** Shevington Road End: 1,467;
Phoenix Stand: 263; Total: 1,730
**DISABLED FACILITIES:** There is a cabin at
the ground which is used for disabled supporters, plus a
section of the terracing (which is open to the elements),
although the cabin only has room enough for six, plus
their helpers. Admission is free for disabled fans and one
helper. When you pre-book your space, organise any
parking requirements that you might have. There are no
matchday commentaries for the visually impaired
available.

**PROGRAMME:** £1.50
Came on in leaps and bounds in 1997-8 and, although it
still is very much a better read for home fans than
visitors, you will easily find enough to keep you going
through half-time.

**FANZINES:**
*The Latic Fanatic*                                    £1
One of the many indicators of where the real balance of
power lies within the town is that the most stinging
attacks are not directed at other local football clubs, but
at Wigan Rugby League Club, although several Wigan
fans I spoke to expressed a desire that the publication
should be less 'lightweight' in its abuse of 'proper'
football teams.

## TRAVEL

**NEAREST RAILWAY STATION:** Wigan
North Western (01942 242231)
Wigan Wallgate station is also situated directly opposite
North Western.

**BUS:** Wigan Central bus station (01942 287811)
The ground is a good 15min walk from the town centre,
so if you want to avoid this, take a 625 which stops on
Springfield Road by the ground.

**BY CAR:**
**NORTH/WEST:** M6 to J27. Take the A5209 to Wigan
(Shevington) and after 0.25 mile turn right onto the
B5206. After a further mile turn left and about 4.5 miles
up the road turn left again into Springfield Road for the
ground.
**SOUTH:** M6 to J25 then take the A49 to Wigan. Turn
left into Robin Park Road and continue into Scot Lane.

Turn right at the third set of traffic lights into Woodhouse Lane, then left at the traffic lights into Springfield Road.

**EAST:** Take the A557 into the town centre and take a left turn into Robin Park Road, then as south.

If, like myself on a recent visit, you find that you have left your directions at home then the best thing to do is ask a policeman. With any luck, you may hit upon the same one that I did who responded 'I could tell you, but it's far too complicated; here let me take you instead'. Whereupon he leapt into his transit, drove round the back streets of the town with me in hot pursuit for about 10min before parking up and telling me that I was in the best street for getting away from, and wishing me an enjoyable afternoon.

If you have to ask anyone you will have to emphasise that it's the football ground you want to go to and not the rugby.

**PARKING:** The parking at the ground is for permit holders only, but there is plenty of on-street parking in the area.

## FUTURE DEVELOPMENT

First things first: it was announced in mid-April that Wigan would play their last season before moving into their new home at the JJB Stadium at Robin Park and not Central Park (home of Wigan Warriors RLFC) as had previously been suggested. From August 1999 the club will take up residence at the new JJB Stadium at Robin Park. The stadium is named after chairman Dave Whelan's sports chain, a move you feel that has been undertaken not to massage Whelan's ego but because he sees at as another way he can invest more money in the club. The new stadium will be state of the art, with a 25,000 all-seater capacity as well as all the leisure/general facilities normally associated with such a development.

## OTHER INFORMATION

The saying that Northerners are the friendliest people in the world has often been disputed by football supporters, although in Wigan it does stand up to stronger examination than in many other places. On every visit to the place I genuinely find myself overwhelmed by the open, helpful and kind nature of the townsfolk and fans, for whom nothing seems too much trouble, and whose personalities make up for the lack of amenities at the ground and make a trip to Springfield Park far more enjoyable than to certain all-seater stadia with all mod cons. Everyone at the club works at making your visit a good one, from the chairman, who ensures that away fans have the same concessions as home supporters, to the people in the tea hut who actually look as if they are happy being there.

If you like a pint then either stroll up from the bus station and pop in at the Old Pear Tree, the Colliers Arms, the Guardians Inn, the Brickmakers Arms or the Springfield before you reach the ground, or walk down the path behind the away entrance to the ground for the Prince Of Wales, Traditional or Belle Vue. For food the chip shop by the Guardians shuts at about 1.15pm on matchdays and so a better bet is a hot pie from the corner shop on Meadow Street, which not only tastes excellent and is cheap (about 60p) but is also served by a really friendly woman who will tell you amongst other things of an excellent short-cut to Wigan Pier, which is also very useful for avoiding the town centre at the end of a match. Other than that, the meat and potato pie at the ground is worth eating, and the tea is hot and strong. If you fancy a spot of sightseeing then undoubtedly this means a trip to the famous Wigan Pier. This area has been developed quite a lot recently, with the Orwell pub being worth a visit.

*Total Football* **Experience Rating: 91**

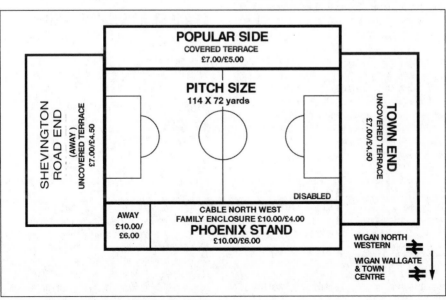

# WIMBLEDON

**ADDRESS:** Selhurst Park Stadium
London SE25 6PY

The sharp-eyed among you may have noted that Wimbledon's postcode differs from that of Crystal Palace. This is not a typo (at least not on my part) but the way the addresses appear in the club programmes, as the club offices are sited at sufficiently different parts of the ground to cause the anomaly.

**TELEPHONE No:** 0181 771 2233
**TICKET OFFICE:** 0181 771 8841
**FAX:** 0181 768 0641
**CLUBCALL:** 0891 12 11 75
**NICKNAME:** The Crazy Gang
**RECORD ATTENDANCE:** 30,115 v

Manchester United Prem Lge 9 May 1993 (L 1-2) Prior to the move to Selhurst the club's record attendance was the 18,000 who turned up for the Dons' Amateur Cup Tie against those crowd-pullers from HMS *Victory* on 2 March 1935 (Wimbledon won 3-0).

## CLUB COLOURS:

**HOME**: Shirts: Dark Blue, Yellow trim;
Shorts: Dark Blue, Yellow trim;
Socks: Dark Blue
**AWAY:** Shirts: Red; Shorts: Red; Socks: Red

**KIT SPONSORS:** Elonex
**MANUFACTURERS:** Lotto

## GROUND INFO

The boom in attendances over recent years seems to have passed the Dons by and, to be honest, this is a ground that if you don't manage to get a ticket for, then you are not really trying. Away fans are (officially) sited in the Arthur Wait Stand, which weighs in at a hefty £20 for what are, to be honest, very ordinary (and that is being polite) facilities. There are concessions available, however. For quite a few matches last season the Top Tier of the Holmesdale Road was not opened — it is annoying to think that the Dons could also make this available to visiting supporters and thus give them not only a better view of the game but also £6 change in their pocket — but the club says this is not possible for safety reasons.

For some games (especially mid-week ones) the atmosphere at the ground can be very down, with games taking place in an eerie half-silence and the players obscenities clearly audible. This has the net effect of making the matches seem not quite real.

**CAPACITY:** Stands: 26,400; Terrace: Nil

**AWAY FANS:** A minimum of 2,987 seats are available in Blocks X, Y and Z of the Arthur Wait Stand. Up to 9,741 are available in this stand for visiting fans.

The Whitehorse Lane Stand (capacity 2,245) can also be made available if demand so requires.

One thing that is worth remembering is that the toilets at Selhurst Park are not one of the nicest places to spend your time.

**DISABLED FACILITIES:** There are 28 spaces available in the Arthur Wait Stand and 20 in the Holmesdale Road Stand. Parking facilities are available in the Sainsbury's car park. Admission for disabled supporters is free, with helpers paying a nominal charge. Pre-booking of these spaces is required; contact the club at least two weeks in advance of a match on the box office number. Twelve seats are available with headphone commentaries for the partially sighted.

**PROGRAMME:** £2.00

Not too bad, although nothing to get over-excited about.

## FANZINES:

| | |
|---|---|
| *Route 1* | £1 |
| *Yidaho!* | £1 |
| *Sour Grapes* | 50p |
| *Hoof The Ball Up* | £1 |

There has been something of a cull within the ranks of Wimbledon fanzines with four that were mentioned last year apparently no longer being produced (although 1997-8 did see the birth of *Route 1*). You never really seem to see that many around. *HTBU* has improved significantly over the last 12 months (and at least is easy to find being sold) and is a good place to keep up with the latest new move plans, the humour content has also increased which means it probably just shades it as best fanzine from *Yidaho!*.

## TRAVEL

### NEAREST RAILWAY STATION:

Norwood Junction, Thornton Heath, Selhurst (0171 928 5100 — Victoria Enquiries)

The three stations are all about the same distance from the ground. Norwood Junction seems to have the best service. See also CRYSTAL PALACE.

**BUS:** London Transport (0171 222 1234)

### BY CAR:

**NORTH:** M1. Take the A406 North Circular Road (heading west) to Chiswick Roundabout (just before you get there you will see Gunnersbury Parkon your right). Take the third exit at the roundabout onto Chiswick High Road, then first left onto the A205 (signposted Kew). After two miles you reach a T-junction at which you should turn left (signposted Putney). Continue until the road merges with the A3, then a mile later turn right onto the A214 (signposted Tooting and Streatham). When in Streatham, turn right onto the A23 Streatham High Road. After one mile turn left into Green Lane (B273) which becomes Parchmore Road. At the bottom of the road turn left onto the High Street. Go straight over at the crossroads with the A212 into Whitehorse Lane and the ground is 300yd on the right.

**EAST:** M25, A20 (signposted London) After approx four miles turn left onto the A224 (signposted St Mary Cray). After three miles turn onto the A232 Spur Road and follow this until you see Shirley Park Golf Club; then right onto the A215 Shirley Road. Turn right again at the top of this road, then first left into Spring Lane (A215). After 1.5 miles turn left onto the B266, and the ground is 0.5 mile on the left.

**SOUTH:** A23 into London, following the signs for Thornton Heath, turn right onto the A235. (NB: you need to go through a small one-way system; this is no more than an overblown roundabout really.) Once on the A235 turn immediately left onto the B266 Brigstock Road which becomes the High Street, then as north.

**WEST:** M4 to Chiswick, then as north.

**PARKING:** There is space for 500 cars at the Sainsbury's car park just off Whitehorse Lane by the ground. There is also plenty of street parking. NB: Because of the tram system being installed in Croydon expect serious congestion in the area.

## FUTURE DEVELOPMENTS

The proposed move to Dublin was scuppered last year by the FAI. Merton Borough Council did offer the club the use of the greyhound track as a ground, but with a very limited capacity — the majority of which would have been on the bends and miles away from the action — this has been rejected. Hull City offered to ground share at a new redeveloped stadium but this has been (sensibly) rejected and at the moment the biggest hopes are either that the Dons and London Irish RUFC may get together and redevelop the Rugby club's Sunbury ground (which currently holds 12,000) or that Wimbledon may strike out alone and develop a site near Gatwick Airport.

Whatever happens (or doesn't happen), expect a lot more red herrings this year and the club to still be playing at Selhurst come 1999/2000.

## OTHER INFORMATION

The Prince George on Whitehorse Road is a good pub, as is the Cherry Trees by Norwood Junction (see Crystal Palace entry for more details) and for grub check out the Chinese chip shop on Whitehorse Road. This does a fine sausage in batter, and chips in brown paper bags which are spot on.

The club revels in its 'Crazy Gang' spirit and, to be fair, there is a lot to be said for this. It has consistently produced great players, who it has sold on for huge profits leading everyone to expect the team to crumble, only for more youngsters to come through the ranks to fill the gaps. The supporters too are an excellent bunch and all the ones I've met have been only too happy to enjoy a couple of pints and put the footballing world to rights. However, it is important not to get too misty-eyed about 'little Wimbledon'. In my opinion, they overcharge for what they offer and while they seem happy to say 'It's not our ground so it's not our problem', that doesn't make it any easier for the visiting supporter and perhaps goes some way to explaining why they are not capturing 'floating' football fans. The club does genuinely believe that it is improving its image a lot, but for the (over)paying customer, there is still a long way to go before this will ever be considered a good day out.

Given all this, the weird thing is you may well end up liking Wimbledon and Sam Hammam, and are perhaps prepared to give them more of a break than you would other teams.

*Total Football* **Experience Rating: 54**

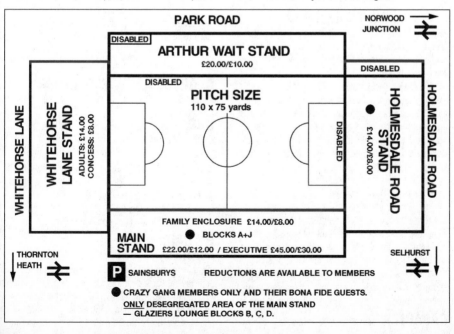

# WOLVERHAMPTON WANDERERS

**ADDRESS:** Molineux Stadium
Waterloo Road
Wolverhampton
WV1 4QR

**TELEPHONE No:** 01902 655000

**TICKET OFFICE:** 01902 653653

**FAX:** 01902 687003

**CLUBCALL:** 0891 12 11 03

**WEB SITE:** www.wolves.co.uk
(official)

**E-MAIL:** info@wolves.co.uk

**NICKNAME:** The Wolves

**RECORD ATTENDANCE:** 61,315 v
Liverpool FA Cup 5th 11 February 1939 (W 4-1)

## CLUB COLOURS:
**HOME:** Shirts: Old Gold;
Shorts: Black; Socks: Old Gold/Black
**AWAY:** Shirts: White/Teal; Shorts: Teal;
Socks: Teal

**CLUB SPONSORS:** Goodyear Tyres

**MANUFACTURERS:** Puma

## GROUND INFO

Away supporters get either the Jack Harris Stand or the John Ireland Stand Lower Tier, depending on the level of support. Leg room is poor and if you are 6ft or over you will feel cramped.

The new Molineux may not have the atmosphere of the old place but of the new all-seater super-stadia this probably comes as close as any to re-creating the noise. If you can't get a ticket for the away end then your best bet is probably the centre of the Billy Wright Stand, but expect a cool reception if this is where you end up. Mind you, getting in the stand is a feat in itself given the number of season tickets the club sells!

Many matches are either sell-outs or near sell-outs which, given the lack of success over recent years, is a tribute to either the loyalty or madness of the home supporters. In view of the high level of ticket sales, it is worth ensuring that you have one before you travel. If you can't obtain a ticket, you may find ticket touts on Waterloo Road towards the Billy Wright Stand (although as this is an illegal activity, I obviously have never used them myself).

**CAPACITY:** Stands: 28,525; Terrace: Nil

**AWAY FANS:** Jack Harris Stand (Block S): 1,500;
(or Blocks); John Ireland Stand;
Lower Tier: 2,971
Note that in the past it has been club policy only to allow concessions on pre-purchased tickets.

**DISABLED FACILITIES:** Generally first-class facilities; there are a total of 90 places in the Stan Cullis and Billy Wright Stands, access being either via the wheelchair lift or six specially designed ramps. There are 16 disabled toilets so, for once, you can expect not to have to queue interminably at half-time; other grounds take note. Admission is free for disabled supporters and £8.00 for helpers. On a slightly less positive note, the club advises that match commentaries are only available for home supporters and that although parking is available, this is for pass holders only.

**PROGRAMME:** £1.80
The home fans rate this publication quite highly, but as a visitor you may well find it does nothing for you.

## FANZINES:
*A Load Of Bull* £1
Get it right, *ALOB* is Bully first and Wolves second; one of the most pointless tasks they must do is having a player of the season vote! However, there is also a generous smattering of anti-Baggies and anti-whoever the Wolves' manager is at the time of writing in its pages as well. I have got to say I've got a bit of a soft spot for it; it may not be the best fanzine you'll ever read, but there's enough to raise a smile, and at least it reminds you of a time (sadly, long gone for many of us) when fans could really build up a relationship with players.

## TRAVEL

### NEAREST RAILWAY STATION:
Wolverhampton (0121 643 2711 — Birmingham New Street Enquiries)

**BUS:** Wolverhampton bus station (0121 200 2700 — Centro hotline)
The bus station is about 300yd away from the railway station, and although it is only 0.5 mile or so from the ground, it can be worth taking a bus just to avoid having to cross a couple of very busy roads.

If you do opt to go by bus, take either a 503 or 504 (one every 10-15min) from stop R.

### BY CAR:
**NORTH:** M6 to J12. Turn right onto the A5, then left after one mile onto the A449 Stafford Road. Continue until you see the Goodyear factory, go straight over the next two roundabouts until (1.5 miles past the factory) you get to the Five Ways roundabout. Take the third exit into Waterloo Road, and the ground is 0.25 mile on your

left.

**EAST/SOUTH:** M6 to J10. Take the A454 (signposted Wolverhampton) and continue on this road until you pass Wolverhampton railway station. Take the second right into Waterloo Road and the ground is 0.25 mile on the right.

**WEST:** M54 to J2. Turn right onto the Stafford Road (A449) and continue until you see the Goodyear factory, then as north.

**PARKING:** The car park at the ground is for permit holders only. There is a car park at the supermarket near the ground, but this is for the supermarket's shoppers only and is protected by CCTV cameras looking for football fans. There are a few small car parks around, but use your common-sense; for example, there is one by the Goal Posts PH right by the ground but this is frequented by a lot of Wolves fans. If you want on-street parking then a good bet is to drive past the aforementioned supermarket and turn onto North Road where there are normally a few places around.

One good thing if you park around the ground is that the police have really got the traffic flows sorted out, which means you can get away and onto the open road easily enough at the end of the match.

## FUTURE DEVELOPMENTS

Nothing major, although the club is continually looking at the service it offers, and if necessary improving it.

## OTHER INFORMATION

The pubs around the ground such as the Goal Posts, and the Hatherton Arms are generally very much the haunt of staunch Wolves fans. The town centre offers a wider (safer) choice and is about a 10-15min walk away.

The toilets at Molineux are large and clean. However, in a classic example of a good idea gone wrong, there is a child's urinal trough which means that kids can go to the loo without having to stand on tiptoes or anything. In reality, because not only kids use it, what actually happens is that while little Johnny is going to the toilet an adult stands next to him. The increased drop for the adult causes 'splashback' and the poor kid ends up getting half drowned (not a nice picture but true).

The food in the ground varies; the pies are excellent and the tea hot and tasty. The burgers are OK'ish but are spoiled by having way too much raw onion on them. Equally the serving counter is a bit small which can cause delays.

Keep an eye out (well you can't really miss them) for the two 'videoboards' which have a horrible computer graphic wolf/mouse type creature trying to animate the fans and perhaps not surprisingly failing miserably. All in all, Molineux is impressive and the (inordinately patient) crowd makes for a good atmosphere, though for an indefinable reason there is something not quite 'right' about the ground and I didn't have the 'great' day out I should have done.

Finally I have got to say that I have come across plenty of horrible merchandising during my travels this season, but the prize for worst of all must go to the 'Wolfie' aftershave sold at the club shop in Molineux. Keep away from this at all costs as somebody managed to spill a couple of drops on me when I was last at the ground and the aroma lingered for weeks and had the effect of sending dogs running away from me howling with their tails between their legs. Horrible!

*Total Football* **Experience Rating: 73**

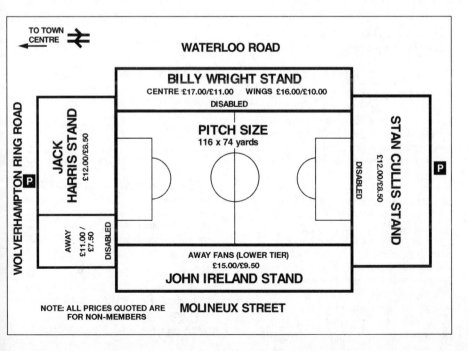

TO TOWN CENTRE

WATERLOO ROAD

**BILLY WRIGHT STAND**
CENTRE £17.00/£11.00    WINGS £16.00/£10.00
DISABLED

**JACK HARRIS STAND** £12.00/£8.50

AWAY £11.00 / £7.50    DISABLED

WOLVERHAMPTON RING ROAD

**PITCH SIZE**
116 x 74 yards

**STAN CULLIS STAND** £12.00/£8.50
DISABLED

AWAY FANS (LOWER TIER)
£15.00/£9.50
**JOHN IRELAND STAND**

NOTE: ALL PRICES QUOTED ARE FOR NON-MEMBERS    **MOLINEUX STREET**

# WREXHAM

**ADDRESS:** The Racecourse Ground
Mold Road
Wrexham
LL11 2AH

**TELEPHONE No:** 01978 262129

**TICKET OFFICE:** 01978 262129

**FAX:** 01978 357821

**CLUBCALL:** 0891 12 16 42

**WEB SITE:** http://www.csm.uwe.ac.uk/~klhender/wxm/index.html

— 'The Webbed Robin' (unofficial). Note: there is a Welsh version of this site on:
http://www.csm.uwe.ac.uk/~klhender/wxm/indecs.html

**NICKNAME:** The Robins

**RECORD ATTENDANCE:**

34,445 v Manchester United FA Cup 4th  26  January 1957 (L 0-5)
Proving that even in the 'good old days' of serious press coverage, journalists were quite happy to throw up a few stereotypes; the headline of one of the 'quality' papers about this match was 'Welshmen too excited to even sing'.

## CLUB COLOURS:

**HOME:** Shirts: Red with White trim; Shorts: White; Socks: Red

**AWAY:** Shirts: Gold & Navy; Shorts: Gold & Navy; Socks: Gold & Navy

**KIT SPONSORS:** Wrexham Lager

**MANUFACTURERS:** Glory Years

## GROUND INFO

Although visitors are encouraged to join their fellow supporters in the Marston Stand (hence the concessions), they can also get admission into the Yale Stand Family Section at reduced rates. The Marston Stand has two massive pillars which if you are not careful can lead to a nightmare view. Either position yourself directly behind the goal, or in the first couple of rows as far to the left/right of the main block of seating as you can. The Marston Paddock wasn't used very much in 1997/98 and as you enter the stand and climb the stairs to your seat you can see loads of wrought metalwork and other assorted rubble which has been dumped underneath the stand. Still closed from 1994/95 was the Mold Stand, which, although the club has tried to hide it by putting boarding around it, is still an eyesore. Its closure wasn't met with too much sorrow as it used to swing in a semi-circle away from the ground, meaning that if you were sat at the furthest point from the pitch, the players appeared to be nothing more than specks on

a distant horizon. The home Kop is quite impressive and is reminiscent of the Fulwell End at Sunderland's old ground at Roker Park. However, the toilets here (as with the Marston Stand) were too horrible for words on my visit to the ground — if I say to take a surf board with you, you'll get the general picture.

**CAPACITY:** Stands: 4,200 Terrace: 7,400; Total: 11,600

**AWAY FANS:** Marston Stand: 2,200; Marston Paddock*: 650; Total: 2,850
* If open

**DISABLED FACILITIES:** There is a little corrugated hut in the corner of the ground between the Marston Stand and the Mold Road Stand into which about half a dozen wheelchair-bound supporters can fit. If you are not one of the six you can still go, but you will be sat along the touchline and exposed to the elements. Helpers are provided with a chair, but this is little comfort. Still, at least you get a warm welcome, you can get a parking space right next to the ground, and enjoy a cup of tea and biscuits at the club house. Away fans are requested to pre-book their visit. Admission is free for disabled supporters and £9 for helpers.

There are no match commentary facilities for the blind.

**PROGRAMME:** £2.00

On the minus side the cost has gone up by 33% but more positively it is an excellent effort and has, I believe, won Second Division programme of the year for the last couple of seasons. When you first look at it the *Robins Review* is just like another typical programme, but every time you open it there seem to be bits and pieces that you've missed and which will keep you going for a little longer.

## FANZINES:

*The Sheeping Giant*               50p
Not baa'd at all (yes, I know it's a crap joke, but I couldn't help myself). Don't expect a politically correct publication; this has actually got a nice in-yer-face feel of the terraces about it.

## TRAVEL

### NEAREST RAILWAY STATION:

Wrexham General (0151 709 9696 — Liverpool Lime Street Enquiries)
There are two stations in the town: Wrexham General, which is adjacent to the ground, and Wrexham Central which is about 1.5 miles away.

**BUS:** King Street bus station (01978 363760)
Buses 11, 18a and 21 run from the town centre to the ground, although we are not talking the longest of walks.

### BY CAR:

**NORTH/WEST:** Take the A483 and Wrexham By-

Pass to the junction with the A541. Branch left and at the roundabout follow signs for Mold. At T-junction turn right into Regent Street which leads into Mold Road and the ground.

**EAST:** Take the A525 or A534 into Wrexham, then follow signs for A541 (Mold), then as north.

**SOUTH:** M54 to J3, then the A41 to Whitchurch. Take the A525 (signposted Wrexham), then as east. This is a scenic route that takes you through such quaintly named villages as Cock Bank, but it's guaranteed you'll be tearing your hair out when your progress is reduced to 5mph, stuck behind a tractor for miles with little or no chance of overtaking.

**PARKING:** Parking is available at Wrexham General station, or in the college grounds near the stadium. Some street parking is available in the vicinity of the ground. The car park at the ground is for permit holders only.

## FUTURE DEVELOPMENTS

The club has been talking about a redevelopment for quite a while, although the only thing that seems to be happening is that the proposed price of the changes has been steadily increasing (£43 million at the last count). However, over the past few months things have begun to firm up, and the club advises that work is due to commence on a new 4,000-seat stand in the not too distant future, which it is hoped will be up and fully operational within 12 months. Naturally as this side of the ground is not currently open, there will be no impact on either home or away fans during construction. Once this has been completed the club will assess what area of the Racecourse to tackle next.

## OTHER INFORMATION

When you enter the ground you may wonder what the cricket pavilion is in the corner, and why all the players waiting to come in to bat are wearing woolly hats and scarves. The answer in fact is that this is the Turf pub balcony overlooking the pitch. From here pub regulars can watch the match for free. A word of warning, don't mention how funny/unique this is to anyone at the club as they get very upset about the whole thing.

The Turf is actually where the football club was founded in 1872. Both home and away fans are welcomed across its portals to drink in the bar which — although fairly large — is generally heaving on a matchday. Alternatives include the Plas Coch, which is also near the ground, or if you are happy to walk 10-15min to get into the town centre to either the Horse & Jockey (a bit small and poky) or the Talbot. If you are a complete wuss, take the road to Chester and continue for about five miles till you get to the Grosvenor, which is just inside the English border. Even further afield is the Mill Tavern in Flint (about 15 miles away on the coast) which, I believe, serves a very decent pint (and which has a Wrexham supporters' travel club attached to it).

For food, The Chippies Open which is left through the archway just past the Horse & Jockey serves good food and excellent fat chips. However, as the words fish and chips go together, so do the words slow and service. If you don't fancy the walk, there are burger vans by the ground. Once inside, the pies are reasonable, but the tea is bitter and the Bovril grainy.

Away fans are well treated, with police and stewards letting you get on with your own thing. If you come from England then don't worry about the fact that a piano version 'Men Of Harlech' is blasted out over the tannoy as the teams take the pitch, as the atmosphere isn't massively anti-English (the town is even called Wrecsam, making it one of the few names in the Welsh language that foreigners can understand). All the same, it is probably best not to mention that you'll be spending the rest of the weekend in your holiday home, whilst enjoying a pre-match pint with the locals.

*Total Football* **Experience Rating: 68**

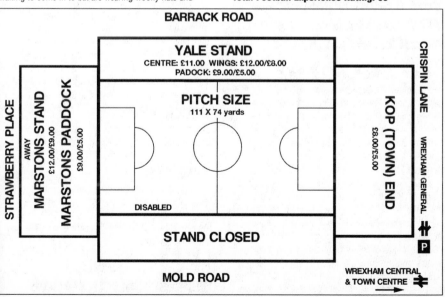

# WYCOMBE WANDERERS

**ADDRESS:** Adams Park
Hillbottom Road
Sands, High Wycombe
HP12 4HJ
**TELEPHONE No:** 01494 472100
**TICKET OFFICE:** 01494 441118
**FAX:** 01494 527633
**CLUBCALL:** 09003 44 68 55
**WEB SITE:**
http://www.wycombewanderers.co.uk
(official)
http://www.ndirect.co.uk/~chairboys/
(unofficial)
**NICKNAME:** The Chairboys,
The Blues
## RECORD ATTENDANCE:
15,850 v St Albans City FA Am Cup 4th 25 February
1950 (W 4-1); 9,007 v West Ham FA Cup 3rd
7 January 1995 (L 0-2)
The first of these matches was at the club's old Loakes
Park Ground; the second at Adams Park.

## CLUB COLOURS:
**HOME:** Shirts: Sky Blue and Navy quarters;
Shorts: Navy; Socks: Navy
**AWAY:** Shirts: Yellow and Navy quarters;
Shorts: Yellow; Socks: Yellow
**THIRD:** Shirts: Red; Shorts: Red; Socks: Red

**CLUB & SHIRT SPONSORS:** Verco
**KIT SPONSORS:** Mizuno
**MANUFACTURERS:** Mizuno

## GROUND INFO
The changes to Adams Park over the last three years have
been incredible. Where once there was only minimal
seating, only one side of the ground remains terraced.
The club has retained the character of the ground by
building one large stand — the 4,990-seat ServisPak
Stand — rather than just standard 'same size'
constructions.

In 1997-8 admission to the away seats rose by £2 for
adults, £3 for juniors, and £5 for OAPs, and I've got to
say that a trip to Adams Park isn't the cheap day out it
once was. Also when dealing with pricing it is worth
noting that in 1997-8 there were over 50 different charges
depending on what part of the ground you were in,
whether you were an adult, OAP or junior and whether
you bought tickets on the day or in advance. While there
are always going to be differences in charges, this does
seem excessive. (The club has said that this will improve

for 1998-9.)

Junior concessions for away fans (and for many home
fans) are none too generous at just £2 less than standard
charges. I've got to be honest and say that, in all my
visits to Adams Park, I have never found the club to be
anything other than friendly and incredibly helpful. The
club says that and recent problems of disabled
supporters being moved for no apparent reasons and of
the club allowing (or at least not stopping) away fans
who had problems with getting into their own sections
going into the Axa Equity & Law Terrace (which is
designated for home fans only) should no longer happen.
You should still be aware that you can see a decent
proportion of any match for free from the wooded hill
which lies behind the stand (although the club says you
will be moved on by the police).

**CAPACITY:** Stands: 7,306; Paddock: 496;
Covered Terrace: 2,195; Total: 9,997

**AWAY FANS:** The Roger Vere Stand: 1,039;
Amersham & Wycombe Stand
(Blocks V & H): 333; Total: 1,372
Also 500 seats in Family Stands with
concessions
The RV Stand offers a decent, unobstructed view, with
reasonable leg room. One area that it does fall down on
slightly is the low number of aisles leading up the stand.
This means that if you want to get a half-time cuppa
slightly early then you have to disturb a lot of people (and
there is not enough room for them to just swing their legs
and let you get past, they will have to stand).

**DISABLED FACILITIES:** There are 50
places (plus 50 helpers) at Adams Park in the Lower Tier
of the ServisPak Stand. Away fans are more than
welcome but must pre-book (as must home supporters).
The cost of admission is £5 for disabled fans and £10 for
helpers (£6 Junior/OAPs). Match commentaries (five
seats) for the visually impaired are also available and
must be pre-booked. There is reasonable parking (13
spaces) at the ground for disabled supporters and it does
not appear that this can be pre-booked, so if you want to
get a space then get down to the ground early.

**PROGRAMME:** £2.00
Last season's effort wasn't quite as good as the previous
year's although there were enough general interest items
to get you through half-time.

## FANZINES:
| | |
|---|---|
| The Adams Family | 60p |
| The Wanderer | 50p |
| One-One | 50p |
Go for TTAF if you can find it, but I have heard it is no
longer in existance.

## TRAVEL
## NEAREST RAILWAY STATION:
High Wycombe (01494 441561)

**BUS:** Central bus station (01494 520941)
A couple of No 300 buses run from the town to the ground. These leave the railway station at 1.55 and 2.25 on matchdays — calling at the bus station 5min later — and prevent a long walk. They are also on hand to whisk fans back to the town after the match, but they do tend to get snarled up in the traffic.

## BY CAR:
If you are coming down the M40 then leave at J4, and follow the signs, taking the A4010. turn left at the first double mini-roundabout, then as north/south/east.

**NORTH/SOUTH/EAST:** M1, M25 westbound (signposted Heathrow), then M40 (signposted Oxford) to J4. Take the A4010 signposted Aylesbury. Go straight over three roundabouts (you should see signs for the ground). After you go over the third roundabout you will go down a longish hill at the bottom of which is a mini-roundabout. Take the first exit (very tight) into Lane End Road, continue to the next roundabout and go straight across, the road is now called Hillbottom Road, and at the top of it is the ground.

**WEST:** A40 towards High Wycombe. Turn right into Chapel Lane, right again at the second mini-roundabout into Lane End Road, then as north/south/east.

**PARKING:** There is a car park (720 spaces at £2) at the ground, and also places around the industrial units in Hillbottom Road. Be warned that the upper car park (which has the old Loakes Park gate at the front of it) is not tarmac. It has been improved through the laying of scalpings but can be slippery in places if wet. If you are reduced to street parking, and you don't arrive early, count on a walk of around half a mile. The nearest public car parks are in High Wycombe which is a couple of miles from the ground.

Be warned the ground is a nightmare to get away from after the match and count on at least a 20min delay if you are at the top end of Hillbottom Road.

# FUTURE DEVELOPMENTS
To be reviewed.

# OTHER INFORMATION
Away fans who are members of their side's supporters or travel club (and have passes to prove it) can buy day membership in the Vere Suite for £1. Given the lack of decent pubs in the vicinity, and the fact that they serve an excellent pint and good food here with a wide variety of choice including chips, it can be well worth the investment. Otherwise there is an off-licence at the junction of Hillbottom Road and Lane End Road or the Hourglass at the bottom of Lane End Road which is half a mile from the ground. It is a reasonable size, but if it gets packed the management seem happy enough for fans to take their drinks and stand in the car park (though it tends to be for home fans only).

There is a chip shop at the ground which is well above average and a cornucopia of mobiles on Hillbottom Road, which offer cholesterol for even the most discerning of appetites. Once actually in the ground the food is excellent, although the servery is small and it can take ages to get served.

Generally it has to be said that Wycombe remains an 'easy' away trip where you are likely to meet nothing but friendly fans and helpful club officials. However, there do appear to be some signs that this is changing — most notably if you look at the prices charged. Similarly (and I reiterate that this is through hearsay rather than personal experience) it appears that there can be problems with organisation if visiting supporters turn up in large numbers. Fans can only hope that Wycombe are not losing sight of what Saturday afternoons are meant to be all about and will return to the days of 1996-7 (and earlier) when this was one of the better days out of the season.

*Total Football* **Experience Rating: 77**

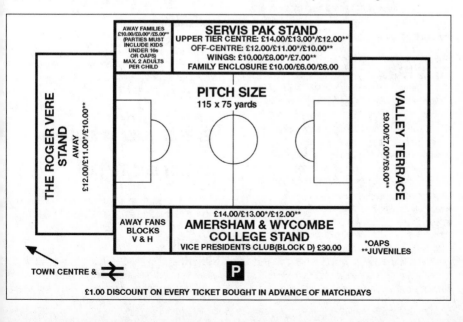

# YORK CITY

**ADDRESS:** Bootham Crescent
York
YO3 7AQ

**TELEPHONE No:** 01904 624447

**TICKET OFFICE:** 01904 624447

**FAX:** 01904 631457

**HOTLINE:** 0891 12 16 43

**NICKNAME:** The Minstermen

**RECORD ATTENDANCE:** 28,123 v
Huddersfield FA Cup 6th 5 March 1938 (D 0-0)

**CLUB COLOURS:**
**HOME:** Shirts: Red with Blue and White trim;
Shorts: Red with Blue and White trim;
Socks: Red/Blue and White hoops
**AWAY:** Shirts: White; Shorts: White; Socks: Navy

**KIT SPONSORS:** Portakabin

**MANUFACTURERS:** Admiral

## GROUND INFO

The first thing that strikes you when you arrive at Bootham Crescent is that it is one of the few grounds where the outside of the Main Stand is done up in a wooden mock-Tudor style (on stilts!). Obviously this has had a depressing effect on the PA announcer who is one of the most morose chaps I can remember hearing, with the (monotone) team changes etc being preceded by large sighs and silences.

Perhaps the most worrying thing about a visit to York is the fact that the ground is outside the city walls, so if the Vikings decide to have a pop at the place while your team are playing, you've had it!

**CAPACITY:** Stands: 3,679; Terrace: 5,309;
Total: 8,988

**AWAY FANS:** Pop Stand Section U: 336;
Grosvenor Road Terrace: 2.044; Total: 2,380
A real mixed bag here; let's get the bad points out of the way first:

• Most annoyingly the club has STILL got perimeter fencing around the away terrace — obviously the numerous incidents when visiting fans ran riot at the Grosvenor Road End remain fresh in the memories of the club (though you'd be hard pressed to find anyone else who could recall such occurrences).

• Secondly there is about three tons of wrought metalwork separating visiting and home fans in the Popular Stand which — along with the pillars in this stand — does not do much to improve the view. Note: if you do want to sit down you should go onto the terrace and pay a £1 transfer as there are no separate turnstiles.

• Finally the toilets on the terrace are of the trough

variety with no roof to protect you from the elements (although as the terrace itself is uncovered I suppose it just means you get a fraction wetter than you might have).

On the plus side, the £8.00 the club charges you to get in is amongst the cheapest you'll find and it does offer excellent concessions for children. The club also has a family section in the Main Stand and offers the use of a family room before and after a game.

In addition, the attitude of everyone at the club towards away supporters is excellent. Helpful and friendly, they will go out of their way to make sure you have a good time at Bootham Crescent, and for that reason alone you will find it easy to forgive them for the majority of the ground's shortcomings.

**DISABLED FACILITIES:** There are 18 places for disabled supporters at the front of the Main Stand, and although booking is not essential, due to the restricted capacity I would recommend it.

Admission for disabled fans is free, and for helpers it is £8.50. The club advises that there is a match commentary facility available. However, there are no parking facilities at the ground.

**PROGRAMME:** £1.80
At first glance it appears to be just full of adverts, but when you go through it you will find quite a lot to read (with more pages for 1998-9) (although, because it is printed in a very small font, it can be a bit headache inducing) with at least half a dozen articles which should be of interest to away fans. One nice touch is as well as having a match to remember — which invariably in other programmes is about the one time that the home side walloped the visiting team 7-0 in 1934 — they also redress the balance with a match to forget column.

**FANZINES:**
None on sale outside the ground though a steward did tell me that there was one available in the York end. However, as he put it 'Bloody hell, you'd be hard pressed to find a City fan who thought it was worthwhile reading never mind anybody else'.

## TRAVEL

**NEAREST RAILWAY STATION:**
York (01904 642155)

**NEAREST BUS STATION:**
Rider York (01904 624161)
There are no buses direct from the station to the ground; instead get either a number 8, 8a or 8b from Rougier Street (by the Tourist Information Centre).

**BY CAR:**
**NORTH:** A1, then the A59 until you cross a railway bridge. Two miles after this turn left into Water End, and at the next T-junction turn right (signposted City Centre).

0.5 mile further on turn left into Bootham Crescent.

**SOUTH:** A64, turning right after Buckles Inn onto the Outer Ring Road. Turn right onto the A19 (following City Centre signs), then 1.5 miles further on turn left into Bootham Crescent.

**EAST:** Get onto the Outer Ring Road, turn left onto the A19, then as south.

**WEST:** Get onto the Outer Ring Road, turn right onto the A19, then as south.

**PARKING:** There is parking at Marygate car park about 0.25 mile on the right after the turn-off to the ground. However, this is quite pricey and puts you at the back of the queue when it is time to go home.

The best bet is to park on the A19 itself; if you leave the car facing the direction you want to head in (and also on the correct side of the road) you can count on saving yourself around half an hour's queuing at the final whistle.

## FUTURE DEVELOPMENTS

None at present.

## OTHER INFORMATION

York is a great city filled with loads to do, lots of good eating/drinking places and very friendly people. If you can, it is well worth stopping a night (there are loads of B&Bs on Bootham Crescent) and sampling the nightlife. If you are just going for the football then drinkwise the pick of the pubs around the ground (ie on the A19 Clifton Road) are The Burton Stone, The White Horse (Thwaites), the Exhibition (John Smiths) or the Bootham Tavern (Tetleys) although if you just go through the wall into the city there is the Hole In The Wall (Mansfields) which is

very welcoming to visiting fans. For food you'll not do better than Polly's Pantry right by the ground. Definitely try one of Polly's beef, horseradish and gravy rolls, but anything from the menu is cheap, tasty and very filling (If you don't want to take my word for it ask the York first teamer who is regularly in on a Saturday settling his tab and eating there shortly before kick-off!!!) As with everyone in York Polly, her husband and their daughter are always up for a chat and a laugh and this is probably one of the top three places for a carryout nosebag in the country. The food inside the ground is pricier but equally tasty. The pies especially are worth a special mention. They are made by a local firm and combine just the right amount of filling with a perfect pastry. One small problem is that there is only one hut which means queues are inevitable, but at least it is within sight of the pitch so you can watch while you wait.

Vegetarians might like to note that there are quite a few good places in the city, the best of which is the Rubicon restaurant in Little Stonegate, which is about a 15min walk from the ground.

Having been fairly positive about York, there are two things that I feel the new visitor should be warned about. Firstly, it is full of people doing street theatre and every act shares — in my humble opinion — two characteristics: being that they are noisy and crap. Secondly, there are many little roads and alleyways in the city that have bizarre titles, so when visiting, should you find yourself up Hornby's Passage just remember it's only a name and nothing to do with the author of a well-known footballing book.

*Total Football* Experience Rating: 83

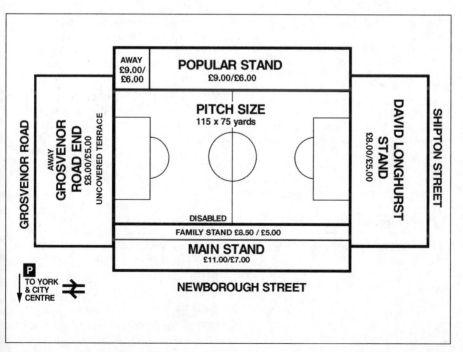

# WEMBLEY STADIUM

**ADDRESS:** Wembley Stadium
Wembley
Middlesex HA9 0DW
**TELEPHONE No:** 0181 902 8833
**TICKET OFFICE:** 0181 902 0902
**FAX:** 0181 900 1045
**INFOLINE:** 0891 60 1996
**NICKNAME:** Venue of the Legends
**RECORD ATTENDANCE:**
126,047 Bolton v West Ham (2-0) FA Cup Final 28 April 1923. And that's just the ones who paid! It's thought there were well over 200,000 in the ground.

## GROUND INFO

Prices for the 1998 Cup Final ranged from £17 to £65, with the Olympic Gallery at £115. Entry to the Olympic Gallery is via turnstiles E and H. There were also a number of restricted view tickets on sale at £15 and 'severely' restricted view on offer at £10. To be honest, if you are lucky enough to be going to see your team in a Wembley sell-out and either of the last two categories is the only ticket you can get, then buy it simply so that you don't miss out on the Wembley experience, but set your video so that at least you can watch the match when you get home.

If you are trying to work out whereabouts in the ground you'll be, turnstiles A-F serve the Tunnel End, and G-M the West End, while the Block Numbers are prefixed by a '1' for Lower Tier, '2' for Upper Tier and '3' for Olympic Gallery.

The seats at the front of the Lower Tier are virtually level with the pitch and have an inadequate rise between each row. In my opinion, the leg room here is laughable, and your seat will not have a back on it.

As a general rule of thumb, many fans in the red seats give up any thoughts of sitting to watch the match. The blue seats on the Lower Tier give perhaps the best view in the stadium as long as you are along the side of the pitch. However, if the people in the red seats are standing up, then so inevitably will you want to be. It is important to note, however, that ground regulations state that all fans should be seated and those refusing to do so may be ejected.

In the Upper Tier, the seats at the front are good, though as you move backwards there are various pillars and obstructions virtually guaranteed to get irritatingly in your way at vital moments.

The Olympic Gallery offers a terrific view of the pitch, but you will need 20/20 vision to be able to make anyone out in any detail.

With the introduction of the Criminal Justice Act, touting is illegal, but there are still plenty of touts by the tube station though they now tend to congregate less on Wembley Way and more by a nearby hotel. If you must buy a ticket from one of these gentlemen, never forget to check your ticket for a hologram and watermark (and remember that stolen tickets can be sold in this way).

**CAPACITY:** Stands: 80,000
**DISABLED FACILITIES:** There are 40 spaces for disabled supporters which are split between bays 101 and 148.

There are no match day commentaries available but there is designated parking available, this however is by prior arrangement only.

For club matches the individual teams are responsible for allocation. If you are going to an international, get in touch with the box office who hopefully will be able to sort you out.

**PROGRAMME:** Looks and reads to me like a new car brochure, and costs between £4 and £6. Out of date in places as well. The A4 size is very cumbersome and, to be honest, if you do want one then you could order it by post and save yourself the heartache of having to lug it round all day (because at that price you're not going to want to try and fold it up and put it in your pocket).

## TRAVEL

### NEAREST RAILWAY STATION:
Wembley Stadium (0171 262 6767), Wembley Central (01923 245001)
Wembley Stadium station is at the bottom of South Way and is served by Marylebone-Banbury trains on the Chiltern Line. Very handy, but trains are infrequent.

Wembley Central is about 10min walk from the stadium, and is served by Euston-Watford/Milton Keynes/ Northampton services.

### NEAREST TUBE STATION:
Wembley Park (Jubilee and Metropolitan Lines).
The tube station is about 5min from the ground when you arrive for a game (and is the recoomended means of public transport access), but after a match it is a different story entirely and you should allow at least 20-30min getting from the ground to the station.

Parents with young children should be aware that some of the queues that can develop going to the station can be frightening (although the tunnel, with the exception of the road underpass, adjacent to the station, has been opened out), especially given that once you're in one, it is very difficult to get out.

**BUS:** London Transport (0171 222 1234)
Buses 18, 83, 92, 182 and 297 serve the stadium.

### BY CAR:
**NORTH/EAST:** North Circular (A406) to right turn into Neasden Lane. Keep straight on for Forty Lane and

Empire Way; turn left into Engineers Way for car parks.

**SOUTH/WEST:** North Circular (A406) to left turn into Harrow Road. Bear right past Wembley Stadium railway station and take the second right for car parks. Alternatively, take the North Circular to left turn into Drury Way, then left at the second (Tesco) roundabout into Great Central Way. Follow the road for car parks.

The road to Wembley is well signposted from all parts.

**PARKING:** There is car parking for about 7,000 by the stadium, but expect to pay between £5 and £10 for the privilege. Also expect to spend an awfully long time trying to get out of the car park.

## FUTURE DEVELOPMENTS

In December 1996 it was announced that Wembley would remain the site of the new national stadium and during 1998, despite a late bid from Arsenal, the stadium was due to be purchased by the English National Stadium Trust. A massive upgrading of facilities will commence in 1999 with the aim of being finished by 2002.

The capacity will be 80,000 (for football) and it is likely that fans will be nearer the pitch. Other details regarding the redevelopment have yet to be confirmed.

Importantly, access will also be improved. Wembley station will be rebuilt and local roads, including South Way and Great Central Way, are to be upgraded and connections with other major roads improved.

## OTHER INFORMATION

For a pre-match drink, the Torch is one of the best places to go. It may be lacking in refinement but does serve a reasonably-priced pint quickly. The staff and management understand that it is a big day out and are happy to let the fans have a good time. Turn left out of the station and it is 200yd on the right. If you do go to the Torch then on the way to the ground there is a chip shop, which is well worth popping in at to refuel.

Wembley Stadium Ltd asked me to point out that the stadium is home of the England football team and amongst other events hosts the FA Cup Final sponsored by AXA and the Worthington Cup Final. (Blimey! Who'd have believed it, the publishers should bump the cover price of this book up for that kind of information.)

Alternatively there are a couple of (very expensive) off-licences at which you can buy cans and then drink on Wembley Way (thumbs up to the Met for letting fans enjoy a beer outside the ground). Inside the ground I think the food and drink is expensive — although probably no more expensive than similar fare at other major venues — and, in my opinion, tastes awful. A small bottle of lager is £2.50 and the burgers get up to the £5 barrier. There are loads of toilets but still they can't cope with the volume of people who hit them at half- and full-time and it can get a bit grim with any wall often becoming a urinal.

Having moaned about Wembley, I have to say it is still the most magical ground in Britain. Just walking down Wembley Way, towards the twin towers, raises goosebumps and as you walk around under the stand the ghosts from English football's past abound. Whoever you support, I pray that they get the opportunity to play there at least once during your supporting life, because nothing else compares.

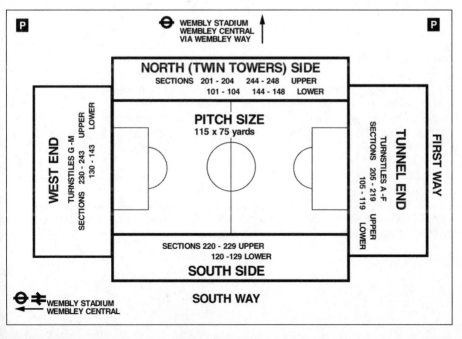

# GROUND INDEX